BERNARD MADOFF AND HIS ACCOMPLICES

BERNARD MADOFF AND HIS ACCOMPLICES

Anatomy of a Con

LIONEL S. LEWIS

 PRAEGER ™

An Imprint of ABC-CLIO, LLC

Santa Barbara, California • Denver, Colorado

Library of Congress Cataloging-in-Publication Data

Names: Lewis, Lionel S. (Lionel Stanley) author.
Title: Bernard Madoff and his accomplices : anatomy of a con / Lionel S. Lewis.
Description: Santa Barbara : Praeger, 2016. | Includes bibliographical
    references and index.
Identifiers: LCCN 2015038749 | ISBN 9781440841934 (hardback) |
    ISBN 9781440841941 (ebook)
Subjects: LCSH: Madoff, Bernard L. | Swindlers and swindling—United States. |
    Investment advisors—Corrupt practices—United States. | Ponzi schemes—
    United States. | Bernard L. Madoff Investment Securities, LLC. | BISAC:
    BUSINESS & ECONOMICS / Finance. | BUSINESS & ECONOMICS /
    Personal Finance / Money Management. | BUSINESS & ECONOMICS /
    Investments & Securities.
Classification: LCC HV6692.M33 L493 2016 | DDC 364.16/3092—dc23
LC record available at http://lccn.loc.gov/2015038749

ISBN: 978–1–4408–4193–4
EISBN: 978–1–4408–4194–1

20 19 18 17 16   1 2 3 4 5

This book is also available on the World Wide Web as an eBook.
Visit www.abc-clio.com for details.

Praeger
An Imprint of ABC-CLIO, LLC

ABC-CLIO, LLC
130 Cremona Drive, P.O. Box 1911
Santa Barbara, California 93116-1911

This book is printed on acid-free paper ∞

Manufactured in the United States of America

Contents

List of Illustrations

*Table appears in Notes, in the book's back matter.

Acknowledgments

I am grateful to the Hon. Barbara Howe, Erie County surrogate judge, and Curtis J. Mettlin, director of cancer control and epidemiology and chief of epidemiological research emeritus at Roswell Park Cancer Institute, for their innumerable intellectual and editorial suggestions. I am also grateful to the reference librarians—Nina Cascio, Joseph L. Gerken, and Marcia L. Zubrow—at the Charles B. Sears Law Library at the University at Buffalo and to Jay Deveau, Branch Librarian, Second Circuit, U.S. Courts Library, who provided valuable and timely assistance in finding a wide assortment of essential documents. Moreover, special thanks are due to Nicole M. Hayden, manager, Software and Computer Productivity Programs, Organizational Development & Training, and to Guangxu Xun, a student in the graduate program in the Department of Computer Science and Engineering, both at the University at Buffalo, for their assistance in preparing my manuscript for publication. Finally, it was a pleasure to work with Hilary Claggett, a senior editor at Praeger, who edited and guided *Bernard Madoff and His Accomplices: Anatomy of a Con* through publication.

Author's Note: Throughout the book, with the kind permission from the copyright holder Springer-Verlag GmbH, I draw on my essays on the Madoff con published in *Society* in 2013 and 2014 (50, numbers 3, 4, 5, and 6, and 51, number 1).

Williamsville, New York
Fall, 2015

Introduction

This book examines Bernard L. Madoff's oversized confidence game; it focuses on what went on behind the scene at his investment firm, Bernard L. Madoff Investment Securities (BLMIS), and on those who enabled his confidence game to succeed for as long as it did.

A confidence game is generally referred to as a con game, or simply a con. There are short cons and long cons. Much of the time, long cons are called big cons. A short con is a quick swindle that may take only minutes. Its aim is to defraud or steal from victims what they are carrying—money, a wallet, a purse, jewelry. A big con unfolds over a much longer period of time. The term *confidence game* possibly originated with situations in which victims were induced or lured to compete in a game of chance from which unknown to them the element of chance had for the most part been eliminated.[1]

In both short and big cons, one individual wins the confidence of another and exploits the trusting relationship to defraud or steal from him or her. The former is a confidence man (or con man), the individual who gains the confidence of others, and the latter is a victim, or in the argot of con men, a mark. The confidence man, the inside man, uses what are generally called outside men to help in his deception.[2] Outside men, the con man's confederates, help in small and big ways. Most are largely invisible working behind the scene, out of sight backstage, to keep the operation running smoothly. They are valued henchmen (accomplices), trusted and trusting. Because of what they do, other outside men are more conspicuous, as they first locate and then entice victims to get involved in a swindle. These outside men are the confidence man's shills or what in the argot are called ropers (those who bring victims and their money to a con game) and steerers (those who pose as satisfied clients). Accomplices, ropers, and steerers are a con man's full complement. Accomplices and ropers are with rare exceptions indispensable to help a con man dupe his victims, and when there are no or too few steerers, they can also be used to bear witness to his cunning.[3]

One present-day short con (already practiced by the turn of the fifteenth century) is "Three-card Monte," in which a shill pretends to conspire with a mark to cheat a con man, the card dealer. In reality, the shill and the con man are working together to cheat the mark. At first, the mark is allowed to win, but then he is confused by the sleight of hand of the dealer and fairly quickly loses his or her money.

Most often short cons occur at top speed and also involve defrauding victims of modest amounts of money. However, the two elements are not always seen together in a con, and this is but one of four possible courses of a con. Long cons can unfold quickly or defraud victims of limited assets. Consequently, it is not always easy to delineate a short con from a long one, a con having a detailed and prolonged plan to defraud. Below is an example:

> A close pal of [Wilson Mizner, the writer, entrepreneur, and celebrity confidence man] was a member of a San Francisco family that had gained enormous wealth in Nevada silver mines. Mizner took the young scion of the Comstock Lode to New Orleans; their mission was to clear out a poolroom with the help of inside racing information. What the young silver mining millionaire didn't know was that the poolroom, with the entire personnel, customers and all, had been organized by Mizner solely for the purpose of getting a slice of the silver millions. Mizner's net profit at the expense of his bosom friend was more than $100,000, and in those simple days it lasted him more than a year.[4]

One present-day long con is a Ponzi scheme, an investment swindle in which high profits are promised and paid early with funds raised from later investors. In a Ponzi scheme, a dollar more for one victim means a dollar less for another victim. Big cons are not necessarily complicated, and generally Ponzi schemes are not elaborate, involving little more than taking money from new investors and giving it to the earlier investors.

The con man Bernard L. (Bernie) Madoff's business, Bernard L. Madoff Investment Securities (BLMIS),[5] was a protracted and massive

Ponzi scheme that lasted from perhaps as early as the 1960s or 1970s until December 2008 and cost investors in the range of more than $17.3 billion up to $18.5 billion.[6]

BLMIS was a Wall Street broker-dealer—that executed orders for stocks and securities on behalf of clients (a broker) and traded stocks and securities for its own accounts (a dealer)—involved in three businesses or activities: 1. the market making business, buying and selling stocks and securities for customers; 2. the proprietary trading business, buying and selling stocks and securities with company money; 3. investment advisory (IA) services, taking custody and managing customer assets. It was within the IA business where the Madoff con game took place.

The BLMIS IA business was a criminal enterprise, an organization set up or controlled for the explicit and sole purpose of executing criminal activity. When IA customers deposited funds to invest in their accounts, BLMIS would not invest the funds in shares of common stock and other securities of well-known corporations as customers had expected, but would deposit the funds in its bank account, and periodically provide customers with account statements showing that stocks and securities had been purchased with their deposits and that these were steadily growing in value. However, none of their money was ever invested by BLMIS. Still, when an IA customer requested some or all funds be returned, the amount was promptly withdrawn from the BLMIS bank account and the money returned. Other money was withdrawn from the bank account to support the lavish lifestyle of Madoff and his family (houses, cars and boats, jewelry, vacations, etc.), to pay confederates (outside men, ropers, steerers, and backstage accomplices) who were helping him con investors,[7] and to prop up the BLMIS market making and proprietary trading businesses that were not always profitable. In the BLMIS Ponzi scheme, every dollar received by an investor above the amount that the investor deposited was one dollar less for the investor to whom the money actually belonged.

After more than six years of investigation, it is still unclear when Madoff's con game began, how much money investors lost, and how many investors were involved. (According to a Complaint filed by the U.S. Attorney for the Southern District of New York, "As of on or about November 30, 2008, BLMIS had approximately 4800 IA client accounts." Looking at this question in another way, by the end of 2013, 16,519 claims had been filed for the return of assets [of which 2,517 had been allowed and 10,921 had been denied because they were third-party claims and not eligible for Securities Investor Protection Corporation (SIPC) insurance]).[8]

Bernard Madoff and His Accomplices: Anatomy of a Con is the study of a big con, specifically of what went on behind the scenes of a big con—of how backstage the con man and his accomplices, as well as ropers and steerers, kept a con game going. It is an examination of Madoff's con game, which first stole millions of dollars from American investors and then billions of dollars from investors from around the world—from Europe, Asia, South America, and the Middle East.

It is worth noting that in this book no attempt is made to ascertain the cause or causes of Madoff and his accomplices' criminal activity. The con was a crime, and crime is a legal category. The only thing that is alike in all crimes—white collar or street crime, confidence games or other frauds—is that they are all violations of law. As MacIver decades ago reminded us, "in that sense the only cause of crime as such is the law itself."

> What is a crime in one country is no crime in another; what is a crime at one time is no crime at another. The law is forever changing, adding new crimes to the catalogue and canceling former ones . . . . Since, then, crime varies with the law, the conditions that evoke it are equally variant.[9]

In a sense, con games violate a fundamental principle of human society, which makes them of particular interest to sociologists. Georg Simmel long ago reminded us: "The first condition of having to deal with somebody at all is to know with *whom* one has to deal. The fact that people usually introduce themselves to one another whenever they engage in a conversation of any length or meet on the same social level may strike one as an empty form; yet it is an adequate symbol of the mutual knowledge presupposed by every relationship."[10] In a con game, victims do not know, they only think they know, with whom they are dealing. Because of this, a great deal can readily go amiss. Simmel adds: "Truthfulness and lie are of the most far-reaching significance for relations among men."[11] Understanding this verity, Jonathan Swift's Lilliputians looked "upon fraud as a greater crime than theft, and therefore seldom fail[ed] to punish it with death; for they allege[d], that care and vigilance, with a very common understanding, may preserve a man's goods from thieves, but honesty has no defense against superior cunning."

Moreover, Goffman has written, "perhaps the real crime of the confidence man is not that he takes money from his victims but that he robs all of us of the belief that middle class manners and appearance can be sustained only by middle class people. A disabused professional can be cynically hostile to the service relation his clients expect him to extend to them; the confidence man is in a position to hold the whole 'legit' world in this contempt."[12]

In 1940, Maurer pointed out:

> In addition to grift sense [the ability of a criminal to live by his wits], a con man must have a good deal of genuine acting ability. He must be able to make anyone like him, confide in him, and trust him. He must sense immediately what aspect of his personality will be most appealing to his victim then assume that pose and hold it consistently. If the mark is a wealthy farmer, he must assume those characteristics which he knows will arouse the farmer's confidence and friendship. He must be able to talk over the farmer's problems with sympathy and understanding . . . .
>
> With business and professional men he reveals other facets of his multiple personalities and in a remarkably short time has established himself on a very friendly footing with them . . . .
>
> Once the outside man has roped a mark, his work is just beginning . . . .[He] puts the mark in contact with the inside man and "ties him up." These steps are, in themselves, little dramas which must be enacted with great naturalness; one false move and the mark suspects that his new-found friend is not all that he seems. If he acts the part well, the mark suspects nothing, for the sequence of events is built up with most convincing logic and plausibility.[13]

A big con is a multi-act piece of theater, the outline of which is scripted by a con man. Before a con begins (before the acting begins) the inside man sets the stage for a performance. He gathers outside men and the props that will enhance success. The first act begins with a confidence man and his outside men finding one or more victims to bilk. In the middle are play-acting, performances, pretending, the utilization of props, and false representations. A successful last act ends by "cooling the marks out," the victims' acquiescing, accepting, or adjusting to the fact that their property is gone—that their money has been stolen and that they have been deceived and cheated.

To see a con game unfold is much like going to the theater. One notable difference, of course, is that the con game's audience does not know that it is part of the performance, in that victims have no idea that they have descended into a world of make-believe. As Maurer put it, "big-time confidence games are in reality only carefully rehearsed plays in which every member in the cast *except the mark* knows his part perfectly."[14]

For Madoff's con game to succeed, it was simply necessary to find those—individuals or financial institutions—with money to invest in the stock market, and that hoped to make more from an investment with BLMIS than with what they believed they could earn elsewhere. To do this, Madoff had to gain the confidence of his investors. His props—all of the accoutrements of a Wall Street financier and a prosperous business—were first positioned, and he began by showing a record of consistent and above-average returns by BLMIS. He also had to show that investors could promptly redeem part or all of their money (both their principal and what was reported in their monthly, quarterly, or annual statements as earnings from their investments). If he failed on either count—finding money and keeping his clients satisfied—his con game would, as would be the case with any con game, quickly collapse.

On December 10, 2008, his two sons' attorney reported to the U.S. Attorney's office that he had told them "in substance, that his investment advisory (IA) business was a fraud, he was 'finished', he had 'absolutely nothing', 'it's all just one big lie.' " It might well be, as some Madoff-skeptics believe, that even this was part of Madoff's performance. In any case, when two FBI agents went to his Manhattan apartment the next morning, Madoff acknowledged knowing why they were there. When told by one agent, "We're here to find out if there's an innocent explanation," Madoff replied, "There is no innocent explanation." According to the senior FBI agent's deposition for the court, "Madoff further stated, in substance, that he 'paid investors with money that wasn't there'. Madoff also said that he was 'broke' and 'insolvent' and that he had decided that 'he could not go on . . . .' " He was immediately arrested, and on March 12, 2009, he pled guilty to 11 counts of securities fraud, investment advisor fraud, wire and mail fraud, money laundering, making false statements, perjury, filing false documents to the SEC (Securities and Exchange Commission), and theft from employee benefit funds. (See excerpts from the transcript of guilty plea proceedings, Appendix 1-A.) On June 29, 2009, he was sentenced to prison for 150 years.

From the beginning, Madoff needed associates in place to help him collect BLMIS investors' money. These ropers readily handed the money over to him so that he could spread it to his family and friends, backstage accomplices at BLMIS, ropers, and steerers who were work-ing his con and, of course, to investors who closed their accounts or requested redemptions. Madoff's backstage accomplices were led by a number of long-term employees who over the years would become familiar with his business and could fabricate documents that would be used to convince his investors, regulators, and others that his ficti-tious investments were generating profits sufficient enough to mini-mize requests to close accounts or for redemptions, and to attract new clients and investments. These backstage accomplices were more vulnerable legally as they were involved in day-to-day activities that were clearly criminal. In the end, in fact, in addition to Madoff, 14 pled or were found guilty of an assortment of white collar crimes. And they were generally not enriched nearly as well as were ropers.[15] Madoff's steerers, his highly visible satisfied customers, were longtime male friends, all of whom were Jewish, as were many, but certainly not all, of his victims (as were many of the attorneys who worked to put him and his backstage accomplices in prison and to return the money to clients that he had stolen). After all, his business and his crime largely took place close to New York City, where the percentage of Jews is larger than in San Antonio or Seattle.

Madoff's Ponzi scheme was fairly straightforward. It was, of course, necessary for Madoff to improvise from time to time on the rare occa-sion when an investor, a journalist, a regulator, or a BLMIS employee not privy to the con asked questions, the full answers to which could quickly lay open what had the appearance of a winning investment strategy, but, was, in reality, nothing more than a lasting performance. This was a manageable problem, however, as Madoff was a practiced liar; he told lies and more lies, and the BLMIS business was immersed in a fog of deception not only through lying but also through distrac-tion, dissimulation, concealment, and misdirection.[16]

As it was, Madoff was a fraud, his success fictitious. He was not a skilled or lucky investor; he was not able to guess correctly over half of the time which way stocks would move. He was at best an indiffer-ent investor. His backstage accomplices at BLMIS and for the most part his ropers and steerers as well as his family were a collection of mediocre, materialistic, greedy, and unconscious individuals.[17]

Yet, Madoff was quadruply lucky as a con man. He was lucky that he could so readily find others to help him carry out his con. Mostly all that he had to do was to reward them sufficiently. He was lucky that late in the twentieth century there were so many people in America and around the world foolish or greedy or trusting enough not to question why the returns he reported on his investments were almost uninterruptedly steady and above average. He was lucky that so many on Wall Street and its regulators had tunnel vision, that even with a number of clues, or red flags, they could not stumble on the fact that he was a con man, that it was artifice, that they were immersed in a fiction. He was finally lucky that by the time he was operating his con, the United States had moved well beyond a country guided by an ethic of production to a nation ruled by an ethic of consumption whereby millions of individuals no longer expected work to yield wealth. Wealth was just as likely to come from family and friends and social connections—an acquaintance or a neighbor, or the friend of an acquaintance or a neighbor, by a chance encounter, or even from a winning lottery ticket or an inside straight draw at a nearby casino. However one came upon it, wealth did not necessarily have to be earned, and whatever its origin, that it was there is all that was important, not how one came by it.[18]

As a result, for decade after decade, Madoff, this very ordinary man with a very ordinary family, with very ordinary relatives and friends, with very ordinary, although expensive, material tastes, fairly easily convinced those who could have readily stayed his con that he was simply a canny investor and that this was evident from his long-term success. However, after the economic downturn of 2007 had taken hold in Europe and the United States, BLMIS began to see more redemptions than new money invested, and Madoff was ultimately forced to confess his ruse. Like millions of poor and rich, laborers without savings and investors with a surplus of money to squander in a con game, around the world after the global recession began, Madoff's luck had run out.[19] In early December 2008, he confessed his crime to authorities, rather than try to flee, hide, commit suicide, or in some other way evade prison.

Madoff's con game did not end well not only for him but also, as is generally the case, for his victims. His victims were left with the Herculean task of trying to recover legitimate claims or a mightier task of trying to recover what had simply vanished or was not recoverable. Those charged with the fairly straightforward task of collecting what Madoff left washing around in the international financial world appeared to be markedly incompetent in completing the task. The legal process that followed BLMIS's collapse reminds one of the epic and never-ending fictional probate-dispute and parody, Jarndyce and Jarndyce.[20] This dénouement left many of his victims feeling outraged and bitter. They were angry at being cheated by Madoff, and relentlessly badgered both regulators for not uncovering Madoff's con and the federal authorities for not promptly making them financially whole, an outcome they believed was both fair and deserved. Few were cooled out,[21] that is, convinced to quietly come to terms with their loss.

As it was pointed out in the first sentence of this Introduction, *Bernard Madoff and His Accomplices* looks behind the scene of Madoff's con; it is a tableau of how it operated. To date, the inquiries into Madoff's fraud by an army of attorneys and journalists have been trying to discover "where the bodies are buried." This book is an examination of "who buried the bodies" and "how they got buried." This seems the more interesting question, the answer to which will take us much closer to understanding the Madoff con game and perhaps other con games as well. To date, there are probably a dozen books, including my earlier one, which primarily looked at Madoff, his victims, and various aspects of his con game,[22] but none have focused on his organization, BLMIS, where his fraud began, was centered, and flourished.

The book describes what Madoff and his associates did to defraud money from BLMIS IA business clients. It begins with looking at how BLMIS's backstage white collar workers routinely, some knowingly and some unknowingly, went about mass-producing false records and documents; it continues with an examination of BLMIS ropers and roping operations (first hustling money largely from middle-class and upper-middle-class investors and steadily moving to those with great wealth); it also reviews accounts by former employees—Madoff's accomplices—detailing what they did and saw in their time at BLMIS.

Much of the material examining how the con game was able to last for decades was found in the court testimony of Madoff and his 14 accomplices who pled or were found guilty of various white collar felonies. What emerges is a tableau of how the con operated, how false records and documents were mass-produced, and how money laundering and other crimes became common practice. It quickly becomes apparent that Madoff's con was built on the deception by more than the 15 implicated in the crime.

Chapter 1 begins by examining five con games in order to isolate their common elements. Two are fiction and three are accounts from the annals of con games. What went on at BLMIS is generally what goes on in most con games: preparation, the introduction of props, play-acting, pretense, false representations, victims convinced that they have much to gain and little to lose, and unremitting efforts to deceive, disorient, and fool. As in a theatrical production, little in Madoff's world was what it seemed to be.

Chapter 2 focuses on the activities of a handful of BLMIS employees who were engaged backstage, hidden from business and government regulators and most investors, to further Madoff's crime. The work of these seven revolved around sustaining the pretense that stocks and securities were being bought and sold, that BLMIS was a profitable business. All of these fairly well-paid accomplices pled guilty to being involved in criminal activities, although only one acknowledged that he knew that his activities were furthering a Ponzi scheme. Regardless of how their attorneys scripted how they would describe their activities in a plea bargain, a culture surrounding their insular workplace developed over time. By 2008, these backstage employees were clearly part of a subculture that had evolved into a wholly criminal enterprise.

The voices of three individuals who worked at BLMIS are heard unfiltered in the following three chapters. The three, Enrica Cotellessa-Pitz, David L. Kugel, and Annette Bongiorno, were among the 15 BLMIS employees, including Bernard Madoff and his brother, Peter Madoff, found guilty of criminal involvement in the con. Deception is at the center of the world described in their accounts of life backstage at BLMIS. Clients, regulators, and other BLMIS employees (some other accomplices) are regularly and repeatedly deceived.

Chapter 6 once again examines the world of make-believe that continued for decades behind the scenes at BLMIS. A review of other con games shows that pretending, misrepresenting, and dissembling are hardly unique to what went on backstage at BLMIS, where Madoff's accomplices, whose work was to deceive, were, like his defrauded clients, often themselves victims of deception.

Chapter 7 looks at how ropers and Madoff worked together to lure new money into his con game. Attention is primarily on four individuals or organizations: first, what began as an accounting firm and evolved into a network of reliable ropers for BLMIS, Avellino & Bienes (A&B); second, Madoff's in-house roping operation, Cohmad Securities; third, Robert M. Jaffe, a well-connected golfer with a low handicap, above-average looks, and a very average IQ whose father-in-law made hundreds of millions of dollars (only some of which had to return after Madoff's con collapsed) investing with Madoff; and fourth, J. Ezra Merkin, a prominent figure among wealthy New York Jews who, like the Puritans, believed wealth placed one close to God.

The key to Madoff's success here, what greatly increased a steady stream of new money to his con game, was simply the greed and naïveté of both his ropers and investors. Madoff generously rewarded the former for their efforts at helping him defraud the latter.

Ropers and roping are again the subjects of Chapter 8. Using an array of documents, the international money-collecting activities of a U.S.-based investment company, the Fairfield Greenwich Group (FGG), and of the international financier Sonja Kohn are reviewed. Although over the years FGG collected approximately $7 billion for Madoff to invest, its executives were almost totally in the dark about what happened to the money after it was directly passed to BLMIS. Madoff was single-mindedly determined to steal as much money from FGG as he could, while the FGG executives appear to be unimaginably dull or perhaps practiced and gifted falsifiers, a combination that greatly enhanced his success as a con man. The case of Kohn shows that there seemed to be almost no limits to what Madoff was willing to pay ropers to keep them engaged finding victims for his con game. Kohn's experience with Madoff shows that being a roper in a con game could be as lucrative as being an inside man, and with a significantly diminished risk of ending up in prison for 150 years.[23]

Big cons increase their chances of success if they have steerers, those who the con game has readily enriched. Steerers serve as exemplars of what may be in the offing for others enticed into the con. Three investors, among many, who used their BLMIS IA accounts to greatly increase their wealth—Jeffry Picower, Norman F. Levy, and Stanley Chais—are at the center of Chapter 9. The knowledge of the existence of but a single steerer by clients and potential clients of BLMIS promoted its fortunes.

Chapter 10 describes how JPMorgan Chase Bank assisted Madoff's con to succeed for many decades. By, for example, turning a blind eye to BLMIS's money-laundering activities, a number of the bank's executives facilitated the continuation of Madoff's con. In a strict sense, the bank did not work for BLMIS, but it was as much at the center of the con as were backstage accomplices. Thus, the bank may not have assiduously laundered money for BLMIS, but year after year, its executives allowed money laundering—the purpose of much of it years after the Madoff con imploded is still for the most part unknown—to become a routine practice.

Chapter 11, "Revisiting the Crime Scene," considers how it was that BLMIS was so criminogenic, and how Madoff was able to keep his con game viable for as long as he did. The criminal subculture with its identifiable and distinctive customs, values, and norms that developed on the 17th floor of BLMIS was one element that surely kept the con viable. The chapter and book conclude with a discussion of how what was learned about Madoff's con and BLMIS furthers our understanding of criminal behavior, particularly the genesis of white collar crime as discussed by Gabriel Tarde and Edwin Sutherland, among others.

The 11 chapters largely show the slow and steady growth of the Madoff con:

- 1960: Madoff qualifies as a general securities representative and general securities principal.
- 1960: BLMIS is founded.
- Early 1960s: Madoff begins using ropers, first Saul Alpern, his accountant father-in-law, and then A&B, the successors at his father-in-law's accounting firm.
- 1983: Madoff Securities International Limited (MSIL) opens in London.
- 1985: Madoff's in-house ropers, Cohmad Securities, is founded by Madoff and his longtime friend Maurice J. Cohn.
- 1989: Walter Noel Jr., through FGG, begins investing with BLMIS.
- 1990: J. Ezra Merkin, through Gabriel Capital/Ascot Partners (1992), begins investing with BLMIS.

In the spring 2008, months after equity markets around the world began sputtering, when a deluge of redemptions started—prompted, for example, by large and continuous withdrawals of its investments by JPMorgan Chase Bank—BLMIS began to collapse. The collapse was complete in little more than six months.

Writing about the pervasiveness of white collar crime just a few years before Madoff launched his criminal enterprise, C. Wright Mills pointed to the necessity of seeing crime's various manifestations as a whole, and of trying to grasp what, taken together, they mean. The prevalence of white collar crime in America suggests, Mills points out, "a crowd of themes," three of which are "the extent of a semi-organized irresponsibility, the extent to which both of this trend readily finds recruits, who, in turn, are further corrupted, and "the supremacy of cash and kudos as the all-American values."[24] *Bernard Madoff and His Accomplices* shows how prescient Mills was in describing life at BLMIS for half a century.

John Kenneth Galbraith has written that there are "three great weaknesses of ... the financial community." First, "there is the tendency to confuse good manners, good tailoring, and, above all an impressive bearing and speech with integrity and intelligence." In short, good actors (as was Madoff) with the advantage of having his wardrobe tailored in London (as did Madoff) or those with the backswing of a pro (as the roper Robert Jaffe), or those who would describe themselves to a fashion publication as a clotheshorse (as did Robert Jaffe), are, obviously, not necessarily a reflection of good character. Second, "there is a troublesome and at times disastrous interdependence. The honest man," Galbraith writes, "becomes committed to the crook before he knows there is anything wrong. Then he must protect him to protect himself or, in the most usual case, refuse to believe there is anything wrong." This might explain what would otherwise be the singular dullness on the part of some of BLMIS's ropers, particularly the executives at FGG. (Upton Sinclair more than once observed: "It is difficult to get a man to understand something, when his salary depends upon his not understanding it!") Third, "there is the dangerous cliché that in the financial world everything depends on confidence." (Galbraith quips: "one could better argue the importance of unremitting suspicion.")

Galbraith adds one more observation: "And we may lay it down as an absolute rule that, given the excess of confidence [during the boom years], there will be confidence men who take advantage of it."[25]

The array of materials collected and analyzed for *Bernard Madoff and His Accomplices* proves Galbraith right on all points.

In the early years of the twenty-first century, farceur corporate criminals seemed to be shoving each other aside to claim who had committed the most colossal crime. First, there was Dennis Kozlowski, whose pay at Tyco—originally formed as an investment and holding company—had soared from $8.8 million in 1997 to $170 million in 1999, and who borrowed $61.7 million in unauthorized, interest-free loans (of which he repaid one-third) in order to purchase a Florida mansion (for $29.8 million), a New York City co-op, a Fifth Avenue apartment, a vintage yacht, a Renoir, and a Monet. In total, he misappropriated approximately $400 million from Tyco. Second, there was Bernard Ebbers, who artificially inflated the stock price for WorldCom—a telecommunications corporation—to keep his own wealth growing. As a result, he helped generate a $11 billion accounting fraud, and within days after Ebbers was forced to acknowledge the true financial condition of WorldCom, the price of its stock lost 90 percent of its value.

Next, there was John Rigas (and his sons), who stole money from Adelphia Communications for almost everything imaginable—from building a private golf course to supporting with millions of dollars an NHL hockey team, and, according to the SEC Indictment, "fraudulently excluded billions of dollars in liabilities" from the company's financial statements. The Rigas fraud was fueled by billion-dollar loans from large commercial banks.

Fourth, there was Gary Winnick, who founded, and then led into bankruptcy, Global Crossing, a firm established to build fiber-optic networks. He used swap transactions, a scheme in which companies exchange the same amount of assets resulting in neither increasing its value, the purpose of which is to make it appear that there are increased revenues in order to boost the share price of company stock. At one point in 2000, the stock price of Global Crossing reached $64 a share; two years later, its shares were worth 15 cents a share. The stock options that Winnick received from Global Crossing enriched him by more than $700 million. Although he had to pay millions of dollars to settle a number of lawsuits, he was never indicted.

Finally, there was the financial corruption at Enron, the energy, communications, and pulp-and-paper company once ranked the seventh largest company in the United States, wherein Kenneth Lay, Jeffrey Skilling, Andrew Fastow, and other executives inflated profits and hid billions of dollars of debt and losses through accounting fraud whereby the debt and losses were simply eliminated from the company's books. As a result, Enron appeared so successful it was named "America's Most Innovative Company" by *Fortune* magazine for six consecutive years, although its revenues and profits were the results of arrangements with "special purpose entities," which enabled Enron to pile on annual losses. As Enron was collapsing in 2001, and as Lay was being paid $104 million in salary bonuses and loans, its share prices decreased from $90.56 to just pennies.

Which of these five is declared the winner in the race to ignominy would depend on what metric is used to measure each mess.

Bernard Madoff and His Accomplices: Anatomy of a Con examines how another farceur brought his mess to pass.

CHAPTER 1

Of Bernard L. Madoff and Others

This chapter begins by examining five con games—known to those who have studied the history of confidence games—in order to isolate common elements. The brief review shows that what went on at BLMIS is generally what goes on in most confidence games: extensive preparations, the use of elaborate props, pretense, victims convinced that they have much to win and little to lose, greed, and the ability to disorient and fool. Moreover, as in most con games, little in Madoff's world was as it seemed to be.

In a confidence game, a victim hands over money or something of value to a con man (or woman) only to have it stolen. One necessary condition in order for a con game to be successful is that the con man creates a world of make-believe by pretense. He or she makes what is not reality, reality. A big con involves a mise-en-scène—an arrangement of performers and props resembling a stage for a theatrical event. To see a con game unfold is much like going to the theater. One notable difference, of course, is that the audience of a con game does not know that it is part of the performance. Victims have no idea that they have descended into a world of make-believe.

Con men often and readily compare themselves with skilled actors. Indeed, their understanding of the con game goes well beyond this simple insight. For example, the confidence man W. C. Crosby pointed out almost 100 years ago: "Confidence is a business, and, like all business, changes and conforms to conditions. ... Social conditions breed, cultivate, and change the practices and devices of the swindler. ... The crook is always attracted to ... sudden prosperity and quick expansion. There he finds loose and easy money."[1] Madoff and his accomplices were able to effectively use computer technology to enable his con to balloon beyond what Crosby and his contemporaries could have ever imagined.

It is not totally clear when Bernard Madoff's giant Ponzi scheme—wherein high profits were promised and early investors were paid off with funds raised from later customers—began, when he began to steal money. We know that it ended on December 11, 2008, when, after he confessed to his sons,[2] Madoff was arrested. For almost 50 years, Madoff's investment company, BLMIS, bought and sold stocks and securities. It was involved in market making (buying and selling stocks and securities for customers), proprietary trading (buying and selling stocks and securities for itself), and investment advisory services (managing the assets of customers). The IA business, where the con game was centered, was largely kept separate from the firm's market making and proprietary trading, as were its books and records. Generally, the IA business did not buy or sell stocks and securities as it purported it was doing.

Money sent to BLMIS by IA customers to buy stocks and securities would not be invested, but would instead be deposited in the BLMIS bank account. On a regular basis, customers would be provided with account statements showing that stocks and securities had been purchased with the deposited funds and that they were continuing to grow in value. When an IA customer requested some or all funds be returned, the amount requested was promptly withdrawn from the BLMIS bank account in order to return the money. (See, Appendix 1-A for Madoff's explanation at his trial of how he "carried out and concealed [his] fraud." Appendices 1-B and 1-C are excerpts from the reports of two forensic investigations into how Madoff began and managed his con game, and Appendix 1-D provides account activities for BLMIS IA accounts. Appendix 1-E is an account by one of Madoff's backstage accomplices of how sham trades and authentic trades at BLMIS differed.)

In short, Madoff was simply keeping the money his customers entrusted to him for their IA accounts. He was stealing it unless they were lucky enough to ask for it back. When requested, he promptly returned it not because he was remorseful, but because he was fearful that if he failed to do so, he would be reported to the authorities and his larger theft would be uncovered. Otherwise, he was transferring the money he kept to the failing parts of his business—the market making and proprietary trading businesses—to help keep them afloat.[3] In actuality, in spite of the fact that the market making and proprietary trading businesses were not profitable, it was necessary for Madoff to keep his legitimate businesses in operation as a façade in order to hide the true purpose of his company.[4]

Madoff, of course, also used the money that he was stealing to support a luxurious lifestyle for his family and friends, to pay redemptions to clients fortunate enough to ask for them while there was still money to return, and to generously reward and support a luxurious lifestyle for those who worked with him to keep them from telling others that they were involved in a criminal enterprise so as to prevent his fraud from being discovered by customers or regulators. Little in Bernard Madoff's world was as it seemed to be.

The testimony Madoff gave during his trial three months after his arrest describes his fraud in the most general terms. He told the court a little of what he did (only that he ran a Ponzi scheme), but nothing about how he did it. In the six years since Madoff pleaded guilty of perpetrating his con game, we have continued to learn more and more about what he did. Some have tried to explain why he did it: Was he a sociopath or psychologically unbalanced in some other way? Was he simply overly materialistic and greedy? Could an answer be found by delving into his childhood or family life? A lot less has been learned about how he did it, in fact, very little. The wide assortment of material collected for this book fills this gap, shedding considerable light on the operations of Madoff's con game.

When Madoff was arrested, thousands of investors quickly learned that they had lost the full value of their accounts. Madoff pled guilty to an 11-count Complaint, and on June 29, 2009, he was sentenced to 150 years in prison.[5]

In spite of the fact that there were numerous errors in the BLMIS trading records for investors and regulators to see—for example, settlements on weekends and holidays and dividends declared, but not recorded—very few individuals were not fooled by Madoff.[6] It was clear not long after Madoff's arrest that his investors who were not part of his scheme (not conspirators) and regulators tasked with looking for irregularities had been deceived for decades. The combination of Madoff's deception, the authorities' incompetence, and the victims' credulity and greed would in large part explain why Madoff's success was so outsized. To the degree that these—cupidity and bureaucratic bungling—are constants, we might expect con games to erupt with regularity over time. Still, with a better understanding of how con games work, we might better detect them and more effectively shut them down before billions of dollars go missing, as was the case with

Madoff. We begin this task of examining Madoff's con game by looking at five con games that long preceded him.

Victims of con games do not readily recognize that they have been entwined in one. If they eventually figure out that they have been part of one, it is well after the fact, after their valuables and the con men have disappeared; they are often unable to provide a very good account of how the swindle was so deftly pulled off. However, fiction and the recollections of con men readily offer examples of the intricacies of con games—and how and why they so readily succeed. Here are five examples of big cons that readily show how con men go about their work.

A Big Con: Example I—*The Sting* (A Movie)

The 1973 motion picture *The Sting*, starring Paul Newman and Robert Redford, with Robert Shaw and Harold Gould, captures one form of a big con called "The Wire," in which a mark is lured into betting on a horse race having been convinced by a con man that the results coming from a telegraph office will be briefly delayed and that with the advanced knowledge he will have, he will surely win the wager.

In the film, Henry Gondorff (Paul Newman), the con man—the inside man, the individual who orchestrates the con—first enlists a number of accomplices and rents an empty basement, transforming it in a few days into what appears to be a prosperous gambling parlor, to prepare for a sting to victimize the story's villain. Johnny Hooker (Robert Redford), is both an assistant inside man and a roper—the individual who brings the victim to the con game, convincing the victim or mark that he will surely win a great deal of money on a horse race. As part of the ruse, an accomplice posing as an announcer in a backroom describes races as if they were happening live, when in fact he is reading from a ticker tape from completed races.

In setting up the scheme, two accomplices go as far as to pretend to be painters in order to get the manager of a Western Union branch to vacate his office in order to convince the intended victim, Doyle Lonnegan (Robert Shaw), that they have access to it. Also as part of the apparatus, they use a pay phone at a corner drug store, where Lonnegan, an underworld financier, waits to receive information.

At the climax of the long buildup, the con men phone a tip to Lonnegan, who is waiting by the phone. After the call, he rushes with a briefcase full of money to the gambling parlor to place a bet. When he mentions to one of Gondorff's backup men, Kid Twist (Harold Gould), that he had bet on the horse to win, he is told that he has made a mistake, that he should have bet on it to place. In a panic, Lonnegan tries to cancel the transaction but is told that he is too late. Chaos ensues. There appears to be two homicides, and he is rushed off the premises being told that by leaving quickly he will avoid any chance that he will find himself in the middle of a homicide investigation.[7]

In *The Sting*, which takes place in 1936, we see a number of elements common to twentieth-century con games.

1. Inside man (Henry Gondorff)—the individual who runs the con game.
2. Assistant inside man and roper (hustler/confederate/capper) (Johnny Hooker)—the member of a con ring who befriends the victim and sets him up for a con.
3. Backup man (Kid Twist)—a con man's close confederate who sometimes acts as a capper.
4. Big store (Gambling parlor)—any confidence game requiring a false front, such as an office, a gambling den, or a bookmaking parlor.
5. "The Wire"—a con game that convinces a gambler that he cannot possibly lose a wager since he will be betting on an already completed horse race, the results of which, coming from a telegraph office, have been briefly delayed.
6. Convincer (The time Lonnegan is allowed to win money from Gondorff.)—a method in which a victim is lured into continuing a con game by allowing him to win a small amount of money to convince him he will, in the end, win a great deal more.
7. Sting—to complete a con game successfully stealing a sizable amount of money from a victim; the actual taking of the money.
8. Cooling the mark out (Lonnegan being hustled out from the gambling parlor)—to keep the anger and disappointment of the victim in sensible and manageable proportions.

A Big Con: Example II—"Salting a Mine"

A number of widely known big cons are recorded, which are not fiction but are just as engrossing and capture the complexity of one just as well as *The Sting*. Perhaps the most notable one in America occurred a hundred years before *The Sting* was filmed. This type of big con is called "Salting a Mine," in which gemstones or gold ore are planted on the landscape to inflate its value and entice investment by marks:

In the summer of 1871, Philip Arnold and John Slack appeared in the offices of a mining promoter, George Roberts, [and asked if he could store some valuables in the safe until the bank opened the next morning.] The bags, [they confided] contained diamonds, emeralds, and rubies said to be found in Apache territory in Eastern Arizona.

Roberts reported the visit to William C. Ralston, head of the Bank of California. Ralston, in turn, called a local jeweler, who placed the immediate value of the gems at $125,000; (Arnold had paid about $12,000 for them in England). [The miners were asked if they were willing to sell their claim. They seemingly were reluctant, but decided to sell part of it. They also agreed to take a blindfolded expert to their diamond field.]

For [four] days, the three men rode in crazy-quilt routes. [When they reached a sandy plateau] the entire area glittered under the sun. A place containing several ant hills was covered with diamond dust, and the mining expert excitedly began to kick the ant hills over, uncovering dozens of diamonds and even a few rubies and emeralds. In a matter of hours, [he] had filled a sack with jewels.

Inept jewelers and so-called experts had convinced Ralston that the gems he had been given by Arnold and Slack were worth more than $1.5 million, when in truth, their real value did not exceed $20,000. Ralston and other potential investors demanded that the two prospectors accompany them to New York, where Charles Lewis Tiffany valuated the gems. [Tiffany reportedly said: "I cannot fix an exact value until my lapidary has had a chance to inspect each stone, but I can assure you that they are worth at least a hundred and fifty thousand dollars."]

As an inducement to the prospectors, the potential investors gave them $100,000 in earnest money, and placed another $300,000 in escrow for them. They also promised a final payment of another $300,000 when the deal, which would give them a half interest in the field, was completed.

Before paying the balance of $300,000 for their half of the diamond field, the financiers insisted on mounting another investigative expedition that would once and for all clear up any doubt of the field's genuineness. [Meanwhile, Arnold and Slack] boarded a ship in New York and sailed to Europe. There, using the funds advanced by Ralston and others, they purchased more flawed and marketless gems for which they spent about $50,000.

[They] returned to America, traveled west, and again salted the 6,500-foot Wyoming mesa.

The two prospectors led their prey once more through a series of canyons and mesas until the prey were properly confused and then into the forty-acre diamond site. Astounded, the investigators began kicking over ant hills, digging with knives, and overturning boulders and rocks to find not only great quantities of diamonds, but rubies, emeralds, and sapphires.

The party dug up about a ton and a half of dirt, their harvest of gems amounting to almost $10,000. Estimating the return from this small amount of superficial spading, [a mining engineer] was more than convinced of a real find. Claiming about 4,000 acres for the investors, he told them they now possessed the richest field in mining history, that the area pinpointed should yield $5 million an acre. "With a hundred men and proper machinery, I would guarantee to send out a million dollars in diamonds every thirty days." The party had turned up 256 carats of large diamonds worth $4,096 at prevailing rates, 568 carats of small ones worth $1,704, and four pounds of rubies worth $2,226.

On the group's return to San Francisco, Ralston and the others frenziedly put together a $10 million corporation of private investors to exploit the field. Arnold and Slack were gotten rid of, being told that they would certainly be fleeced by the energetic money moguls if they continued to insist on shares in the field. Ralston and his powerful associates were unrelenting in their demands, and finally, the two prospectors gave in and accepted [actually, only Arnold, as Slack had disappeared, and nobody ever reported seeing him again] the promised balance of $300,000, signing over all rights to the field, including those gems already in Ralston's possession.[8]

A Big Con: Example III—Using "The Wire" (A Nonfiction Account)

A third example of a big con also shows prominent features that were evident in Examples I and II—pretense, greed, extensive preparation, elaborate props, the ability to disorient and fool, and victims, who need only be convinced that they have much to gain and little to lose.

In his autobiography, J. R. "Yellow Kid" Weil, a busy and enduringly successful con man of the early twentieth century, describes one of his many big con operations wherein being "a smooth and polished actor" enabled him to make a good deal of money for decades. This time, he used "The Wire."

First, Weil placed a newspaper advertisement offering an investment opportunity. Then, much like what Paul Newman did in *The Sting*, he set up what had the appearance of a betting parlor. He also had to find an accomplice who "was a good actor."

The poolroom to which Weil led the victim, whom he called Macallister, the next day, had been arranged for his special benefit. He had rented the banquet hall of a hotel, and outfitted it fully with equipment, which also had been rented for the occasion. There was also a telegraph instrument, which was not connected with Western Union. It received messages from another instrument that had been installed elsewhere.

To be innocent props, he had hired a hundred actors, who looked like real gamblers. The cashier's cage, wall sheets, and telegraph operator also looked authentic. He had other actors in the cashier's cage and others who went to the windows and placed bets.

The wall clock had been set back a few minutes, as the scheme required that there be an actual winner because it would be easy enough for Macallister to check up on this.

When it was time for the sixth race to start, according to the clock, actually the race was already over. The telegraph began to click. The clerk called out: "Colorado is delaying the start." That was the signal the con men had agreed upon. It meant that Colorado actually was the winner.

Macallister hurried to the window, but it was completely blocked by several men arguing. If he had been able to place his bet, he would have won $10,000. Of course, the con men had no intention of letting him do that; that was why the argument had been staged in front of the cashier's window.

> "Look here!" I said to the cashier. "My friend had $2,500 to bet on that last race, but he couldn't get to the window. Those fellows cost him $10,000."
>
> The cashier shrugged. "I'm sorry, but what can I do? I didn't start the argument."
>
> "Hereafter," I said, truthfully enough, "we'll go elsewhere to make our bets."

Macallister told one of the con men how he had been prevented from making the bet. "This is awful," the con man responded.

"What will I tell the New York operator? He's expecting $5,000 out of this deal." "I don't know about you," the other con man replied, "but I'm going to pack my grip and get out of town. I don't want to be around [if it's discovered] you're in the clutches of the loan sharks." "Just a minute," Macallister said. "I told you I'd lend you the $2,500 and I will. It wasn't your fault the scheme failed."

> I accompanied Macallister to the First National Bank, where he withdrew $7,500 and gave it to me. I told him I would deliver it to my brother-in-law when he got off duty . . . .
> Then I met Billy Wall and we divided the profit, which exceeded $7,000, since expenses had been less than $500.

Weil was far from being through; Macallister still had more money to be conned out of, to be handed over.

> Before I decided to take him again, I strung Macallister along for several months . . . .
> Macallister had heard of wire-tapping and the idea intrigued him . . . .
> Joe Moffatt showed us into a room filled with expensive-looking gadgets. He pointed out a "special transformer—a box about three square feet and eighteen inches deep . . . .
> Actually, there was no such device for stopping messages . . . .
> [Macallister] made a deal with Moffatt to buy the mechanism, including the cables and the set of pole climbers, for $12,000 . . . .
> Moffatt's entire business was with con men. He rigged up inexpensive but fancy-looking gadgets to be sold to wealthy suckers . . . .

Macallister was then brought to another betting parlor.

> [He] was one of the most excitable gamblers I ever knew . . . . He almost stumbled over himself hustling to the window. He bet $10,000 and came back with the ticket trembling in his hands. Avariciously, he listened to the account of the race. As the clerk called out: "Jerry Hunt won" he collapsed completely. I revived him. He went to the window and cashed his ticket. Jerry Hunt paid $18,000 for his $10,000 bet. He was so elated that he insisted on cutting me in, and gave me $2,900 as my part of the winnings. I had taken a long chance.[9]

A Big Con: Example IV—Kreuger's Con(s)

There are numerous documented accounts of the deceitfulness of Ivar Kreuger, the brilliant and ambitious international financier and swindler. One that stands out, that burnishes his reputation of a master swindler, who John Kenneth Galbraith described as "the Leonardo of [his] craft,"[10] is how he completely hoodwinked two prominent American bankers and investors charged with ascertaining his trustworthiness.

When [the American banker] Durant arrived, Kreuger assumed the role of the superb imposter. Kreuger seemed relaxed and gave a huge party for his new American friend. The guests were distinguished-looking men and beautiful women, and Kreuger whispered to Durant that most of the men were foreign ambassadors. Yet, none of them seemed able to speak English, or to have the slightest interest in meeting the guest of honor. It was the era when Americans were dazzled by European titles and pomp. Durant accepted it all, never for a moment suspecting that the dazzling men and lovely women were movie extras, complete with wardrobe costumes, who had been hired by Kreuger for the night.

Durant returned to America more pro-Kreuger than ever. However, the replies he brought back to his prepared questions seemed inconclusive and vague as he tried to focus his mind on assembling Kreuger's stupendous facts. The board of directors listened, but were far from satisfied. It then voted to send Percy A. Rockefeller, another board member, to visit Kreuger, the Match King.

Kreuger cannot have welcomed these inquiring visits. Where he had given Durant only superficial treatment, he had to dig deep for Rockefeller. His foremost weapon was the dummy telephone in his office. It rang constantly while Rockefeller sat across the desk, and Kreuger would lift the phone and say, "Certainly, put His Excellency on." Hand cupping the mouthpiece, he would whisper "Mussolini" to the awed Rockefeller. Then, into the phone: "Greetings, Benito, my dear chap. How are you and what can I do for you?" There would follow a long conversation about an Italian match monopoly, and when that call was finished, another would come from Poincaré, Stanley Baldwin, or even—an amazed Rockefeller reported—from Stalin.

Kreuger then took Rockefeller for a weekend at his island home. The phone again rang constantly with calls from international celebrities, for Kreuger had told his executives to call him at intervals during the day and not to hang up, no matter what nonsense he talked. "I am playing a practical joke on my American friend," he explained.

Rockefeller asked about a set of figures Kreuger had three years before given International Match Corporation. To Rockefeller's amazement, "his host reached back into the recesses of his brilliant mind and reeled off, to the very last dollar, long columns of figures the same ones that had been written down." Throughout the rest of the weekend he listened to Kreuger answering questions from memory, and by the time he returned to Stockholm he could see no point in waiting for the records that, Kreuger still insisted, were being prepared by busy accountants.

And Rockefeller returned to the United States even more impressed than Durant.[11]

More on Kreuger is found in Chapters 6 and 8.

A Big Con: Example V—O. Henry (A Short Story)

The final example of a big con is taken from a short story by the great and droll American writers, O. Henry (William Sidney [or Sydney] Porter). If con men from Charles Ponzi to Bernard Madoff read fiction, one could believe that they stole the whole or drew heavily from this O. Henry tale to develop their financial legerdemain. However, compared to O. Henry's con, Kreuger's and Madoff's cons seems less well planned and unnecessarily convoluted, although, of course, fictional con men can always be made to appear more adroit than their real-life counterparts.

O. Henry's con is found in his "A Tempered Wind," and focuses on one episode in the vagrancy of Buckingham Skinner (Buck) and the story's narrator Parleyvoo Pickens, who on reaching New York City join up and underwrite a con envisioned by Romulus G. Atterbury, "a man with the finest head for financial operations I ever saw. It was all bald and glossy except for gray side whiskers. Seeing that head behind an office railing, and you'd deposit a million with it without a receipt. This Atterbury was well dressed, though he seldom ate."

> Atterbury got to liking me and Buck and he begun to throw on the canvas for us some of his schemes that has caused his hair to evacuate . . . . This time he talked bigger things, and he got us to see 'em as he did. The scheme he laid out looked like a sure winner, and he talked me and Buck into putting our capital

against his burnished dome of thought. It looked all right for a kid-gloved graft. It seemed to be just about an inch and a half outside of the reach of the police, and as money-making as a mint. It was just what me and Buck wanted—a regular business at a permanent stand, with an open air spieling with tonsillitis on the street corners every evening.

So, in six weeks you see a handsome furnished set of offices down in the Wall Street neighborhood, with "The Golconda Gold Bond and Investment Company" in gilt letters on the door. And you see in his private room, with the door open, the secretary and treasurer, Mr. Buckingham Skinner, costumed like the lilies of the conservatory, with his silk hat close to his hand. Nobody yet ever saw Buck outside of an instantaneous reach for his hat.

And you might perceive the president and general manager, Mr. R. G. Atterbury, with his priceless polished poll, busy in the main office room dictating letters to a shorthand countess, who has pomp and a pompadour that is no less than a guarantee to investors.

There is a bookkeeper and an assistant, and a general atmosphere of varnish and culpability.

At another desk the eye is relieved by the sight of an ordinary man, attired with unscrupulous plainness, sitting with his feet up, eating apples, with his obnoxious hat on the back of his head. That man is no other than Colonel Tecumseh (once "Parleyvoo") Pickens, the vice president of the company.

"No recherché rags for me," I says to Atterbury when we was organizing the stage properties of the robbery .... "Cast me for the role of the rhinestone-in-the-rough or I don't go on exhibition ...."

"Dress you up"? says Atterbury; "I should say not! Just as you are you are more to the business than a whole roomful of the things they pin chrysanthemums on. You're to play the part of the solid but disheveled capitalist from the Far West. You despise the conventions. You've got so many stocks you can afford to shake socks. Conservative, homely, rough shrewd, saving— that's your pose. It's a winner in New York. Keep your feet on the desk and eat apples. Whenever anybody comes in eat an apple. Let 'em see you stuff the peelings in a drawer of your desk. Look as economical and rich and rugged as you can."

... I could hear Atterbury saying to victims, as he smiled at me, indulgent and venerating: "That's our vice president , Colonel Pickens ... fortune in Western investment ... delightfully plain manners, but ... could sign a check for half a million ... simple as a child ... wonderful head ... conservative and careful almost to a fault."

Atterbury managed the business. Me and Buck never quite understood all of it, though he explained it to us in full. It seems the company was a kind of cooperative one, and everybody that bought stock shared in the profits. First, we officers bought up a controlling interest—we had to have that—of the shares at 50 cents a hundred—just what the printer charged us—and the rest went to the public at a dollar each. The company guaranteed the stockholders a profit of ten percent each month, payable on the last day thereof.

When any stockholder paid in as much as $100, the company issued him a Gold Bond and he became a bondholder. I asked Atterbury one day what benefits and appurtenances these Gold Bonds was to an investor more so than the immunities and privileges enjoyed by the common sucker who only owned stock. Atterbury picked up one of them Gold Bonds, all gilt and lettered up with flourishes and a big red seal tied with a blue ribbon in bowknot, and he looked at me like his feelings was hurt.

"My dear Colonel Pickens," says he, you have no soul for Art. Think of a thousand homes made happy by possessing one of these beautiful gems of the lithographer's skill! Think of the joy in the household where one of these Gold Bonds hangs by a pink cord to the what-not, or is chewed by the baby, caroling gleefully upon the floor! Ah, I see your eye growing moist, Colonel—I have touched you have I not?"

. . .

Atterbury attended to the details of the concern. As I understand it, they was simple. The investors in stock paid in their money, and—well, I guess that's all they had to do. The company received it, and—I don't call to mind anything else. Me and Buck knew more about selling corn salve than we did about Wall Street, but even we could see how the Golconda Gold Bond Investment Company was making money. You take in money and pay back ten percent of it; it's plain enough that you make a clean, legitimate profit of 90 percent, less expenses, as long as the fish bite.

. . .

It costs us $500 for office rent and first payment on furniture; $1,500 more went for printing and advertising. Atterbury knew his business. "Three months to a minute we'll last," says he. "A day longer than that and we'll have to either go under or under an alias. By that time we ought to clean up $60,000. And then a money belt and a lower berth for me, and the yellow journals and the furniture men can pick the bones."

Our ads. done the work. "Country weeklies and Washington hand-press dailies of course," says I when we was ready to make contracts.

"Man," say Atterbury, "as an advertising manager you would cause a Limburger cheese factory to remain undiscovered during a hot summer. The game we're after is right here in New York and Brooklyn and the Harlem reading-rooms." . . .

Pretty soon the money began to roll in. Buck didn't have to pretend to be busy; his desk was piled high up with money orders and checks and greenbacks. People began to drop in the office and buy stock every day.

. . .

Just as Atterbury said, we ran along about three months without being troubled. Buck cashed the paper as fast as it came in and kept the money in a safe deposit vault a block or so away. Buck never thought much of banks for such purposes. We paid the interest regular on the stock we'd sold, so there was nothing for anybody to squeal about. We had nearly $50,000 on hand and all three of us had been living as high as prize fighters out of training.

. . .

[On the morning a newspaper published a story unmasking the Golconda Gold Bond and Investment Company], me and Buck hurries down to the office. We find on the stairs and in the hall a crowd of people trying to squeeze into our office . . . . Me and Buck judged they'd been reading the papers too.

Being fictional, O. Henry's con men feel remorse for having cheated too many common men and women, young and old, factory workers and mill-hands, and return what they have stolen. Not unsurprisingly, "some of the stockholders that had been doing the Jeremiah act the loudest outside had spasms of restored confidence and wanted to leave the money invested." However, the con game was ended. Before rushing, they told the nemesis newspaper reporter:

"You can't understand it, of course," says Buck, with his hand on the door knob. "Me and Pick ain't Wall Streeters like you know 'em. We never allowed to swindle sick old women and working girls and take nickels off of kids. In the line of graft we worked we took money from the people the Lord made to be buncoed—sports and rounders and smart Alecks and street crowds, that always have a few dollars to throw away, and farmers that wouldn't ever be happy if the grafters didn't come around and play with 'em when they sold their crops. We never cared to fish for the kind of suckers that bite here. No, sir. We got too much respect for the profession and for ourselves...."[12]

Deception is plainly at the core of con games.

Madoff's Deceptions

An examination of Madoff's con reveals that many aspects of what went on at BLMIS is very much like what generally goes on inside most con games. Madoff behaved much like how inside men behave orchestrating a con. His IA was much like any big con; it was much like a theatrical performance. And his victims were much like victims of other con games. Blum has concluded:

During the course of work with confidence men and their victims, we observed a strongly theatrical quality in what transpired. The con men play roles for which they rehearse and make up, they hire one another to do bit parts, they set up stages for action and, when all is ready, they invite the victim not only to be an audience but to participate as an actor in the star role. The victim, in accepting the invitation, moves from the humdrum into a world of impersonation and fantasized gain. It can be amazing to see how readily ordinary folk enter into these dramas, how easily the theater begins, and how practiced they are in impersonating themselves as they would be if they were what their hearts desired.[13]

Next are three snapshots of Madoff in the midst of his con game. The three excerpts here are representatives of the daily complexity of keeping the con game on track. The examples also show that the Madoff scheme had all of the elements—and the drama—of a big con, and can most readily be understood as representative.

Madoff's Deception: Example I

Acting as his own roper, Madoff induced a childhood friend to invest in his con game. The schoolmate described to a Madoff biographer how he was ensnared. After a 50-year hiatus, he telephoned Madoff with some questions about where best to invest the proceeds from his recently sold business. Madoff threw out a few facts about his own asset management fund.

> But when [the friend] popped the question about getting into the fund, Madoff declined. "I can't," he said. "It's a closed fund." At that, Bernie told him there was someone in his office who wanted to speak with him. He handed the phone to Ruth [Madoff].
>
> They chatted "excitedly," until she interrupted him in midsentence.
>
> "Bernie wants to talk to you again," she said. Bernie took the phone back. "You know what . . . we've known you a long time, and I'll open it up for you to come in . . . . But can you meet the minimum?" Bernie cited $2 million. "I can meet that . . . . Do you mind if I bring others in with me, some family?" "Not at all," Madoff said.

The appreciative childhood friend and his wife then "took Bernie and Ruth out to dinner."[14]

Madoff's Deception: Example II

Jeffrey Tucker, an executive at the FGG, one of BLMIS's principal ropers (see Chapter 8) had been invited by Madoff to the BLMIS offices for an impromptu due-diligence visit. With the help of his backroom accomplices, Madoff hoped to convince Tucker that all of the equities he claimed he had been purchasing were safely held in an account at Wall Street's central clearinghouse, the Depository Trust Company (DTC). With a well-prepared theatrical performance, his polished presentation, and a small supporting cast, Madoff was easily able to fool Tucker.

Going well beyond the usual practice of using fraudulent trade confirmations and account statements generated by BLMIS employees to routinely deceive clients, with the Tucker staging, props were introduced and utilized to make it appear that actual trades were with regularity being conducted and equities were accounted for—and in safe hands. At the center of the ruse was Madoff simulating that he was connected to a DTC computer terminal, while in reality he was communicating with a BLMIS employee in front of another computer terminal in another room, a few feet away. Here is Tucker's testimony[15] of his visit:

Q: And going back to what you were saying. In 2001, did you visit Madoff's offices for a meeting with Bernard Madoff and Frank DiPascali?

A: DiPascali?

Q: DiPascali, yes.

A: Yes.

Q: So, could you please describe that meeting?

A: Yes. In 2001, one or two articles had been published; the first was in *MARHedge* and the second was in *Barron's*, and they were about Madoff and his business. The *Barron's* article clearly, was somewhat, critical. Much of it I thought was frankly just irresponsible journalism. However, Madoff called me, as I said—I think it was after the *Barron's* article—and said: "You know, do you—are you getting feedback from your clients?" And I said: "We have some who are concerned, but that the principal concern I have is that the assets are there." And so he said: "Come up this afternoon." He indicated that . . . who was one of the principals of . . . was in New York, and he was going to invite . . . as well. And I went up there that same day in the afternoon and met with Bernie and Frank. The meeting started with Bernie saying: "Pick any date that you want," and I selected a couple of days which I believe were [from] the prior October. Bernie then told Frank to go and get the ledgers or journals and he came back five or ten minutes later and opened up what he purported to be a P&S (Purchase & Sell) blotter, which was a record of each trade, the amount of shares, the price and the counterparty. And he let me just thumb through the pages and there were—it was a big journal with quite a few pages for that particular day. There were small trades, 700 shares, 1,500 shares, and there were some treasury trades in there as well. So it would have been a time when we were either selling or buying treasuries and I believe it was probably a point where we were selling treasuries to get out of cash and into the market. He then opened up another journal which was purportedly the stock record for Madoff Securities and let me, again, turn through it. And he said:

"Pick any two stocks." I picked AOL/Time Warner. We turned to that page and the page had the—a total and below it a listing of each—purportedly of each client and their positions in shares. And I saw that we were the first name because it was done in size. . . . was right next to us, there were some similar funds, and I would say probably 100 names on the list. My recollection is there were four-million-plus AOL/Time Warner shares in the firm, purportedly. He then activated—he and Frank activated—a screen that he said would get us into their DTC account. And then they continued to move pages on the screen until they got to the AOL page, and with the stock record I could compare the total number of AOL shares according to the Madoff stock record with the Madoff account at DTC, which were the same. And I knew that the position I saw for us was roughly what we had because I was somewhat familiar with our size in shares. And . . . essentially he said to me: "You know, I've got confidentiality agreements that I'm breaching, but I think it's important that I show you this to you." That was basically the meeting.

Q: So, how did you know that the screen you were looking at was the DTC screen?

A: It had a logo. It had a DTC logo. It was not a full-sized screen like this one here [the screen of the individual transcribing the testimony] . . . . But it had a logo, and then I could see the pages being turned electronically until they got to the AOL page.

Q: Had you ever seen a DTC screen before?

A: No.

Q: So, this was the first time you'd seen a DTC screen?

A: Yes.

Q: And you believed it was a DTC screen because it had a logo. Did it say DTC?

A: DTC?

Q: And because it was telling you that; because Madoff told you that?

A: Yeah, of course.

    . . .

Q: So, you compared what was on that purported DTC screen with the AOL holdings on Madoff Securities stock records. Is that correct?

A: Yes.

Q: And did they exactly match up or were they roughly the same?

A: Yes, exactly.

Q: They exactly matched up, okay. And did you get a printout of the DTC screen?
A: No.
Q: Did you repeat the review with any other equity or option, or was it just the AOL shares?
A: I think just AOL.
Q: Okay.
A: Again, I saw the pages turn, but that was the only one we stopped on.
Q: Did the DTC screen mention FGG as the beneficial owner?
A: No.
Q: So, it was in the name of Bernard L . . . .?
A: Madoff, yeah.
Q: But there's no beneficial owner listed?
A: I did not see anything.
Q: Okay. Now, did you ever repeat that review, the comparison of the DTC screen against the Madoff stock record?
A: No.
Q: Are you aware of anyone else at FGG who ever repeated that review?
A: Not that I know of.
Q: Okay.[16]

Between 2001 and December 2008, Madoff helped to make Tucker even richer.

Madoff's Deception: Example III

It was essential for Madoff to work with others who would help him carry out his complex criminal activity, and who he could trust not to betray him. He needed individuals who he could depend on year in and year out. Family members are oftentimes such individuals; at least, this was the case with Bernard Madoff and his younger brother, Peter. Bernard Madoff was able to use Peter to work with him to help his con game to continue and to grow exponentially. Peter Madoff's role was a manager of Bernard Madoff's con game who had a somewhat circumscribed charge of BLMIS, and for decades he proved to be an able and steadfast ally, more loyal to his brother than his brother was to him. In the words of one FBI agent involved in gathering evidence for the government, "Peter Madoff played an essential enabling role" in Bernard Madoff's "house of cards."[17]

With a law degree and some knowledge of computer technology, Peter Madoff was viewed as a talented senior executive at BLMIS. He was the chief compliance officer, senior marketing director, and head of the market making and proprietary trading operations. He was in place to be an ideal hustler/confederate/capper—or outside man.

Like his older brother, Peter also greatly enjoyed acquiring considerable wealth, material things—houses in Old Westbury, Long Island, and Palm Beach; a Park Avenue co-op; a 1995 (355 Spyder) Ferrari and a vintage Aston Martin ($140,000 and $274,563, respectively, paid for by BLMIS), etc. And, in addition, according to a court document submitted by the SIPC trustee, "On April 14 and June 2, 2004, $450,000 and $4,000,000, respectively, were wired from [an IA account] to Peter in connection with the purchase of [his] apartment located at 975 Park Avenue."[18]

In early May 2012, the SIPC trustee filed an expanded $255.3 million lawsuit against members of the Madoff family who had worked at BLMIS—Peter Madoff; Mark (who had committed suicide) and Andrew Madoff, Bernard Madoff's sons; Shana Madoff, Peter's daughter and a compliance officer in the firm; and their families (wives, ex-wives, and children). The amount of money the SIPC trustee wanted returned for the benefit of the victims had grown from, initially, $198.7 million in October to $226.4 million in November 2009. From this total, the trustee sought the return of $90.4 million from Peter Madoff.

As the SIPC trustee saw it, Peter Madoff had over too many years been particularly derelict. Quite simply, his "duties and responsibilities [as CCO (chief compliance officer)] were well-defined by law. Yet, he failed miserably to meet them." His older brother claimed that he had other companies handling his IA trading, but it is difficult to imagine Peter Madoff not having asked him why this trading was not done at BLMIS: "Why aren't you trading with us?" or "Who are you trading with?" (Of course, many other BLMIS employees might have asked these same questions.)

According to the SIPC trustee's accounting, Peter Madoff had been paid $36,245,000 in salary and bonuses for the 15 years prior to the collapse of BLMIS in 2008, and "he received over $3.8 million paid either directly to him or to vendors on his behalf as a 'draw' during that same period . . . . Peter also directly received, and/or benefited from, over $1.5 million in salary from his wife Marion Madoff's 'no-show' job with BLMIS." (Actually, the figure appears to be closer to $1.6 million.) He, of course, was able to avoid the detection of tax authorities by disguising the payments he took from BLMIS as loans or back-dated stock trades.

Moreover, the only contributions Peter Madoff appears to have made to his two BLMIS IA accounts over the years totaled $32,146. Yet, the record shows that he redeemed $16,252,004 from this investment. (In one egregious instance of how his BLMIS IA account accumulated such a large sum of money, his March 2002 account statement shows that approximately $15.4 million worth of Microsoft stock was acquired ["purchased"] for his account in December 2000 and "sold" in January 2002, earning him $8,752,620. In May, he withdrew nearly $6 million of this money. From April 2003 through May 2005, he withdrew an additional $6.9 million from the same account.)

In effect, Peter Madoff, as with all other BLMIS employees who assisted Madoff in his fraud, was rewarded with both an inflated salary and BLMIS-created investment earnings.

In testimony in his own trial, Peter Madoff denied knowing his brother had been stealing the money investors had been handing over to him, but he did not deny that he too was a criminal. He had worked for BLMIS since the late 1960s, and at the time the fraud was uncovered, he was not only the firm's chief operating and compliance officer but also the general counsel. He owned only a very small part of the firm's London money-laundering operation; he did not own any of BLMIS.

Peter Madoff faced far fewer criminal charges than his brother, only two felonies: participating in a conspiracy to commit fraud, to falsify books, records, and statements; making false filings to the government; committing mail fraud; and obstructing or impeding lawful government functions. Three years after his brother was sent to prison, in his mostly scripted 17-minute allocution he admitted his guilt to a federal judge.

> PETER MADOFF: Your Honor, I am here today to plead guilty to conspiracy and falsifying records of an investment advisor . . . .
>
> On several occasions my brother and I engaged in money transfers in ways specifically designed to avoid the payment of taxes . . . . In addition, at my request, my wife was placed on the . . . payroll and for many years received compensation for a no-show job . . . .
>
> With respect to the conspiracy charge, I am pleading guilty because I conspired with others to commit several violations of the law: attempts to interfere with the administration of the

Internal Revenue Laws; falsifying the books and records of an investment advisor; false filings with the SEC [Securities and Exchange Commission]; and mail fraud and securities fraud.

...I conspired with others to prevent the IRS [Internal Revenue Service] from collecting proper tax revenue—to my and my family's benefit—in three different ways: [1] [Failing to report] various fringe benefits. [2] My brother gave me a substantial sum of money .... [A]t the same time, I also asked for an equal amount of money to give to my daughter .... [I]n order to avoid the payment of a gift tax ... we treated the stock transaction as though it had occurred in my account rather than my brother's. In 2002, in order to avoid the payment of a gift tax on a transfer from my brother to me, we treated a similar stock transaction as though it had occurred in my account rather than my brother's .... [3] In 2005, 2007, and 2008, I received gifts from my brother which I used to provide my children with substantial sums of money. Although I had no expectation of repayment, I required my children to execute promissory notes for the amounts I provided in order to avoid gift tax. On these and other occasions, my brother provided me with gifts of substantial sums of money which I had no intention of repaying, and some of these transfers were documented as loans in order to avoid a gift tax.

... [In addition], in 2006 through 2008, I knowingly signed and/or approved false compliance documentation ....

... [As] chief compliance officer, I failed to implement any meaningful supervision over my brother's management of the customer business and failed to confirm his representations that he was trading and managing investment advisory accounts in compliance with the customers' directions. Nevertheless, I approved and/or signed as chief compliance officer documents falsely certifying that I had [fulfilled my responsibilities] .... I knew at the time that these statements were false ....

In addition, in 2006 and 2007, I allowed my brother to file with the SEC an investment advisor registration form ... I knew contained false and misleading statements. For example, at Bernie's direction, the form falsely stated that BLMIS had only 23 investment advisory accounts. Although I did not know the true number of the accounts, I did know there were more than 23 accounts. I failed to include ... the material fact that my brother was only registering for a limited number of accounts or money under management .... I knew that these misstatements on the form allowed my brother to conceal the true extent of my brother's customer business, as well as the fact . . . that the form was required to be filed with the SEC and that it would be available to customers.

I also conspired with others to falsify employment and payroll records of BLMIS including false reports that were filed with the Department of Labor . . . .

Finally . . . in December of 2008 [as Bernard Madoff was confessing his crime], I agreed to assist my brother who was planning to pay out remaining customer funds to a limited number of customers—specifically, family, friends and employees— thereby depriving investors the opportunity to share in those funds . . . .

In addition, the next day [after he and his brother discussed the latter's criminal activity], I had taken out $200,000 from the firm . . . .

As previously explained, I approved and/or signed documents that included false statements . . . . [For example], when I signed the [2007 Annual Review] . . . I knew that it was false.[19]

There is no record of Peter Madoff being asked or responding to the question of what made him believe that trading was being carried out in the IA business. He knew that there was an office staff on the 17th floor, but he never saw an assemblage of brokers buying and selling securities. He saw a record in his monthly statements of trading— always buying low and always selling high—making him increasingly wealthy. Yet, he never saw evidence of trades being made. He had no idea who his brother's counterparties were in his options trading. He must have believed that, whoever they were, they were uncommonly stupid or unlucky or profligate. His brother was never on the losing side of a transaction with them. Many others at BLMIS, beginning with his daughter and nephews, could have been asked the same question.

As he admitted in court, Peter Madoff was clearly a party to some of his brother's crimes. Through his own criminal activities, he contributed to Bernard Madoff's con. In spite of what he admitted about himself in his court testimony, he spoke out about his brother's "atrocious conduct," never about his own crimes. Echoing Claude Rains in *Casablanca*, he said that he was "in total shock" and "shocked and devastated" when he learned that his brother was a con man.

Whether or not Peter Madoff knew that his brother was stealing all of the money his IA customers had given him to invest, or only some of the money, or perhaps only a little of the money is not a particularly important fact to establish. It is immaterial to determine if there was a single inside man, a sole architect of the con, if Bernard Madoff kept secrets of his criminal activity from his brother. It is also immaterial whether or not, as it has been widely claimed, Peter Madoff felt intimidated by his brother. Bernard Madoff may have bullied and intimidated his younger brother, but his beneficence was never refused. In fact, Peter Madoff also appeared to ask for more and more—a no-show job for his wife, additional money for his daughter. As Chapter 6 most clearly shows, Bernard Madoff readily deceived not only his victims but also his accomplices. What is important is that Peter Madoff, Frank DiPascali, Jr., as well as other accomplices contributed to a series of crimes. They knowingly participated in a criminal conspiracy. They did not passively fall into crime; they did not casually ignore the rules. They set out to break them. As the assistant U.S. Attorney pointed out to the judge during Peter Madoff's trial, when he "signed many weeks of compliance reports in one sitting [he] intentionally chang[ed] pens and ink colors in order to disguise the fact that he had created them at one time and that they were false." Both Madoff brothers are felons.

It is unlikely when he was engaged in criminal activity that Peter Madoff believed that only he and not his brother was breaking the law.

For being a party to the crimes within BLMIS and for his silence, Peter Madoff was generously rewarded. At his trial, the U.S. Attorney's office emphasized the government's claim made earlier that over a 10-year period, from 1998 through 2008, he "received at least $40 million" from the firm. He is much more than a footnote to his brother's decades-long con. As an Internal Revenue Service official put it, the Madoff "scheme relied on sophisticated teamwork to prevent its discovery." Clearly, Peter Madoff was a central part of the fraud.

Contrary to his fatuous falsehood that he had acted alone, not long after Bernard Madoff's arrest, the evidence began to quickly mount that others—many others—had assisted him in carrying out his con game.[20] Actually, from the day of his arrest in 2008, it was inconceivable that he could have acted alone. It was a collective effort that he could not have done by himself. He needed at least three types of support. First, he needed assistance to create and maintain the BLMIS books and records. He needed to maintain two sets of books and records, one that reflected the true state of his business and one to show to taxing authorities and regulators. Second, he needed computer systems support to fabricate information about trades (although they were fictional), to keep track of customer accounts, and to produce and distribute customer account statements. Third, he needed clerical help to manufacture documents for taxing authorities and regulators. For example, although there was no actual income, he had to create a record of income. Moreover, because there were no trading counterparties, he was not receiving automatically generated data that he otherwise would have if there were any.

In order to successfully defraud victims in a confidence game, it is necessary to deceive them at every turn. As with every con, Madoff's con was replete with deception—among other things, an inoperative trading strategy, imaginary trades of stocks and bonds, mass-producing fabricated monthly statements for customers, claiming business relationships that never existed, bluffing customers, employees, regulators, and the public, pretending competence, feigning friendship with those being victimized.

The next chapter focuses on those implicated in assisting Madoff in furthering his con game, those for whom deception was routine. At its center are excerpts from court testimony of former Madoff employees as each describes their participation and practice. Taken together, this testimony provides a number of details of how Madoff's big con worked.

Appendix 1-A

Excerpts from the Transcript of Guilty Plea Proceedings for Bernard L. Madoff, March 12, 2009

The essence of my scheme was that I represented to clients and prospective clients who wished to open investment advisory and individual trading accounts with me that I would invest their money in shares of common stock, options, and other securities of large well-known corporations, and upon request, would return to them their profits and principal. Those representations were false for many years. Up until I was arrested on December 11, 2008, I never invested these funds in the securities, as I had promised. Instead, those funds were deposited in a bank account at the JPMorgan Chase Bank. When clients wished to receive the profits they believed they had earned with me or to redeem their principal, I used the money in the JPMorgan Chase Bank account that belonged to them or other clients to pay the requested funds. The victims of my scheme included individuals, charitable organizations, trusts, pension funds, and hedge funds.

. . .

To further cover up the fact that I had not executed trades on behalf of my investment advisory clients, I knowingly caused false trading confirmations and client account statements that reflected the bogus transactions and positions to be created and sent to clients purportedly involved in the split-strike conversion strategy, as well as to other individual clients I defrauded who believed they had invested in securities through me.

. . .

In more recent years, I used yet another method to conceal my fraud. I wired money between the United States and the United Kingdom to make it appear as though there were actual securities transactions executed on behalf of my investment advisory clients. Specifically, I had money transferred from the U.S. bank account of my investment advisory business to the London bank account of Madoff Securities International Limited (MSIL) a United Kingdom corporation that was an affiliate of my business in New York.... I caused money from the bank account of my fraudulent advisory business, located here in Manhattan, to be wire-transferred to the London bank account of MSIL.

. . .

I caused the fraudulent investment advisory side of my business to charge the investment advisory clients four cents per share as a commission .... I did this to ensure that the expenses associated with the operation of my fraudulent advisory business would not be paid from the operations of the legitimate proprietary trading and market making businesses.

(Transcript: *United States of America v. Bernard L. Madoff*, 09-CR-213 [Denny Chin, District Judge], 24–30.)

Appendix 1-B

Excerpts from a Report of the Forensic Investigation into the Financial Affairs of the BLMIS Con by Examiner Joseph Looby, October 16, 2009

Organization of BLMIS

9. BLMIS was organized into three business units, the market making unit, the proprietary trading unit, and the investment advisory business.

13. BLMIS employees generally referred to the IA business as "House 17" and the market making and proprietary trading businesses combined as "House 5."

16. The House 17 AS/400 was used only in connection with the IA business. The House 5 AS/400 and other computer systems were used in connection with the market making and proprietary trading businesses.

BLMIS Bank Accounts and Customer Deposits

17. BLMIS used two primary bank accounts to fund its disbursements, one held at Bank of New York Mellon (the "621 Account") and another held at JPMorgan Chase Bank (the "703 Account").

18. The 703 Account was primarily used for customer deposits and withdrawals from the IA business. Amounts invested in BLMIS by customers were deposited into the 703 Account. Similarly, the majority of redemptions by [IA] customers were withdrawn from the 703 Account.[21]

19. Remaining cash balances in this account at the end of each day were transferred to affiliated overnight investment accounts at JPMorgan Chase Bank and other investments until additional monies were needed to fund additional withdrawal requests by customers, capital needs of the broker-dealer operation at BLMIS, or Madoff's (and other insiders') personal needs.

22. By early December 2008, BLMIS generated client account statements for about 4,900 customer accounts (the "November 30, 2008 statements"). When added together, and after netting out approximately $8.3 billion of amounts shown as owed to BLMIS, these statements erroneously showed approximately $64.8 billion of investments with BLMIS. In reality, BLMIS had assets on hand worth a small fraction of that amount.

23. The $64.8 billion balance recorded on BLMIS customer statements is net of "negative" accounts that approximate $8.3 billion. The total amount shown on the November 30, 2008 customer statements for the 4,900 accounts with purported positive equity balances totals $73.1 billion.

The Proprietary Trading and Market Making Businesses

27. Review of the financial history of BLMIS demonstrates that neither of these [proprietary trading and market making] business units would have been viable without the fraudulent IA business, the proceeds of which were used to sustain those business operations from at least 2007 forward.

The IA Business

32. Outwardly, the IA business functioned as both an investment advisor to its customers and as a custodian of their securities. The precise date on which BLMIS began purportedly engaging in investment

advisory services has not been established, but it appears that BLMIS was offering such services as far back as the 1960s.

33. There were 25 individuals that worked for the IA business of BLMIS.

38. There were essentially two groups of IA business customer accounts, the split-strike conversion strategy accounts, administered by Frank DiPascali, and the non-split-strike conversion accounts, administered by other BLMIS employees.

40. The House 17 AS/400 was designed to record and assist with the printing of the fictitious securities purportedly bought and sold by BLMIS, customer cash transactions, customer statements, trade confirmations, management reports, and Internal Revenue Service 1099 forms.

41. Importantly, the House 17 AS/400 was not connected, inter-faced, and/or reconciled to any of the systems used to facilitate or execute the purchase and sale of securities at BLMIS. It was a closed system, separate and distinct from any computer system utilized by the other BLMIS business units. [This is] consistent with one designed to mass produce fictitious customer statements.

42. As of November 30, 2008, DiPascali was identified in the House 17 AS/400 as administering 4,649 active customer accounts, primarily the split-strike conversion accounts.

43. As of November 30, 2008, the House 17 AS/400 identified 244 active accounts administered by other BLMIS employees.

47. Because fictitious trades require no opposite broker to execute and complete the trade, no counterparties existed and none were iden-tified in the House 17 AS/400 system. None of the split-strike trades entered into the House 17 AS/400 were reconciled (or reconcilable) with the DTC

The Split-Strike Conversion Strategy

50. The split-strike conversion strategy involved the purported sale of the baskets [of equities], moving customer funds completely out of the market to purported investment in treasuries, money market funds, and cash reserves until the next presumed trading opportunity arose. At the end of each quarter, all baskets would be allegedly sold and alleg-edly invested in treasuries or money market funds, and cash reserves.

51. However, no securities were actually purchased by BLMIS for its customers and the money received from a customer was not invested in securities for the benefit of that customer, but was instead primarily used to make distributions to, or payments made on behalf

of, other investors as well as withdrawals and payments to Madoff family members and employees.

56. At no point while customer funds were purportedly either in the market or out of the market, however, were such funds invested as shown on the fictitious statements. Instead, to the extent that such customer funds had not already been expended, they were held in the JPMorgan Chase Bank 703 Account.

57. In fact, one of the money market funds in which customer resources were purportedly invested through BLMIS, as reflected on customer statements as late as 2008, was the Fidelity Brokerage Services LLC's Fidelity Spartan US Treasury Money Market Fund. However, Fidelity has acknowledged that from 2005 onwards, Fidelity did not offer participation in any such money market fund investment.

64. Once a basket [of equities] trade was identified as one that achieved the fictitious return desired, certain employees, known as key punch operators, were provided with the relevant basket information that they entered manually into the House 17 AS/400. The basket trade was then routinely (e.g., monthly) replicated in the selected BLMIS split-strike customer accounts automatically and proportionally according to the fraction or number of baskets each customer's purported net equity could purportedly afford.

66. With the benefit of backdating (i.e., the knowledge of previously published priced history), Madoff and his employees at BLMIS were able to consistently generate purported annual returns for split-strike conversion customer accounts generally between about 10% and 17%.

The Non-Split-Strike Conversion Strategy Accounts

75. The non-split-strike conversion strategy customer accounts included many long-time customers … and accounts held by various Madoff family members and employees.

76. The non-split-strike conversion strategy customer accounts reported unusually high rates of returns, often in excess of 100% [a year].

Appendix 1-C

Excerpts from a Report of a Forensic Accounting Analysis by Bruce G. Dubinsky of the IA Business of BLMIS, November 22, 2011/ January 6, 2012

19. There is no evidence that the purported investment transactions for House 17 customers ever occurred at least as far back as the 1970s.

In fact, the evidence shows that trading did not occur. Reconciliations of: 1. House 17 equity positions to available DTC records and 2. Option trades with the available Option Clearing Corporation records indicate that no securities transactions were executed by House 17.

20. The convertible [a security that can be converted into another security] trading strategy purportedly implemented by BLMIS in the 1970s utilized fictitious trades that in many instances exceeded the entire reported market volume for the particular security on the day it was purportedly traded. On numerous trading days, trades were reported at prices that did not represent true prices, as the prices reported for the purported trades were outside the range of market reporting trading prices on a given day. Dividend payments and/or accrued interest were not reported by House 17 on many customer statements even though the real convertible securities paid such dividends and/or interest. Further, convertible securities were reported by House 17 as being traded on days after the actual date of conversion reported by the issuing corporation, thereby evidencing the fictitious nature of the purported trades . . . .

21. The split-strike conversion strategy, purportedly put into place by BLMIS in the 1990s, utilized fictitious trades that in many instances exceeded the entire reported market for the particular security on numerous trading days. Many reported trades were recorded at prices that did not represent true prices as the prices reported were outside the range of reported trading prices on a given day. House 17 supposedly executed 83% of buy transactions by share volume below the "Volume Weighted Average Price" and executed 72% of the sell transactions above the "Volume Weighted Average Price," statistics that evidence the fictitious nature of the trades.

22. Purported trades were recorded as being settled on weekends or holidays when the US stock and option exchanges were closed, and were also supposedly settled after the normal acceptable industry mandated time period, . . . again supporting the opinion that these trades simply never occurred. In addition, billions of dollars of purported dividends earned that was reported on House 17 customer statements were fictitious and were never received by BLMIS, again showing the fictitious nature of the trades.

23. House 17 created fake reports from the DTC trading clearinghouse . . . . House 17 customer statements contained fictitious trades that were back-dated using special software modified in-house to reprint customer statements after the fact. Also, extensive in-house computer programs were created to conceal the fictitious investment transactions.

27. As further proof, a solvency analysis was conducted and it was determined that BLMIS was insolvent as of at least December 11, 2002. BLMIS's customer liabilities were approximately $12 billion as of December 11, 2002, far exceeding the fair market value of its assets by $10 billion.

212. BLMIS was registered with the SEC as a broker-dealer as of January 19, 1960, and it was not until 46 years later that it was registered, beginning in 2006, as an investment advisor.

214. On [that] application, BLMIS reported representation of 23 customer accounts and assets under management of approximately $17.1 billion. In actuality, in or around January 2008, BLMIS had approximately 4,900 active customer accounts and purported assets under management of approximately $74 billion.

241. In order for House 17 to have realized the investment returns as reported on its customer statements and continue to make cash disbursements to customers from these earnings, the purported trades would have had to have been actually executed in the market. They were not.

249. The investigation and analysis of cash flows and cash transfers between House 5 and House 17 show that aside from the House 17 liquidity crisis and transfers during the waning days of BLMIS in December 2008, House 5 did not provide financial support to House 17. Furthermore, other than during the House 17 liquidity crisis, the investigation shows that House 17 received no financial support from third parties, i.e., loans. Therefore, any distribution to House 17 customers came from other people's money.

250. In fact, monies were being diverted not from House 5 to House 17, but from House 17 to House 5.

302. [According to an analysis of valuation] the resulting negative $9.95 billion demonstrates that BLMIS was deeply insolvent as of December 11, 2002 [6 years before BLMIS was placed into bankruptcy].

Appendix 1-D

Table 1.1   BLMIS Disbursements to Investors, 1981–2008

Year	Number of Disbursements in Excess of Deposits	Aggregate Value of Disbursements in Excess of Deposits	Average Disbursement Amount	Number of Accounts
1981	10	$239,466	$23,947	9
1982	36	$487,199	$13,533	23
1983	37	$2,431,473	$65,715	19
1984	38	$782,991	$20,605	23
1985	192	$7,135,066	$37,162	71
1986	375	$18,858,068	$50,288	92
1987	497	$14,174,763	$28,521	111
1988	722	$35,995,555	$49,855	164
1989	992	$49,914,278	$50,317	184
1990	1,122	$45,713,503	$40,743	225
1991	1,469	$71,552,235	$48,708	283
1992	1,858	$519,368,321	$279,531	313
1993	2,500	$228,463,943	$91,386	424
1994	2,667	$282,226,802	$105,822	447
1995	3,133	$479,946,926	$153,191	456
1996	3,932	$539,182,466	$137,127	528
1997	3,003	$668,343,286	$222,559	703
1998	2,443	$786,614,902	$321,987	483
1999	2,995	$999,865,155	$333,845	625
2000	3,848	$1,149,561,399	$298,743	848
2001	4,340	$1,352,096,251	$311,543	922
2002	4,974	$1,391,790,937	$279,813	1,082
2003	6,278	$1,675,967,743	$266,959	1,288
2004	6,913	$1,572,900,380	$227,528	1,439
2005	7,453	$1,576,183,767	$211,483	1,627
2006	8,739	$1,227,904,383	$140,509	1,840
2007	9,573	$1,732,389,729	$180,966	2,072
2008	9,220	$1,901,590,538	$206,246	2,090
Total	89,359	$18,331,681,525		

Source: Letter from Stephen P. Harbeck, president of SIPC, to Congressman Scott Garrett, January 24, 2011, 12–13.

Appendix 1-E

Description by Frank DiPascali, Jr. of Sham and Authentic Trades at BLMIS[22]

Q: How would you get that information for the options trading for the IA business?

A: Initially?

Q: Generally over time?

A: Bernie had a list of clients that they had agreed were going to start to trade options to hedge their accounts. Some of those clients were Annette's clients, so I would get information from her and then provide Annette with option to trades that would do exactly what Bernie wanted.

Eventually, some of those clients became my clients directly. I would do the research as to pricing mechanisms. I would write the tickets, and then I would give them to Annette . . . I was providing the information and writing some of the tickets.

Q: When Mr. Madoff asked you to do these index options after the stock market crash, did you realize that the trading in the IA accounts wasn't really happening?

A: Correct, yes.

Q: The trading was fake?

A: Yes.

Q: Did you nonetheless go ahead and provide him with the index options information that he wanted?

A: Yes.

Q: Who managed most of these client accounts in the latter part of the 1980's?

A: Annette.

Q: On the accounts that you worked on, did Ms. Bongiorno continue to have involvement?

A: She was processing the work that I created.

Q: Who were some of the clients that you dealt with?

A: Fred Wilpon and his family, his lawyers and his partners, some high-net-worth individuals that were clients of Bernie's. A fellow by the name of Richard Schafler was one of my first clients. He had a series of accounts for his mother's trust, for his sister, for his business. It was a pretty small list of clients.

Q: The trading that was happening in all these accounts, was it real?

A: No.

Q: Was any of that trading happening at all?

A: No.

Q: Did you ever hear Ms. Bongiorno discussing with her clients that the trading was coming from BLMIS trading room?

A: Occasionally.

Q: What does it mean that the trading was coming from the BLMIS trading room? Or what would that mean?

A: It would mean that the trades were being done in the trading room and that her part of the process was to ascertain which trades were done for this client, and then post them to that client's account and process that client's confirmations and statements, and so on. It presumes these trades are happening in the trading room when you say I'm waiting for my work from the trading room or whatever, yes.

Q: Going back to the 1970s, if a trade were happening in the trading room, what would have to happen?

A: There would have to be communications with a counterparty— another dealer or some other broker-dealer. It's a relatively complex little free-for-all that goes on for a trade to happen, especially in arbitrage, especially convertible arbitrage. You're trying to execute a transaction with two different brokers, possibly in two different markets, and trying to get this done in as little time as possible so that you don't have any risk . . . .

Q: You have to look at real-time information about the prices of stocks, right?

A: Correct.

Q: Over the years in the 1970s and the 1980s, did you see Ms. Bongiorno looking at real-time prices for stocks?

A: No.

Q: How did you see her trades being put together?

A: She would get information from David [Kugel] which was being culled from back-dated newspapers.

Q: From yesterday's *Wall Street Journal*?

A: Yes.

Q: Can you buy stock using yesterday's *Wall Street Journal* at the prices you see in there?

A: No.

CHAPTER 2

Backstage, the Accomplices

This chapter continues the examination of how Madoff's con game worked by focusing on the activities of the BLMIS backstage employees who were hidden from regulators and most clients. The chapter centers on seven relatively well-paid office workers who pled guilty to being accomplices and engaging in criminal activities. Of the seven, only one acknowledged that he knew he was furthering a Ponzi scheme.

Bernie's Version

After his arrest, when Madoff hollowly claimed that he was able to carry out his con unassisted, few, if any, believed him. Many more were put on guard never to believe any of his subsequent claims. It was not uncommon to hear him described as delusional. (See Introduction and Chapter 1.) Whatever his grasp on reality, in over a half dozen interviews granted to journalists in his early years in prison, he revealed little about his activities at BLMIS, and a good deal of the little that he did share appears to be false, contradicted by facts uncovered by government prosecutors and defense attorneys or by the accounts of others.

More than one of the journalists was told by Madoff that until the early 1980s his investment strategy had worked well, that his clients' accounts saw large returns. It was not until the stock market's steep decline of 1987, he claimed, that the con game began in earnest. It was then that four large investors insisted on selling their holdings that he was unable to do without having to sustain heavy losses. He was at the mercy of them, and their greed. In the decade that followed, the stock market did not have enough volatility to allow him to overcome this setback and return to his earlier successes. He simply was not able to produce substantial profits to meet his clients' expectations of above-average returns. The Ponzi scheme began in 1992 when he routinely used new deposits to pay returns on other accounts. After that there were simply no trades and he began forging trading slips.[1] With this neat account, Madoff would like to largely exonerate himself: "I was simply a victim of an economic cycle and the greed of others that pushed me into it." However, there is enough material in this chapter to refute his version of events.

It might be true, but nonetheless too facile to simply label Madoff as delusional. One would expect little else from the conversation of someone who early in his entire adult life became a performer creating the persona of the astute investor, a successful businessman, and a worldly and important personage. During the time his con operated, Madoff had to constantly perform these roles; he was continually on stage. He was creating an impression for his audience of investors, BLMIS employees, the world of Wall Street, government regulators, and, maybe or maybe not, family members. Others, wittingly and unwittingly, helped him put on his show, sustain it, and witnessed it, but it was largely his show. He had to be persuasive enough to prevent his audience from learning that there was no character behind the character he invented.[2] Being a consummate actor was how Madoff understood the world, and the little he has said since his arrest suggests that he still understands the world that way.

By withholding the secret of how his con game worked, Bernard Madoff, although a disgraced man, business failure, and convicted felon surely in prison for the remainder of his life, retained for a few months a power that seemed uniquely his own—like the most adroit conjurer—the knowledge of how he carried out his deception. As the considerable dimensions of his con game became clearer, his claim that he had acted alone began to seem ludicrous; it was implausible, simply not possible. It was not long before, in the face of pressure from authorities, some of his conspirators broke their silence—agreed to a plea bargain—and, backstage at BLMIS, where Madoff's accomplices were helping him defraud investors, what once seemed mysterious and intriguing proved to be somewhat banal.

The more that was revealed about the magnitude of Madoff's con game, the clearer it became that there was a fully committed supporting cast who worked together on the set, backstage, as part of Madoff's con. Goffman sees a set or setting—"involving furniture, décor, physical layout and other background items which supply the scenery and stage props"—as a standard part of any performance.[3] In a con game, the set is often referred to as a boiler room (or bucket shop).

In comparing a theatrical performance and a staged confidence game, Goffman notes that both require "a thorough scripting of the spoken content of the routine; but the vast part involving '—expression given off' is often determined by meager stage directions. It is expected that the performer of illusions will already know a good deal about how to manage his [or her] voice, his [or her] face and his [or her] body, although he [or she]—as well as any person who directs him—may find it difficult indeed to provide a detailed verbal statement of this kind of knowledge."[4] This was the template for Madoff's con. Planning was involved; what occurred was far from being extemporaneous. At the same time, the improvisations and reversals Madoff was forced to make as events unfolded over the years showed that he was far from completely prepared for the full range of unanticipated eventualities.

The chapter begins with a listing of the 15 individuals who were found criminally responsible for participating in the Madoff con.

Fifteen Criminally Responsible for Participating in the Madoff Con

Annette Bongiorno: Bongiorno was a BLMIS employee for 40 years, and was one of Madoff's most trusted aides. She handled a wide range of administrative chores, and appeared to do about everything he asked of her well—and she was well rewarded for her work: in 2007, alone, her salary was tripled from $200,200 to $624,000. She and those whose work she supervised spent much of their time recording transactions that had never occurred using stock tables published days, weeks, or months earlier in order to fabricate customer account statements so that they would show steady returns even during economic downturns. She also acted as a roper, inducing family and friends to invest with BLMIS. Before BLMIS's failure, Bongiorno had over $50 million in her IA accounts, two luxury homes, and three luxury automobiles.

Daniel Bonventre: Before joining BLMIS in 1968, Bonventre had worked briefly as a bank auditor. In less than a decade he rose from his position as an accountant to become the firm's director of operations. He worked closely with Madoff on a scheme of using investor money to artificially improve BLMIS's revenue and income. He oversaw the ledger entries and financial statements to conceal the illegal cash infusions. Bonventre also helped arrange millions of dollars in illegal payments and loans to Madoff family members and other BLMIS employees to enable them to purchase, among other things, luxury homes. Moreover, he was able to enrich himself with fake transactions in his IA account.

Enrica Cotellessa-Pitz: Beginning in 1978, Cotellessa-Pitz worked for BLMIS for 30 years; between 1998 and 2008, she was the firm's controller, closing the books each month and preparing reports for regulatory agencies. She began working in a clerical position at BLMIS to help transition the firm from paper to computerized accounting. At the time of Madoff's arrest, her salary was $450,000 a year, and the final balance in her IA account was about $3.5 million.

Jo Ann (Judi) Crupi: Crupi was an account manager at BLMIS who worked to create false account statements and maintain false books and records. She was central to an effort by BLMIS to survive a major audit for which she received a bonus of over $2 million. She joined BLMIS in 1983 as a keypunch operator and steadily advanced to positions in the IA business requiring more responsibility. Although she never had a formal title or clearly delineated responsibilities, by the mid-1990s she was put in charge of the bank account (the 703 Account) of the IA business. She also oversaw the IA accounts of several large BLMIS clients, the balance of which was close to $1 billion.

Frank DiPascali, Jr.: DiPascali referred to himself as a "director of options trading" and as "chief financial officer" at BLMIS. He oversaw day-to-day operations of IA business at BLMIS with an annual salary of over $2 million. He was the person many investors dealt with regarding their IA accounts. He joined the firm in 1975, one year after graduating from high school. DiPascali withdrew more than $5 million from his IA account to which he had not made any contributions. After pleading guilty to 10 counts of fraud relating to the con, he testified that he learned by the late 1980s or early 1990s that no trading was occurring in the BLMIS IA accounts, that Madoff was operating a Ponzi scheme.

David G. Friehling: The BLMIS outside accountant, Friehling was also the tax accountant for other Madoff family members.

He was the sole practitioner in a small accounting firm, having worked there for 20 years, and began auditing Madoff's financial statements in 1991. It was his responsibility to verify the existence of assets Madoff reported he held and securities trades BLMIS reported it made. Instead he gave his imprimatur to numbers Madoff passed to him. He falsely certified audits and financial statements submitted to government regulators. The sham audits and documents prepared by other BLMIS backstage accomplices that he put his imprimatur on readily fooled regulators and enabled Madoff to perpetuate and to greatly enlarge his con. For his work, between 2004 and 2007, he was paid between $12,000 and $14,000 a month. Friehling was charged with multiple counts of fraud and filing false reports. In his July 10, 2009, plea bargain, he readily admitted to a handful of felonies.

Paul J. Konigsberg: An accountant, tax attorney, roper, and longtime friend of Bernard L. Madoff. Among other things, Konigsberg prepared tax returns for the Madoff family foundation and for some of BLMIS's larger clients. Madoff steered wealthy clients to Konigsberg, who helped, with the assistance of BLMIS backstage accomplices, to cover up fraudulent transactions by fabricating books and records. At the time BLMIS collapsed, Konigsberg handled various accounting assignments in connection with more than 300 of its customer accounts. (He typically received duplicate monthly statements for his customers.) He used false back-dated trades provided by BLMIS to prepare tax returns. He received tens of thousands of dollars a month to advise the MSIL operation (of which he was the only nonfamily shareholder) and to funnel client checks to the London office for Bernard Madoff's own use.

Craig Kugel: Craig Kugel, David L. Kugel's son, joined BLMIS four years before it collapsed. In his brief time in the firm's human resources department, he colluded in a scheme to pay salaries or benefits to a number of individuals, for example, Peter Madoff's wife and housekeeper, Bernard Madoff's housekeeper and boat captain, DiPascali's boat captain, Irwin Lipkin, and Daniel Bonventre's son, who were not employed by the firm. One consequence of his, and his father's, work as Madoff's 17th floor accomplices is that BLMIS issued a letter, so that he could obtain a bank loan, showing that his IA account had as much as $885,000 in it while the actual amount was $289,000. He also failed to report to the IRS that he used the BLMIS credit card for personal expenses of "roughly between $15,000 and $30,000 a year"—for, among other things, vacations, "a trip to Paris [and] a trip to the Cayman Islands."[5]

David L. Kugel: David Kugel was hired as an arbitrage trader for BLMIS beginning in the 1970s, and before long was helping Madoff to falsify these trades. Like a number of the 17th floor accomplices he provided historical trading information, which he obtained from the *Wall Street Journal* and other sources, primarily to Bongiorno but also to Crupi so that they could create fraudulent trade confirmations, customer statements, and other records. And like a number of the 17th floor accomplices he appeared to be blindly loyal to Madoff: "If he asked me to do something, I gave it to him. I didn't question him. I believed him." The SIPC (Securities Investor Protection Corporation) trustee stated he believed that Kugel was the architect of the Madoff "strategy." Over the years, he withdrew almost $10 million in profits, which were not from actual trading activity, from his BLMIS IA account. Given the relatively large amount of his assets, it is unclear why he allowed his son to put himself in legal jeopardy.

Eric S. Lipkin: Lipkin began as a teenager working part time at BLMIS, handling clerical duties, and after college he followed his father, Irwin, into the firm. Like a number of other backstage accomplices, he helped research stock prices using stock tables published days, weeks, and months earlier. For his assistance on a project designed to mislead outside auditors and examiners, he received a bonus equivalent of five weeks' salary. After BLMIS was found to be bankrupt, forensic accountants found an unusual extensive record of fictitious trading in his and his family's IA accounts.

Irwin Lipkin: Lipkin was BLMIS's first employee. The two met through Lipkin's wife, Carole Lipkin, who had handled administrative chores for Madoff before he established BLMIS. He began working at BLMIS in 1964, and was there for almost 35 years before retiring in 1998. He had a close personal relationship with Madoff, writing a letter at that time in which he referred to Madoff as "the brother I never had," and after his retirement, Madoff permitted him to stay on the payroll. For many years Lipkin was the BLMIS controller responsible for the internal books and records, which he admitted to falsifying. He also performed internal audits, and assisted Madoff in reviewing customer accounts.

Bernard L. Madoff: Madoff was the con game's inside man. With deception and deceit, and occasional bullying, he guided his stable of ropers and BLMIS 17th floor employees, some knowingly and some unknowingly, in cheating investors out of their money. IA business customers were told and sent account statements showing them that their money was being invested in stocks and other securities when it was actually being used to pay other IA business customers or to support the lavish lifestyles of members of Madoff's inner circle what they were falsely led to believe were the earnings on investments. From modest beginnings, Madoff's con—due to the steadfast loyalty of his employees, members of his inner circle, the ineptness of regulators, the misplaced faith and greed of investors—became a worldwide Ponzi scheme.

Peter B. Madoff: Peter B. Madoff was seven years younger than his brother, Bernard L. Madoff. An attorney, he worked for his brother beginning in the late 1960s, and was the firm's chief operating officer, running the firm's daily operations for half of that time. He also served as the firm's general counsel, chief compliance officer, and senior managing director. He was widely regarded as the number two executive at BLMIS. He oversaw the creation of the company's innovative electronic trading systems. He brought his daughter, Shana, also an attorney, into the firm as a compliance officer. (Shana married Eric Swanson, an SEC assistant director, whom she had met at the time he was part of the SEC team conducting an examination of BLMIS, in 2007, the year after he left the SEC.) Not satisfied with the millions of dollars he stole from BLMIS, he took an additional $200,000 immediately after his brother confessed to the con. He pled guilty to participating in the fraud on June 29, 2012.

Jerome O'Hara and George Perez: O'Hara began working at BLMIS in 1990, and Perez in 1991. Both were computer programmers, who designed computer codes and algorithms used to generate millions of fake trade confirmations, account statements, trading blotters, and other books and records. Using their mastery of the computer, they worked together, largely at the direction of Frank DiPascali, Jr., to create BLMIS's fictional paper trail.

In maintaining the computer system used for the IA business, they added and deleted files in an effort to hide Madoff's con. The computer they used for their work for the IA business did not electronically receive trading data from third parties. There is some evidence that before BLMIS collapsed, both tried (unsuccessfully) to extricate themselves from the fraud, while there is no evidence other backstage accomplices appeared to have had reservations about assisting Madoff with his con.

There is little question that the work of each of these 15 individuals was vital to the longevity of Madoff's con, although only Bernard Madoff and Frank DiPascali, Jr. acknowledged that they knew it was a Ponzi scheme. Ten, including Madoff, his brother, and DiPascali, in the face of the irrefutable evidence against them, agreed to plead guilty to a variety of white collar felonies. Five of the fifteen claimed that they had not knowingly committed crimes, in spite of considerable evidence showing that they were willing participants; they fully rejected all charges that they were in any way complicit in Madoff's con. After a lengthy trial lasting more than five months, the five were convicted for working as Madoff's backstage accomplices. (The regular work of a number of other employees at BLMIS—for example, individuals performing routine clerical tasks—of course, furthered Madoff's con, but they did so seemingly unknowingly and were of little interest to the SIPC trustee or criminal investigators. There is no way to determine their number, and the number of others at BLMIS who understood that they may have been committing fraud, with any precision.) Chapters 3, 4, and 5 look more closely than these brief descriptions at the participation of Enrica Cotellessa-Pitz, David L. Kugel, and Annette Bongiorno in the Madoff con.

The Boiler Room

Madoff's boiler room, the setting for the pretense that a legitimate business was operating, was located on one floor (the 17th) of his business that occupied most of three floors in a 34-floor skyscraper on Third Avenue (between 53rd Street and 54th Street) in Manhattan. Clients sent their money—with the expectation that it would be invested, that stocks and securities would be purchased for their accounts—to the boiler room where Madoff's IA staff worked. The boiler room, however, only pretended to trade stocks and securities. It was little more than scenery—desks, people at work, computers, ringing telephones, paper, and (unlike the BLMIS office space on the 18th and 19th floors) cluttered—with an affordable company of actors and actresses improvising, like repertory players (or performers hired by Henry Gondorff or J. R. "Yellow Kid" Weil), as they—with the exception of Madoff, who more than occasionally behaved erratically—mostly matter-of-factly faced and overcame one financial challenge after another interspersed with their routine clerical functions.

As noted above, some of those involved clearly knew that they were helping perpetrate some form of fraud, and were knowingly and willingly Madoff's accomplices. There appears to have been other 17th floor employees who were simply following directions, not really reflecting on what they were doing. The claims of those who worked just as diligently as Madoff's conspirators to further his con that they had no idea they were doing so is and was believable to some, but inconceivable to others.

Six of the seven, who in their plea bargains admitted they were knowingly and willingly Madoff's accomplices, spent much of their time in the boiler room working to hide the fact that it was a set-up for the single purpose of defrauding investors, not assisting them to invest.

Madoff clearly needed a great deal of committed assistance from his accomplices in order to keep the con game going year after year. To assure unquestioned loyalty and secrecy, it was necessary that he reward all quite well. He obviously understood that generosity would minimize the possibility of betrayal. In fact, the not inconsiderable wealth each accomplice accumulated over the years of employment at BLMIS was a factor that readily identified them all as part of the fraud, of the conspiracy. Government documents show, for example, Daniel Bonventre (who continued to maintain his innocence after being found guilty of being an accomplice and whose office was not actually on the 17th floor) was paid (going back to 1993) a total salary of $7,439,693, $1,396,674 in bonuses, and $422,592 (in unexplained payments). Over the years, he also withdrew $3,386,833 from his IA account. The government's Indictment against Bonventre begins: "Between 2002 and 2006, Bonventre received the benefit of more than approximately $1.8 million in three separate back-dated, fictitious, securities transactions in [his] account that were not, in fact, actually executed . . . . On or about November 12, 2002, Bernard L. Madoff signed a check drawn on the . . . made out to Daniel Bonventre, the defendant, and his wife, in the amount of approximately $999,375 ('check No. 1') . . . . On or about May 25, 2005, a check was drawn

... in the amount of approximately $400,000 ('check No. 2') was made out to Daniel Bonventre, the defendant, and his wife .... On or about April 6, 2006, Daniel Bonventre, the defendant, received a check ... in the amount of approximately $577,954.81 ('check No. 3')."

Beginning with the testimony of Frank DiPascali, Jr., here is how each of these seven BLMIS backstage accomplices, all who fairly readily pled guilty, described his or her criminal activities in court.

Accomplices: Example I—Frank DiPascali, Jr.

After pleading guilty to multiple counts of fraud, DiPascali outlined to the court how the con game worked.

FRANK DIPASCALI:	From at least the early 1990s through December 2008, there was one simple fact that Bernie Madoff knew, that I knew, and that other people knew, but that we never told the clients nor did we tell the regulators like the SEC. No purchases or sales of securities were actually taking place in their accounts. It was all a fake. It was all fictitious ....
THE COURT:	When did you realize that?
DIPASCALI:	In the late 1980s or early 1990s.
	I would like to address some of the counts in the Information. Regarding Count One, [which is] conspiracy, Count Two, [which is] securities fraud, and Count Three, [which is] investment advisor fraud.
	From our office in Manhattan at Bernie Madoff's direction, and together with others, I represented to hundreds, if not thousands, of clients that security trades were being placed in their accounts when in fact no trades were taking place at all.
THE COURT:	How did you do that? [Was it] through documents or through oral communications?
DIPASCALI:	Both.
THE COURT:	Both?
DIPASCALI:	Most of the time, the clients' money just simply went into a bank account in New York that Bernie Madoff controlled. Between the early

1990s and December 2008 at Bernie Madoff's direction, and together with others, I did the following things: On a regular basis, I told clients over the phones and using wires that transactions on national securities exchanges were taking place in their account when I knew that no such transactions were indeed taking place. I also took steps to conceal from clients, from the SEC, and from auditors the fact that no actual security trades were taking place and to perpetuate the illusion that they actually were.

On a regular basis, I used hindsight to file historical prices on stocks. Then I used those prices to post purchases of sales to customer accounts as if they had been executed in real time. On a regular basis, I added fictitious trade dates to account statements of certain clients to reflect the specific rate of return that Bernie Madoff had directed for that client.

On a regular basis, I caused the U.S. mail to be used to send fraudulent account statements to clients from our office in Manhattan. The account statements listed security transactions that had supposedly taken place in the client accounts, although I knew that no such transactions had indeed taken place. For example, in December of 2008, I caused fake account statements to be mailed from the Madoff firm to a client in Manhattan.

On a regular basis, I caused money to be wired from bank accounts in New York to bank accounts in London, and other places abroad. For example, in March of 2007, I caused about $14 million to be sent by wire from a bank account in London to a bank account in New York in furtherance of this fraudulent scheme.

THE COURT: How did it further this scheme?

DIPASCALI: Bernie Madoff was trying to present the scenario, Judge, to regulators and others that he was earning commission income on these fictitious trades in order to substantiate the ruse. He had me wire funds—excuse me. He had our London office wire funds to New York that represented the theoretical amount of those commission incomes, had the regulators come in and added up all the tickets, if you will, to see our customer commissions. And in the example I cited in that particular instance, had we actually done those trade we would have earned $14 million in commission income. So he had the London office wire to the New York office a figure of about $14 million.

THE COURT: What was your role in connection with those wire transfers?

DIPASCALI: I calculated the theoretical commissions and advised the London office where to send the money. [See Appendix 2-A for a fuller account by DiPascali of how MSIL was used by BLMIS to launder money.]

. . .

Sir, international money laundering, between 2002 and 2008, I caused money to be wired from a Madoff firm bank account in New York to a Madoff account in London, which again was used to continue this fraud. I participated in falsifying documents that were required to be made and kept accurately under the SEC rules and regulations, including ledgers, trade blotters, customer statements, and trade confirmations.

. . .

Between 2004 and 2008, the firm was a registered broker/dealer. Between September 2006 and December 2008, when the firm was also registered as an investment advisor, it was required to keep accurate books and records under the SEC rules. In January of 2006, together with others, I used data from the Internet to create fake trade blotters that were made and kept and produced for the SEC.

In April of 2008, together with others, I caused fake trade blotters, ledgers, and other books and records to be made and kept by the firm.
. . .

On January 26, 2008, at Bernie Madoff's direction, I lied to the SEC during testimony I gave under oath in Manhattan about the activities of the Madoff firm. ... I did all of these fraudulent activities Your Honor in Manhattan.

THE COURT: Let me ask you about the perjury count. There are a number of specifications of false statements, eight, in particular with an underlying portions which I gather are the false or allegedly false statements. . . .

At the time you uttered these statements—this is a transcript of your testimony, is that correct?

DIPASCALI: It is indeed a transcript describing the Madoff trading operation, which I knew, at the time when I was describing it, was entirely fraudulent.

THE COURT: So you anticipated my next question. You knew at the time you made these statements that portions of the statements, in particular the underlying portions, were false?

DIPASCALI: Yes, sir.
THE COURT: You did this to mislead the SEC?
DIPASCALI: Yes, sir.
THE COURT: For what purpose?
DIPASCALI: To throw them off their tracks, sir.
THE COURT: Did you have a sense they were on the track?
DIPASCALI: Yes, sir.
THE COURT: At that point?
DIPASCALI: Yes, sir.
THE COURT: These statements were made all on one occasion, January 26, 2006? [See Appendix 2-B for excerpts from DiPascali's testimony before a committee of the SEC. In his testimony, DiPascali tries to appear both seductive[6] and harmless.]

DIPASCALI: Yes, sir.

THE COURT: And where was that?

DIPASCALI: Down at the SEC offices in the World Trade Center.

THE COURT: World Financial Center?

DIPASCALI: Correct.

THE COURT: I interrupted you. I think you were proceeding on to another count.

DIPASCALI: Judge, thousands of clients, institutions, individuals, funds, charities, were all misled about the status of their accounts, what was being done with their money, and what their accounts were worth.[7]

Accomplices: Example II—Irwin Lipkin

Hired in 1964 when Madoff worked alone with the help of only his wife, Irwin Lipkin was a longtime BLMIS employee. In the decades of his employment until his retirement in 1998, he helped oversee the company's steady and rapid growth. It was well understood that he was part of the company's inner circle; he considered himself close to Madoff. As the BLMIS controller, he was responsible for the company's internal books and records, including the general ledger, stock records, and the FOCUS reports (Financial and Operational Combined Uniformed Single report for the federal government). Among his regular duties, he assisted Madoff in reviewing customer accounts and in performing internal audits of the purported securities positions BLMIS held. Being responsible for overseeing the BLMIS IA business, he was surely central in facilitating its illusion of legitimacy.

In its relatively simple two-count Information, the office of the federal prosecutor charged Lipkin with conspiracy to commit securities fraud, conspiracy to falsify records, and for making false filings and statements to the government. More specifically, it was alleged that he created false books, records, and documents.

Before Lipkin pled guilty in his brief court appearance, the federal prosecutor made it clear that the government was prepared to "establish each of the following elements beyond a reasonable doubt: first, that the conspiracy charged in the Information in fact existed, in other words, that there was in fact an agreement or understanding to either violate the laws of the United States or to defraud the United States; second, ... that the defendant knowingly, willingly, and voluntarily became a member of the conspiracy charged; and third, that any one of the conspirators, not necessarily the defendant, knowingly committed at least one overt act . . . in furtherance of the conspiracy during the life of the conspiracy." In addition, the government was prepared to "prove beyond a reasonable doubt . . . that at the time of the alleged offenses [falsifying statements], the defendant made a false statement; second, that the defendant knew the statement to be false; and third, the defendant made a false statement in a document required by ERISA [Employee Retirement Income Security Act]."

After the preliminaries in the courtroom, Lipkin was asked by the presiding judge to make his plea, and to elaborate "What makes you guilty of the two crimes?"

I. LIPKIN: Your Honor I appear today pursuant to an agreement with the government regarding my entering a guilty plea to the crimes of conspiracy and falsifying certain financial records of my employer of some 35 years, the securities firm formerly known as BLMIS. I was Madoff's first employee starting in 1964. Eventually, I became controller of BLMIS. I retired in 1998. I remained on the Madoff payroll along with my wife Carole to enable both of us to appear eligible for continuing financial perks [perquisites] such as health insurance and 401(k) benefits, and in Carole's case Social Security benefits.

By maintaining two no-show jobs for Carole and me and my false filing [the Labor Department's] ERISA 5500 forms, I perpetrated criminal acts.

While the conduct I am pleading guilty to today relates to my employment at BLMIS, I would like the Court to know that at no time before I retired was I ever aware that Mr. Madoff or anyone else in the company was engaged in the Ponzi scheme reported in the media.

My belief in Bernie Madoff's trading skills was such that I encouraged my own family to invest their money in accounts managed by Mr. Madoff. In fact, my wife, my sons, and my grandchildren invested and lost virtually all of their money with Mr. Madoff. As it turns out, these investments never existed, and the family faces financial ruin.

While working for Bernie Madoff, I made accounting entries in financial records that I knew were inaccurate. Moreover, I knew the documents containing these false entries were to be filed with various regulatory authorities. These filings helped Mr. Madoff run the Ponzi scheme that harmed thousands of people.

I am truly sorry that I contributed in any way to the massive harm done to so many victims.

As Madoff's controller, I was responsible for preparing and maintaining certain financial books and records, which included (a) the general ledger, (b) the stock records, (c) FOCUS reports, and (d) the firm's annual financial statements. I understand that the numbers in the general ledger and the stock records, some of which were false, went into the firm's financial, annual financial statements, which, in turn, were sent to some customers. The FOCUS reports were to be filed with the SEC on a monthly, quarterly, and annual basis. I knew these reports were to be accurate and certified as accurate when filed. Until 1998, I signed FOCUS reports that I knew to be inaccurate as directed by Mr. Madoff. By following Mr. Madoff's direction, I violated the federal securities laws.

Sorry, Your Honor.

I also assisted Mr. Madoff in performing internal audits of the many securities positions held by him and the company.

I helped Bernie Madoff create records and books, the general ledger, and the FOCUS reports so he could deliver promised financial returns to his customers. In a nutshell, the entries typically came at the end of the financial reporting period. They were created to enable the company to report particular profit and loss numbers. I changed the P&L [profit and loss] numbers when Bernie would tell me what he wanted.

I made false entries in the company's books and records to reflect the adjustments to the value of certain securities. At Bernie's direction, I would change the value of certain securities in our records, and from time to time, as directed, I entered false securities in our stock records to artificially depress P&L and to impact Bernie's tax liability.

Bernie was frequently audited by both the IRS [Internal Revenue Service] and the New York State taxing authorities. It was common in our business. The company's income was reported on Mr. Madoff's tax returns, which I believe was inaccurate. Since Mr. Madoff directed our outside accountant how much income to report, I made changes to the general ledger as Mr. Madoff instructed me.

During these tax audits, the books and records were altered to corroborate the information that Bernie was supplying to the IRS. For example, during the IRS audit in 1992, at Bernie's request, I made revisions to the 1992 general ledger several years after the fact so documents would appear to be consistent with Bernie's tax return.

I also made sham trades in our families' investment accounts in November 2001 when I called Annette Bongiorno and asked her to locate a transaction to enable me to reduce my long-term capital gain for that period. She canceled the original purchase of Johnson & Johnson shares after the original transaction occurred.

In December of 2002, I again asked Annette to create losses in my IA account and those of my sons'. According to my monthly statements, I learned she created back-dated trades that reflected purported purchases of the stock of Micron Technology which resulted in the losses I sought. Finally, since Carole and I were represented to be employees of BLMIS, when we were not, the Labor Department [ERISA] 5500 form was false, which violated federal law. Not only was the 5500 form unlawfully provided to the Department of Labor, it was also provided to the third-party administrator of the Madoff health plan.

. . .

THE COURT: Was your wife improperly carried on the 5500 form while you were still controller?

I. LIPKIN: Again, I don't really remember because it was so long ago. She may have been; I am not sure.

    . . .

I. LIPKIN: Your Honor, in discussing with my attorney, I remember that, yes, she was on the 5500 form at my awareness . . . . It had to be probably late in the 1990s, because at some point in time she was on the books and had actually worked there [at BLMIS].

    . . .

THE COURT: You told me that you changed P& L numbers, you put in stock record information that was wrong, and you knew that documents that you were putting that information into would be going to customers, going to the SEC under certain circumstances. When you put those numbers in at Mr. Madoff's request or otherwise, did you know at the time that they were wrong, that they were false?

I. LIPKIN: Yes Your Honor.

THE COURT: Are you sure? Are you sure that you knew they were false? I am asking if you are telling me the truth on that.

I. LIPKIN: To my recollection, yes.

THE COURT: Did you know that what you were doing was wrong and illegal at that time?

I. LIPKIN: Yes Your Honor.[8]

After Lipkin completed his testimony, the federal prosecutor told the court that through witness testimony, documents, and other evidence, the government could have proven that beginning at least as early as the mid-1970s

Mr. Lipkin made false entries with respect to BLMIS' P&L in the books and records of the firm. On an approximately monthly basis, Lipkin changed the P&L numbers at the direction of Bernard Madoff. As a result of these false entries made in the BLMIS books and records by Lipkin and the BLMIS director of operations Daniel Bonventre, BLMIS' general ledger, stock records, FOCUS report, and other documents were false and misleading . . . . When Mr. Lipkin retired from BLMIS in or around 1998, he instructed Enrica Cotellessa-Pitz on how to manipulate the revenues of BLMIS in order to reach a particular P&L results and allow the fraud at BLMIS to continue.

In addition, since in or about at least 1975, Lipkin and his wife Carol maintained their own personal IA account at BLMIS. On multiple occasions, Lipkin requested that Annette Bongiorno execute fake, backdated trades in his personal account and the accounts of his family members. In order to reduce Lipkin's capital gains income, at his request, Bongiorno would either (1) cancel the sales of shares in Lipkin's account well after those sales purportedly had occurred or (2) document purported purchases of shares near the monthly high price and purported sales of these shares near the monthly low price weeks later. No such trades actually occurred.

In fact, Your Honor at paragraph #28 of the Information, the government has included the text of one of Mr. Lipkin's written requests to Annette Bongiorno which Ms. Bongiorno reflected upon. The text of that note reads: "Dear Annette, Please set up losses in the following accounts." It then goes on to list Mr. Lipkin's accounts where he requests a $125,000 loss to one account, a $40,000 loss to another account, and a $30,000 loss in the final account. The note continues: "These are about what each will need. Thanks. I will see you in Florida next month. Love, Irwin"

With regard to the no-show jobs Your Honor, Lipkin arranged for him and his wife to have no-show jobs at BLMIS from which they received income from a purported salary. They received health care benefits and 401(k) and other benefits to which they were not entitled. Ms. Carole Lipkin was never an official employee of BLMIS and she was never officially part of the books. There is some indication that Mr. Lipkin has a side agreement with his own wife in which he would share half of his salary with her. However, at no time was Ms. Lipkin ever on the official books and records of BLMIS as an employee.

Now, of course, after Mr. Lipkin retired in 1998, both he and his wife remained employees, well, had no-show jobs at BLMIS where they were reflected on the 5500 forms that were sent to the Department of Labor. As Eric Lipkin, Mr. Lipkin's son, reported and previously testified when he pled guilty, he reported a higher numbers of employees on the 5500 forms than, in fact, worked at BLMIS. So, in fact, Mr. Lipkin caused false filings to be made through the 5500 forms to the Department of Labor.

Perhaps due to his ill health, the plea bargain Lipkin was offered was quite lenient.

Because of this, it is almost inexplicable why he would attempt to continue his deception in his brief courtroom appearance, why he would risk irritating the judge, perhaps undermining the agreement he and his attorney had made with the prosecutor. However, like Bernard Madoff, the man he saw as a relative rather than an employer, he seemed to prefer lying even when it is difficult to see what benefit might be derived from doing so.

Accomplices: Example III—David G. Friehling

From 1991 through 2008 the accounting firm Friehling & Horowitz purportedly audited Madoff's financial statements. David Friehling, who had joined the accounting firm in 1989, took on the responsibility of auditing Madoff's books just a few years later at about the time his partner and father-in-law, Jerome Horowitz (who as a young man had worked for Ruth Madoff's father) retired. Friehling was also the tax accountant for Peter Madoff, and other Madoff family members. As Madoff's auditor for 17 years, in the last years that Madoff's con game was viable, he (since he was the only professional member of the firm) was paid over $150,000 annually, approximately $12,000 to $14,500 a month. (In its Complaint, the SEC put the total annual figure at $186,000.) In more recent years, Friehling would work in the BLMIS offices approximately one day a month and for approximately two weeks at the end of each year.

Shortly after Madoff was arrested, it was discovered that there had been no independent verification of Madoff's business revenues, assets, liabilities, bank accounts, or trading records.

Basically, Friehling put his imprimatur as a certified public accountant on documents prepared by Madoff's staff, those assisting Madoff in carrying out his con. These were then forwarded to various government entities. Over the years, Friehling's IA account with Madoff increased substantially; between 2000 and 2008, about $5.5 million was withdrawn from his and his family's accounts.

In court testimony after pleading guilty to nine counts of fraud and deceiving the government, all of which taken together threatened him with a maximum total of 114 years in imprison, he detailed "the specifics of [his] conduct" as an auditor and tax preparer for Bernard Madoff and others.

FRIEHLING:	With respect to conducting GAAS (Generally Accepted Auditing Standards) and GAAP (Generally Accepted Accounting Principles) ... I did not conduct independent verification of ... assets, review material sources of ... revenue, rigorously examine bank accounts ... , or verify the purchase and custody of securities .... Instead, I relied on the financial information provided by Bernard Madoff and [his] other employees ... which I took at face value and used ... to prepare ... financial statements. I certified that these statements were accurate ....
THE COURT:	You could not express an opinion as to the fairness and accuracy of the financial condition of the company and of its operating profits without going through all of these independent verifications?
FRIEHLING:	Yes.
THE COURT:	Didn't you put your signature on there just as if you had done all of these verifications?
FRIEHLING:	Yes.
	...
THE COURT:	So you knew that when you put on your opinion it was a false opinion?
FRIEHLING:	Yes.
	...
FRIEHLING:	I also prepared tax filings for Bernard Madoff and others. In that capacity I prepared personal tax returns that contained information I knew that was not accurate and assisted in the filing of those returns with the IRS.[9]

Accomplices: Example IV—Enrica Cotellessa-Pitz

Enrica Cotellessa-Pitz began her 30-year career at BLMIS in 1978 while still a college undergraduate majoring in economics. By 1998, she had become the company's controller, responsible, for among other things, closing the books each month and preparing the reports that needed to be submitted to regulatory agencies. Basically, much of her work at BLMIS was to hide Madoff's criminal activity. Most central to this was recording as revenue, and diverting it for use by Madoff's failing market making and proprietary businesses, hundreds of millions of dollars that was being stolen from IA customers.

According to the SIPC trustee and court records for the liquidation of Madoff's business, Cotellessa-Pitz was paid "$3,255,588 in compensation for her role in the fraud ... at least $467,316 in 2008 alone." In addition, she and her husband had two IA accounts "from which they withdrew at least $489,059" over the years.

For her part in the conspiracy and for falsifying documents, which together left her facing 50 years of imprisonment, Cotellessa-Pitz was asked to plead guilty to four different felonies. Before the court she detailed a number of her crimes:

COTELLESSA-PITZ: I am here to plead guilty to the counts in the Information filed against me and to accept responsibility for what I have done.

From approximately 1999 through 2008, while working for Bernard Madoff, I made accounting entries in the books and records of his business that I knew were false and inaccurate, and I filed documents with regulatory authorities and others that I knew repeated these falsehoods and inaccuracies. I now know that these acts helped Bernard Madoff and others perpetuate a fraud that harmed thousands of people . . . .

During the period when I was controller of BLMIS, I agreed with and worked together with other ... employees to violate the laws of the United States, and I took a number of actions over the years ... that constituted violations of U.S. laws. . . .

My conduct included a number of acts that I would like to describe.

From about 1999 through December 2008, I worked with others to make false entries in the books and records of BLMIS and to cause the filing of false documents with the SEC ... . At the direction of [Bernard] Madoff, [Daniel] Bonventre, and others, I caused inaccurate ledgers and other books and records to be created and kept by BLMIS, including inaccurate general ledgers and stock records. I then transferred the same inaccurate

entries into FOCUS reports and annual
financial statements that I knew would be
sent to the SEC . . . .

The following are a few examples of the
types of false records I created and maintained.

From about 1999 through December 2008,
I made false and inaccurate entries in the
books and records of BLMIS relating to
transfers of funds from BLMIS's IA business.
At various times, I believed these transfers to
be the interest or commissions from securities
trading in the personal accounts of Bernard
Madoff or the accounts of customers of the
IA business. Nevertheless, at the direction of
[Bernard] Madoff, [Daniel] Bonventre and
others, I booked these transfers improperly to
the accounts of BLMIS's proprietary trading
and market making businesses, and recorded
these false entries in . . . [the] trading ledgers,
general ledgers, and other supporting books
and records . . . .

In addition, at the direction of [Daniel]
Bonventre and others, I booked the transfers
of funds at times into specific securities or
trading positions and accounts that were part
of the firm's proprietary trading and market
making businesses. I knew that these transfers
bore no relation to these securities or position,
and that the funds did not result from trading
in these securities through the firms
proprietary trading and market making
businesses and, therefore, that my entries
were false. I understood that my entries falsely
inflated the revenue, increased the profits, and
hid the losses of the proprietary and market
making businesses and at the same time did
not accurately report the financial condition
of BLMIS as a whole.

In addition, in 2005 the SEC audited
[Madoff's] businesses. At [his] direction and
in response to this audit, I together with

others, created false books and records to be shown to the auditors.

For example, the SEC requested a list and description of all ... trading accounts as well as a report reflecting the monthly profit and loss for each of the trading accounts for a three-month period in 2005. In response, I together with [Daniel] Bonventre, [Jerome] O'Hara, and others created several false trading account reports that were given to the SEC. In those reports, among other things, we intentionally omitted an account affiliated with the IA business ... .

Separately, I assisted [Bernard] Madoff and other BLMIS employees in defrauding the United States by preventing the IRS from collecting the proper amount of income taxes from Madoff. I did this in 2007 ... as well as on other occasions. [Together with others, I fabricated and back-dated documents] in order to support Madoff's false tax returns ... . I knew that the back-dated stock positions were not real and that the false general ledger and trading ledger were being created in order to deceive the IRS tax auditors in connection with Madoff's tax returns.

The altered back-dated documents that I helped to create were shown to the IRS auditors.

THE COURT: And to confirm, you knew at the time that you made these false records and false submissions that you have described that the information in them was false?

COTELLESSA-PITZ: Yes, Your Honor.[10]

After these admissions, the attorney for the government reassured the court that if the case had gone to trial "The evidence would show that Ms. Cotellessa-Pitz [and her co-conspirators] engaged in a scheme to create many false and misleading entries in the books and records of BLMIS that lasted for decades."[11]

Accomplices: Example V—Eric S. Lipkin

Brought into the criminal network by his father, Eric Lipkin began working for BLMIS part-time while still in high school, and after completing college he joined the company in 1992. Initially, he served as one of Madoff's assistants in various capacities until formally being given the title of the company's payroll manager.

Lipkin was one of a handful of second-generation employees who worked at BLMIS, following his father (and, by some accounts, his mother) into the firm. It will be recalled that his father was Madoff's very first employee and eventually became the company's controller. According to the SIPC trustee, between July 1990 and July 2008, Irwin Lipkin withdrew $2,102,590 from his IA account. Eric's mother and Irwin's wife, Carole Lipkin, had (putatively) also been a longtime employee at BLMIS before retiring in 2001. Carole Lipkin's IA account at BLMIS had a balance of $7,934,500 in December 2008 when Madoff was arrested. Not counting Eric's $2,854,880 IA account at that time, there were two other IA accounts for Lipkin relatives, one for $1,353,960 and the other for $997,469. (By 2008, Eric Lipkin's annual salary was $225,000, and in addition, he had been given, without having signed a promissory note or discussing repayment, $720,000 by Madoff to build a home.) These figures from two sources taken together show how generously Madoff rewarded the Lipkin family for their many years of employment and loyalty—and service to his con.

Before too long, Eric Lipkin began creating fraudulent documents, becoming an integral part of Madoff's criminal enterprise, a few years after joining BLMIS when he moved from the payroll and benefits department and began working in the IA division. After that, using historical prices for stocks and bonds, he worked with others to calculate the value of IA accounts based on the rate of return promised by Madoff. In short, he, along with others, was manufacturing false portfolios. He also falsified payroll records, adding individuals who did not work for the firm, enabling them to receive retirement and other benefits to which they were not entitled.

The government was particularly interested in establishing that Lipkin worked with a number of other BLMIS employees to create these counterfeit and misleading documents. In his testimony, he readily admitted that there was a conspiracy and that for a number of years he was central to it.

E. LIPKIN: With regard to the conspiracy charged . . . , I worked with BLMIS's employees to deceive others. I created fake DTC [Depository Trust Company] reports . . . .

I knew that these documents were false because they were created by me and not by the DTC. I created them to match documents given to me by other BLMIS employees. My understanding was that the DTC reports that were being prepared were being given to the auditors to mislead them.

Also in part of the conspiracy charged . . . it was my job to prepare the BLMIS payroll documents and records. As part of my job from at least 1996 . . . , I created fake, false payroll records and also submitted to the Department of Labor inaccurate 5500 forms [which are intended to assure that employee benefit plans are operated and managed in accordance with certain prescribed standards that, among other things, "certify monies . . . are in a 401 (k) plan"]. These forms falsely showed that a number of people were employees of BLMIS when in fact I knew they were not working for BLMIS.

For instance, sometime in 2008, Daniel Bonventre instructed me to include one of his sons as an employee when I knew he wasn't working there, and I agreed to do it; and I created BLMIS payroll records to reflect that he worked there,

Further, beginning in 2007 . . . , I knowingly certified on the 5500 form that there were people who worked at BLMIS when in fact they did not. I also understood that the 5500 form contained a certification that all information on the form was accurate, and I signed it knowing it was not accurate and then I submitted it to the Department of Labor . . . .

Regarding Count Two, conspiracy to commit bank fraud, and Count Six, bank fraud, I was attempting to get a construction loan. In order to ensure I receive the loan, I went to Frank DiPascali to create a new BLMIS account in my name that falsely said my account value was greater than it was. I knew I could ask Frank DiPascali to do this for me because I knew it had been done previously for other BLMIS employees. . . .

Once I got the fake statement, I sent it from New York City to a bank in Florida. I knew that the account did not have the money in it that the statement said it did and that it was wrong to mislead the lender to get the loan . . . .

THE COURT: When you did these things that you have described, did you know that what you were doing was wrong and illegal?

LIPKIN: Yes.[12]

Accomplices: Example VI—David L. Kugel

David Kugel began working at BLMIS as an arbitrage trader primarily in the proprietary trading business in 1970; he remained with the firm for nearly four decades, eventually assuming a managerial position on the trading floor, even taking on the task of trading floor compliance analyst. In the 1970s, Madoff asked him to begin providing the IA operation with back-dated and bogus arbitrage trades, some of which were based on information he found in previously published newspaper stock tables.[13] The false trades he helped create—that there was an appearance of profitable trades, when, in fact, no trading had occurred—continued for three decades, stretching much longer than Madoff publicly acknowledged. Kugel's son, Craig, worked for BLMIS or its affiliated company, Primex Trading (run by Madoff family members), performing administrative functions, from 1997 until it collapsed after Madoff's arrest. (In a document filed in court, the SIPC trustee stated: "Between 2005 and 2008, he [Craig] visited the floor that housed the IA business on nearly 250 different occasions," which, of course, is compelling evidence that David Kugel was like Madoff, a criminal paterfamilias who recruited a son to a career as a criminal. (See the following section.)

During the course of his work, David Kugel applied the fabricated and highly profitable trades to his own IA account with BLMIS. From one such fabricated and highly profitable trade in 2007, his account grew by $375,000 in just a few weeks. Between 2001 and 2008, he withdrew nearly $10 million from his IA accounts. (As part of his plea bargain, he agreed [like all of the other conspirators] to forfeit all of the wealth he had accumulated, from his homes in Florida and Long Island to his collection of watches.)

After Madoff was arrested and the firm collapsed in December 2008, Kugel was charged by the government with conspiracy, securities fraud, and bank fraud, and agreed to plead guilty to six criminal counts. He admitted that he knowingly, willingly, and voluntarily was part of a larger conspiracy.[14]

> **D. KUGEL:**   I provided historical trade information to other BLMIS employees, which they used to create false, profitable trades in the IA accounts .... Specifically, beginning in the early 1970s, until the collapse ... , I helped create fake, back-dated trades. I provided historical trade information first to Annette Bongiorno and later to Jo Ann Crupi, and others which enabled them to create fake trades that, when included on the account statements and trade confirmation of [IA] clients, gave the appearance of profitable trading when in fact no trading had actually occurred. I helped Bongiorno, Crupi and others create these fake, back-dated trades based on historical stock prices and were executed only on paper.
>
> Many of these false trades were based on trades that previously had been used in the proprietary operations of BLMIS. I was aware that the trades would be reported to BLMIS customers on their monthly statements and trade confirmations, and that the information was false. ...
>
> I acknowledge from at least 2002 through 2007, on several occasions, I caused false financial information to be submitted to various financial institutions on my behalf and on behalf of other potential borrowers. The false financial information was submitted in connection for applications for mortgage loans.
>
> I asked Jo Ann Crupi to prepare documents that did not accurately reflect my assets and the assets at BLMIS, and she did so. These documents overstated the total value of my own and other potential borrowers' holdings in accounts at BLMIS. These fake documents were submitted to financial institutions on my behalf and on behalf of other potential borrowers.

THE COURT:	Thank you. I have a couple of questions for you. You used the term "conspired" in relation to Counts One, Three, Four, and Five. What do you mean by that?
D. KUGEL:	When I conspired, I worked together with them to create the false trades that appeared on the IA clients' statements and confirmations, pursuant to agreement and understanding.
THE COURT:	You had an agreement and understanding with the other individuals you mentioned in order to create the false trades?
D. KUGEL:	That applied to historical information, yes.
	. . .
THE COURT:	And the financial institutions to which the false mortgage information, application information, was given were banks; is that your understanding?
D. KUGEL:	Yes, Your Honor.
	. . .
THE COURT:	And when you were dealing with the false trading history information and the false financial information did you know that that information was false?
D. KUGEL:	Yes, Your Honor.
THE COURT:	And did you know that what you were doing was wrong and unlawful?
D. KUGEL:	Yes, Your Honor.[15]

Accomplices: Example VII—Craig Kugel

Craig Kugel, David Kugel's son, had been employed first at an affiliate, Primex Trading, than at BLMIS for a total of eight years before Madoff was arrested. For much of that time, he was responsible for or assisted in, among other things, budget forecasting and the administration of the company's benefit and health care plans.

Seven months after his father pleaded guilty for his involvement in Bernard Madoff's crime, Craig Kugel, facing the same judge on June 5, 2012, pled guilty to five felonies, including conspiracy to obstruct the IRS, making false statements in relation to documents required by ERISA, and filing false tax returns. Specifically, he admitted to declaring in documents that Marion Madoff, the wife of Peter

Madoff, was an employee, with an unspecified "managerial position," of BLMIS. Although she was not—she had "a no-show job"—she was paid a total of almost $1.6 million between 1996 and 2008. In its information to the court, the government maintained that he "created and maintained false internal BLMIS records reflecting individuals who did not work at BLMIS: a retired employee of BLMIS who had worked there for nearly 40 years, the son of another employee [Daniel Bonventre] of BLMIS who had worked there for 40 years . . . ."

Kugel also admitted that for the relatively short time that he was employed at BLMIS he charged to his corporate credit card personal expenses—including luxury clothing, jewelry, and vacations, amounting to over $200,000—and not declaring that as income. Senior management at BLMIS, of course, knew of this fact. As part of his guilty plea, Kugel agreed to forfeit $2.3 million.

After pleading guilty, Kugel added: "I am sorry for my lapse in judgment." He outlined, at times very generally, his crimes:

> **C. KUGEL:** Your Honor, I was employed by Primex Trading, LLC, a company affiliated with BLMIS beginning in 1999 and subsequently hired by BLMIS starting in 2003. At Primex I performed duties as controller and at BLMIS my responsibilities included budget forecasting for operations and overseeing BLMIS health care plans. In my capacity of reviewing internal BLMIS employee records, I together with others was aware that there were certain individuals on the payroll who did not work for the firm but who nevertheless received salary and benefits. I, with the help of others, sent employee lists which were provided to me by others containing individuals who did not work for the firm to our third-party health administrator.
>
> From 2003 on, I signed and submitted 5500 forms to the Department of Labor on behalf of BLMIS as required by ERISA using the numbers provided to me by others knowing that the information was inaccurate and swearing to its truth, thus violating the law.
>
> Beginning in 2001 and through 2008, I charged personal expenses on the corporate credit card and did not report this money as income to the IRS as required by law. In filing federal income tax returns

for the years 2005 to 2008, I agreed with another person to omit these expenses which I received as income, thereby preventing the IRS from collecting taxes that should have been assessed.

...

THE COURT: Thank you. Now, I notice that you were reading from a document as you gave this account. Does that document accurately reflect your conduct and the facts known to you?

C. KUGEL: It does Your Honor.

THE COURT: And do you swear that the information is true?

C. KUGEL: I do swear that it's true.

THE COURT: You mentioned something called a 5500 form. Is that a report that is required to be prepared and submitted to the Department of Labor in connection with employee benefit plans under ERISA?

C. KUGEL: It is Your Honor.

THE COURT: And you signed such forms knowing that employee census information in them was incorrect?

C. KUGEL: That is correct Your Honor.

THE COURT: And when you did these things, did you know that what you were doing was wrong and illegal?

C. KUGEL: I did Your Honor.

THE COURT: Mr. Moore [Assistant U.S. Attorney], does the government wish any further factual matters to be addressed in the plea allocution?

MR. MOORE: No, Your Honor.

THE COURT: Mr. Moore, would you please summarize the government's case against Mr. Kugel?

MR. MOORE: Yes, Your Honor. Had the case proceeded to trial, the government would have proven through testimony and evidence beyond a reasonable doubt the facts set forth in the superseding Information, specifically, the government would have proven that ... Mr. Kugel was aware there were individuals on BLMIS's payroll who did not work for the firm but who nevertheless received salaries and benefits. The defendant created and maintained false internal BLMIS records for individuals who did not work at BLMIS.

In addition, Your Honor during his tenure at BLMIS, Mr. Kugel charged significant amounts in

> personal expenses to a corporate American Express
> card. None of these expenses charged by Mr. Kugel
> were reported by BLMIS or the defendant himself to
> the United States IRS as salary, bonus, or any other
> form of compensation. As a result, for several years
> Mr. Kugel filed false U.S. income tax returns.[16]

When possible, these BLMIS backstage accomplices preferred to paint themselves as victims. They hoped to shift the blame to others—often to Bernard Madoff. They could not deny their crimes outright, as there was an obvious conscious attempt on their part to mislead others. It is difficult to imagine that they just accidentally committed fraud or that they helped Madoff further his fraud simply because they were naïve. Being part of a complicated scheme the intent of which was to harm others, it was best to attempt to convince the authorities or the public that they were the ones duped.

Undoubtedly, having vast numbers of counterfeit and misleading documents produced in order to deceive customers and regulators is what made it so easy for Madoff to so readily raise money to further his con for so long, moreso perhaps than his vaunted manipulative skill. As will become clear in Chapters 8 and 9, it took a great deal more time to fool clients than to find them. Finding victims for his con proved to be relatively easy. Many of Madoff's victims, in fact, eagerly and patiently waited to be given permission to hand over money to Madoff or to one of his ropers.

One would think that the employees who entangled themselves in criminal activity at BLMIS understood for years that they were participants in a criminal conspiracy. The often heard claims of those—from Peter Madoff to Craig Kugel—who had spent years (and some careers) diligently defrauding clients and enriching themselves that they truly believed they were engaged in something less than organized criminal conspiracy is doubtful, perhaps just another pretense. It seems unimaginable that only one of these enablers, Frank DiPascali, Jr., admitted knowing that he was enmeshed in a con, in Madoff's Ponzi scheme.

In a sworn deposition, an FBI special agent, who at one point led the agency's Madoff Fraud Task Force, describes one such memorable moment when DiPascali, Bonventre, and Madoff conspired together to further the con:

> I have learned that Bonventre, among other things . . . , prepared
> DiPascali to pose falsely as BLMIS's director of operations

during one or more visits by [a] European accounting firm to the BLMIS offices in order to be able to respond to inquiries about the "back-office" operations related to BLMIS's IA activities.

According to DiPascali, in or about 2005 ... , Bonventre helped to prepare DiPascali for the on-site review of BLMIS operations by representatives of the European accounting firm. Bonventre attended meetings with Madoff and DiPascali to prepare for the visit, and helped to prepare DiPascali to play the role of BLMIS's director of operations. Specifically, Bonventre taught DiPascali terminology, instructed him about paper and information flow, and provided him explanations about the firm's banking arrangements so that he could respond knowledgeably to questions. [See Appendix 2-C for the DiPascali account of temporarily being thrust into the role of the principal or leading man, and Appendix 2-D for the Bonventre denial of this account.]

These rehearsals generally proved to be successful.

The contention that all of these seven accomplices, but one, believed they were involved in something less than a Ponzi scheme is hardly likely. Could it be that only Bernard Madoff and Frank DiPascali, Jr. knew that they were entangled in a con game? In the face of the mountain of evidence amassed by prosecutors, the eight (including Peter Madoff here) fairly readily admitted to defrauding BLMIS customers, to committing felonies such as conspiracy, but each attempted to distance himself from Madoff's Ponzi scheme. Why not? The defense of ignorance can be successfully used to evade responsibility. There are countless examples of it being believed, of it being effective. It was used with some success, for example, at the Trials of War Criminals before the Nuremberg Military Tribunals. Indeed, millions of Germans and Poles went to great lengths convincing themselves and others that they were ignorant that the Holocaust was killing millions in Western Europe (a defense used not only by Wernher von Braun and his rocketeers but also by some employed in Death Camp activities), and it appears to have worked.

In addition to the claim of ignorance, that they were unwittingly involved in helping Madoff to commit crimes, some of his backstage accomplices also claimed that they were simply following orders, another defense liberally used at Nuremberg and, of course, before and since, in courtrooms around the world.

Frank DiPascali, Jr. (Accomplice I): "By 1990 or so Bernie Madoff was a mentor to me, and a lot more. I was loyal to him. I ended up being loyal to a terrible, terrible fault .... From our offices in Manhattan at Bernie Madoff's direction, and together with others, I represented to hundreds, if not thousands, of clients that security trades were being placed in their accounts when in fact no trades were taking place at all .... On a regular basis, I added fictitious trade dates to account statements of certain clients to reflect the specific rate of return that Bernie Madoff had directed for that client."

David G. Friehling (Accomplice II): "In what is surely the biggest mistake of my life I placed my trust in Bernard Madoff. While I am amongst thousands of people who now make the same claim, I wish for Your Honor to understand how I came to make this mistake, but also how I came to suspend my judgment in committing crimes with which I am charged."

David L. Kugel (Accomplice VI) (October 30, 2013): Madoff "was my boss. If he asked me to do something, I gave it to him. I knew it was wrong, but I didn't question him .... I believed him."

The Response to Authority

This testimony sound very much like: "Madoff made me do it; I was simply following orders." This, of course, would appear to be little more than a defensive and ineffectual excuse. However, if looked at in the context of a line of research by social psychologists, which has examined the tension between obedience to authority and personal conscience, these attempts to explain are suggestive of much more.

Long before there were psychiatrists, social psychologists, or social science disciplines, it was well understood that people are loath to blame themselves for what goes wrong. They readily and often shift the responsibility for unhappy outcomes to others, not least of all to those with authority over them. To better understand how people respond to authority, in 1961 the social psychologist Stanley Milgram launched a series of studies to better understand the influence of authority figures on behavior. This was a year after the Adolph Eichmann trial in Jerusalem, and Eichmann's well-known defense that he had no choice but to follow the orders of his superiors, that he was bound by an oath of loyalty to the German government and the army in which he served, was still reverberating from Israel to Europe and America. His entreaty that the matter was out of his hands was hardly surprising. What else could he say in the effort to save his life? What some of the BLMIS backstage accomplices claim, and appear to believe, is also hardly surprising. Indeed, Milgram's research findings show how individuals (not least of all Madoff's backstage accomplices) respond to authority, making the common claim: "I was simply following orders" understandable.

In Milgram's initial study of the obedience to authority, which was a controlled observation, 40 subjects were each in turn directed to administer ever-increasing powerful electric shocks to a victim who appeared to be having difficulty learning a task. The subjects were told: "We want to find out just what effect different people have on each other as teachers and learners, and also what effect *punishment* will have on learning in this situation." In reality, there was no shock and no victim. The victim was an actor (really an accountant) who was a confederate of Milgram's, and the machine, with an array of flashing lights and buzzers, that ostensibly administered severe shock only looked like it could do so. Every detail of the machine that supposedly emitted the shocks was made to look authentic: "No subject in the experiment suspected that the instrument was merely a simulated shock generator."

At the urging of the experimenter, of the 40 subjects 26 administered what they believed was the final massive 450-volt shock to the victim acting obviously distressed. To be sure, most subjects were uncomfortable administering the shocks. However, their obedience to authority outweighed their understanding that what they believed they were doing was hurtful and immoral.[17] (The conditions under which normal inhibitions against harming others are weakened are considered in Chapter 5.)

In short, Milgram's findings strongly suggest that people will do much more than dispensing painful shocks if prompted to do so by an authority figure. After analyzing his results, Milgram wrote: "The experiment yielded two findings that were surprising. The first finding concerns the sheer strength of obedient tendencies manifested in the situation. Subjects have learned from childhood that it is a fundamental breach of moral conduct to hurt another person against his will. Yet, 26 subjects [out of the 40] abandon this tenet in following the instructions of an authority who has no special powers to enforce his commands . . . . The second unanticipated effect was the extraordinary tension generated by the procedures. One might suppose that a subject would simply break off or continue as his conscience dictated. Yet, this is very far from what happened. There were striking reactions of tension and emotional strain." Milgram was not the first to observe that the situation an individual finds himself or herself in goes a long way in explaining behavior. And the implications of the research are evident: "The obedience experiments presented a disturbing view of human behavior. Milgram, his colleagues, and later the public were surprised by the sheer power of an authority to compel someone to hurt an innocent person, despite the absence of any coercive means to back up his commands."[18] Madoff had means to back up what he expected from his employees—money, a seemingly unlimited amount of other people's money.

Milgram was appalled by what he had found. In September 1961 he wrote to the head of social sciences of the National Science Foundation: "The results are terrifying and depressing. They suggest that human nature—or more specifically, the kind of character produced in American society—cannot be counted on to insulate its citizens from brutality and inhumane treatment at the direction of malevolent authority. In a naïve moment some time ago, I once wondered whether in all of the United States a vicious government could find enough moral imbeciles to meet the personnel requirements of a national system of death camps, of the sort that were maintained in Germany. I am now beginning to think that the full complement could be recruited in New Haven. A substantial proportion of people do what they are told to do, irrespective of the content of the act, and without pangs of conscience, so long as they perceive that the command comes from a legitimate authority." Some presently might also be appalled by the activities of Madoff's backstage accomplices, but 50 years after the publication of Milgram's research, no one should be surprised.

The collective findings from the behavioral study of obedience research are convincing. Milgram's results, and those of the countless others who have replicated his research, would suggest that it is more than the obvious greed of Madoff's backstage accomplices that would explain their diligence. (Milgram wrote more than once: "Obedience is as basic an element in the structure of social life as one can point to.") These accomplices could hardly refuse a request from a workplace supervisor. Helping to mass-produce records, the purpose of which, at least at first was unclear, until it became routine, was something one could readily learn to do as a matter of course. And before Madoff was arrested there were considerable rewards for making BLMIS function effectively.

Some of his victims have acknowledged that their greed as much as Madoff brought them into his con game.[19] A smaller percentage of his backstage accomplices allow that they were motivated by greed. It is not an easy matter to concede; its connotations are invariably unpleasant. Moreover, to admit to greed is tantamount to admitting that one consciously participated in a crime, and even that one may have knowingly participated in a con game. From prison, Madoff repeated more than once that greed was at the heart of his con. One early interviewer reported Madoff told him that he warned investors not to risk money that they could not afford to lose, but, he added, "everyone was greedy." When they, as Madoff characterized it, begged him to invest their money, "I just went along," he rationalized.

Greed on Wall Street, of course, can be found well beyond BLMIS. It is part of the Wall Street culture, a very conspicuous part. It has the power not only to build but also to destroy companies. For example, in his account of the 1984 unraveling and sale of the venerable brokerage firm Lehman Brothers, Kuhn, Loeb to Shearson/American Express, the journalist and Wall Street insider Ken Auletta writes: "*Greed* was the word that hovered over the troubled partnership. To their faces, [Lewis L.] Glucksman [the firm's CEO] accused [Eric] Gleacher [a Lehman partner] and the senior bankers of *greed* for money. Behind his back, senior bankers accused Glucksman of *greed* for power. Traders said the bankers were *greedy* because they were privately angling to sell the firm. Bankers said the traders were *greedy* to steal their shares and to take such fat bonuses. Greed was a melody running through the debate that autumn about 'capital adequacy.' "[20]

But Much More Than a Skit

Madoff and his accomplices did much more than create documents and reports. They were playwrights, producers, and directors. They prompted performers and performances. They created facts. They created narratives and stories. They created myths. They created fictitious money and profits. They created co-workers. They created illusions.

It can be said that life backstage at BLMIS was in large part about performance. It was not only about individual performances. The accomplices were interconnected; they worked together. Their network can be viewed as more than individuals with a shared identity, goals, and norms. Sociologically it was clearly a formal group. Its structure and activities were rationally organized and standardized, with prescribed rules, goals, and leaders. Beyond this, however, it had many elements common to a crime family, a term generally reserved for discussions of organized crime. In one sense, Madoff's backstage accomplices could be aptly described as an organized gang of criminals. For some, membership was based on blood relationships, built on family ties. Membership for others was intergenerational; in other cases, it was neighborhood ties or associations—where families lived in close proximity to each other.[21]

At times, the backstage accomplices at BLMIS were nimbly able to act much like what Goffman called "a performance team"—"any set of individuals who cooperate in staging a single routine"[22]—who are involved in impression management. More so than most other performance teams it was imperative that they *always* cooperate in their performance. Their definition of the situation had to prevail unchallenged. Even after Madoff's con was uncovered, there were numerous examples of how they typified performance teams. First of all, the privilege of familiarity, "a kind of intimacy [even] without warmth" that slowly developed over time on the 17th floor, was evident in the testimony of many. From what they said and did, from what could be found, there seemed to be an understanding "informally to guide their efforts in a certain way as a means of self-protection." Moreover, they were "dissimilar in important respects, and hence desirous of maintaining social distance from one another." Most importantly, they were clearly "bound together formally or informally into an action group in order to further like or collective ends by any means available to them."[23]

For purposes of the discussion here, a performance team can be seen as little more than "a grouping not in relation to a social structure or social organization but rather in relation to an interaction or series of interactions in which the relevant definition of the situation is maintained."[24] It was much less important that Madoff's 17th floor accomplices worked for BLMIS than what they shared with each other from their work there.

In the 2013–2014 criminal trial of five of the 17th floor accomplices, the judge defined for the jury the term *conspiracy*, for which, among other things, all five were charged, as a criminal agreement of two or more persons to violate the law. She explained that conspiracy involved individuals knowingly (acting voluntarily and deliberately rather than mistakenly and inadvertently) and willfully (acting knowingly and purposely) joined together in "a kind of criminal partnership" and that any act to affect the object of the conspiracy—to deceive investors, to falsify the BLMIS books and records, to use the mail to defraud, to make false filings with the government, to provide false information to a bank—is a crime.[25] Moreover, although a substantive crime may not in the end be committed, an understanding to violate the law—even if the conspiracy is not successful—is a crime.

Much of the time a conspiracy is secret in its origin and execution. However, taken together and considered as a whole, the many documents produced by the BLMIS 17th floor accomplices over decades and passage after passage of testimony from the trial transcript show a conspiracy as conclusively as would direct proof that they sat around a table and entered into a solemn pact orally or actually wrote down a plan to violate the law. Clearly, more than the five on trial or even more than the other accomplices who pled guilty worked together for decades as a performance team in a conspiracy. The authorities chose to give these others—Robert Jaffe or Frank Avellino or Michael Bienes or Shana Madoff or Marcia Cohn or Ezra Merkin—a pass.

Goffman concludes his initial discussion of performance teams by noting: "A team, then, has something of the character of a secret society .... Individuals who are on the staff of an establishment are not members of a team by virtue of staff status, but only by virtue of the cooperation which they maintain in order to sustain a given definition of the situation."[26] There were numerous examples of a member of a BLMIS backstage accomplice's team—before clients, regulatory officials, and other BLMIS employees—able "to act in a thoroughly calculating manner, expressing himself [or herself] in a given way solely in order to give the kind of impression to others that is likely to evoke from them a specific response he [or she] is concerned to obtain."

Example after example throughout the book shows Madoff's backstage accomplices working together to fool individual clients and to fool institutional investors. Some took care of the IA accounts of other accomplices. Some helped other accomplices commit crimes. Some helped other accomplices hide crimes. In one brazen charade alluded to earlier, one even took on another's identity for a few days.

It is not possible to know if the virus of the culture of crime and the corresponding criminal activity spread by Madoff would have been so infectious within BLMIS had not Annette Bongiorno and Frank DiPascali grown up as neighbors, or had not Madoff's brother had a law degree and some familiarity with recent advances in technology, or had not both Irwin Lipkin and David Kugel had sons educated and prepared to work in the world of finance, even in an institution that was at its core crimogenic.

Other BLMIS employees, besides these seven who pled guilty, worked faking records, keeping a second set of books, backdating fictitious trades, cheating on taxes, helping to launder money, and lying to customers.. The con could not have been carried out without backdating the buying and selling of stock and bonds. A clerk (not a backstage accomplice) explains how backdating was routinely done:

Q: What about the term *backdating trades*, did you ever hear her [Annette Bongiorno] use the term *backdating trades*?
A: Yes, I've heard that term.
Q: And in what context would she use the term *backdating* with regard to trades?
A: In other words, if this was the month of October, we may backdate a trade to June or July in order to make the trade ticket.
Q: And how far back did you see, during the time that you were working for Ms. Bongiorno, trades back-dated?
A: I've seen it as far back as a year.
Q: What was a more typical amount of time that trade would be back-dated?
A: It could be 30 days, it could be a week.
Q: Now, after all of the information was gathered and given to Ms. Bongiorno, did you observe her doing her own calculations with regard to these trading?
A: Yes.
Q: And then, ultimately, would she give you additional instructions in her process?
A: Whenever she would give us the trading sheets, she may tell us—if we were writing it up—she may say, okay, this particular customer, I need to have a set amount of trades, a certain amount, like 100,000 shares, but we may need to break it up and not just do a lump of 100,000 shares, 25, 50, you know, another 25. And then she would give it to us and tell us that basically it was written up properly for the proper customer what the amount of shares.
Q: And then after it was all written up, what happened?
A: Once the trades were written up and she had applied the cost basis, we would then give it to the computer room, the keypunch operators, to input the information into the system . . . .
Q: What do you mean when you say keypunch?
A: They would—whatever the information was on the sheet—they would input that into the system, into the customer's account.
Q: So they would literally punch in the information that she instructed?
A: Right.
Q: Now, during the time that you were working with her, did you ever see what were known as trade confirmations?
A: Yes.

Q: What were trade confirmations?

A: Trade confirmations were after the keypunch operators input the information into the computer system it would generate a confirmation sheet that basically gave me the information that had been written out on that—the initial write-up of what we had done on the trade sheet.

Q: From the time that you gave that information to the keypunch operator, how long did it take to generate the trade confirmations?

A: Well, it depends. Sometimes, if they weren't really busy, it could be punched out in a matter of a few minutes. If it was given in at night, I would receive it back the next morning.

Q: But sometimes you would give them that information and you'd get the trade confirmations within minutes?

A: Yes.[27]

Moreover, BLMIS employees had to make sure that customer accounts were kept at an acceptable level at the end of a reporting period. If returns were short of targets or expectations, then extra profits had to be generated. Additional trades had to be generated and computer programs adjusted. This additional work prevented customer dissatisfaction and withdrawals.

For the most part, BLMIS backstage accomplices maintained that they were not committing crimes. As they defined their actions, they were simply following or passing on instructions. Their contention was that they had no idea the IA business was a fraud, and because they did not understand the larger picture, they would not accept as fact that they were involved in a massive criminal conspiracy. To be sure, they may not have understood that they were furthering a Ponzi scheme, but they clearly comprehended that they were helping to carry out a charade, propping it up and concealing the fact from regulators, auditors, taxing authorities, lenders, and investors. A number knew, for example, that personal items, such as vacation expenses, were routinely charged to BLMIS credit cards, and that income taxes for these expenses were evaded. Others knew that the IA business did not have nearly the number of employees to carry out the securities trading that it claimed were being completed, even if most trades, as they were falsely told, were presumably being done in Europe. Some knew that the company kept other Madoff insiders, not only Peter Madoff's wife, in no-show jobs (like Gogol's "Dead Souls"). In short, other backstage accomplices besides these seven knew about and were committing crimes for which they were relatively well paid.

In the next three chapters is the 2013–2014 court testimony of Enrica Cotellessa-Pitz, David L. Kugel, and Annette Bongiorno of what each saw and did on the 17th floor at BLMIS—of how each contributed to Madoff's con and how each understood their role—over a number of decades.

The performance of each served, as Goffman anticipated, "mainly to express the characteristics of the task . . . and not the characteristics of the performer." Moreover, the personal front was employed "not so much because it [allowed him or her] to present himself [or herself] as he [or she] would like to appear, but because his [or her] appearance and manner [did something] for a scene of wider scope."[28]

Appendix 2-A

Testimony of Frank DiPascali, Jr. Describing How MSIL Was Used by BLMIS to Launder Money[29]

This is Bernie speaking: "I'm going to call these guys in Europe. They've got a big bunch of money just sitting around in British treasury instruments doing nothing, and they always have this balance, they've got this balance in which they call gilts, which is the British term for a treasury instrument. So BLMIS has these gilts, a whole bunch of them, they are sitting around doing nothing anyway. I'm going to tell these guys that I'm not getting the rate of return that I want on that, that I'm going to have my desk in New York trade U.S. Treasury paper—U.S. Treasury paper.

"What I want you to do, Frank, is occasionally you will write a treasury ticket into the MSIL IA account, and then you will fax that ticket over to the guys in London requesting that they wire money from their Barclays [bank] account into BONY [Bank of New York] to pay for the treasury that we are presenting they just purchased."

That's what I explored doing, how we would mechanically set that up.

Now, the amount of the treasury purchase, Bernie further explained, needed to be equivalent to the amount of theoretical commissions that the special IA customers had generated.

. . .

Then I would look for a treasury bill and purchase an equivalent amount of treasury bills equal to that number, so that when I sent that confirmation via fax to [the] back-office in London, they would wire from their Barclays account that amount of money, so they would have a flow of money from Barclays equal to commission equivalents.

It had nothing to do with I'm not getting a good enough rate of return in London. It had nothing to do with that they had excess money; it was convenient that they did. The purpose of this exercise was simply to have a line item on the books and records of the business, also known as the BONY bank statement, that a wire of X came in on this date for this amount of money.

That date, and that amount of money, was generated by the trading activity of the IA clients and how much commission equivalents the trading activity theoretically generated. It was an almost foolproof way for [BLMIS] to get a legitimate entry on an illegitimate trade and its commission. Madoff was very excited that he had thought about it.

. . .

Q: What, in terms of paperwork, is done on the IA business once that first step occurs?

A: In order to inform them that they have purchased U.S. Treasuries, we generated a "confirmation of purchase" for their account that had the description of the U.S. Treasury and the net amount of the purchase cost of that ticket. Then we would photostat that, leaving the bottom section. It is only 8 by 5. When you photostat and you put it in the top of the photostat machine, it's justified to the top, which would give us the opportunity to write the wire instructions on the bottom.

We would write "please wire to BONY," and then we would draw an arrow or something to the net amount of money for settlement date November 3rd, and thanks, and we would fax it over to a fellow by the name of Chris Dale, who was one of the employees at MSIL.

. . .

Q: What was the next step that was taken?

A: A sale ticket for that same treasury would be written and the same process would occur. We would put the entry into the system, which would then therefore make the MSIL account no longer own that treasury. That confirmation of trade was Xeroxed, and the illustration of what we were going to do with the proceeds was then written on the bottom.

It would typically have the sale ticket on top, and then it would say something like: "Hi, Chris: We will wire to your account at Barclays for settlement date November 7th and of the ticket, $8,537,432." That ticket would get to Chris via fax so he would look for a wire hitting his BONY account on that settlement date, which was going to be either that day or the next day.

Q: Would funds be wired from BLMIS to MISL?

A: Yes.

Q: From what account were those funds wired from?

A: From the 703 Account.

. . .

Q: What did this movement of funds have the effect of doing in terms of funds going from the 703 Account and into the 621 Account?

A: It had a lot of different effects, one of which was a way to increase the cash in the business account. The operating account of the business would therefore be funded with the proceeds of the 703 Account. Then the other purpose was to have an entry on the books and records of money coming in from overseas—from Barclays—that hit the operating account that could be called the repatriation of commission equivalents from settlements in London. Those were the two major results of this triangle.

Appendix 2-B

Testimony of Frank DiPascali, Jr. before a Committee of the Securities and Exchange Commission, January 26, 2006

In three-and-a-half hours of testimony before the three-member committee, DiPascali spent much of the time attempting to confuse it with mostly an arcane lexicon, as if he were practicing a black art, or mythicizing Madoff.

First, dazzling with jargon:

A: If you go long in a security, like gold, soy beans, anything, any, you know, asset, if you bought a put, you mitigate the risk of the downside depending on the premium you pay for the put. It's insurance on the downside loss.

For a bazillion years, people were buying General Motors, buying a put on General Motors and possibly selling the call on General Motors. Now there are two ways to play that: Guys that were just simply looking to earn a return that was somewhat just a click over the cost of money would buy General Motors at, let's say whatever price, 50 something, then they would buy the put at X and sell the 55 call at Y.

If the sum total buy stock, buy put, sell call, when you consider the dividend income in the cycle, would allow for a return that was marginally above, let's say, 90-day paper.

So if you are borrowing at 90-day paper, you would borrow money, put the strategy on, take a $10,000 investment and make $10,300. That's called a forward conversion. That's a standard stock market strategy as opposed to a reverse conversion, which is the exact flip side of that.

It's a short stock, short put, long call scenario. And if you use the same strikes you were at, absolutely no risk, as long as you set that up for a net cost or a net proceed, depending if it's a reverse conversion or a forward conversion, when considering the dividend.

For illustrative purposes, let's say you set it up for 50.5 and the dividend is 50s, and you used a 50 strike put and a 50 strike call, you were at zero economic risk because on expiration date, you are going to put that stock at 50 or it's going to get called away from you at 50. It cost you 50.5 to set up, you are going to catch a half dollar dividend. You are at zero profitability and zero risk.

However, when you shorted the stock on a reverse conversion, you had to go out and borrow those shares. So when you borrow reverse conversion shares, to make your delivery, you need to make the delivery, in effect—I don't know if they do that today because I am not involved in that. But in the old days, the period of time we are talking about, when you made your delivery, the broker delivered two pages.

You took the cash and that's the cash that you posted collateral to the loan officer that lent you the stock to make the delivery in the first place.

For the privilege of doing that, that loan—they would rebate back to you, sometimes 60, 70, or 80 percent of the cost of those funds. So you had a strategy on that , had a zero risk, and a zero profitability, but you were cash flow positive, because for the time the strategy was on, you were catching a stock loan rebate from the stock loan officer. The reverse conversions were the way of the world in the 1970s and 1980s.

. . .

So his room probably has a pocket of money that was set up in reverse conversions and catching positive cash flow from the stock rebate.

He probably had positions on forward conversions and other stocks where he was earning a rate of return slightly above, you know, short-term paper, maybe because at the time he had a pool of short-term paper that he, for whatever reason, wanted to hold onto.

Instead of taking a treasury-bill deal, you take a forward-conversion deal, and you pick up 10 or 12 or 15 basis points. This is the type of . . . very astute trader he is.

[The reason some of the conversions … actually occurred was] because that's when index options became available as a trading tool. Because a lot of the questions dealt with, okay, can you use an index option to do the same thing that we are doing with equity options in forward and reverse conversions.

That's a very complicated question, and the answer I learned is "yes," it can be done as long as the securities that are in place, whether they are long or short, whatever the stock side of the ledger looks like, had better be in the index.

If it's not, you've got some severe risk, especially if you are doing a bona fide reverse conversion or forward conversion where the profit potential was already determined to be zero and you are looking for only cash flow returns from, let's say a stock loan rebate or you are looking for a nominal rebate paper, you can't afford to have the long side or the short side.

I will use the term basket of securities disjoint from the index, because now you are at serious economic risk.

Second, working to mythicize Madoff:

Q: Do you have any idea when he decides that?
A: Probably 50 years of doing this game . . . . Are you familiar with who my boss is in the business?
M: Yes.
A: He owns and has developed the most technological firm on Wall Street. There is no doubt in anybody's mind. Over the years, he has—I don't know who built it for him, but there are momentum tools that are obviously working, and there are, you know, he is an astute market trader, if you had to put a label on him.

The way Warren Buffett can buy a company that's undervalued and do whatever he does, and all of a sudden it's a valuable asset.

As a trader, he is the Warren Buffett of Wall Street, if you want to call him that. He is everybody that you think he might be. Trust me, I am looking at the guy, he is amazing. Peter may come off as a jerk sometimes, I don't know if you've experienced that, but sometimes he is jerky. The guy is a genius; there is no doubt about it. He has the gut sense of what's good economically, currency, stock "market-wise," "real estate-wise."

The guy is astute—and he is a trader. He has a good sense—based on a bazillion different tools—that he has developed over the years of when to enter any particular market.

. . .

So give me what I'm supposed to buy [he tells his employees] and I will tell you when I am buying it, in essence.

. . .

Q: Is there anybody else at Madoff, the company, who can make these judgment calls other than Mr. Madoff?

A: No.

Q: What happens when he goes on vacation?

A: He is never on vacation. Bernie Madoff is available 24 hours a day, seven days a week, and 365 days a year, anywhere on the planet.

Q: Does he have the models available to him?

A: He has the same data as I have in the office. He has an office in France, Montauk, Manhattan his home in Palm Beach, and his boat in Palm Beach.

. . .

Q: How does he select the dealers to talk to?

A: He's got a London office he developed, I guess probably in the mid-1980s. He has relationships in Europe, extensive relationships for over 20 some-odd years with banks and other large institutions. I mean he's got quite a network of various sophisticated institutional dealers in Europe; he is on a first-name basis with the people who are running the derivative desks.

Q: How does he —

A: Most of them are banks.

Appendix 2-C

Testimony of Frank DiPascali, Jr. Relating to an Unwanted Audit[30]

Q: Now, as the time approached for when KPMG was going to come in, did Mr. Madoff have discussions internally about how the firm was going to prepare for this audit?

A: Yes.

Q: Who was involved in those discussions?

A: I was and Jodi was.

Q: And —

A: And Mr. Bonventre was.

Q: With respect to Mr. Bonventre, what was discussed in those meetings that you were present at?

A: When the format request from KPMG London came to Bernie, it very clearly said that they wanted to spend time with the director of operations. When Bernie went to Danny with that letter, he told him he wasn't going to be available to handle that inquiry with KPMG, he's not going to be in the office on those days.

Q: And that was what one of the discussions were about, correct?

A: Yeah, because I was brought into those discussions.

Q: And when you were brought in, what were—when you were brought in to discuss those specific things, who did you talk to about it?

A: Those specific things were talked about in Danny's office with me and Bernie.

Q: And was Mr. Bonventre there?

A: Yes.

Q: Okay. And in those discussions amongst the three of you, what was decided—how was it decided that that was going to be handled?

A: That I was going to play Danny to the auditor, that I was going to somehow learn the intricacies that one would know of a back-office environment, being the director of the back-office. Bernie was literally going to introduce me to the auditor as the director of operations, and in the interim between that meeting and the actual audit, Bernie directed Danny to teach me what I needed to know to make that happen.

Q: Now, did you have the expertise at that point to be the director of operations at BLMIS?

A: Not entirely, no, not by a long shot.

Q: Okay. And what sorts of things did you need to learn about?

A: How the settlement process actually worked. I had my own, in my mind, concept of some things that were right. There were lots of buzz words and bells and whistles that I wasn't familiar with. I needed to learn the buzz words, basically.

Q: And in that meeting with you, Mr. Madoff, and Mr. Bonventre, did Mr. Madoff express that you were going to learn to play this role in connection with this KPMG audit that was going to happen?

A: Crystal clear to that.

Q: After that conversation, did you have meetings with Mr. Bonventre one-on-one?

A: Yes.

Q: And in those meetings, what did Mr. Bonventre say to you and what did you say to him?

A: He basically taught me how the clearance and settlement of a stock happens, and we chatted about the various methods of clearance and settlement and how we could build a scenario on the IA side that that was happening as well.

Q: Now, you said build a scenario, what do you mean by that?

A: The trades weren't happening; so, therefore, the trades were really not settling. There were no settlements with counterparties; there were no trade entry to some clearing organization. These trades simply did not exist, and we've got an auditor coming a week from Wednesday that is going to want to see the internal controls of our back-office. He's going to want to walk through, and he said so primarily in the letter, the flow of a trade from point of origination to complete and total settlement, and who touches that trade and how it gets processed and what environment, what platform, what clearing organization. He wants to see flows of money.

He wants to see securities, how they're delivered, who actually makes the deliveries, what system you use to make the deliveries. He's checking to make sure that he is, and he says so in his letter, going to be happy that we have certain controls in place where none of our employees could steal form his client. [He wants to know] who initiates a wire and how many people have to sign off on the initiation of a wire when money goes out of the account, and how do you verify a signature. [He wants] to make sure that the process you have for moving securities and moving money is, in their opinion, satisfactory according to accounting principles and auditors.

...

Q: When the auditors arrived, did you speak with them?

A: At length.

...

Q: Once they were situated, who met with them on that first day?

A: Bernie did kind of like the introductions. I don't know what was discussed, then I walked in, and he introduced me as his director of operations.

Q: After that, did you proceed to interact with these auditors?

A: Yes.

Q: Did you lie to them?

A: Absolutely.

Q: Can you give us a sense of how the interactions between you and they occurred in terms of requests they would make and responses you would give?

A: They first wanted an understanding of the scope of the business and a description of what we do for our mutual clients. Then, as those discussions were progressing, he [or they] would say things like: "So I would expect to see such and such."

For instance, in the discussions of clearance and settlement where we are custodying [*sic*] securities for the benefit of his clients and those securities are custodied to DTC, he would say something like: "So I would expect to see a third-party confirmation of that." and I would say: "Yeah, sure, if that's what you want?" And so on and so on.

At almost every junction of his getting an understanding from my explanation of how we operated the business, he was then coming back and saying things like: "So I would expect to see a stock record segregated for the benefit of customer?" Yes. And I would expect to see: "Let's say, how would you have these trades recorded in your system? I would guess that you would have some sort of a document." Yeah: "It's called a trade blotter."

"OK, so you would have a trade blotter that would show me the origin of the trade?" "Yes." "And what would that look like?" "Well, you would see the customer trade and you would see therefore who we actually purchased that security from in the open marketplace that eventually wound up with the customer."

As we talked about things like the customer always receiving an average, price of many, many transactions, he would say something like: "So I would expect to see from your blotters all the little individual transactions at many market prices?" "Yes." "And if I ran a tape of those and averaged them, I would come up to the customer's price?" I would say something like: "Give or take the commission equivalent mark-up or mark-down, yes."

Then he would be taking notes to himself that this is something that somewhere down the road he is going to perform a little acid test on. That's how his requests developed. He first needed to get an understanding of what I was explaining to him on how we treated these customers, and then his expertise took over as to what documents he would need to verify what I was saying.

Q: When he would ask you about specific types of documents he would expect to see, were you able to provide answers?

A: Yes.

Q: How did you know about those various documents that he was asking you about?

A: I was given a condensed back-office 101 course by Dan.

Q: When you brought up document to give them, were those documents false documents?

A: Yes.

   ...

Q: How long was KPMG at BLMIS?

A: Pretty much that entire week.

Q: How much of your time was spend dealing with them, KPMG?

A: The entire week and every night of that week to prepare for the next day.

Appendix 2-D

Four Examples of Daniel Bonventre Contradicting the Testimony of BLMIS Colleagues[31]

Bonventre denied DiPascali's account in Appendix 2-C; in fact, a number of times in court testimony, Bonventre contradicted the testimony of other former BLMIS colleagues.

   (A)

Q: Mr. DiPascali testified that you prepared him to pose as director of operations in preparation of the 2005 KPMG audit; do you recall that testimony?

A: Yes.

Q: Was that true?

A: No.

Q: Did Mr. DiPascali ever talk to you about your duties as director of operations?

A: Yes.

Q: Explain.

A: He and Bernie came to my office. They asked me a series of questions. It took approximately ten minutes to answer and they left.

Q: What did they ask you about, if you recall?

A: They asked me how we got our dividend information, how we got our reorganization information, how we reconcile our trades, and what do those reconciliations look like.

   ...

(B)

Q: Mr. Bonventre, before December 11, 2008, did you know that Mr. Madoff was running a Ponzi scheme?

A: No.

Q: Before December 11, 2008, did you know that Mr. Madoff was doing anything fraudulent.

A: No.

(C)

Q: Do you recall Craig Kugel testifying that you attended budget meetings?

A: Yes.

Q: Did you ever, in 40 years, attend a budget meeting at Mr. Madoff's firm?

A: No.

Q: Do you recall Craig Kugel testifying that someone in your group at the firm dealt with funding of the firm's 401(k) plan?

A: Well, the funding came through the cage. They handled all of the money flow, but the instruction for the amount and details came from Eric Lipkin.

Q: Was he in your group?

A: No.

Q: Craig Kugel testified that he spoke to Mr. Madoff about getting [your son] Daniel medical insurance. Do you recall that testimony?

A: Yes.

Q: Did you ever discuss this particular issue with Mr. Madoff, himself? And by "Mr. Madoff" I mean Bernard Madoff.

A: No.

(D)

Q: Before this case, were you ever aware of any form that reflected the number of employees of BLMIS who qualified for the medical plan?

A: No.

Q: Did you ever discuss any such form with Craig Kugel?

A: No.

Q: Did you ever discuss any such form with anyone?

A: No.

CHAPTER 3

Deception: Backstage with Enrica Cotellessa-Pitz[1]

It has been observed that "nothing is more common on earth than to deceive and be deceived." Deception is surely pervasive in American society. Among other things, Shulman reminds us that deception "offers people hope that perceptions can replace reality. Deceivers want how they seem to be taken for how they are."[2]

The centrality of deception backstage at BLMIS from all quarters evident in Chapters 1 and 2 comes as no surprise. As it is well understood, deception can be coercive: "When it succeeds, it can give power to the deceiver—power that all who suffer the consequences of lies would not wish to abdicate."[3]

Deception, of course, is a necessary component of crime, and is at the core of a con game. However, the deception here poses a special problem. As Simmel pointed out, deception can be particularly disruptive in advanced societies:

In a richer and larger cultural life, however, existence rests on a thousand premises which the single individual cannot trace and verify to their roots at all, but must take on faith. Our modern life is based to a much larger extent than is usually realized upon the faith in the honesty of the other. Examples are our economy, which becomes more and more a credit economy, or our science, in which most scholars must use innumerable results of other scientists which they cannot examine. We base our gravest decisions on a complex system of conceptions, most of which presuppose the confidence that we will not be betrayed. Under modern conditions, the lie, therefore, becomes something much more devastating than it was earlier, something which questions the very foundation of our life ... [For] modern life is a "credit economy" in a much broader than a strictly economic sense.[4]

It is the culture of lying that makes Madoff's con of particular interest sociologically, not the length of time he managed to escape detection or the amount of money gained by some and lost by others. The various forms of deception introduced by Madoff and his backstage accomplices (lying [making up information the opposite of or quite different from the truth], equivocation [providing ambiguous or contradictory statements], concealment [omitting relevant information], exaggeration, and understatement) were all readily evident. Not only Madoff but also others at BLMIS seemed constantly entangled in deception in its various forms. As Shulman has noted: "The very normative expectation of deception makes lying a coin of the realm that becomes its own rationalization: not only should you lie because it is expected that you will, but you are foolish if you don't, because 'nice guys finish last.' "[5]

At the same time, the claim by so many backstage accomplices that they were unaware of the con and attendant deception, although seemingly wholly unbelievable, is perhaps not impossible, and cannot be dismissed out of hand.

Chapters 3 and 4 are extended accounts of two of Madoff's backstage accomplices—Enrica Cotellessa-Pitz and David L. Kugel—of what each saw and did as 17th floor employees at BLMIS. This chapter begins with excerpts from the court testimony of Cotellessa-Pitz as a prosecution witness in the criminal trial of five of her former BLMIS colleagues two years after her own guilty plea. In great detail, she elaborates on her earlier acknowledgment of the growing and unbroken deception that created a great deal of illusionary wealth.

Q: Ms. Cotellessa-Pitz, did you ever work at BLMIS?
A: Yes, sir, I did.
Q: How long did you work at that company?
A: 30 years.
       . . .
Q: What was your last job?
A: In my last job my title was controller.
Q: How long were you the controller at BLMIS?
A: About ten years.
Q: What did that entail?

A: Part of the job was filing financial papers for the company, FOCUS reporting, short interest reporting. I helped with the annual audit, various other financial documents that had to be submitted to the regulators in addition to other work that I did in the operations department at BLMIS.

...

Q: I want to move on to your training at BLMIS. Can you explain how it is that you first began to learn what your job was at BLMIS?

A: I worked for Dan Bonventre for the entire time I was there. He trained me initially in dividends and interest. I was paying bills. Anything related to the back-office operations of the firm I learned from Dan.

Q: When you first started working there at the direction of Dan Bonventre, what exactly was it that you were doing?

A: Initially, it was dividends. The companies pay quarterly dividends; most of them pay quarterly dividends. It was appropriately putting the entries through associated with those payments.

...

Q: What was it that you had to do in connection with dividends at BLMIS?

A: I had to put through the appropriate entries to the traders in our trading room on a certain date. Then, at a later date I had to balance that position with settled positions in the back-office, and then on payable date receive the moneys or pay out the moneys to anybody that was due.

Q: You're talking about the traders. Which part of the business are you talking about when you talk about traders?

A: I'm talking about the market making and proprietary trading division.

Q: Which floors was that business housed on?

A: The 18th and 19th floors when we were up at Third Avenue.

...

Q: In terms of the calculations that had to do with dividends, who owned the securities that you are talking about in terms of these dividends?

A: Mr. Madoff, Bernie.

Q: They were firm securities?

A: They were firm securities, yes.

...

Q: What did Dan tell you to do? Can you explain the process by which he showed you how to do this dividend work?

A: At that time it was very manual. There was no automation, computer automation at the time. There were entries that had to be written up on an instruction sheet for the data entry clerks. The traders were either given money or charged money depending on their position. Then, subsequently, on a later date, there would be additional entries that went through.

Dan showed me trading symbols, CUSIP numbers. There were calculations that had to be made as far as what the actual amounts were. He followed me through that process, trained me how to do dividends.

Q: This all had to do with real stocks?

A: Yes.

  . . .

Q: Can you explain in brief summary what was your job as the controller? What was your understanding of what your job was as the controller?

A: Predominantly, my job was to file the financial documents. I really had very little control over all the entries that were being conducted in the firm.

Q: What do you mean when you say you really had very little control?

A: I was the controller in title only in that I took numbers from somewhere else and put them on reports.

Q: Who was the person that supervised you as the controller of BLMIS?

A: That would have been Dan and Bernie, Bernie Madoff.

  . . .

Q: After you took the test, what happened? Did you pass?

A: Yes, I passed.

Q: When was that?

A: That was in 1999.

Q: During the time that you were taking that class, was there ever anything that you were taught that made you say: "Whoa, what Dan Bonventre taught me about accounting before was totally incorrect?"

A: The test was different than the general accounting of the firm, so some of—a lot of the things that were on the test did not relate to a lot of the work that we were doing in the market making and proprietary trading businesses.

Q: I guess my question is, was there anything that you were taught that was in conflict with your training at BLMIS?

A: Yes.

Q: Like what?

A: There was a lot of information about margin. I had no idea what margin was. There was a lot of information about customers which we did not have on our books and records. It was a difficult test for me to pass in that a lot of what was directed at in that course did not apply to the work that I was doing on the 18th floor.

Q: So are you talking about things that were in conflict, or are you talking about things that were just different from what you were working on?

A: Different.

   ...

Q: Can you tell me, just in essence, what it was that you did that falsified the books and records of BLMIS?

A: Well, there were a number of instances when that occurred. We were transferring money from one division to the next. We were changing the records for tax purposes. We modified records during audits with the SEC. There were numerous occasions when the records were altered.

Q: And in terms of the activity that you engaged in modifying these records for these various purposes that you were talking about, did you engage in that activity with other people?

A: Yes.

Q: Who were the other people that you engaged in that activity with?

A: Dan Bonventre, Bernie Madoff, Frank DiPascali, Jerry O'Hara, and Eric Lipkin.

Q: And so one of the things that you mentioned just a second ago was that you were moving money from one division to the next. What do you mean by that?

A: We were transferring money from the 17th floor IA businesses onto the books and records of the market making and proprietary trading business and recording it to securities that had nothing to do with the money that was being transferred.

Q: What do you mean when you say that these securities had nothing to do with the money that was being transferred?

A: We were just crediting accounts, trading accounts, putting profit into securities essentially to hide the money. We were putting the profit into security positions that had a substantial loss so as to disguise it and to basically inflate the firm's profits and losses.

Q: In terms of that movement of money, who was responsible for identifying where you would move these—this money from the 17th floor in terms of where in the trading positions it would be moved.

A: Dan Bonventre.

Q: Can you explain what you mean by that?

A: Well, initially, when we started, when this money started to be moving—moved over, he would instruct me where to put the money, what account the money should go into. Over time, I realized that it was essentially going to the losing accounts, and I was able then to pick up as to where it could go on a monthly basis without him. But initially, he would tell me where to put the money.

Q: And when he was telling you where to put the money, did the trading positions that he was having this money from the 17th floor being moved into, did that have anything to do with real trading transactions?

A: Not from the 17th—not from the 18th floor, no.

Q: How is it that you were able to look and determine which trading position you were going to move the hidden money into?

A: It was practically one account that had very large index options positions and carried large monetary profit and loss balances; so generally it would go into those accounts.

Q: Did those accounts have any particular name within the firm?

A: It was—we referred to them as the box spreads, the spread account.

Q: Now, when you were engaging in this money movement—did you ever have any discussions where it was referred to as interest from the 17th floor?

A: Yes.

Q: Can you explain the nature of those discussions?

A: Initially the interest would come over—would be transferred over at the end of the year, and Bernie referred to it as interest that he had to report under the business tax ID [number], and we had to record it as such on the books. However, it was not going into interest income. It was going to trading.

The interest, which we used to take in in just December, eventually changed over time and we started to receive the money more frequently, on a more of a monthly basis instead of just waiting for December. Again, it was not being recorded as interest. It was being reported as trading revenue.

And at some point, the interest was changed, and it was no longer being called interest. It was being called commissions, commission equivalents, and again, we were still putting it into— at one point, we were still putting it into the options. At another point, we were putting it into individual securities. So it changed over time, but essentially it was still money being transferred over and being recorded in the proprietary trading business and these were trades that were taking place on the IA business side.

Q: Now, one of the things that you've said is that, at some point, it changed over and started being referred to as commissions?

A: Yes.

...

Q: Do you ever remember having any meetings where any of the changes that took place with regard to the movement of this money were discussed?

A: There were meetings with regard to how it was going to be recorded differently over time.

Q: Can you tell me about the nature of any of those meeting that you remember?

A: I recall at one point we were putting it into individual securities. We had been taking the money over as interest, and Bernie decided he wanted to change it. And we started taking it into individual securities as commission on individual stocks, and then it changed into going into one symbol, COMEQ, and then eventually into commission income.

Q: Who participated in these meetings?

A: It was Bernie and me. Dan was involved. Frank DiPascali was involved.

Q: Do you remember ever participating in a meeting in the latter part of 2005 that related to the movement of money at all?

A: Yes.

Q: Can you explain where that meeting took place?

A: There was a meeting in Dan's office, and it was towards the end of the SEC audit that we were undergoing in 2005. And it was regarding how the money was going to be transferred from— the source of where the money was going to be transferred from.

Q: You said this meeting took place in Mr. Bonventre's office?

A: Yes.

Q: Who was present for this meeting?

A: It was me, Bernie, Frank DiPascali, and Dan Bonventre.

Q: What happened at the start of this meeting?

A: It was a closed-door meeting, and Bernie had called the meeting. And we were sitting in Dan's office, and it was really the first time that I was in a closed-door meeting with them. And he said—Mr. Madoff said—he sat down and he said, you know, you all know what we do here.

Q: He said: "You all know what we do here?"

A: Yes.

Q: What was your understanding of that comment?

A: I was not really sure what we do here. I was in this position. I was almost embarrassed because I felt that he was my boss—I did not know what to think of that, and it was kind of that situation where you think you're supposed to know what your boss is referring to and you don't, and you just keep quiet because you don't know what he's talking about, and there was a silence in the room. Nobody was saying anything.

     And Bernie continued the conversation, and he said he wanted to make it appear that the money was coming from overseas. And we had been transferring commission money, commission equivalent money, for quite some time at that point, and it had been coming from various brokerage firms. It was my understanding that they were commissions on trades being executed overseas.

     And we had London office, which is where I thought the trades were being conducted through, and I said, well, I said: "If we're doing the trades overseas, why isn't the money coming in from the London office?"

Q: What was the reaction in the room when you said that?

A: It was still quiet. It was still, quiet, and it was just odd, a very—an uncomfortable quiet. And Bernie said: "Well, yeah, we can do that. We can think about doing that." And what I remember after that the meeting was over very quickly.

Q: And after that meeting, did the money start coming in from London?

A: Yes.

Q: Now, were you ever aware of an account at BLMIS that was referred to as Annette's checkbook?

A: Yes.

     . . .

Q: Can you explain what that was?

A: Annette's checkbook was where customer checks were written from and where—I guess, where wires came into, but mostly customer withdrawals, distributions.

Q: And do you know what the number or what any of the numbers were of that account?

A: Just the 703 Account.

Q: How is it that you were aware of the existence of this account?

A: Well, I knew about the account for quite some time; I was designated signer on the account. I signed checks for it.

Q: Over what time period were you signing checks for the 703 Account?

A: 1998 on.

Q: Did you have any responsibility for any accounts connected to the 703 Account, other than signing checks?

A: No.

Q: And how is it that you, working on the 18th floor, became responsible for signing check for the 703 Account?

A: When I took over someone had retired . . . .

Q: Now, over the course of the time that you were doing this, did you end up signing many checks?

A: Yes.

Q: Did anyone explain to you what the specific purpose was of each of the checks that you signed?

A: No.

Q: What was your understanding of, overall, what the checks were for that you were signing that came from the 703 Account?

A: Customer withdrawals.

. . .

Q: Now, you, yourself, did you have an IA account at BLMIS?

A: Yes.

Q: Can you explain how it is that you first—or how it is that you came to have an IA account at BLMIS?

A: It was back in 1986, and I had refinanced my mortgage on my house. And at that time, the interest rates were very high on mortgages, and I was taking some equity out of my house. And I asked Bernie, what to do with the money that I was going to take out, and he extended me an offer to open up an account.

Q: Did you take him up on the offer?

A: I did.

Q: Why?

A: Well, he was going to pay a very high rate of return. It was 24%.

Q: He told you that it was going to be 24%?
A: Yes.
Q: And what was your understanding of what was going to happen with the money in your IA account?
A: He told me it was a fully managed account, which meant that he had all the investment decisions to make on the account and that if I wanted to buy 100 shares of IBM or anything like that, that I had to go elsewhere to do that, that I would have no say over what was in the account, and that was the deal.
Q: But was it explained to you that within his discretion, it would be stocks and bonds or whatever they were buying, stocks?
A: I understood it to be, yes, stocks, stocks predominantly, yeah.
Q: And so in terms of this account, how much money was it that you put into it initially based on this refinancing of your home?
A: Oh, it was $30,000.
Q: Over time, did you ever come to put more money into the account?
A: Yes.
    . . .
Q: Well, can you explain how it came to be that you ended up putting in more than the initial amount that you invested into your investment account at BLMIS?
A: Well, some of it came from savings, and most of it came from refinancing my house.
Q: So did you end up refinancing again?
A: Two more times.
Q: Two more times. And each time that you refinanced, did you put the money into your BLMIS account?
A: Yes.
Q: Why were you refinancing your house to put money into and investment account?
A: Because I was getting a very good return.
Q: Now, ultimately, at the time of the collapse of the firm, how much money did you have or did you understand yourself to have in your BLMIS account?
A: About $3.5 million.
Q: Did that represent all of our savings?
A: Yes.
Q: What happened to that money?
A: It's gone.

Q: Was there ever a point during the time that you were working at BLMIS that anyone advised you that you should take any money out of your account?

A: Yes.

Q: When was that?

A: That was probably in 2005, 2006, I think, 2006.

Q: Where did that conversation take place?

A: That was a personal conversation between Annette Bongiorno and me.

Q: Where were you?

A: We were—We had the conversation more than once. I think once we were at lunch. Another time it might have just been in the office.

    . . .

Q: So what was communicated to you by Ms. Bongiorno?

A: She had said to me that she noticed that there was a lot of money being withdrawn from the customer accounts. I understood it to mean the family accounts, the Madoff family accounts, and she just suggested to me, as her friend, that I should think about taking money out.

    She said she didn't know what the reason was that everybody was taking money out, but that perhaps I should consider taking out enough for my daughter's college education because then I would have it. She said that she was taking money out, and that I should think about doing the same.

Q: What did you end up doing after that?

A: I went to Bernie?

Q: And did you have a conversation with him?

A: Yes.

Q: What happened during that conversation?

A: After the conversation with Annette, I actually went home and discussed it with my husband and asked: "What should we do?" And he suggested I speak with Bernie. So I did, and I said to Bernie: "Look," I said, "everything I own everything I have is here. You know, should I think about taking some money out at this time; should I diversify?" And he said to me: "Absolutely not. There's no need for you to ever worry about your money here."

Q: Did you even up taking the money out of your account?

A: No.

    . . .

Q: So let me ask you, did you ever ask Mr. Bonventre any questions that related to the bookkeeping practices of the 17th floor?

A: Yes.

Q: What kind of questions did you ask him?

A: Well, I had asked him why they didn't have a general ledger on the 17th floor.

. . .

Q: Did he say anything else?

A: He said that he had been telling Bernie to have a general ledger on the 17th floor and that Bernie didn't want it, and I said: "How do they balance their work without one?"

Q: What was his response?

A: He said he didn't know.

Q: Now, you had this conversation. Do you remember when it was you had this conversation, or was it just one conversation?

A: I remember having the conversation twice, probably twice—twice, two different occasions in his office. I'm not even quite sure what had prompted the conversation. It could have had to do with a canceled check or something like that, but it was just purely speculative. We balanced our work every day on the 18th floor.

Q: And in terms of what was on the books and records of BLMIS as reflected in the work you were doing on the 18th floor, was the 17th floor—were the 17th floor monies reflected on those books and records?

A: Not entirely, no.

Q: What about the 703 Account, was that reflected on the Madoff books and records that you worked on?

A: No.

Q: Are you familiar with an individual named David Friehling?

A: Yes.

Q: Who is David Friehling?

A: He was Bernie's accountant.

Q: How is it that you came to know David Friehling?

A: I worked with David Friehling on the audit—the annual audit.

Q: What was the nature of that work?

A: David would come in to do the annual audit in November. I would give him the documents associated with the financial statements, and he would write them up, but I had already done all the work associated with the documents.

Q: Was there ever an occasion where David Friehling asked you about the 17th floor being reflected in the books and records?

A: Once.

Q: What happened?

A: David was in my office, he was sitting at my desk, and he was going through some of the paperwork for the audit. And he stopped and he said: "The customers are in here, right?" And I paused because I knew the customers weren't in there, and I said, just a minute. And I went out and I said to Dan—and I said: "David's asking about the customers being in the numbers; so—"

Q: What did Mr. Bonventre say?

A: He paused for a moment and he said: "Tell him they're in there." So I went back out to David and I said: "Danny says they're in there."

Q: Now, you knew, in fact, that the customers were not in the books and records?

A: Yes.

Q: So why did you tell Mr. Friehling that?

A: I just repeated what Dan told me.

Q: Did you ever see Mr. Bonventre handling any IA account securities?

A: Umm.

Q: Let me be clearer: Did you ever see him handling securities that belonged to customers of the firm?

A: I—I'm not sure under—

Q: Well, I guess the question I'm asking is: Were you aware of the fact that the firm had these customers on the 17th floor?

A: Yes.

Q: Did any of your work with Mr. Bonventre actually involve securities that were owned by customers?

A: Not in our business. Not on our side of the business, no.

Q: What about with regard to loans that the firm obtained; did you ever have any dealings in terms of loans that the firm obtained that had to do with customers?

A: We had—We had some loans on our side, yeah.

Q: Did any of those have any relationship to customer securities?

A: Yes.

Q: What was the relationship?

A: We used bonds that belonged to customers to obtain bank loans.

Q: What do you mean by that?

A: It means that we used securities that the ultimate owners of the bonds or securities belonged to, customers, that had IA accounts, and we represented them as our own.

Q: And when you represented them as your own, what were you doing with them in terms of the bank?

A: Using them as collateral

Q: And did the firm actually end up obtaining money falsely representing customer securities as their own?

A: Yes.

Q: Was Mr. Bonventre involved in that?

A: Yes.

Q: Who are some of the customers whose securities that you used in order to obtain loans?

A: Carl Shapiro, Noel Levine, Norman Levy, Stan Chais, and Jeffry Picower.

Q: Were there any particular accounts at BLMIS where you specifically kept customer securities that you utilized?

A: Well, we had a trading account for our customers where we had some customer securities. That was the seven accounts.

Q: Are you familiar with an account that was known as the Geo-Serve account?

A: Yes.

Q: What was the Geo-Serve account?

A: The Geo-Serve account was a custody account at Chase, JPMorgan Chase Bank, that held bond positions.

Q: And whose bond positions were kept in the Geo-Serve account?

A: Customer bonds.

. . .

Q: What was Mr. Bonventre's role?

A: He monitored on a monthly basis the accuracy of the positions on the 18th and 19th floor to reconcile with the positions held at DTC. Actually, it was audited monthly but the positions were verified daily.

Q: Did you actually see Mr. Bonventre looking at DTC reports?

A: Yes.

Q: Did there ever come a time when you became aware of an effort at BLMIS to create reports that looked like actual DTC reports?

A: Yes.

Q: Do you remember when that was?

A: It was a long time ago, probably in the 1990's or before; early the 1990's or before. It was a long time ago.

Q: Who did you observe was involved in that effort to make these reports that looked like actual DTC reports?

A: I observed Dan Bonventre, Bernie Madoff, and Ken Hutchinson.
. . .

Q: Can you tell us, how long this project was going on, from your observation?

A: I would say probably close to maybe a couple of months, six to eight weeks.

Q: What did you observe?

A: I just observed different renditions of the document—different types of paper, different types of fonts that we used in the creation of the document, different layouts, format—until it was right.

Q: What do you mean until it was right?

A: Until it reached [looked like] a real DTC position statement.

Q: You're describing an evolution of documents that ultimately culminated with a document that matched up with the real DTC report?

A: Yes.

Q: Where were you seeing these documents as they evolved?

A: In Dan's office.

Q: Who did you observe Mr. Bonventre communicating with regard to these documents that were being created?

A: It was Bernie and Frank looking at them. Ken I really didn't see. Ken was more of—he was the programmer. When he was complete with the project, I saw him. He came to me and was kind of like gloating that he had completed the project.

Q: The individual you referred to is Ken Hutchinson?

A: Yes.
. . .

Q: Ms. Cotellessa-Pitz, without referencing anything anyone said, did you have occasion during this project to observe any specific aspects of the report that evolved with the evolutions of the DTC report?

A: Yes.

Q: What aspects?

A: I saw the change of paper, the change in the font, the format changes. I saw the evolution of the work.

Q: Were there any particular characters that you saw on the documents that were different from one version to the next?

A: I particularly remember asterisks, the asterisks on the page, boxes around each position. The DTC position statement was an unusually formatted report.

Q: What did it look like in terms of the final product of what you saw in terms of the simulated DTC report?
A: It looked like a DTC report. It was the same green and white paper. It was the same font. It looked like a DTC report.
Q: Do you know why these other individuals were working on this document?
A: No.
Q: Were you yourself personally involved in the creation of the simulated DTC reports?
A: No.
  . . .
Q: You mentioned that one of the things that you did in connection with some of the crimes that you participated in at BLMIS had to do with the movement of money. Are you familiar with the term at BLMIS that was known as "CP adjustments?"
A: Yes.
Q: What does "CP adjustments" refer to?
A: "CP adjustments" referred to the movement of money between the IA business and the market making business.
Q: When you say the movement of money between the IA business and the market making business, can you explain in a little bit more detail what you mean in terms of the "CP adjustments?"
A: It was transfers of money between the two divisions involving bank loans and increasing the profit and the capital on the side of the market making business.
Q: When were these "CP adjustments" made?
A: I participated in them at the end of the month when necessary, but to my knowledge it occurred inter-month as well.
  . . .
Q: And you also mentioned a specific SEC audit that took place in 2005?
A: Yes.
Q: Did you participate in that SEC audit?
A: Yes.
Q: And was your guilty plea at all related to what you did in connection with that SEC audit?
A: Yes.
Q: How so?
A: I altered many books and reports to give to the auditors from the SEC in connection with that audit.
Q: Did anyone work with you on that activity?

A: Yes.
Q: Who worked with you on that activity?
A: Eric Lipkin, Frank DiPascali, Bernie Madoff, Dan Bonventre, and Jerry O'Hara.
Q: Now, first of all, what was your understanding of what the SEC was while you were working at BLMIS?
A: Who they were?
Q: Yes, who they were.
A: A regulator.
Q: And so how was it first explained to you that the SEC was going to be coming in to conduct an audit?
A: Either Bernie or Dan made an announcement. Bernie made the announcement, I would say, and Dan distributed the work that had to be done.
Q: What do you mean by that?
A: The SEC would send in a request saying that they were coming and submitted an initial document request in relation to what they were auditing when they came.
. . .
Q: In the course of beginning to prepare for this SEC audit, did you participate in any meetings that related to how you all were going to respond to this audit?
A: Yes.
Q: Can you explain what the nature of those meetings was?
A: Well, I wouldn't say they were exactly meetings. They were more directives from Bernie at the time as to how he was going to respond to everything in this audit. He was quite frenzied with this audit.
Q: What do you mean when you say he was quite frenzied?
A: He was agitated about this audit, and I really did not know the reason why. But he responded in a very nervous way with this audit and demanded that things be done very quickly, like wanting things done yesterday.
Q: And so to the extent that Mr. Madoff was giving these instructions, who else was around when Mr. Madoff was in this frenzied state and giving instructions?
A: Frank, Dan, Eric, and I were around. That's who I remember.
Q: Were there any discussions at the firm about how you were going to respond to that request?
A: Yes.
Q: What was the nature of those discussions?

A: The nature of those discussions was that we had had a lot of money in a particular account that reflected a lot of transfers from the IA business, and Bernie wanted that account eliminated.

Q: What do you mean when you say eliminated?

A: He didn't want to show it to the SEC.

Q: So what happened?

A: So in the list of trading accounts that we gave them, we eliminated the account and in subsequent papers, eliminated all the money that had gone into that account as well.

Q: And you said this is the account that related to a lot of the money that was coming over from the 17th floor?

A: Yes.

Q: Who was involved in those discussions about eliminating this account?

A: Myself, Bernie, Dan, and Frank.

Q: Was anyone else involved?

A: Jerry O'Hara.
    ...

Q: Ms. Cotellessa-Pitz, you mentioned earlier in terms of the crimes that you participated in at BLMIS some activities related to tax audits.

A: Yes.

Q: What was your role in these tax audits as related to what you pled guilty to?

A: I participated in altering trading documents for Bernie to submit to the IRS or New York State tax authorities to correspond about what he reported as income on his tax returns.

Q: What do you mean when you say you participated in altering documents?

A: I put trading positions in that weren't there and took trading positions out, decreased/increased positions, all to get to a certain number that he wanted to appear on his tax returns— that he had previously reported on his taxes.

Q: Did anybody work with you in that activity?

A: Yes.

Q: Who was that?

A: Dan Bonventre and Jerry O'Hara.

Q: What was Mr. Bonventre's role in this activity that you were engaging in with regard to these tax audits?

A: We did it together. There was a series of numbers that we had to get to, and there were selections of securities that could potentially fit the numbers that we were trying to get to. Sometimes they worked and sometimes they didn't, but eventually we got to a set of numbers that fit what Bernie wanted.

Q: What do you mean when you say you got to a set of numbers that fit what Bernie wanted?

A: There was designated number for various tax years. They differed in every year that Bernie's income had to be reduced by. We altered the trading documents so that it would match what he had reported.

Q: Where did this designated number come from? Did it have any relationship to his actual income?

A: I don't know where the number came from. I know the number that he wanted. I don't know where the reduction came from that he reported. In one year we had to reduce his income by $29 million, $26 million, and $43 million. It was different all the time. We fabricated documents to give him and his accountant what he wanted.

Q: What was your understanding of what the impact would be of fabricating these documents in connection with these audits?

A: Bernie's tax liability would be reduced substantially.

Q: You mentioned that there were IRS audits and there were also New York State [tax] auditors?

A: Yes.

Q: Did you participate in both kinds of audits?

A: Yes.

Q: Over what time period did these audits stretch?

A: The audits themselves usually were over a three-year period. There might have been one for 2004, 2005, and 2006 and another one for 2001, 2002, and 2003; and 2001, 2002, and 2003; 1997 or 1998 through 2001. It varied, but usually they were all in three-year intervals.

Q: How far back were you involved in participating in the creation of these fabricated documents for the tax audit?

A: The early 2000's.

Q: Was Mr. Bonventre working with you throughout that entire time?

A: Yes.

Q: What was Mr. O'Hara's role in this process?

A: He made the changes that he was directed to do.

. . .

Q: I think you already mentioned your familiarity with a person named David Friehling?

A: Yes.

Q: Did he have any role in these tax audits?

A: Yes.

Q: What was his role?

A: He dealt with the auditors.

Q: What do you mean by that?

A: He was the one that presented the material pursuant to the audit that was taking place.

Q: The process that you engaged in in order to alter the documents that you fabricated in connection with these audits. Was this a simple process?

A: No.

Q: Why do you say that?

A: It was a very cumbersome task to get a set of securities to fit the numbers that Bernie wanted, and it was three years running. So what you did in the first year had to carry forth to the second year and then subsequently to the third year. I found it to be quite difficult.

Q: Why was that a cumbersome process in terms of figuring out the numbers on this?

A: Because you had to take a cost basis which was much lower than the current market price, you had to mark it to the market based on year-end prices, you had to take into account the profit or the loss that you were taking in one year and bring it forward to the next. And trading documents had to be altered for every year.

Q: After all of that process, what was the ultimate thing that was produced?

A: An altered trading ledger with changed positions and general ledgers and balance sheets and year-end statements that changed the trading inventory and the capital and the profit and loss.

     . . .

Q: And was that number going to go into any document?

A: This document was going to be rerun and given to the auditors.

Q: The rerun version?

A: Yes.

Q: And was the rerun version going to have accurate information about the finances of BLMIS in it?

A: No.

     . . .

Q: And what was your understanding of what is being reflected here in terms of this $71 million number that is connected to this $99 million number?

A: The trading profit is being reduced by $28 million.

Q: Why would you reduce the trading profit here by that much money?

A: Because Bernie reduced it on his income tax by that amount, and he needed the documentation to support that.

. . .

A: This is a balance sheet for December 31, 2003.

Q: And there's writing in the right-hand margin of this balance sheet. Can you explain what the writing in the right-hand margin in the balance sheet is?

A: It is the adjusted numbers for the 2003 balance sheet to correspond with Bernie's tax return.

Q: The handwriting that's on the right-hand margin, do you recognize any of it?

A: Most of it is mine, and the number that is crossed out is Dan's.

. . .

Q: What do you mean when you say the printed number is a number reported?

A: That's the capital of the firm as we had reported through the years, through the year anyway, and then the written number is the adjusted number to correspond with Bernie's taxes.

. . .

Q: Did this have any relationship to actual stocks that had been traded at BLMIS?

A: No.

Q: So what did this refer to?

A: A potential security that we could add to the trading ledger.

. . .

A: The number that Bernie used, the number that Bernie reported.

Q: So what you're talking about is one column showing the number Bernie had reported on his taxes and the others showing what the books and records of the back-office reflected?

A: Yes.

Q: Why was it important to differentiate between those two numbers in connection with these tax audits?

A: We had to change the back-office numbers to agree with Bernie's numbers.

. . .

Q: But this was referring to nonexistent trades?

A: Nonexistent positions, yes.

Q: And those actually ended up being reported on the books and records that related—that were being kept on the 18th floor?

A: Just for tax purposes.

Q: Tax versions of the books and records?

A: Yes.

Q: And then what happened to those documents?

A: They were given to the auditors.

Q: Now, you mentioned that you gave these to Jerry O'Hara to create the documents?

A: Yes.

Q: And what exactly did you give to him in terms of creating the documents?

A: We gave him the trading account, the security position, the quantity, the price that needed to be inserted into the trading ledger.

. . .

Q: Who gave you that information?

A: Dan.

Q: What did you use it for?

A: To finally get to the final number, the final profit and loss total for the month.

Q: The final profit and loss total for the month that you produced to the SEC, was that number accurate?

A: No.

Q: How was it inaccurate?

A: Because it had a lot of adjustments made to the content of the number. The overall number agreed with what had been previously reported, but the breakdown of the number [was] inaccurate.

. . .

Q: After you got this third request from the SEC, were you part of any discussions that related to how you were all going to respond to this request?

A: Yes.

Q: Who was involved in those discussions?

A: Bernie, Dan, Frank, Eric, and I were involved in this one as well.

Q: What was the nature of the discussion with regard to this request from the SEC?

A: This request presented a problem because this was asking for the gross revenue. What we had been previously giving to them was net income. We had deleted really all the information, much of the information, associated with this request on the prior submissions to them.

Q: Why was that a problem?

A: Because showing it now seemed to be contrary to what we already had given them.

Q: The previous false information?

A: Right.

      . . .

Q: What is depicted on page 4 of this document, Ms. Cotellessa-Pitz?

A: This is the amount of money that was transferred—this is the amount of commission equivalent money from the 17th floor by fiscal year and by calendar year.

Q: Where did you get this information?

A: I got this from Frank.

Q: Frank DiPascali?

A: Yes.

Q: Can we go to page 5 of this document. What is this? What are we looking at here?

A: This is the breakdown by department per the SEC request for the various, the market making, the proprietary trading, and the commission equivalents.

Q: There is some handwriting on this. Do you know whose handwriting that is?

A: It's mine.

Q: Why did you write "new" at the bottom?

A: That this is a second version or a version. There was a previous version.

Q: In the previous version was the information different?

A: Yes.

Q: Why was the information changing from version to version?

A: There were a number of reasons. The commission equivalents number that I had reflected in my work for this time period was different than the commission equivalents number that actually went on the report. We had designated traders, certain traders, as proprietary traders who in previous early years 2002 and

2003 we were designating as market making traders. There was different information that was used to compile the request for the SEC.

Q: We were just talking about the SEC audit 2005. In the time period of 2005 and 2006, were you ever involved in obtaining large loans from banks in connection with BLMIS?

A: Yes.

Q: What was your role in that process?

A: I generally typed the letters requesting the loans.

Q: What do you mean when you say letters requesting the loans?

A: Usually, there was a letter written to the bank requesting the loan and what was going to be used as collateral and where the funds should be transferred. That was faxed over to them as a loan request.

. . .

Q: What is this communication?

A: This is a letter of instructions to JPMorgan Chase Bank authorizing them to receive $100 million worth of federal home loan bonds into our Geo-Serve account on November 4, 2005.

Q: This $100 million dollars worth of federal home bonds loan that were being delivered to JPMorgan Chase Bank, were they being represented in connection with this loan as assets of BLMIS?

A: Yes.

Q: Were they actually BLMIS assets?

A: No.

Q: Who did they belong to?

A: They belonged to a customer, an IA customer.

Q: Can you read what is written in this letter

A: "As per your telephone conversation with Dan Bonventre, we would like to borrow $95 million using our account G13414 as collateral. Please credit our account number 140081703 with said funds. Thank you for your assistance with this matter."

Q: Ms. Cotellessa-Pitz, who signed this letter?

A: Bernie Madoff and I.

Q: Why did you write this letter to JPMorgan Chase Bank?

A: I was instructed by Dan to request the loan and I wrote the letter.

Q: Did Dan tell you why he wanted you to request this loan?

A: No.

Q: Why did you indicate "Please credit our account" and identify the 703 Account?

A: That's what I was instructed to type.

Q: Instructed by who?

A: By Dan.

Q: The 703 Account, was that associated with any aspect of the business at BLMIS?

A: Yes. It was Annette's account, the IA business.

. . .

Q: What does this document indicate, Ms. Cotellessa-Pitz?

A: This is a loan statement from the bank, in this case JPMorgan Chase Bank, indicating the amount of interest charged by day, how many days at what percentage rate. It is a statement of interest due to the bank for the amount that they charged us.

Q: Does it indicate that there is a particular loan outstanding for BLMIS?

A: Yes.

Q: For how much?

A: $95 million.

Q: Does this relate to the letter that you wrote and the letter that Mr. Bonventre wrote previously?

A: Yes.

. . .

Q: Do you know why it doesn't appear?

A: Because it was added after the fact.

. . .

Q: Why were 11 million shares of Amazon added in connection with a tax audit?

A: It was, again, the same scenario, to alter the books and records to reflect a position based on Bernie's tax return.

. . .

Q: What is the difference between the first document we looked at and this document?

A: This document has 1,278,000 shares of Apple posted to it.

Q: Can you explain how the change between the first and the second document occurred?

A: It was placed there. It was just placed there for tax purposes.

Q: By whom?

A: By myself and Dan and Jerry.

Q: Jerry O'Hara?

A: Yes.

. . .

Q: Ms. Cotellessa-Pitz, can you explain, why was the Apple position that is reflected here added?

A: This was the trading account that was chosen. The LL account was generally an error account. This was just the account that was chosen for the tax purposes this time.

. . .

A: We added a short position . . . for Bernie's taxes.

Q: When you say "we," who are you talking about?

A: Dan and myself.

Q: What does this mean in terms of what the purported gain or loss would be?

A: It reduces the profit for the period.

Q: Is this an $82 million loss, essentially?

A: The $54 million at the year-to-date column indicates the loss. The $82 million indicates a change in the position.

Clearly, Cotellessa-Pitz saw and engaged in much more criminal activity—and deception—at BLMIS than she had previously acknowledged in court. By active participation in creating a world of fiction, little was real at BLMIS. Chapter 4 shows the same was true for David L. Kugel.

CHAPTER 4

Deception: Backstage with David L. Kugel[1]

This chapter consists of numerous excerpts from the court testimony of David L. Kugel, who like Cotellessa-Pitz was a prosecution witness in the criminal trial of five former BLMIS colleagues. Like Cotellessa-Pitz, Kugel, of course, hoped by again testifying to receive a lighter prison sentence.

Like in the case of Cotellessa-Pitz, Madoff and other backstage accomplices drew readily from their quiver of deceptions to lure Kugel into the con. Before long, he too readily engaged in pretense.

The particular value of Kugel's testimony is that it clearly shows how Madoff's backstage accomplices were so easily attracted by money, a great deal of money over many years, so as to be invariably and progressively drawn into the vortex of his con. This process, of course, necessitated Madoff sharing more of the money he was stealing from investors with individuals outside of his family circle. However, as the amount of money invested in the BLMIS IA business continued to grow larger and larger, this never posed a problem. In fact, Madoff appeared to become more reckless in what he doled out to his backstage accomplices. He appeared to like the idea of appearing to be generous. And he surely fully understood that money bought loyalty, loyalty by some that persisted even as they awaited long prison terms for their work helping his con thrive.

Q: When did you begin work at BLMIS?
A: I started in April 1970.
Q: How long did you stay there?
A: Until the fraud, December 2008, plus three months extra for the [SIPC] trustee.

Q: Over the 38 or so years that you worked at BLMIS, did you commit any crimes there, sir?

A: Yes, sir.

Q: Tell the jury what crimes you committed?

A: Security fraud and mortgage fraud.

Q: Did you commit those crimes alone, or did you do them with other people?

A: With other people.

Q: So, first, can you tell the jury what you did, in general terms, to commit securities fraud?

A: I gave historical information to create fraudulent trades, fabricated trades that were for the clients. Confirmations [of these trades] were sent out, and they appeared on the monthly statements of clients.

Q: Tell the jury who were the people that you worked with to commit securities fraud?

A: Bernard Madoff, Annette Bongiorno and Jodi Crupi—and others.

Q: And you said you also committed mortgage fraud?

A: Correct.

Q: Tell the jury generally what you did to commit mortgage fraud?

A: I, on my mortgage application, put down assets from my brokerage account that weren't there.

Q: Your brokerage account at BLMIS?

A: Yes, sir, I'm sorry, at BLMIS. Yes.

Q. And did you commit that crime alone or with others?

A: With others?

Q: With whom did you commit mortgage fraud?

A: Bernard Madoff and Jodi Crupi.

Q: And when did you start committing crimes at BLMIS?

A: I would say the mid—about the mid-1970s.
    . . .

Q: What were you doing in the trading room?

A: I was a market maker, as I described before, someone, another brokerage firm, would call up and ask the price that I was willing to buy stock for or willing to sell stock for. And if I liked either one of the prices, they would either buy stock from me or sell stock to me.

    I also did my own trading. If I saw one of these discrepancies that we spoke about, the arbitrage discrepancy, on my own, I would go out and execute and try to do the trade myself.

Q: And when you say on your own, do you mean with your personal money?

A: No, I'm sorry. I explained it bad. When I say on my own, I mean buying from another brokerage firm where it was initiated, where someone called me up on the phone. In other words, I would watch the markets, and when I say on my own, proprietary, company money. I would just—there would be—obviously, there would be a broker on the other side, but I would initiate—or I would initiate the trade as opposed to someone coming to me with a trade and they would initiate it. That would be the main difference.

Q: Okay. So some of what you were doing was market making, correct?

A: Yes.

Q: And some was proprietary trading?

A: Correct, correct.

Q: And to be clear, this was all real trading, correct?

A: A hundred percent. Yes.

Q: Real securities?

A: Real securities.

. . .

Q: Are you familiar with the DTC or Depository Trust Corporation?

A: Yes, sir.

Q: Did the DTC exist in the early 1970s?

A: I believe DTC was—it existed I think in the—starting in the mid-1970s, if I remember correctly.

Q: So prior to the mid-1970s, or whenever the DTC was created, it was, obviously, not part of this process of trading, correct?

A: Correct.

Q: And then once the DTC was created, how did the process of completing trades change?

A: It turned into what's called a book entry delivery. In other words, there was settlement, the stocks were kept—DTC stands for Depository Trust Corporation, and stocks were kept on deposit in what is commonly known as the DTC for your account.

So if you had—if you show that you own stock—and I sold it to Merrill Lynch, an entry would be made. I would give instructions to the DTC to deliver the stock to Merrill Lynch, and it would be basically a book entry type of delivery.

Q: And when you say book entry, you mean the physical securities didn't change hands?

A: Correct.

Q: It was just recorded as a move?

A: Correct.

Q: Was it physical?

A: No.

Q: It was just recorded as moving from BLMIS to Merrill Lynch, in your example?

A: Correct. Correct.

Q: So prior to the creation of the DTC in the early 1970s, who kept track of who owned a security?

A: At BLMIS, you're asking me? I'm sorry.

Q: Yes, at BLMIS.

A: Sorry. The back-office would keep track of the physical stock. It would be commonly referred to as "what's in the box," meaning actual securities, and they would do a balance of the securities every day to make sure they matched the positions that the firm had.

Q: So the back-office kept an inventory of the firm's securities?

A: Yes, sir.

Q: And, again, that was the back-office that Mr. Bonventre and Ms. Bongiorno sat in?

A: Correct.

. . .

Q: And generally speaking, who served as transfer agents for securities?

A: It was generally the bank, a bank.

Q: So also like a third-party bank, just like a conversion agent?

A: Yes, sir.

Q: And at BLMIS, when a security was traded, who was responsible for registering with the transfer agent the sale or purchase?

A: The back-office.

Q: When you were first hired at BLMIS, were you aware that there was also an investment advisory [IA] business?

A: No.

Q: When did you become first aware that there was an IA business at BLMIS?

A: I believe the first—the first time I became aware of it was when Bernie Madoff asked me to drop off an envelope for one of his clients, and that was in probably sometime after I started.

Q: Do you recall how long after you started? Was it weeks, months, years?

A: I would say probably within the first year, from memory.

Q: And other than dropping off an envelope with a client, did you have any conversations with Mr. Madoff in which you learned that there was an IA business?

A: Sometime after—he mentioned—he told me that he was doing investing for close friends and family.

Q: Did he ever ask you questions in connection with the IA business?

A: Yes.

Q: And what's the first question you can remember Mr. Madoff putting to you about the IA business?

A: I believe the first question was. Excuse me. He told me that he did—that he was trading convertible securities, and he asked me to review the return on it, just do the math on it to see what the profit was.

Q: Was Mr. Madoff good at math?

A: Certain aspects, yes; certain aspects, no.

Q: What aspects, yes, and what aspects, no?

A: He had trouble with long division.

Q: I'm sorry?

A: He had trouble with long division.

Q: Bernie Madoff couldn't do long division, you said?

A: That was my understanding, yes.

Q: Other than Mr. Madoff, do you know who was involved in the IA business in the early to mid-1970s?

A: Yes.

Q: Who else was involved in the IA business?

A: At the time Annette Argese—Annette Bongiorno. That was her maiden name at the time.

Q: How do you know she was involved in the IA business?

A: I'm trying to think. The couple of times Bernard Madoff would say give the information to Annette regarding the IA account or regarding the investors, and I think that when I got the envelope, I might have picked it up from Annette.

Q: You're saying when you got that first envelope?

A: Yeah.

Q: You think you got it from Ms. Bongiorno?

A: Yes.

Q: And also that you gave certain information to Ms. Bongiorno?

A: Yes.

. . .

Q: And what sort of information—at the very beginning? What sort of information did Mr. Madoff ask you for?

A: What he asked me for is if I saw an active arbitrage situation, to let him know.

Q: And what was your understanding of what an active arbitrage situation meant?

A: Stock that had volatility, meaning trading range, and volume.

Q: And what was your understanding of what Mr. Madoff was going to do with that information?

A: He was looking for ideas to trade, to make trades in these particular securities. I was trying to give him ideas for this security or whatever else he was doing.

Q: Other than you, was anyone else actually trading convertible securities at BLMIS in the early 1970s?

A: Yes.

Q: Who else?

A: Peter Madoff did a few, a few type of securities at that point.

Q: Was Peter Madoff trading the same convertible securities that you were?

A: No.

Q: So when Bernard Madoff asked you for information about your own trades, were you concerned that he was going to be trading in the same securities?

A: Bernard Madoff? Yes, I did ask him. I said to him: "Why don't you let me—how come I'm not doing it? How come I'm not doing these trades?" And I also said I was concerned how it would affect my profitability, since I was doing these securities. And he assured me that it wouldn't affect me. He told me that he was dealing with banks, mutual funds, large investors that I would not deal with in the trading room, and I took his word at that point.

Q: Tell us about the next request that Mr. Madoff made of you?

A: I would say after I started giving him names, and I gave them like instantaneous, from the trading desk as I was doing it. He asked me to give him examples of stock—set up an example for him or a few examples where they made a certain return. He asked me to set up for a certain percent, and I wrote down as examples what it was, what the examples were in arbitrage.

Q: When you say examples, what do you mean?

A: I meant I actually set up, a hypothetical trade based on the way the stocks traded that I traded. So I would give him an example where I would buy the preferred, the convertible, exchangeable security. I would give him the sale of the common [stock], and he would ask me for a certain percent. And I gave him—based on his request, I gave him what he needed.

Q: So you gave Mr. Madoff information about historical trades that returned a certain percentage?

A: Yes, sir.

Q: And do you know what Mr. Madoff was doing with that information?

A: I knew he was using it for investments, for investors. I didn't know how at the time.

Q: How did you know he was using it for investors?

A: Because he indicated to me that he was trading convertible securities for investors based on the examples he asked me to check previously.

Q: When you say you didn't know how he was using them, what do you mean?

A: I didn't know what he did with it after I gave it to him, at first.

Q: You didn't assume that he was just doing those trades?

A: At that point, initially, no; initially, no. I did not realize what he was using it for.

Q: Let me ask it a different way. Could he have just done those trades?

A: Yes.

Q: How could he have done the trades that you were giving him based on historical information?

A: He could have just—Well, first of all, I just gave him prices I didn't give him the number of shares. I just gave him—I just gave him prices; so it could have been done to any amount of money. Like I said before, he asked me for examples of arbitrage situations, or to tell him when something was active. So I just—when he asked me to do that, I figured it was all the same.

Q: What do you mean, it was all the same?

A: Meaning it was all arbitrage situations that he was asking me for.

Q: Does that mean that he wouldn't have been doing the exact thing that you wrote down?

A: At the time, I didn't know.

Q: At some point, did you realize what Mr. Madoff was doing with the information that you provided?

A: Yes.

Q: And when was that?
A: After a few times of doing this, he asked me to give the information to Annette Bongiorno.
Q: Okay. And when was that?
A: Probably, again, in the mid-1970s.
Q: And how did that help you realize what Mr. Madoff and Ms. Bongiorno were doing with the information that you provided?
A: Once I did that, I then started getting—I would say—regular requests, probably once a week, asking for a certain dollar amount of trades that would earn a certain percent.
Q: And you said you got those requests about once a week?
A: Yes.
Q: From whom did you get the requests?
A: From Annette Bongiorno.
Q: Once Mr. Madoff asked you to start working with Ms. Bongiorno, what was his, Mr. Madoff's, involvement in this process?
A: Virtually nothing.
Q: Specifically what information did Ms. Bongiorno ask you for and what information did you provide. When you got these weekly requests from Ms. Bongiorno, what sort of information specifically did she ask you for?
A: She would give me a number, which I believe represented what money had to be invested. So, for example, she would ask, let's say, I need $1 million. On a sheet of paper it would say $1 million. She would request the number of weeks that she wanted the arbitrage to run for, usually anywhere from four to eight weeks, and a monthly percent return.
    And it would be on a sheet of paper, and I understood it to be that I had to look back historically and pick out trades that would meet these requirements.
Q: So the request that you got from Ms. Bongiorno was a dollar figure, a percentage return and the duration for the deal?
A: It was a monthly return of 2½%.
Q: And typically, what was the duration of deals that Ms. Bongiorno asked for?
A: Five or six weeks.
Q: And typically, what was the amount of money that Ms. Bongiorno asked for?
A: It varied each week. I would say the range was between $1 million and $3 or $4 million.
Q: And, again, we're still in the mid-1970s, correct?

A: Right, right. I believe that's what it was.

Q: And if you could just do the math for us. If trades are returning 2½% a month, what would the annualized rate of return be?

A: Well, 2½% a month times 12 is 30%. I think it was a little lower because there was some low period . . . .

Q: There were some low periods?

A: I mean that money wasn't invested every time it finished.

Q: How do you know that?

A: Bernard Madoff explained it to me once.

Q: Now, when Ms. Bongiorno asked you for this information, what information did you provide in return?

A: Okay. The information that I provided, first of all, it was all historical information, things that already took place. I provided the symbols of the exchangeable security, the common symbol. I provided what's commonly called the range, which means on the buy side—the low price you could buy it and the high price you could buy it.

   On the sell side, I also provided a range and, again, this represented the high price—the low price you could sell it and the high price you could sell it. I wrote the trade date down that the trades took place—that the trade would have taken place on. I wrote what each preferred or exchangeable security, whether it was a bond or preferred, what the terms were. If it was a bond, I wrote down the interest rates. I also wrote down how much money was to be used for that particular security.

   So I had, in other words—what I felt would have represented an actual trade that might have taken place. So I put down how much money, maximum money, to be put—to be used for this trade. I also wrote down the requested—let's say for six weeks at 2½%, I wrote six weeks, 2½%, and at certain times I was given the name of the client that was—that they were asking for, and I would—if it was given to me, I wrote it back on the ticket.

Q: And?

A: I think that was—yeah, that was basically it, I believe.

Q: So taking the last part of that first, you said if a name of a client was given to you . . . .

A: Sometimes on the sheet—yes.

Q: Who would give you the name of the client?

A: Annette Bongiorno.

Q: And as you sit here, do you recall the names of any of the clients that you provided this information for?

A: Yes.
Q: What names do you remember?
A: I remember there was an account called A&B, and then there was another group, it was [Chais's] Popham, Lambeth, and Brighton [funds].
Q: Prior to Mr. Madoff's arrest, did you know what any of those things were?
A: Outside of the name? A&B, I learned, was for Avellino and, I think, Bienes was his name. The other three names somehow were associated with Stanley Chais, who was an investor also.
Q: So in your example, if Ms. Bongiorno asked for a $1 million of investments and you put down $100,000 for a particular trade, how would you get to the other $900,000?
A: I would continue doing it until I found enough trades that met the requirement to get up to a $1 million.
Q: Okay. So if you were asked for a $1million you might give several different trades to get that?
A: Correct.
Q: You said that all of the information was historical information?
A: Yes, sir.
Q: Where did you get that historical information from?
A: From the *Wall Street Journal*.
Q: And typically how far back did you go?
A: We went—usually it was given—the information was usually given to me on a Tuesday or a Wednesday, and I went back to the previous Friday.
Q: The information was given to you by Ms. Bongiorno?
A: Yes.
Q: So you went back a week?
A: I went—no , it was given to me on Wednesday, let's say , a Tuesday, or a Wednesday, and I gave it back the previous Friday; so that's only four days.
Q: Where did you get those *Wall Street Journals* from the 1970s? Would you have to go to the New York Public Library?
A: No. You could, but, no, Annette Bongiorno kept daily—I asked her for them. She kept daily *Wall Street Journals*. She kept them; so if I needed them, I asked for them.
Q: And how far back did she keep them?
A: That, I don't know.
Q: But at least several days old to do what you needed to do?
A: Yes, at least.

Q: Now, you also said one of the pieces of information you provided was a range of prices?

A: Correct.

Q: Where did you get that range of prices from?

A: Either from the *Wall Street Journal* or from my knowledge of the stock being traded.

Q: And why provide a range of prices as opposed to a particular price?

A: Because even though I was asked for a particular percent, 2½%, they needed other prices.

Q: Let me interrupt you. Who are they?

A: I'm sorry. Even though Annette asked me, Annette Bongiorno asked me for a particular percent, it was—they needed other percents that might have been lower than 2½%.

Q: Who are they? And what's your understanding of why Bernard Madoff and Annette Bongiorno needed to be able to do different percents?

A: Different clients got different percents based on what Bernard Madoff told the—you know.

Q: And were you involved in that process?

A: No.

Q: So who was it that picked the actual price to use for an historical trade?

A: Whoever set up the trade.

Q: And?

A: The fake trade.

. . .

Q: If you had $72,000 to invest for 7 weeks at 3% a month—do you follow me?

A: Yes, sir.

Q: How would you take the information that you provide and turn it into a fake trade?

A: The first thing you would do or someone would have to do, it's 7 weeks, the 3% means I make 3% a month. It's based on a 4-week month. You would divide 3% by 4, and that would give you, I don't know if you can see it, .75% each week. It is 7 weeks, so we have to do times 7 times ¾ to get the percent for 7 weeks, for the whole deal. It comes out 7 times ¾ is 5¼%.

My investment is $72,000. I know I have to make 5¼%. I would times that by 1.0525. That means the original investment plus the return for 7 weeks at %, that's right, 7 weeks at 3%, means that

I would have to have sales equaling $75,780. That would give me the sale.

Q: Now, the next step, you were about to provide a price, correct?

A: Yes, and I'll use these prices.

Q: So in reality, you would have provided a range of prices to Ms. Bongiorno?

A: Correct.

. . .

Q: You said it was used to create fabricated or fake trades. Did you understand at the time that these trades were not happening, that they were fake?

A: Yes. Yes.

Q: And since when did you understand that the trades in the investment business were fake?

A: I suspected almost probably a little after I started doing it. It was confirmed when I opened my account and I saw trades appeared in my account.

Q: When was that?

A: I opened the account in 1977; so that confirmed what I thought.

Q: And how did opening your own account confirm that the trades were fake?

A: Because a number of the deals that I gave showed up in my account.

Q: So you testified earlier that you wouldn't see the trade confirmations and account statements that were generated based on the information you provided; is that right?

A: Yes.

Q: But you're saying, at some point, you opened your own account and so you saw that information?

A: Right, right.

Q: And why was it that seeing the trade confirmations and account statements led you to conclude that the trades were definitely fake?

A: Because I knew what trade—what securities I gave them.

Q: So that was the first time that you knew for sure that the information you were providing was used on customer statements?

A: It's the first time I was able to prove conclusively that those trades were all being fabricated based on the information I was giving.

Q: And that was 1977?

A: Yes, sir.

...

Q: Who were the people that you provided the historical trading information to?

A: Well, Annette Bongiorno, Jodi Crupi.

Q: And when did you start providing the information to Jodi Crupi?

A: Maybe the late 1980s to the early 1990s, give or take.

Q: At that point, what was, to your knowledge, Ms. Bongiorno's role?

A: She was supervisor of that department.

Q: When Ms. Crupi took over the job from Ms. Bongiorno, did you have to train her?

A: I didn't, no.

Q: Were you providing essentially the same kind of information about convertible arbitrage trades, fake trades?

A: Exactly the same information.

Q: And so Ms. Crupi would have had to do the exact same math that we just went through?

A: Yes.

Q: And did she have questions about how to do the calculations?

A: Again, probably the biggest question was, I can't read your handwriting, or it's possible sometimes when I gave her the numbers, it didn't work out. In other words, it didn't meet the requirements, and I checked it.

Q: So in other words, Ms. Crupi would come to you and say, this doesn't actually work for what I requested?

A: Correct.

Q: And was she correct when she came to you with those issues?

A: Sometimes.

Q: And sometimes she wasn't correct?

A: Right.

Q: And, still, for the trades, the information that you provided to Ms. Crupi, as the information you provided to Ms. Bongiorno, she was the one who picked the exact price point?

A: Yes, whoever fabricated the trade.

Q: And when you say "whoever fabricated the trade," what do you mean?

A: The person who I gave the information to, Jodi Crupi and whoever fabricated the information used—whoever fabricated the trade.

Q: I see. So you're saying you gave the information to Ms. Crupi, and then you don't know what happened with it exactly afterwards?

A: Correct.

Q: Were there instances, as with Ms. Bongiorno, where you actually sat with Ms. Crupi as she did the calculations?

A: I don't recall a particular instance.

. . .

Q: Well, you testified earlier about trading in your own account?

A: Correct.

Q: Were you referring to your own IA account?

A: Yes, sir.

Q: At what point did you begin trading your own IA account?

A: I believe it was around 1998.

Q: And at what point did you become a supervisor on the trading floor?

A: Actually, probably around the same time.

. . .

Q: You became a supervisor at about the same time you also started actively trading your investment account?

A: Correct.

Q: And when we say actively trading your investment account, are those real trades?

A: No, sir.

Q: So explain to the jury what you were doing from 1998 on?

A: In my account, I created fabricated trades of stocks, not arbitrage, but stocks to put in my account.

Q: And who did you work with in connection with that?

A: Bernard Madoff and Annette Bongiorno.

. . .

Q: Someone else?

A: At times, I gave the information to Jodi Crupi.

Q: When you say you gave the information, what sort of information are we talking about?

A: At the end of the month, I would give a buy—whatever the case may be, a buy or sell trade, an actual—what looked like information that was a trade. There was no other information that was needed. For example, I would give, buy a thousand shares of IBM with a price, and I would write the trade date.

Q: Okay. So unlike with the arbitrage, where you were providing ranges of prices, in the late 1990s and 2000s, you were providing exact historical fake trading information?

A: Correct.

Q: Okay. From the late 1990s onward, did you have—besides trading in your own account—did you have any other interaction with the IA business?

A: Yes.

Q: So describe that?

A: At times, Annette would ask me questions about a stock, like what happened to a particular stock or what—was there a name change or related things. Sometimes it's hard to find; so she would ask me information about stocks.

Q: And you said one example was if a stock had a name change?

A: Correct.

Q: Okay. So let's talk about your own IA account at BLMIS. I think you testified earlier that you opened the account in 1977; is that right?

A: Yes.

. . .

Q: What is [that document]?

A: That was a deposit, $25,000, when I opened the account with my wife.

Q: So was this your original account opening deposit in BLMIS?

A: Yes, sir.

Q: What's this?

A: That's a check I used to deposit the money from my checking account, our checking account.

Q: From August 30, 1977 on, did you continuously have an account or accounts at BLMIS?

A: Yes.

. . .

Q: Where did the money come from to open this original BLMIS account?

A: My wife inherited her father's house, and after he passed away, she sold it, and that's what we put in.

Q: So you testified earlier that when you opened your account, you were certain that the trading was fake, that you suspected it before that; is that right?

A: Yes.

Q: Why—why, Mr. Kugel, would you invest your money in an IA account that you suspected was fake?

A: Because I thought the money was being used—Bernard Madoff was using the money to make other investments, and this is the way that he paid back clients for the money that was invested in the account, in the IA accounts.

Q: Did you ever have a conversation with Mr. Madoff about that?

A: Yes, I did.

Q: Tell the jury about that conversation?

A: I asked him: "Where are you investing the money?" And he told me that he was investing the money in shopping centers, foreign currency, and other investments, which he never clarified, and that was basically the conversation.

Q: And so you thought the money in your IA account was going towards shopping centers and foreign currency?

A: Other investments that he was making, yes, yes.

...

Q: This was part of your annual salary that you just left at BLMIS?

A: Correct. I could have withdrawn the money, taken the money the year I earned it, but I deferred it.

Q: How did you come to be able to defer your compensation at BLMIS? Were you able to do that right from the beginning?

A: It started, I believe, in 1980. There was a conversation with Bernard Madoff. I had a very good year. I asked him to be a partner. I inquired about being a partner. He said, I have no partners, but if you invest, I will give you a [substantial] return, I will invest the money for you. That's what I did.

Q: Over the years can you approximate how much of your actual salary you deferred into your IA account?

A. I would say approximately $5 million.

Q: $5 million of actual salary?

A: Yes, sir.

Q: You put into your IA account?

A: Yes. That was deferred, yes.

Q: The whole time you knew that those statements were fake?

A: Correct.

Q: At some point in the late 1990s, you just testified, you began providing the exact fake information that went on your [account] statements; is that right?

A: Yes, sir, most of it, yes.

Q: Why?

A: I had a conversation. When I stopped trading, the account built up with the profits, and the money I put in I think was something around, at that time somewhere around $10 million. I went to

Bernard Madoff and I asked him if I wanted to take money out, how would I [be able] do it. He said—it wasn't a definitive.

But whatever it is, after the conversation it was my understanding that he wanted me to do it from the IA account rather than giving me a bonus from the trading room, which it should have been. But he wanted to do it from the trading account. So he told me to put through trades up to the point, up to the money— I'm sorry—where the profits would be up to the money in my account—that showed in my account.

Q: Let me see if I can break that down. You deferred compensation into the investment business, correct?

A: Yes, sir.

Q: When you did that, did the money that you deferred show up on your monthly account statements?

A: No, sir.

Q: Did it show up on some other kind of internal BLMIS document?

A: Yes.

Q: What kind of document?

A: It was called a portfolio management report.

Q: Also known as a PMR?

A: Ok, yes. I'm sorry. Yes.

Q: Had you ever heard that acronym when you were there?

A: No.

Q: What did you call in back then?

A: Portfolio management report.

Q: Who showed you portfolio management reports?

A: Annette Bongiorno.

Q: Did you have access to them in the computer systems at BLMIS?

A: No, sir.

Q: You couldn't pull it up at your desk?

A: No, sir. It reflected the money plus the profits earned on the account.

Q: When you say the profits earned, what was the basis for those profits?

A: The returns that Bernard Madoff gave me.

Q: What were those returns based on?

A: Whatever he told me it was. He never really clarified how he came up with a percent. He just told me at the end of the year what I earned on the money.

Q: But it was a percent?

A: Yes, sir.

Q: He just told you that you made X percent this year?

A: Correct.

Q: Typically, what kind of returns did you get?

A: 21%.

Q: The portfolio management report, you testified, showed the money that you deferred plus this 21%?

A: Correct.

. . .

Q: You put fake trades in your account so that the monthly account statements would get big enough to match the portfolio management report?

A: That was the objective, yes.

Q: Why did you need to do that?

A: Under Bernard Madoff's instructions.

Q: Could you take the money out if it wasn't shown on your account statement?

A: I could have. I never had any question that I could have, but I just felt he wanted to do it this way. I didn't argue. I just complied.

Q: When you spoke to Mr. Madoff about doing these trades, these fake trades in your own account, were there any rules or parameters about how you were supposed to do the fake trading?

A: Yes.

Q: What were those rules? Can you tell the jury about this?

A: Basically, don't make it look ridiculous. In other words, don't buy a stock at let's say $1 and let it go to $100. I bought stocks, for example, quality stocks like IBM, Home Depot, Intel, and Microsoft. The guidelines were don't make a huge profit in one trade, to make it look [reasonable]. And I complied with that.

Also, he told me to do it within the month. I did it within the month. Whatever trade I did, I looked back at the end of the month and looked to the beginning of the month, and I picked a stock that had a little head start that was up a little, and I put the trade through. At the beginning I showed him what trades I did, and he said that it was okay.

Q: Did you ever actually give the trades to Mr. Madoff?

A: I showed them to him. I didn't give them to him, but I showed them to him.

Q: Were you the one who entered them into the systems?

A: No, sir.

Q: Who did you give the trades to?

A: I gave it to Annette Bongiorno and at times to Jodi Crupi.

. . .

Q: Generally speaking, as a result of the fake trading in your IA account, did you get tax advantages?

A. Yes.

Q: For example, declaring money as a long-term capital gain instead of income?

A: Correct.

Q: That was all fake, correct?

A: Yes.

Q: You submitted fake returns to the IRS, didn't you?

A: Yes.

Q: You also committed tax fraud?

A: Yes, sir.

Q: To your knowledge, was "short against the box" [short selling securities that you already own] a strategy that was used only by you in your personal IA account?

A: No.

Q: Where else was it used in the IA business?

A: For other clients.

Q: How do you know that?

A: A couple of reasons. One, some of the people in the office used a "short against the box" [strategy]. That's how I realized it, I think, in the first place. Second of all, I was asked tax questions about "short against the box" at various times.

. . .

Q: You said a moment ago that in 2008 you wanted to take $6 million, $3 million for yourself and $3 million for your wife, out of your BLMIS account, correct?

A: Yes, sir.

Q: At that time did your account statements, as opposed to your portfolio management reports, reflect enough money to be able to do that?

A: No.

Q: How were you able to take money out of BLMIS?

A: I went to Bernard Madoff, explained to him what I wanted to do, that I wanted to take some money out. He said to me that you can take it as a bonus. I said great, rather than go through the whole thing of doing the trades. I said I wanted to take out $6 million. And that's how it happened.

Q: For 2008 you withdrew a bonus of $6 million?
A: Yes.
Q: What did you do with that money?
A: I deposited it in my IA account.
Q: Where?
A: At Bernard Madoff.
Q: You took a $6 million bonus from Bernie Madoff and deposited it right back into your BLMIS IA account?
A: Yes.
Q: When was that?
A: In March, I believe it was February or March 2008.
Q: Why did you do that?
A: I'm sorry?
Q: In other words, you said this was for estate planning purpose. Why didn't you put it into some other bank, for example?
A: Once I deposited the money, it actually showed as an asset. Again, I had a partnership with Phyllis, my wife, and myself. Once the $6 million was in the account, it satisfied my estate obligation. The other reason I deposited it is I didn't know what to do with the money. I didn't want to go to 60 banks and open up accounts, and I wasn't sure what to do with it at that particular time. I thought the money would be earning a return while it was in there, and that's why I did it.
Q: Why would you have to put your money into 60 banks? Why not just put it into one bank account at Citibank?
A: Two reasons. One, if I put in it a bank, at least I wanted to get the best available interest rate. Two, at the time FDIC insurance, the Federal Deposit Insurance Corporation, only guaranteed the account for $100,000.
Q: So anything after that first $100,000 wasn't safe?
A: Wasn't insured. But basically, yes.
Q: Does that mean you thought your money was safer in BLMIS than at a bank?
A: I thought it was safe. I don't think I made a conscious decision that one is safer than the other, but I felt it was safe there.
Q: Once that $6 million was deposited into your IA account at BLMIS, in your words, it showed on your account statements, right?
A: Yes.
Q: What happened to that money?
A: A trade was put through by the IA department.
    . . .

Q: Did you ever meet any of the IA clients?
A: From time to time, yes.

   . . .

Q: Now, you also mentioned Stanley Chais, and I think you testified earlier that sometimes when Ms. Bongiorno asked you for historical trade information, she would write down either Chais or the name of those accounts, that you understood were affiliated with Chais; do you recall that testimony?
A: Yes, sir.
Q: What were the circumstances under which you met Mr. Chais?
A: Mr. Chais was a college friend of Marty Joel; so I met him through Marty. Mr. Chais came up to the office occasionally. Marty was a friend of his, and he came up to the trading room, and I said hello.
Q: Did you ever have a conversation with Mr. Chais about his investment account?
A: No.
Q: You knew you had been providing information that was used to create fake trades in his accounts, correct?
A: Correct.
Q: You never said anything to him?
A: No, sir.
Q: You never talked to him about the fact that you thought the money was somewhere else?
A: It never came up.

   . . .

Q: Did you ever have a [BLMIS] corporate credit card?
A: Yes, I did.
Q: And you wouldn't consider that a perk?
A: It was given to me for business expenses.
Q: When did you get the credit card?
A: I believe sometime in the mid-1990s. I'm not sure.
Q: What did you use it for?
A: I used it either for business expense or personal expense. Sometimes I put personal expenses on it.
Q: So a second ago you said you got it for business expenses, but you just testified that you used it for personal expenses?
A: Correct.
Q: And you wouldn't consider that a perk?
A: Whatever I put on as a personal expense, I paid back; so, no.

Q: I'm sorry, you paid it back?

A: Yes, sir.

Q: Who did you pay back?

A: To Bernard Madoff.

Q: So whenever you used your corporate credit card for personal expense, you paid BLMIS back?

A: Yes, sir.

Q: And how did you—who decided whether something was a personal expense or a business expense?

A: I did.

Q: And how did you make that decision? For example, if you took a client out to dinner and you brought your wife, was that a business expense or a personal expense?

A: The answer is, what I did—whatever went on the credit card, I deducted. I didn't start nitpicking which is business and which is personal. Just whatever the bill was for the credit card, rather than get into a trying to figure it out, I just deducted the whole credit card bill.

Q: Deducted it from what?

A: From my salary.

Q: Meaning you paid back everything that you charged on the corporate credit card?

A: Yes, sir.

Q: Even if business expenses?

A: Yes, sir.

Q: Were there any restrictions on your ability to use the credit card?

A: Yes. It was—one time—first of all, it was a Platinum Card. I used it to put a cruise on there because there was benefits for doing so with the Platinum Card, and after I used it—or after the bill arrived, Bernard Madoff said: "You know, don't put that on it. Even though you're paying for it, don't put it on there anymore." And I didn't.

Q: How much was that cruise?

A: I believe it was about mid-20.

Q: Mid-20 what?

A: Thousand. I'm sorry. Excuse me.

Q: So other than this one cruise that was mid-20, were you ever told that you wouldn't or shouldn't charge something to the corporate credit card?

A: No, that was the only time that I recall.

Accounts

The testimony by Enrica Cotellessa-Pitz and David L. Kugel in Chapters 3 and 4 are perfect examples of *accounts*, "statements made to explain untoward [or deviant] behavior."[2] In the fullest accounts one can find story-like constructions containing recollections of events, including plot, story line, affect, and attributions.[3] Accounts are self-protective; they can be useful in preserving self-esteem. They differ from explanations, which are statements "about events where untoward [or deviant] action is not an issue and does not have critical implications for a relationship."[4]

There are two basic types of accounts, excuses and justifications. Excuses are accounts in which there is an admission that the act in question was bad, wrong, or inappropriate, but also denial of full responsibility. A sometimes useful excuse is the appeal to defeasibility—not being fully informed, or not being completely free, or not truly intending the actions, not intending the consequences. Another excuse is to scapegoat, contending that the actions were in response to someone else. Justifications are accounts in which one accepts responsibility for his or her actions, but denies anything negative associated with them. Common justifications in accounts of white collar criminal activity are to minimize the amount of injury caused or an appeal to loyalty. Both a variety of excuses and justifications were generously sprinkled throughout Cotellessa-Pitz's and Kugel's testimony in their efforts to neutralize what they had done, to minimize their criminality. Both offered many more excuses than justifications, of which there were an infinite variety.

The accounts of both are useful to gain additional insight into the culture of the IA business at BLMIS as generally experienced and understood by backstage accomplices. As Kenneth Burke would have described it, the account-making by these BLMIS backstage accomplices was a simple effort to convince themselves and others of the credence of their reality.[5] Over the years, their reality had little credence.

Cotellessa-Pitz begins her account describing herself as little more than a file clerk. She next tells of how fresh out of high school, she began dating Frank DiPascali, Jr., who was soon to become Madoff's right-hand man, and then how she put her career at BLMIS in jeopardy by ending the relationship.

Cotellessa-Pitz goes on to claim that she was led to believe that the securities she kept track of were owned by Madoff. She builds on the theme that she was involved in straightforward clerical work; she did not imagine that there could be anything deceptive about her clerical duties: "Predominantly, my job was to file the financial documents. I really had very little control over all the entries that were being conducted in the firm ... I was the controller in title only." Moreover, even after being trained at BLMIS, her work was mostly supervised. In short, she was trained and told what to do by males who directed the affairs of BLMIS. These superiors seem to have a full grasp of the extent of the firm's finances, although there were too many aspects of these she did not understand. In her early years at BLMIS she was led to believe that she was working with Madoff's money. She was peripheral to decisions and events. At times she barely had any idea "what [others were] talking about." Her work became part of the deception: "To hide the money ... to disguise [losses]" or that "Bernie wanted to make it appear the money was coming from overseas." She was involved in BLMIS, representing customer bonds as its own in order to easily obtain bank loans. She describes how BLMIS employees forged documents.

After a few years at BLMIS, she was fully immersed in the world of deception: "I altered many books and reports to give the auditors from the SEC." She relates how she also helped Madoff deceive the IRS to resolve a tax problem. However, all the time she was trying to be an effective employee, Madoff and others continued to lie to her, continued their deception.

According to Kugel's account, he was for the most part oblivious that he was committing criminal acts. For a time, for over a half dozen years, he did not become aware that the IA business was "fake": "I suspected almost probably a little after I started doing it. It was confirmed when I opened my account," when he found out inadvertently.

Kugel inadvertently became involved in the con. At first, he merely served as a link between the three BLMIS businesses and Bernard Madoff and Annette Bongiorno, simply preparing or passing information to one or the other. Madoff, after first deceiving him, lured him into the con. He often worked with others. In fact, he never committed crimes alone, but only with others. He did not initiate fraud. In fact, it found him. He was little more than a cipher at BLMIS.

Kugel testified that when he asked Madoff what he did with the money IA clients invested in BLMIS, Madoff lied that he invested it in shopping centers and foreign currency. This furthered his belief that it was possible for one to accumulate millions working with

Madoff, which continued until the con collapsed and all IA accounts were worthless.

Not surprisingly, both Cotellessa-Pitz and Kugel in these accounts are mostly trying to distance themselves from the artifice backstage at BLMIS that they first only witnessed and then fully participated in. As Benson concluded after his interviews of 30 individuals convicted of white collar crimes:

> The investigation, prosecution, and conviction of a white collar offender involve him in a very undesirable status passage. The entire process can be viewed as a long and drawn-out degradation ceremony with the prosecutor as the chief denouncer and the offender's family and friends [and some interested public] as the chief witnesses. The offender is moved from the status of law-abiding citizen to that of convicted felon. Accounts are developed to defeat the process of identity transformation that is the object of a degradation ceremony. They represent the offender's attempt to diminish the effect of his legal transformation and to prevent its becoming a publicly validated label.[6]

Cotellessa-Pitz's and Kugel's accounts are two more examples, to the letter, of what Benson found.

The detailed description of sham trades and how money was laundered at BLMIS by Frank DiPascali, Jr. in Appendices 1-E and 2-A brings home how deep seated the criminogenic culture backstage was, and how there were no limits to what Madoff or an accomplice might do to keep the con viable. (Excerpts from some of DiPascali's other testimony in Appendix 2-C and 6-B are just as telling.) In fact, in working alongside Madoff and keeping the con on track in Madoff's vacations and other absences, DiPascali probably even knew more than Peter Madoff about the infancy and development of every facet of the con. Although sometimes seemingly attempting to shift the blame for his involvement in the con to others and not always trustworthy in some matters, DiPascali is still the most reliable source in plumbing the depths of dishonesty at BLMIS.

In Chapters 3 and 4, Cotellessa-Pitz and Kugel both confirm and fill in important gaps in the details provided by DiPascali. In discussing various aspects of the con, other accomplices have mostly confirmed or filled in gaps in his various and extensive accounts.

Lying was quickly and readily learned by all of Madoff's backstage accomplices. It was just something everyone did. It was like background noise. It was a first step to other types of deceit, all with the single purpose of successfully stealing money.

There was a strikingly wide range of deception backstage at BLMIS—most particularly, lies (making up information), concealments (omitting relevant or important information), and exaggerations—experienced and witnessed by Cotellessa-Pitz and Kugel, and, of course, countless others. Bok has suggested that "those who learn they have been lied to in an important matter ... are resentful, disappointed, and suspicious. They feel wronged ... and they look back on their past beliefs and actions in a new light of the discovered lies. They see that they were manipulated."[7] However, being constantly deceived was something both Cotellessa-Pitz and Kugel seemed to accept as a matter of course. There is no evidence that it led either to feeling betrayed or to become increasingly distrustful. However, they were deceivers themselves. Perhaps they concluded that as such they had forfeited the hope that they could take for granted being told the truth. It would be hypocritical for them to expect that others have not upheld the rule of telling the truth, a rule that they have continually broken.

As deceivers, perhaps both expected to be deceived themselves, or perhaps both intuitively understood that one of La Rochefoucauld's *Maxims*, "Social Life would not last long if men were not taken in by each other," was most applicable to Madoff's con rather than Bok's foreboding. Also, their greed (particularly Kugel's cupidity) may have inoculated them from the realization of how toxic BLMIS's 17th floor had steadily become.

It is possible if there were not others, who were not part of the con, working alongside the backstage accomplices that the 17th floor would have simply imploded. They had no reason to continually distort or twist, and this may have served to prevent the haze from enveloping all. Bok asks:

Imagine a society, no matter how ideal in other respects, where word and gesture could never be counted upon. Questions asked, answers given, information exchanged—all would be worthless .... There must be a minimal degree of trust in communication for language and action to be more than stabs in the dark. This is why some level of truthfulness has always been seen as essential to human society, no matter how deficient the observance of other moral principles. Even the devils, as Samuel

Johnson said, do not lie to one another, since the society of Hell could not subsist without truth any more than others. A society, then, whose members were unable to distinguish truthful messages from deceptive ones, would collapse.[8]

Yet, the BLMIS IA business did quite well for the longest time. Satisfying the greed of backstage accomplices surely contributed to allaying feelings of betrayal or distrust.

CHAPTER 5

Deception: Backstage with Annette Bongiorno[1]

As was the case with Enrica Cotellessa-Pitz in Chapter 3 and David L. Kugel in Chapter 4, much of Chapter 5 consists of many salient excerpts from the lengthy transcript of over 11,000 pages from the five-month trial of five BLMIS backstage accomplices that began October 16, 2013, and ended March 24, 2014. In this chapter, all of the excerpts are from the testimony of Annette Bongiorno. Bongiorno's account of her years as a backstage accomplice at BLMIS provides one of the most detailed and helpful picture of the Madoff con.

Bongiorno, one of the five defendants, gave extensive testimony describing her 40-year career at BLMIS. Her testimony was many times evasive—her attempts at concealment were many and mostly obvious—but also many times forthright. The reader need not consider this material as would a jury member or jurist figuring out when she is evasive and when she is not. It is not necessary to determine guilt or innocence, but simply to appreciate how BLMIS's backstage accomplices were taught, learned, and taught others—on the social-system level in a criminogenic environment—to commit criminal acts rather than assimilating criminal values and behavior through membership in broader social groups, for example, from a community.

The testimony of the three backstage accomplices in Chapters 3 and 4, and now Chapter 5, also provides a hint as to why Madoff's con was so enduring and successful: he was offering everyone involved in the con—family members, backstage accomplices, ropers (see Chapters 7 and 8), and even clients[2]—plausible deniability. With a good part of the paper trail not recovered, all could—and almost all did—safely deny knowledge of the con. After they closed ranks, reaching the standard of proof "beyond a reasonable doubt" necessary in criminal prosecutions for knowing about Madoff's Ponzi scheme was greatly limited or simply not possible.

Q: Ms. Bongiorno, how long did you work at BLMIS?
A: 40 years.
Q: During your career there, your 40 years there, did you ever intend to participate in a crime?
A: No.
Q: Did you ever understand, during all that time that Mr. Madoff was running a Ponzi scheme?
A: Absolutely not.
Q: Did you ever understand, during all that time, that Mr. Madoff was committing a fraud?
A: No.
Q: Did you ever understand that the account statements that you helped to prepare were false?
A: No.
Q: Did you ever commit a fraud yourself?
A: Never knowingly.
. . .
Q: Were you offered a job at BLMIS?
A: Yes.
Q: What type of job were you offered?
A: Well, it was kind of like a bunch of things. I was going to be typing, doing some adding for them, opening mail, mailing things out, sort of like what I did for the bank, only—and I took a pay cut, by the way, to go to work for that man [Bernard Madoff]. He told me there was a lot of overtime; so that would make up for the money that I was going to lose in my pay. They said they would pay time and a half; so I would make it up and then some.
. . .
Q: At the time you first went to work there, had you had any experience with the securities industry at all?
A: None.
Q: And how old were you when you first went to work at BLMIS?
A: Nineteen.
Q: What was your job title?
A: We didn't have titles. I don't know. I didn't have a title.
Q: And what sort of things were you doing at BLMIS?

A: Typing, I was opening mail. We'd get comparisons or what they call comparisons, comps, so I'd open those envelopes. I did a little bit of everything. I was like a girl Friday ... When the tickets came out of the trading room, I would multiple the shares by the price and put it on the ticket, and then I typed the ticket, and I'd mail the ticket, whatever there was to do.
. . .

Q: Did there come a time shortly after you started to work there when you met Mr. Madoff?

A: The first day.

Q: Were you asked to take a lunch order for him?

A: Yes.

Q: Do you remember what happened?

A: I was told when I was interviewed that part of the money that they'd make up in my salary would be if—he said when they worked through their lunch hour—Bernie paid for everybody's lunch. So that first day that I worked, he asked me to take a lunch order .... And back in those days, Bernie stuttered. So when I got to him and I asked him what he wanted for lunch, he started to stutter. He was saying—he wanted to say that he wanted a ham and cheese sandwich, but he said that he'd like I have a "ha-, ha-, ha-." He said: "Just get me a ham sandwich." So knowing that he was trying to say ham and cheese, and I knew that—

Q: How did you know that?

A: Well, because my brother had a stutter in those days too, and so I was just used to hearing that and I knew what he meant. So when I placed the order, I place the order for the ham and cheese sandwich and ....

Q: Did you deliver it to him?

A: Yeah. When the order came up, I delivered everybody's lunch to them.

Q: And what was Bernie's reaction when he actually got the ham and cheese?

A: He was very happy. He looked and gave me the thumbs up and said: "You're going to do really good here." That was almost like the first and second things he said to me: "Just get me a ham sandwich," and "You're going to do really good here." He didn't talk to me much that first day. He was busy at the desk.

Q: After you started work there, were you working overtime a lot?

A: A lot.

Q: How often were you working overtime?

A: From the first night, they asked me to stay over. There was a lot of paper and, you know, we were a small office. There weren't a lot of people; so we all had to pitch in, which is why I took the job. I wanted the overtime. I wanted to make the extra money. So the first night he asked me—Irwin asked me because Irwin was in charge back then. He asked me if I could stay late, and I said yes, and I worked late. And when you work late for him, he bought everybody dinner, and he sent us all home in cars, in cabs or a car service, whatever we could get at the time.
. . .

Q: So you rode home in a car almost every night?

A: I did. I rode home in a [car]. Peter, Bernie's brother, worked part time. At the time, he worked after school and weekends, and he lived in Howard Beach by me. So sometimes we shared a cab if he was in [the office]. Otherwise, Irwin would get a car for me, and there was another girl that worked every single night too, Sylvia. He made sure that she had a cab, and that we would get home safely.
. . .

Q: Who did you talk to [about working in the evenings]?

A: I spoke to Irwin first, and I told Irwin that my dad wants me to quit, and he said: "Why?" And I explained why, and he said: "Oh, well, I can't give you fewer hours. Part of the reason we hired you is because we needed somebody to work late at night . . . ." He said he was going to tell Bernie about it, and he did. And then Bernie called me into his office or into his brother's office because he didn't have his own office, and he said to me: "You know, gee, Annette, I hate to lose you so quickly. You're doing so well." He said: "I have an idea." I said: "What's your idea?" He said: "How about you have Ruth and I come over for coffee maybe one day over the weekend so that we can meet your parents, and they can see that we're nice people." So I said: "That might work. Let me see if my mother will go for that."

So I went home, and I asked my mom if she'd like to meet them. I asked my father, and my father said: "All right. You know, if you want, if that will make you happy." And my mother said: "You can have them come for dinner." So that Sunday, Ruth and Bernie and Peter and Marion came and had dinner with my mom and dad.

...

Q: Did you understand what arbitrage trading was then?

A: I'm trying to think if we started then. Well, I didn't know anything about it. I was taught what it was.

Q: Were they starting to do arbitrage trades at about the time that you went back?

A: Right, we did.

Q: Can you describe the process of how the arbitrage trades were done?

A: I got a ticket for every buy and every sell and a fractional share note from David Kugel. Every single arbitrage trade for every single customer had a ticket .... I would post it. I would keep it all organized so that at the end of the month I could type the statements. Everything was done manually.

Q: And in terms of the trades, did there come a time when you actually broke the trades down and allocated them to various customers?

A: Yes. And I believe that started after we moved. Bernie asked me one day to try to be more helpful to David [Kugel] because David couldn't keep up. He wasn't giving us the work on time. So he asked me to please learn how to break them down and to help David in that way.

Q: And breaking them down, what does that mean?

A: Breaking down meant instead of him giving me a buy and two sells and a fractional share for every single customer, he gave me one buy and one sell. And on each ticket he gave me a range of prices, a range of percentages because each person—each account, got a certain percentage, and how long it was. He would tell me, this trade should last about five weeks, eight weeks, 12 weeks, whatever it was.

So he would give me what Bernie said was like a block of preferred or a block of bonds and a block of common stock, and they'd give me the ranges. And based on what he wanted his client to receive from this ticket, I would break them down. I would distribute for client A, who had X amount of dollars, how many shares, and client B. And so I started breaking it down. I still got the tickets from David. The original tickets that came out of the trading room came from David, and I would just break it down by customer.

...

Q: Was there anything in that change in your role, where you were breaking down the tickets and figuring out how much each customer would get from these trades, was there anything about that that made you suspect three was any kind of fraud going on?

A: No.

Q: Did David Kugel suggest to you that there was anything wrong about what you were doing?

A: Not at all.

Q: Did Bernie suggest to you that there was something wrong with what you were doing?

A: No.

. . .

A: Well, first, he laughed, but when I didn't show up the next day, he started calling me and telling me come in and let's talk about it. And I said: "I really wanted to be your secretary. That's what I always wanted to be and you hired a secretary, it's unacceptable." And then he said to me—well, he told Irwin to call me. He had Sylvia call me. He had Peter call me, and then he said: "Meet me at Goldie's Diner," which was in the neighborhood.

Q: You said: "In the neighborhood." What neighborhood?

A: It was not far from where I lived in Howard Beach. I was in Queens at that point. So I went to Goldie's Diner and he sat there and he said: "Come back." He said: "I don't want to lose you over this, it's stupid." He said: "I promise you no secretary of mine will ever be more important to me than you are. They will only be there to help you. You will not be doing anything for them."

. . .

Q: Did you go back?

A: I did.

Q: All right. Did you have a job title at that point?

A: Well some kind of assistant, I guess. Titles weren't important in our firm; they just weren't.

Q: As time went on after you moved to 110 Wall Street, did you start supervising others?

A: Well, yeah. We had to hire more people because the work just kept coming and coming. When we went on computers, I stayed every night. I put every brokerage firm on Wall Street on the computers for him, keypunching, putting all the information on, and we were very busy. I mean, Danny [Bonventre] told you how we worked around the clock. We stayed over some nights.

Q: How many people did you have working for you in those early days at 110 Wall Street?

A: Working for me or working in the firm?

Q: Working for you.

A: Working with me personally? [I had] maybe two people.

Q: And did you hire a number of people for the firm over time to work with you?

A: Over time, yeah.

Q: Did you give them the orders that Bernie had given you about not discussing your job outside the office?

A: Yes, that was part of what we were all told, that it was personal to him.

Q: And when you gave those orders to the people that worked for you, did you have any idea you were helping to commit some kind of fraud?

A: No.

. . .

Q: Did your relationship to Mr. Madoff develop over time?

A: Yeah.

Q: Did you come to feel you were close to him personally?

A: Yeah. I loved Bernie. He was like my big brother. I had a lot of respect for him and love, yeah.

Q: Did you find him a generous person?

A: Very.

Q: When you got married, what sort of wedding gift did he give you?

A: He paid for my honeymoon.

Q: Where did you go on your honeymoon?

A: We went to Paris and to England.

. . .

Q: Over time, did you ever ask Mr. Madoff if you should get a securities license?

A: Yes, I did.

Q: What did he say to you?

A: Actually, I asked him that in the early years and then again later on.

Q: You asked him that more than once?

A: Yes.

Q: What did he say to you about that?

A: He said: "You don't need it. Everything you need to know I'll teach you." He didn't want me out of the office, and he didn't want me to go back to school.

Q: Did you ever ask him if you should go back to school?

A: I did.

Q: — and get a college degree?

A: Yup. He didn't want me to go back to school. I thought that you needed to have a college degree to have a Series 7 [license]. I didn't know. He said you didn't, and I didn't need it anyway.

Q: And did you just accept that?

A: Yes. He said I didn't need it because I wasn't going to be on the trading desk.

Q: Were there times when you asked him where the trades that you were putting in your customer's accounts were coming from?

A: No. I didn't ask him. He told me.

Q: What did he tell you about that?

A: He told me he did these trades [came from] downstairs in the trading room. He said he bought these big blocks of stock, and they were in his account, and he would distribute it with my help to his customers.

Q: And did you understand that he was distributing the stock after the trades had occurred?

A: Yes.

Q: From an inventory that he had?

A: Exactly.

Q: Was there anything about that explanation that he gave you that made you concerned about what he was describing to you?

A: No. And from the beginning, the customers were always second anyway. I mean, you didn't rush to get the customer ticket out. You got the brokerage tickets out, the ones that went to Bear Stearns, etc. Those had to go out every day, but the customers went out when you got around to it. It never seemed to be a problem that they were not in the mail the same day like the brokerage ones.

Q: During the years that you worked at BLMIS, did you believe that the trades that were put on statements for your clients, did you believe they had actually been executed?

A: Yes, I did.

Q: Where did you think those trades had been executed?

A: On the trading floor.

Q: The trading, floor, you mean at BLMIS?

A: Yes.

Q: Did you work on the same floor as the traders?

A: I did for a while, and then he moved us to the 17th floor.

. . .

Q: During the trial we have heard a lot about how trades were entered into clients' accounts after the trades had occurred or apparently after they had occurred. Do you recall hearing about that?

A: Right.

Q: Did that happen at BLMIS?

A: Yes.

Q: When did you begin to enter trades into customers' accounts after the fact like that?

A: Almost always.

Q: Almost from the time you started?

A: Well, in the very, very early days we were able to do both in the same day, get everything out at once. But over time, the bigger the firm got, the more behind we got on that part of the trading. I mean, David gave me trades once a week. So yes, they were always back-dated.

Q: At any point during your career at BLMIS, did anyone suggest to you that this was a problem?

A: No.

. . .

Q: Do you recall a Madoff customer named Jeffry Picower?

A: Yes.

Q: Was that a customer in whose accounts trades were back-dated?

A: Always.

Q: How often did you enter trades into Mr. Picower's account?

A: Most of his accounts, once a month we did the whole month at the month end. But he had one or two accounts we did once a year.

Q: When you would do those accounts once a year, how far back would the trades be that were entered into those accounts?

A: Through the whole year.

Q: So 11, 12, months back?

A: Sure.

Q: At the time that you were entering these trades into Mr. Picower's accounts, did it seem strange to you to be entering them after the fact like that?

A: No.

Q: Did you ever have any discussions with people associated with Mr. Picower's office about what trades would be placed in their accounts?

A: They would make suggestions, and Bernie would say "yes," we will do it or "no," we won't. But it was never a mystery that they were back-dated. They knew it.

Q: Did they ever suggest there was something wrong with this practice?

A: The only person that ever suggested that to me was you.

. . .

Q: The very first note, the first line says: "Conf. call." I assume that's a conference call.

A: April and Bernie.

Q: April and Bernie. Who was April?

A: April [Freilich] was Jeffry Picower's assistant.

Q: The date there, May 14th, what date is that?

A: May 14th? What do you mean?

Q: Is that the date that the call occurred?

A: Oh, yes.

Q: The second line says: "She needs some gains during January and February 2006." Did I read that correctly?

A: Yes.

Q: That happened a lot with April from Jeffry Picower's office?

A: All the time.

Q: When that happened, when Bernie was on the phone with you and April, did anyone suggest to you that this was improper?

A: No.

. . .

Q: From time to time did Mr. Joel give you trades that he would ask to be placed in his account?

A: Yes.

Q: Were those trades in your experience for transactions that had already occurred?

A: Yes.

Q: When he gave you these transactions that had already occurred and asked you to put them in his account, did he suggest to you that you were doing anything wrong?

A: No.

Q: How would he give you the trades that he would ask you to place into his account?

A: He might write them on a piece of paper and hand them to me. He might have called up and I might have written them down.

Q: Did you ever put anybody like that's trades through without talking to Bernie first?

A: Never.

Q: What would you say to Bernie when Marty Joel would give you a piece of paper with trades?

A: I would call him up and say: "I received this from Marty." I would read them to him, ask him what he wanted me to do with them, and follow his instructions.

. . .

Q: So does this indicate that Mr. Joel was asking you to put trades into is account that were back-dated?

A: Yes.

Q: Did that surprise you when he asked you that?

A: No. All the trades were back-dated for these portfolio accounts.

Q: And it didn't surprise you that the customer would ask for that?

A: No.

. . .

Q: And can you read us what you said to Marty Joel here in your note?

A: "Marty, a few of the prices had to be changed. They were circled. The rest went through. A."

Q: And "A" is who?

A: Me.

. . .

Q: And this note, what did you do with it, to the extent you remember? Would you give that to Marty?

A: I don't know if I faxed it to him, or if I gave it to him, or if I saved it for him. I don't remember.

Q: Now, when you did this for Marty Joel, entered trades in his account that had happened in the past, did you think you were doing anything wrong?

A: No.

. . .

Q: What, if anything, did you hear Mr. Madoff say about the volume of his trading activity during the time that you worked at BLMIS?

A: Oh, I've heard him say he does 20 to 30, sometimes even 40% of the entire market in a given day. He'd brag about that once in awhile.

Q: And did you believe him when he said that?

A: Yes.

Q: Why did you believe him when he said that?

A: Why wouldn't I? I don't know. I just did.

Q: On occasion, did you ever hear Mr. Madoff discuss his own investments, the investments he made personally?

A: Outside of the office?

Q: Yes.

A: Yes. He told us he owned cattle ranches and shopping malls and restaurants and foreign banks, and once he told me he had a diamond mine. And he asked if I wanted any diamonds. He always talked about all of that to all of us.

Q: And did you ever take him up on that—on the offer of diamond?

A: No.

Q: Did you ever ask him questions about how it was that he was able to give away trades in a down market?

A: I did once ask him how we were making money when everybody else says they're losing money and—not everybody else, but here and there I would hear something like that. And he said that he could make money even in a down market by shorting stock, and he said that even if he didn't make enough money in one given day to support what he promised his clients, if he didn't make it in the stock market, he made it elsewhere.

Q: And when you say what he promised his clients, what are you referring to there?

A: He told his clients, before they even opened accounts: "Historically, I've been making this much a year" for each account. I remember it being as high as 36% in the very beginning, and I know it went down to 12% and 15% at the end. So he kind of said that based on what he was doing, this is what I can give you. That's what he would tell them. So that's what I mean.

Q: And was that a sort of target rate or return for the clients?

A: Yes, it was the benchmark rate of return.

Q: And was that how it was referred to at BLMIS?

A: Yes.

Q: And was there a particular document that reflected the benchmark return clients had been promised?

A: Yes, that was called the portfolio.

Q: Was there anything called a portfolio management report?

A: That was it, a portfolio management report.

Q: At any point in your career at BLMIS, did the fact that Mr. Madoff was promising his clients a particular return cause you concern about the legality of what you were doing?

A: No.

Q: Why not?

A: I don't know. I just believed him, and I believed what he told me. I never even thought of the word illegal.

Q: How long in your career was this promise of a benchmark return made by Mr. Madoff?

A: Well, not the very first or second year because I wasn't doing it then, and I don't even know if he was, to be honest. But for as long as I could remember, since those portfolio accounts started, and before that the arbitrage accounts, had a benchmark. They didn't have portfolios, but he promised them a certain amount of money every year, yeah.

Q: At any point in your career at BLMIS, were you actually picking the trades that went into customer's accounts?

A: Yes.

Q: Describe how that happened? Can you tell us how you would pick arbitrage trades that would go into a customer account?

A: Well, David [Kugel] would give me—say he gave me five different situations—arbitrage set-ups, and I would determine what was due for each account: how much money, which trades to give them until the stock was gone. Because don't forget what I told you yesterday, they told me they were buying blocks of bonds, blocks of preferred stocks, and they were selling blocks of common stocks.

So it all had to be distributed to the customers, and David taught me how to do that, step by step, to figure out how much each individual account needed to buy and how much each individual account needed to sell in order to make the profit that Mr. Madoff said they were going to make.

Q: And you would do that by referencing this benchmark figure?

A: Yes, that was written on the top of every client ledger sheet, and later on, when the portfolios came into being, it was in the portfolio.

Q: And so how many of these trades at a time might Mr. Kugel give you?

A: It could be a range. I mean, the earlier days when there were fewer customers, less money, there were fewer trades. Maybe he'd give me three a week or four a week. Later on, he could have given me as many as 12 or 15 a week. I don't remember, but he gave me tickets for every single one of them.

Q: A buy slip and a sell slip?

A: A buy and a sell. And on the buy slip was the conversion, like one bond equals, I don't know how many shares, 50 shares or one preferred equals 2.5 shares, and he would tell me how long the trade would take, and he would tell me the percentage range.

Q: And then using that information, you would figure out which customers for which trades?

A: Exactly.

Q: Okay. Later on, did there come a time when you stopped doing the arbitrage trading business?

A: Well, there was that group, and I had more help. I showed the other girls how to do it. I showed them how to do the set-ups and determine who gets what, and David continued to give them tickets. And then Bernie started doing the portfolio accounts, which I would help him with.

Q: And when you say "the girls," who were the girls that were then doing the arbitrage accounts?

A: Well, Jodi Crupi did it for a while. Joann Sala did it until she retired. There was a girl there, Francine. I don't know her new last name. Her name at the time was Barbato. I think Semone [Anderson] and Wini [Jackson] helped with all of that.

Q: And did there come a time when the arbitrage trading just sort of petered out?

A: Yes.
   . . .

Q: And you went on, I think you said to do portfolio-type trades, other types of trades other than the arbitrage business?

A: Yes.

Q: Can you describe what those were, and how that worked?

A: Well, from the early days, Bernie every now and then bought a stock here and there for some of his clients, and that started to grow. And that worked where he would give me a ticket and I would punch it and type it and send it out.

   Those are the accounts we're calling portfolio accounts. As they got bigger, they became computerized. We made up a program for it so he could keep track of it on the computer rather than having me do it manually at the end of that month in order to figure out what their equity was and what it should be, based on his benchmark.

   He taught me how to check all of that. And when I started doing that, when that became heavier, more and more volume, that's when I stopped doing the arbitrage and passed it off to somebody else to do it, and I was helping him with the long positions instead.

Q: And how were you helping him? What were you doing?

A: Well, he would tell me he bought a block of IBM on such and such a date, and it would be similar to the arbitrage. I would know who sent in a check, like Jeff Picower sent in a million dollars. He'd say, break it up; give him half, put half of that in IBM, put half of that in this. He'd give me the day and tell me to write the trades on a sheet and give it to the girls to punch.

Q: And did you ever help Mr. Madoff find blocks of stock that would work to satisfy the benchmarks for your clients?

A: Sometimes.

Q: Tell us how that worked?

A: I kept a sheet. It was like a spreadsheet that showed all the stock every month end and the price, if they had a split, if they had a dividend, all this information was kept in my room and I would check it sometimes. And he'd ask me: "Does anything have a huge increase from February until now?" And I'd look it up and call him back. I'd say: "Yes, IBM is up 30%," or whatever, and then he would tell me what to do with it.

Q: And when he told you what to do with it, would he tell you that he had bought IBM stock?

A: Yes.

Q: And what would he tell you to do with it then?

A: To see how many shares I needed to buy for Jeffry or whoever, whatever the customer [who] had cash.

Q: At any point, did this interaction about hitting the benchmark or satisfying the benchmark for your customers strike you as inappropriate or problematic?

A: No.

...

Q: Is this part of that project of converting to the computer system that you have described?

A: I believe it is, yes.

Q: Was it this note or some similar notes that you gave to Mr. Bonventre?

A: This was something very similar to this, yes.

Q: In this note you write: "No trades should show as-of unless I want them to," is that correct?

A: Yes.

Q: Why did you write that?

A: Because all the trading that was done for the customers was done as-of. None of them were done on the day that the trade was made.

Q: Why would you want to keep that from the customers?

A: I didn't keep it from them. What do you mean?

Q: Were you trying to hide something from the customers?

A: No, not at all.

Q: You also write in this note: "No comps should have an entry date."

A: Because all the comps needed a trade and a settlement date.

Q: Were you trying to hide anything from your customers by asking the computer to be programmed in this way?

A: No, not at all.

Q: Did you intend to commit any kind of fraud when you wrote this note?

A: No, I did not.

Q: Did you intend to defraud your customers when you wrote this note?

A: No.

Q: Did anyone suggest to you that this was a fraud?

A: No.

Q: That what you were doing was wrong?

A: No.

Q: Did you keep this note?

A: Yes.

Q: Was the computer system ultimately set up in the way that you requested?

A: Yes.

. . .

Q: Ms. Bongiorno, did there come a time when you opened an IA account for yourself at BLMIS?

A: Yes.

Q: Do you remember when that was, approximately?

A: Very, very early. Maybe it was in the very early 1980s.

Q: Where did the money come from that you deposited into that account?

A: From my salary, maybe gifts that I got.

Q: Did the amount in your account increase over time?

A: Yes.

Q: Did it go up as much as 25% in a year some years?

A: Yes, some years even more.

Q: What caused the account to increase in this way?
A: The trading that was being done.
Q: Those were all trades that were back-dated?
A: Probably.
Q: Were the trades that you were putting in your own account any different from the trades that were being put into other customers' accounts?
A: No.
Q: Who decided what trades would be put into your account?
A: Bernie.
Q: But were you, in the industry, aware of good years in the market and bad years in the market?
A: Yes, because I would hear people talking about it.
Q: I'd like to show you what is in evidence as Defendants' AB-1000-3. I don't know how clear that is, but that is a chart that shows the Dow Jones Industrial Average. Do you know what that is, Ms. Bongiorno, the Dow Jones Industrial Average?
A: Can I explain to you what it is? No.
Q: Do you know what it is?
A: *I guess it's an average of all the stocks and bonds that are bought during the course of a day.* [Italics added.]
Q: Did you understand that the Dow Jones Industrial Average was increasing during the year that you worked at BLMIS?
A: Some years I would hear that the market was up. Nobody ever said the Dow Jones [Industrial Average], simply that the market was up or the market was down.
Q: [Here] is another chart that shows the closing increase or decrease in the Dow Jones Industrial Average at times. Am I correct that there are some years when the Dow Jones Industrial Average increased as much as 30% in a single year?
A: I don't see 30%.
Q: How about the very top one?
A: Now I can see it. 38.32%. There is a 27%.
Q: Now, by December of 2008, your accounts at BLMIS had a total of approximately $50 million in them, is that correct?
A: That's correct.
Q: Did that seem ridiculous to you?
A: No.
Q: Why not?
A: Well, because I had this great account that made a great return. The early years I saved as much as I could and spent as little as

possible. I saved. My husband and I were always savers. I didn't have children. They are a huge expense. I wasn't a clothes horse. I didn't spend a lot on money on shoes and pocketbooks. I don't spend a lot of money on vacations. I spend a lot of money on food and get-togethers, but I wasn't a big spender.

I was able to save a lot. I took money out of my accounts to pay bills. I have nice homes, I live[d] nice. But, they are not decorated like palaces. I think that's because between the income that he provided, the return on my accounts, and the fact that I wasn't one that splurged on anything major, I think that that's why.

Q: Did it strike you as absurd that someone who just had a high school education should have that kind of money?

A: No. I thought I was very, very lucky once.

Q: Kind of like hitting the lottery?

A: Kind of like hitting the lottery. I also worked very hard. I was there 24-7 on call for 40 years.

Q: Did it occur to you that because you had this great account and it was worth so much, there must be something fraudulent about it?

A: No. I never thought of the word "fraudulent."

Q: Were there other employees who had accounts at BLMIS?

A: Yes.

Q: What types of employees had accounts at BLMIS?

A: The traders did. Almost anybody that had savings had an account there. Do you want names?

Q: Why don't we try categories? You mentioned traders. Were there other categories of employees that had IA accounts?

A: I believe all the managers did, all the different department supervisors did.

Q: The Madoff family members at the firm?

A: Yes, all the Madoffs did.

Q: Some of the people who had these accounts, were they licensed in the securities business?

A: I think so. I believe so.

Q: I think you described a practice you had of delivering statements to the employee at the firm.

A: Yes.

Q: That was once a month?

A: Yes, it was once a month, so that they could have everything in one envelope. Whatever trades went through, the confirmations, the statements, the memos, everything was put in an envelope. Once a month I would take the envelope and hand it to them personally, unless they weren't at their desk. If they weren't there, it came back up to my office.

Q: What would you do with it?

A: I'd wait until they came to get it or the following month try to deliver them once again.

Q: When you were delivering these packages to the supervisors, the traders, the other people who had IA accounts at BLMIS, did anyone who you gave these to complain to you that something seemed wrong about these statements?

A: No.

Q: What complaints, if any, did you ever hear about the nature of the statement that you were handing out to the people who had IA accounts?

A: What complaints? I never heard complaints. If somebody thought there was an error, maybe they would say this doesn't look right, this is an error. I don't know. I never heard a complaint.

Q: What did you hear any of them say about how unusual this was?

A: I never heard anybody say it was unusual.

Q: Do you recall what sort of rates of return the other employees at the firm got?

A: He told me that my account would make 2% more than everybody else's. My account was opened and stayed open forever until it was gone. But sometimes on other accounts for people in the office he did trades just when he wanted to; he didn't constantly do the trading that he did for me every month. I don't know what they made in the end. I don't know what their net percentage was at the end.

Q: But you were familiar with their benchmark rate?

A: The benchmark was about, I believe, 24% for everybody except me. I think mine was 26%.

Q: What did Bernie tell you about why you got the extra two points?

A: He said because I was there from day one and I was part of the foundation of his firm.

Q: Did you withdraw money from your IA account from time to time?

A: Yes.

Q: When did you start to withdraw sums of a million dollars or more?

A: I think it was in 2006.

Q: That was toward the end of your career at BLMIS?

A: Yes.

...

Q: When you began withdrawing large sums from your account, did you withdraw a large part of your balance?

A: Oh, no. It was a fraction of my balance.

Q: What were you doing with that money that you withdrew?

A: I was putting it in a bank. I just felt like—I didn't have a savings account anywhere in the whole world, just BLMIS. I decided that I wanted to take some of my eggs out of that basket. I started with a million dollars one year, and then a year later I took another million out, and I put it in a bank, just to have it someplace else, just to separate it.

Q: Were you concerned that there was something wrong with Madoff and that's why you should withdraw the money?

A: Absolutely not.

Q: What prompted you to decide you didn't want all your eggs in one basket?

A: Well, in 2006, Bernie started having some of the employees catch up on whatever he owed them. I noticed people taking money out. I thought to myself, am I the only one in this whole place that doesn't withdraw a penny? I do withdraw money to live and to live comfortably, but I didn't have savings anywhere else.

    I thought my father, if he was alive, he would say I was crazy, that you don't put all your eggs in one basket. So I went home to my husband and said I'm going to take some money out and put it in a bank. He said: "Whatever, whatever you want." I took out a million dollars, which was nothing in comparison to what I had at the time.

...

Q: Ms. Bongiorno, I think you mentioned earlier something called a RuAn [Rudy-Annette] account. What were the RuAn accounts?

A: The RuAn accounts back in the 1980s were a bunch of my cousins, they lent me money. I had Bernie invest the money, and I paid them interest on it.

Q: About how many cousins got involved in that?

A: Maybe four or five. It was at a time when we were all engaged in saving for our weddings.

Q: They were members of your family?

A: Yes. I think I was already married, but I think they were all getting married. Yes. Originally, they were all just members of my family, right.

Q: As time went on, did others open RuAn accounts with you?
A: Yes.
Q: What others opened RuAn accounts?
A: Aunts and uncles, my cousins' in-laws, my cousins' friends, my friends like Wanda and Isaac Maya. You met Isaac yesterday. It just kind of snowballed because the return was so good.
Q: About how many people were invested in RuAn accounts at the maximum?
A: Oh, God, 20, 25.
Q: There were all people that were either members of your family or friends?
A: Yes, or friends of my family.
Q: Were you intending to get these people involved in a fraud?
A: Absolutely not.
Q: To open these accounts, did you have to ask anyone's permission?
A: To open them?
Q: Yes.
A: Just Bernie.
Q: What did he say about opening these accounts for you?
A: He didn't really say much. He didn't want to open individual accounts, because they were small amounts. That's why he said: "You know, you could borrow the money." He's the one that recommended that I do it that way, borrow the money and pay them the interest on it. At the end of the year I had to issue a 1099 [IRS form] to them and supply it to the government, which I did every year. He told me how it should work.
Q: Did he suggest to you that you should earn a little money in connection with it?
A: Oh, yes.
Q: How much?
A: Because I was doing the work on it. That varied over the years. I think it was like 4% or 5% in the beginning. Then maybe it went down. Some years it went up. It varied.
Q: Did the RuAn investors know that you were earning a little money in connection with these accounts?
A: Yes, they did.
Q: Did there come a time when these accounts were closed?
A: Yes.
Q: When was that, approximately?
A: Right after the A&B upset, he [Bernard Madoff] came to me and said to me that he wanted me to close that account, too. And

there was other group accounts that he had whose names escape me, I don't remember them, that he didn't want these joint accounts anymore, because he said that although our account was small and something like the A&B account, he just didn't like that whole flavor he got from the A&B account. He said that he would never want anything like that to happen to us and that I had to close the account.

Q: Did anything about that discussion make you suspicious?

A: No.

Q: Did some of the RuAn investors then reinvest directly with Bernie?

A: Yes. He said that if they had a certain amount of money on their own, he would open a personal account for them. So RuAn was closed, every penny given back, the interest that they earned up to that point given to them, and RuAn was gone. Those that were able opened an account directly with Bernie.

Q: Those accounts, were they accounts that you managed going forward?

A: I didn't manage accounts. I took orders on accounts. I didn't manage anything.

Q: Those accounts, the ones that were reopened at BLMIS, were they in your side of the business?

A: They were put into arbitrages originally. I don't remember if I was doing it then or if JoAnn [Crupi] had taken over. I don't remember who was doing them. But they became part of Frank's options group, so eventually they ended up in options.

. . .

Q: In April of a typical year, people, that's tax time, correct, April?

A: Mm-hm.

Q: Did you ever get requests from accountants to open accounts for Madoff?

A: Yes.

Q: When would that happen?

A: Almost every year in April, February, or March.

Q: Did you take those requests to Bernie?

A: Yes.

Q: What did Bernie tell you about those requests?

A: Some maybe he opened, but a lot of times he said that he wasn't doing any more accounts, that we were very busy with what we already had and he didn't want to open any new accounts. He did that occasionally; he'd just say: "I'm not taking any more money; I'm not taking any new investments." I thought nothing of it.

. . .

Q: Do you recall hearing some testimony about a man named Jacques Amsellem?

A: Yes.

Q: Do you recall that account?

A: I recall it, yes.

Q: Do you recall that Bernie told you at some point that you needed to get that account in line?

A: Yes.

Q: Getting an account in line, was that a kind of shorthand expression that was used at BLMIS?

A: That was an expression that Bernie used.

Q: When Bernie said to you that you needed to get an account in line, what did you understand him to mean?

A: The portfolio accounts, the accounts that ran at a certain percentage that had long positions and short positions, because of the market going up and down, sometimes they were out of line. Sometimes they were under where he said that they would be, and sometime they were way over where he said they would be.

   It was my understanding, as it was with me, and as it was with the people I heard him talk to, it was my understanding that he had an agreement with all the people about what they were going to make on an account.

Q: What was getting an account in line? What was that?

A: It meant that an account was either way over where it should be and he had to put through trades to bring it down to where it should be or it was way under and he had to put through trades to bring it up to where it should be.

Q: And did you get a number of accounts in line over time while you worked at BLMIS?

A: I did.

Q: When you would get an account in line, did you ever believe you were doing something wrong?

A: No.

Q: With respect to Mr. Amsellem's account, do you recollect that his account was gotten in line after he passed away?

A: I didn't, but I heard that said here; so yeah.

Q: Did you think that there was something wrong about that getting the account in line like that?

A: No, I didn't.

Q: How long had Mr. Amsellem been an investor by the time you got it in line?

A: Years. I don't know many years.

Q: Did his account grow over time?

A: Oh, sure.

Q: Do you recollect that getting his account in line meant reducing the amount in the account?

A: Well, I remember it now.

Q: Having seen it?

A: Having seen it recently, yeah.

Q: At the time that his account was gotten in line, had he earned a profit for a number of years?

A: Oh, yes.

Q: Do you recollect whether he made withdrawals from his account over time?

A: I'm sure he did.

      . . .

Q: Ms. Bongiorno, over the years, did you become familiar with a customer at BLMIS named Stanley Chais?

A: Yes.

Q: Who was he?

A: He was also a friend of Bernie's—maybe from college or something—a very close friend, and he was a client.

Q: A client. Okay. And did he have accounts that you monitored or worked on?

A: Yes.

Q: Was there a time when you were asked to get Mr. Chais' accounts in line, similar to the way you were asked to get Mr. Amsellem's accounts in line?

A: Yes.

Q: And by doing so, were you reducing Mr. Chais' returns?

A: Yes.

Q: At the point where you were asked to get Mr. Chais' accounts in line, how long had he been a customer of the firm?

A: For as long as I can remember. It was probably from the beginning.

Q: Who asked you to get Mr. Chais' accounts in line?

A: Bernie. I was in Florida. He called me, and he asked when I was coming home because he had this major job he wanted me to do.

Q: And was Mr. Chais alive at that point?

A: Oh, yes, very much so.

Q: Did you discuss this with Mr. Chais or anyone from his office?

A: I only spoke to Mr. Chais. I never spoke to anyone from his office, and I did because I had to ask him to return statements to me that he already had.

Q: And was that practice when statements were revised, you asked for the originals back?

A: Oh, yes.

Q: And did you explain to him what you were going to do?

A: No. He knew.

Q: How do you know that?

A: Because he told me he spoke to Bernie, and he knew we had a big job to do.

Q: And when you got his accounts in line, were you reducing the amount of his profit?

A: Yes.

Q: And Mr. Chais didn't have a problem with that?

A: Obviously not. He sent all the statements. He sounded fine. He wasn't annoyed. He was okay with it.

Q: Did anything about that process, that the client didn't protest, did anything like that cause you to be suspicious?

A: No, but I did ask Bernie why, and he told me that they were way over line and if something happened to Stan, it would be a problem for him.

Q: For Bernie?

A: For Bernie, right, because he and Stan had an agreement, and he didn't know if Stan's children knew about their agreement.

Q: And when you say he and Stan had an agreement, an agreement about?

A: About what his return would be, the way he had an agreement with everybody, what he thought he was going to make for each of them, and his account was way over. His accounts, because he had a lot of accounts. Stan opened two or three accounts for every one of his kids and then his grandkids; so we had to correct quite a few accounts.

. . .

Q: And can you read us that note?

A: "Stan Chais, month end"—"ME" stand for month end—"April, no trading this month. Create gains and losses. Good loss at high, buy at low."

Q: When you wrote the phrase "create gains and losses," what did you mean?

A: I don't know because the top says "no trading this month."
Q: Did you mean to refer to fictitious trading?
A: No.
    . . .
Q: Do you recall the occasion when Frank [DiPascali] went to work at BLMIS?
A: I remember.
Q: Who helped him to get that job?
A: I did.
Q: Did anyone ask you for that help?
A: I was with his mom sitting outside one evening.
Q: On the stoop?
A: On the stoop. The old days, after dinner, we would take our folding chairs and sit outside and talk to the neighbors. And his mother was crying, and I went over to sit on her stoop. I went to ask her what had happened. She was crying. I asked if everything was all right.
Q: After you had this conversation with Frank's mother, what did you do?
A: I asked Bernie—I knew Bernie was looking for somebody to work in the research department, and I asked him if he would interview him [Frank]. I said: "He's a very smart young man, and he's pumping gas and he needs a job." I said that I've known him for many, many years. He's a good kid. "Would you interview him?" And he said: "Of course, bring him in." So I brought him in, and he hit it off with Bernie immediately and they hired him. I want to say he was interviewed by Peter; so I know whoever interviewed him was very happy with him and hired him on the spot
    . . .
Q: You've mentioned at various points A&B. Do you remember generally the situation where there was a lot of account statements changed at A&B?
A: Yes.
Q: Was Mr. DiPascali a fringe player in that process?
A: A fringe player? What does that mean?
Q: Okay. I'll withdraw the question. Did you take orders in that process from Mr. DiPascali?
A: I did.
Q: Did Mr. Madoff explain to you what happened at A&B?
A: What he told me was that they didn't get a license that they needed in order to do what they were doing, and so they were

closing down their business and he had to now get the accounts in line, which means if they were below profit or over profit, whatever. He would put through the proper trading to get the accounts in line so he could close all the accounts out and send them back the money.

Q: And what type of accounts were the A&B accounts?

A: You know, I think some were long-position accounts at the time, portfolio accounts, but I also believe they had some arbitrage accounts. I really can't—I'm not a hundred percent sure what they had. I think they had a mixture of both.

Q: And in addition to Mr. DiPascali, did anybody else give you orders as to what to do about the A&B accounts?

A: Well, Frank told me what to do based on Bernie telling him to work with me on it. I didn't take orders Frank, but Bernie told me that Frank was going to help out with it.

Q: When you worked on this A&B problem, changing these account statements, did you understand that you were committing a fraud?

A: No.

Q: Did anything that either Mr. Madoff said to you or Mr. DiPascali said to you about A&B made you think you were doing something wrong?

A: No.

Q: Had you gotten accounts in line before this time?

A: With them?

Q: With Bernie?

A: Oh, yeah.

Q: At that point in time, did anything that was said to you indicate to you that you were fooling the SEC in some way?

A: They never mentioned the SEC. They never mentioned audits, which I know came out here. They never mentioned that to me. Bernie only told me what Bernie needed to tell me to get me to do my job. He didn't explain things like that to me. I wouldn't have understood it if he did explain it, but he didn't explain it.

Q: And because Bernie didn't explain things like that to you, did that make you suspicious?

A: No.

. . .

Q: After the A&B revision of all those account statements was done did those—did any A&B individual customers reinvest their funds at Madoff?

A: Yes, a lot of them did.

Q: Did you help with that process?

A: Yes, I did.

Q: What did you do to help with that process?

A: I opened accounts up, filled out maintenance sheets for them, gave them numbers, and assigned them account numbers.

Q: Who monitored their accounts after they came back?

A: I think I did—some of them. And I think some went straight to Frank.

Q: And what type of accounts was Frank working on, as you understood it?

A: He was doing option accounts, I believe, back then. I think that when they first came back, they all went into arbitrage. I'm not sure if they went somewhat over to Frank's side. I'm not sure if he was doing options at that point.

Q: Did there come a time when the bulk, the majority, of the A&B customers did migrate to Mr. DiPascali?

A: Yes.

    . . .

Q: Who were the customers [that stayed with you]?

A: Stan Chais, Carl Shapiro, Jeffry Picower. [Also] some of people who worked in my department, in my office, the whole office, the firm I should say: Martin Joel.

Q: Folks who had been with the firm a long time?

A: Yes, and customers with the firm a long time.

Q: When the A&B customers migrated back to BLMIS, did Mr. Madoff ask you to take Frank under your wing and work with him?

A: He asked Frank if he would like to work with me.

Q: Did Frank tell you what his response to that was?

A: He said he's rather have needles in his eyes.

Q: Did he explain what he meant by that?

A: Because Frank was very laid back. He came and went as he pleased. I tried to run my department pretty much according to the way Bernie wanted it run. The job was 9:00 to 5:00. He expected us to be dressed decently, no jeans, not sloppy. It wasn't Frank's style. I was a bit of a pain about that stuff. So he didn't want to work for me.

    . . .

Q: You mentioned Mr. Picower as one of the accounts that stayed with you. Do you remember an account called ACF Corporation pension account?

A: Yes.

Q: How often were you entering trades in accounts that were associated with Mr. Picower's account?

A: He had a lot of accounts. Some were done monthly, and some were done once a year. I think ACF might have been the one that was done once a year.

Q: Was there a time when that account was switched from securities to T-bills or something like that that you remember?

A: Yes, I do remember that. I remember doing that, right.

Q: Did you make any changes to the account without getting Mr. Madoff's approval?

A: No. I didn't do anything without his approval.

Q: When you made the changes to the accounts, was there anything about that process that made you think you were involved in a fraud?

A: No.

Q: When you made changes to an account like that, what was the process of getting the old statements back?

A: I would just call April [Freilich], if she had them, and say, return the statements, we are sending you new ones, corrected ones. But I think ACF [Corporation] was done once a year. I don't know that she would have even had them. I'm not really sure if she had them or not. But that's the procedure with his other accounts. Anything they had, I would call up and say I need you to return the statements to me, we have corrections for you.

Q: Who did she [April] work with?

A: Jeffry Picower.

. . .

Q: But were you aware of them [audits]?

A: I was aware that there would be agents auditing the books, but that was all I was aware of. They were there. I passed them; I would see strangers in my travels throughout the office.

Q: Were there times after you and Mr. DiPascali separated and Mr. DiPascali began working on options accounts when you would ask him for options trades?

A: Yes. Bernie once in a while would say to me, for example, and this I remember clearly—Mr. Horowitz would get an option trade once every quarter—and Bernie would say: "Ask Frank for the option trade, give him the amount of money that you need." And I would do that, go to Frank and ask for whatever it was, $20,000, or whatever.

Q: Was there anything about that process that seemed unusual to you?

A: No.

. . .

Q: During your testimony a couple of days ago, you described the benchmark concept that applied to your customers, do you remember that?

A: Yes.

Q: Did different customers have different benchmarks?

A: Yes, they did.

Q: Did that strike you as odd?

A: At the time I didn't think of it at all, it didn't strike me as odd. Later on, during the past few years, when I think back on it, I would say that it wouldn't have—if I did think about it at all—I would have thought that it's no different from any bank.

You go into a bank. Every bank has a different percentage that they pay out based on what you are putting your money into: Checking account, savings account, CDs. All percentages are different. If you do into four different banks, you get all different percentages.

I still didn't see that there was anything wrong with that. I didn't think about it then. But when I thought about it when I was asked about it by you, that is how I would have thought about it.

Q: Do you recollect situations where different customers were getting stocks, the same stocks, and getting them in their accounts at different prices?

A: Yes.

Q: Getting them placed in their account at different prices, I should say?

A: Right.

Q: At the time did that strike you as odd?

A: Not at all.

Q: Why not, ma'am?

A: Something similar to the percentage returns. A container of milk costs different amounts of money depending on where you buy it. If you buy it in a big supermarket or small little convenience store, everybody sells things for what they want to. He [Madoff] told me that they were his stock and he could sell them when he wanted at whatever price he wanted as long as the price was in [the price] range for the day. That was from day one.

Q: When he [Madoff] told you that, where did you believe he was getting the stock that he was selling to his customers?

A: On the trading desk. He was trading for his own account and then giving the stock out to his customers.

Q: As you understood it, how long did he have to assign this stock to his customers?

A: I don't know. There is no one answer for that. In the very early days, when it was some stock here and there, we got the stock and he distributed it on the same day. When David [Kugel] was doing arbitrages, he was buying blocks of stock, and he was giving me information once a week. Later on, when long positions came into play, portfolio accounts, then he was doing it a month out, a year out, in some cases, as we saw, even more than a year out.

I don't know. That's the answer. I really don't know that there was anything wrong with that, either. I didn't think that there was.

Q: Nothing about that process struck you as suspicious?

A: No. The only rule that we had with that was when we were completing a trade, like when we did a sale, he never wanted to have to redo a 1099 [IRS form]. Madoff wanted all the sales which got reported to the IRS to be done in the correct year. In other words, he might go back a couple of years on a buy side, but he wouldn't do that on the sale side, because the sales got reported, and he never wanted a corrected 1099 [IRS form]. There were corrections, but that was the general rule.

Q: Bernie expressed to you the view that he didn't want to correct a 1099 [IRS form]?

A: Yes.

Q: Did that make you suspicious that there was some kind of tax fraud going on at Madoff?

A: No. I thought he was being extra careful not to have any problem with taxes. You know, the 1099 [tax forms] had to go out every year by a certain time. He didn't want a correction after that date to go out.

Q: Nothing made you suspicious about that, either?

A: No.

. . .

Q: You recall that when we broke we were talking about your going to Frank DiPascali to get options trades for your customers in some cases. Do you remember that?

A: Yes.

Q: Why weren't you doing that yourself, finding the options trades?

A: I never knew anything about options. I didn't know how they worked. Plus, Bernie said: "Get this trade from Frank." I went to Frank for it.

Q: Did anyone ever explain to you what the split-strike conversion strategy was?

A: You know, I might have asked him to explain it to me. But the question is did I get it? I never understood it, I never got it.

Q: Was that something that you were doing for your customers in the long accounts?

A: No. Most of the options, any options, that went through in a long account for one of the customer that were on my side of the office, they were done by Frank, not by me. I didn't know how to do an option account or an option trade.

    . . .

Q: You mentioned this morning and you mentioned the other day David Kugel. How long did you know David?

A: I think since 1971. When I came back to work for Madoff after I was laid off, he was already there at that point. I think that was in 1971.

Q: Over time did you become friendly with him?

A: No.

Q: Did you meet his wife?

A: I did meet his wife. We went out to dinner once in a while, yes. [We had] that kind of social relationship, yes.

Q: Did he own a home not far from you in New York?

A: Yes, he owned a home where I live now.

Q: Did he also own a home not far from you in Florida?

A: Yes.

Q: How close were your homes in New York and Florida?

A: Just a few blocks away.

Q: Did Mr. Kugel, and his family, own or have IA accounts at BLMIS?

A: Yes, they did.

Q: What members of his family had IA accounts, as you recollect it?

A: He did. He had some kind of a partnership. It might have been with his brother—I know he had a brother—his son, and his daughter.

Q: As you recollect it, who decided what kind of trades would go into those accounts?

A: David's account was probably decided by David but then approved by Bernie.

Q: Were those trades back-dated, as you have described?

A: All the trades were back-dated.

Q: Did you suspect there was anything wrong with what was going on in Mr. Kugel's accounts?

A: No.

   ...

Q: What do you recognize that to be?

A: It looks like trades in these different stocks that he wanted sold short.

Q: Is this the type of instruction Mr. Kugel would give you for trades in his accounts?

A: Yes.

Q: When he gave you an instruction like this, what would you do?

A: I would call Bernie, and I would go over the trades with Bernie and ask him if he wanted them to go through.

Q: What would Bernie say to you?

A: "Yes"; most of the time he said yes.

Q: Were there ever times that Mr. Kugel would give you instructions that you didn't even understand what he wanted?

A: Yes.

Q: What would you do then?

A: Well, it wasn't about trading. It was about something going on with his portfolio. The portfolio management report, he gave me instructions on it. I asked him to explain it. He did. I didn't understand him at all, nothing about it. I said, all right, just leave it with me, and he left.

   I called Bernie, and I said: "I got these instructions from David; I don't understand them. I asked him to explain it, and he did two or three times. However, I still don't understand what he is asking me to do." Bernie told me to read it to him, and I read it to him. He said to me: "Okay, just put it through, it's fine." So I put it through.

Q: That's what you did?

A: Right.

   ...

Q: And did you get to know Enrica Cotellessa-Pitz well?

A: Very well.

   ...

Q: Did she have an IA account?

A: Yes.

Q: Who decided what sort of trades would be put into that account?

A: Bernie Madoff.

Q: Did there come a time, Ms. Bongiorno, when you gave Ms. Cotellessa-Pitz some advice about withdrawing funds from her account?

A: I didn't give her advice, but I mentioned to her that maybe we should do that.

Q: Do you remember about when that was?

A: 2004, 2005, 2006, one of those years.

Q: And why did you talk to her about that?

A: Because, and I think I mentioned this before, I didn't have savings anywhere else; so I asked her if she did. And she wondered why. And I said: "Well, I have all my savings at Madoff and maybe it's time to put my eggs in a few other baskets." And I was just letting her know that I was going to do that and that if she had them all there, maybe she should consider that too.

Q: At that point, had you seen others taking money out of the firm?

A: Yes.

Q: Who had you seen taking money out of the firm?

A: Mark Madoff, Andy Madoff, and David Kugel. I can't remember all the names.

Q: When they made their withdrawals, those people, did any of them explain why they were doing it, to you?

A: No. I wouldn't have asked them that.

Q: Was there a time when Mr. Bonventre withdrew money from the firm?

A: Yes, yes.

    . . .

Q: Ms. Bongiorno, we've heard reference to something called "Annette's checkbook"; do you remember that?

A: Yes.

Q: Do you remember what bank account that was?

A: Yes.

Q: What bank account was it?

A: It was at JPMorgan Chase Bank.

Q: Were you monitoring that account in December of 2008?

A: No.

    . . .

Q: Ms. Bongiorno, do you recall getting a call from Mr. Madoff on December 10th of 2008?

A: Yes.
Q: What did Mr. Madoff ask you to do?
A: He asked me to come to work.
      . . .
Q: What did you do after Mr. Madoff asked you to come to work?
A: I put the clothes down that were in my arms, and I went home, I showered, I dressed, and I went to work.
Q: When you got to the office on December 10th, was Mr. Madoff there?
A: No.
Q: Was Frank DiPascali there?
A: No.
Q: How long was it until one of them arrived?
A: Oh, not too long. It was under an hour.
Q: Who came first?
A: I believe Frank.
Q: Did you speak to Frank when he came to the office?
A: Yes.
Q: What, if anything, did you ask Frank?
A: I asked him why I was there.
Q: And what did Frank respond to you?
A: He said: "What are you asking me for?" So I said; "Bernie told me you needed me to help you with something." And he said: "Oh, so he decided to go through with that?" And I said: "Go through with what?" And this is where it's fuzzy. I'm not sure if he actually told me or if, at that point, Bernie was upstairs and they told me to go upstairs and he then gave me the instructions and told me why I was in.
Q: And did either Mr. DiPascali or Mr. Madoff instruct you to do something?
A: Yes.
Q: What did they order you to do?
A: They ordered me to close out all the accounts of everyone that worked in Madoff in the office and the family and friends of those that worked for Madoff.
Q: And were you given a list of accounts you were expected to close?
A: No. I was asked to go downstairs and make a list of them and then go over it with Frank.
Q: And did you do that?
A: I did.

Q: In the course of that conversation, did you make a remark about your taxes?

A: I sure did.

Q: What do you recall saying about your taxes?

A: I said: "I'm going to have to pay all these taxes in one year?"

Q: And what were you referring to?

A: My accounts.

Q: And why were you concerned about paying taxes if you had to close the accounts?

A: Because when you close the accounts and you make sales, you have to pay taxes on your capital gain.

Q: Why weren't you worried about the collapse of BLMIS at that point?

A: I didn't know BLMIS was collapsing at that point. I had no clue.

...

Q: What did you do after you spoke to Mr. DiPascali and Mr. Madoff about closing the accounts?

A: I went downstairs to my office, I got the list of accounts out, and I got the portfolio management report out. And I started ticking off all the accounts that would come under the heading of employees or family and friends of employees.

Q: And did you ask anyone to help you with this project?

A: Frank.

Q: And did Frank help you with that project?

A: Yes. We had a couple of questions and we made the list.

...

Q: As you were doing this task, did you show lists of stock prices to Mr. Madoff?

A: Yes.

Q: What kind of stock price lists were you showing him?

A: Bloomberg.

Q: Why were you doing that?

A: Well, we had to look up the stocks on the Bloomberg to see what the prices were and where he would want to put these trades through.

Q: And what did Bernie do with those lists?

A: He gave them back to me and told me what to do.

Q: And when he told you what to do, what was he telling you?

A: He was telling me to write the trades up and put them through. "Put them through" means give them to the computer room.

Q: And put them through at a particular price?

A: Yes.

Q: And did you do what Mr. Madoff ordered you to do?

A: Yes.

Q: Were checks ultimately issued?

A: Yes.

Q: Do you recognize this to be the sort of checks that were issued after you closed accounts?

A: Yes.

Q: Were you able to get these checks signed?

A: No.

. . .

Q: But you did know that A&B had customers right?

A: Yes.

Q: And that those customers were giving money to A&B, which was then being invested with BLMIS, right?

A: Yes.

Q: You knew that because you managed the accounts on a daily basis, right, Ms. Bongiorno?

A: I didn't manage the accounts. I just took orders.

. . .

Q: You're doing this [A&B] project because the SEC is looking at A&B, right?

A: I'm doing it for that? No.

Q: You knew that the SEC was looking at A&B.

A: No.

Q: You knew that A&B was being investigated by some authority, right?

A: Yes.

. . .

Q: And the RuAn accounts were investors that you knew who provided you with funds that you then invested with BLMIS; is that fair?

A: In the very early day, yes.

. . .

Q: I believe you testified on direct that these RuAn accounts were managed by you until around the time of the A&B events?

A: After that.

Q: Okay. Well, at some point, you had to disband the sort of main RuAn account, and then if people were able, they would reinvest individually with BLMIS, right?

A: Yes.

Q: I believe you also testified that a lot of these people were friends, right?

A: Yes.

Q: I think a fair number of them were your family or distant family members?

A: Yes.

. . .

Q: I think you testified . . . that you, in fact, earned a percentage of what they had invested in BLMIS, right?

A: That's correct.

Q: It was between, I think, 4% to 5%?

A: I don't remember, but I think that sounds about right.

. . .

Q: And I believe you testified that Mr. Madoff had suggested that you were entitled to this percentage because you had to work on these accounts and do the paperwork and just perform those types of duties; is that fair?

A: Because I had to take what he was doing and break it down on my spare time at home at night, he said that I should do that, yes.

Q: And because you were doing that work, that you were entitled to 4% to 5% of the earnings they made on their accounts?

A: Right.

Q: Now, when the RuAn account itself was disbanded in the mid-1990s, did a number of these investors reinvest in BLMIS?

A: Yes, they did.

Q: And at that point, their accounts were directly with BLMIS and you were no longer the intermediary; is that fair?

A: That's correct.

Q: Because before, you had handwritten statements that you would send to the clients, right?

A: Correct.

. . .

Q: Isn't it a fact that even after these accounts closed, you still received a percentage of the profits that were earned by these very same clients?

A: I did.

Q: Right. Even when you were doing none of this paperwork?

A: Right.

Q: You still got money based on these accounts, right?

A: I did, yes.

. . .

Q: And we saw that he wired in $125 million, right?
A: Yes.
Q: And we saw that you went through and picked stocks that had the biggest swing going back four months, right?
A: Yes.
Q: So by picking those, Mr. Picower got back-dated trades of the biggest movers in the market going back four months, right?
A: That's how it looked, right.
   . . .
Q: But when you redid them, you "flipped" what was in those accounts, didn't you?
A: I don't know what you mean by "flipped." First of all, I didn't flip anything. I did what I was told to do.
Q: Well, Ms. Bongiorno, you had the statements right?
A: Right.
Q: They were all sent back to you?
A: Right.
   . . .
Q: And you got these sent back to you from the client, right? Then you put completely different, completely different securities in them, didn't you?
A: I didn't put them in.
Q: Did you redo the statements?
A: Yes.
Q: Did you sit down and write out what was going to go into those statements?
A: Yes.
Q: And instead of stocks, was it now bonds?
A: But it was based on bonds given to me by Bernie. I didn't do it.
Q: Well, did you have the old statement in one hand, correct?
A: Correct.
Q: And you could get the new statement in the other hand, right?
A: Yes.
Q: And you could use your eyes to see they were different, right?
A: Yes, correct.
Q: And you were the one that made the new one different, right?
A: Yes.
   . . .
Q: You went back and wrote January 2002 when you redid the January statement, right?
A: Right.

Q: And you redid the February statement by saying it was February 2002?

A: Right.

Q: And they were completely different, right?

A: Right.

. . .

Q: To be clear, you were earning a percentage on the profits of these trades, right?

A: Of the trades?

Q: Of the profits in the RuAn accounts.

A: No. I was getting a percentage of their investment, based on the investment, I believe.

Q: You were getting money based on the full amount invested?

A: I think so.

Q: That would actually be more than the profits on the trade?

A: Right.

Q: So about 8% was coming from?

A: I'm getting confused. Yes, I think it was on the investment, not on the . . . . I'm not sure.

Q: You were getting 8%, 7%, 6% over various times, right?

A: Right.

Q: As you sit here today, you're not sure if that was on the profit or the full investment?

A: It was the full investment; I'm 99% sure, yes.

Q: Earlier . . . you testified it was the profits, right?

A: Yes, I believe I did. I made a mistake.

. . .

Q: Do you remember seeing this folder on your direct examination?

A: Yes.

Q: Who wrote "Andy" at the top?

A: I did.

Q: Who does "Andy" refer to?

A: Andy Madoff.

Q: This is Andy Madoff's deferred compensation account, right?

A: Yes.

Q: You worked on some of the deferred compensation accounts for certain employees at BLMIS?

A: I worked on their portfolio accounts. It wasn't all compensation.

Q: Looking at this deferred compensation account can you tell us what the opening balance is?

A: The initial investment says $17,376,497.84.

Q: This is for the time period January 2005 to December 2005, right?
A: Yes.
Q: Can we go to the next page. This is the same deferred compensation account, but this is for the year 2006, right?
A: Right.
Q: That is the same account that we have just been looking at for Andrew Madoff, isn't it?
A: Yes.
Q: But this time it's for the year 2007, right?
A: Right.
Q: You worked on a project in which you adjusted these numbers in his account, right?
A: Yes.
Q: Isn't it a fact, Ms. Bongiorno, that what you were doing was making it look like Mr. Madoff had less money because he was getting divorced by his wife?
A: I didn't do anything of the kind.

    . . .

Q: Here you have written a note to yourself that you are going back to change just the December statements, right?
A: Right.
Q: The December statements would show the end of year compensation or the end of year balance in these accounts by Andy Madoff, right?
A: Right.
Q: You actually went through multiple iterations of changing the numbers in this account, didn't you?
A: I did.
Q: Looking at the very bottom of the document, as of December 31, 2007, you have it as having $200,186.50. Do you see that?
A: I do.
Q: Can we highlight that, please? Also at the bottom we saw in the prior documents that at the end of 2007 Andy Madoff had around $33 million in this account, right?
A: Right.
Q: Through the adjustments that you have made, it's down to $200,000, right?
A: Right.

    . . .

Q: You testified on direct [examination] that you knew that all the trades were back-dated?

A: Yes.

Q: You testified that that is something that did not seem unusual to you?

A: Because it was since day one, that's right.

This testimony by Bongiorno provides a fairly exhaustive picture of how Madoff was able to manipulate a backstage accomplice to help him further his con. None of her answers to the different questions and attorneys contradicts the accounts of other backstage accomplices or the paper record, and, more importantly, she adds many finer points to what was heretofore less than fully understood about how the con played out.

There is much in Bongiorno's testimony that is remarkable. She repeatedly denied that she had any idea that she was at the center of a con game, or of any fraud or crime. She, in fact, maintained that she only vaguely understood how the world of investing worked. After 40 years of working at BLMIS and, with her husband, accumulating more than $50 million in her BLMIS IA accounts, she worked to portray herself as still an artless 19-year-old from Howard Beach, who was only doing her job, only following orders. At times, she seems artless.

It might be, as she claimed, that Bongiorno was not a Madoff confidante. She was, however, without question, a trusted—one of the most trusted—BLMIS accomplices, involved in some of the most unusual aspects of the con. Notably, she was charged with juggling the accounts of BLMIS's largest individual clients, for example, those of Stanley Chais and Jeffry Picower (whose part in the con is discussed more fully in Chapter 9). She was asked to use her clerical and bookkeeping nimbleness on a task that on its face was illegal, to save Andrew Madoff millions of dollars in a divorce settlement. In addition to her long-term clerical and managerial responsibilities at BLMIS, Madoff recruited Bongiorno to be a roper so as to bring to BLMIS a pool of money that otherwise might have eluded the Ponzi scheme. Although insisting not to know what the Dow Jones Industrial Average meant, Bongiorno knew enough to keep track of the money solicited from family and friends that she brought to BLMIS in order to collect the commissions Madoff promised her even long after her involvement with these accounts had ended.

Expanding the Web

In addition to what the many hours of questioning from both defense and prosecuting attorneys brought forth, it was revealed by others that Bongiorno worked closely with the accountant Paul J. Konigsberg, a longtime Madoff associate, who in 2014 pled guilty to a three-count Information charging him, most particularly, with conspiracy to falsify the books and records of BLMIS and to obstruct the administration of the tax laws. The Konigsberg's criminal Information details how he and Madoff with the help of Bongiorno worked together to change monthly and yearly account statements for numerous BLMIS clients so that their accounts showed earnings that had been promised by Madoff, and also to change U.S. federal tax obligations.

15. For the majority of Madoff's clients, the fraudulent trading activity was back-dated within a single month. ... For others, however, BLMIS was able to create fake trades that were back-dated by many months in order to manipulate the returns in their accounts, sometimes for tax purposes.

16. When that happened, BLMIS employees sometimes asked certain customers to return account statements to the firm so that they could replace the original statements with "amended" ones reflecting new or different false trading activity. Madoff could ask this of only certain clients, since replacing a statement— sometimes one several months old—that reflected particular securities positions with "amended" statements reflecting entirely different positions, and resulting in entirely different account values, risked exposing the fraud.

17. For example, in or about early 2003, Bongiorno created a year's worth of profitable, back-dated trades in the account of a BLMIS client, who was also a client of Paul J. Konigsberg. Specifically, the client suffered losses in a number of different investments in 2002, causing the client's net worth to decline dramatically. In order to restore the client's wealth, Konigsberg and the client went to Bongiorno's office at BLMIS, and sat with her as she created and back-dated an entire year's worth of profitable securities transactions and corresponding account statements for the client's IA account. Bongiorno then instructed Konigsberg and the client to return the original statements before receiving the new, "amended" statements. Bongiorno's notes in connection with the "amended" statements read: "Do not send corrected statements until we get Paul & the client's copies." Konigsberg then prepared the client's tax returns based on the "amended" statements.

18. Likewise, in or about 2008, Bongiorno created "amended" statements for another IA client of BLMIS, who used the accounting services of Konigsberg. In or about August 2008, Konigsberg was present for a conversation between Madoff and the client, in which Madoff stated that he would no longer support the client financially. Specifically, the client owed Madoff approximately $1.6 million, and unbeknownst to Konigsberg at the time, Madoff planned to recoup that money by backdated trades in the client's account. In order to accomplish that goal, both the client and Konigsberg, who received duplicate account statements, needed to return the original statements first. And in fact, the original statements—crossed-out to reflect that they were no longer current—were returned to Bongiorno. A note on the original February 2008 statement stated: "Rec. only Paul's copy, not the client's copy of 2/29/08." A similar Post-it note was on the original, crossed-out April 2008 statement. And another note made by Bongiorno read:

Corrected statements
Keep in hanging folder.
Do not mail out!
We never received his original statement back.
He told Bernie he sends everything to Paul &
Paul told Bernie he shreds whatever he doesn't need!

19/20. In or about 1992 ... Madoff offered Konigsberg, an additional cash payment of approximately $20,000 per year. Konigsberg instructed Madoff to pay [it to] a relative of Konigsberg's, who had previously worked at BLMIS. For example, in a note dated April 14, 1992, Bongiorno recorded a conversation she had with Konigsberg:

Paul called.
Said [two particular investors] will be sending in additional $150,000—for their accts.
They get 18% on that.
[Relative] gets 2% to be added to pay ck.

21. Between approximately 1992 until the firm's collapse in December 2008, the [relative] was listed as an employee at BLMIS and was enrolled in the firm's employee benefits plans, despite not working at BLMIS. During that time period, therefore, the relative received more than approximately $320,000 in cash compensation on account of a "no show" job at BLMIS, plus employee benefits.[3]

Once again, in order for Bongiorno and Konigsberg to successfully complete some of this legerdemain, he was permitted to come to the offices of BLMIS (and to bring a client along)—although he had never been employed there, so that the two could work side by side.

Finally, Bongiorno's unconvincing claim that she did not nearly know the full extent of Madoff's con and that she was not a knowing participant was made by most Madoff accomplices, most notably Peter Madoff. In fact, this excuse by others that they had little idea of what Madoff was doing or what he had them doing was repeated so often that it seemed threadbare well before it was time for Bongiorno to begin to defend herself in court. The claim made under oath by Peter Madoff that his older brother kept him mostly in the dark did not keep him from prison, and a jury did not accept Bongiorno's repeated contention that she had no idea she was committing crimes daily.

Bongiorno's unfailing obedience to authority, and the shifting of responsibility for 40 years of this unfailing obedience, is hardly surprising given Stanley Milgram's innovative and revelatory research discussed in Chapter 2. One would expect her to try to evade responsibility for centrality in Madoff's con, at least when this served her purposes. She had little interest in acknowledging what was so evident to others, that her decades of work at BLMIS had entangled her in the Madoff con and that by arranging for her to accumulate tens of million of dollars in her IA accounts, Madoff was well aware of this even if she hoped to deny it.

Twenty-five years after Milgram completed his initial research on the psychology of authority, two other social psychologists, Herbert C. Kelman and V. Lee Hamilton, building on Milgram's findings and insights, examined why so many people participate in behavior harmful to others, why so many participate so readily in "crimes of obedience."[4] They examine in detail how and why people react to the expectations of authorities even when they go beyond the bounds of morality or law. Two of the three social processes Kelman and Hamilton identify, relevant for understanding the Madoff con, that create the conditions by which moral inhibitions against harming others are weakened are *authorization* and *routinization*.[5]

Authorization and Routinization

An explanation for the criminal activity of Bongiorno and her BLMIS backstage colleagues that essentially relies on their psychological make-up or dispositions would surely be inadequate. It is unlikely that as they were growing up, there was a cluster of experiences that pointed them to white collar criminal careers. The answer as to why the usual moral restraints that prevent most individuals from rushing into white collar crime would seem to be more sociological than psychological, although it is possible the psychology of individuals might suggest who most readily would be a candidate to pursue a white collar criminal career.

To explain the criminal activities at BLMIS, it might be best to look at two processes isolated by Kelman and Hamilton under which the usual moral inhibitions against stealing become weakened—how these white collar crimes become possible—authorization and routinization.

Kelman and Hamilton are fully aware that "authorization processes in crimes of obedience must be understood in the context of authority in general. Legitimate authority creates the *obligation* to follow rules, regardless of personal preferences or interests: Without this obligation it is difficult to maintain a dependable and equitable social order. Crimes of obedience ... become possible when individual abandon personal responsibility for actions taken under superior orders, continuing to obey when they ought to be disobeying."[6]

With authorization, the situation is unequivocally defined so that the individual is absolved of the responsibility of having to make a moral choice. White collar crime had become part of the culture on the 17th floor of BLMIS. Creating false documents or lying or helping others avoid paying taxes was expected and encouraged. These had become commonplace. It was known that Bernard Madoff ordered employees to commit crimes. The readiness to do so in such an environment was greatly enhanced. This alone carried automatic justification to do what so many others were doing—creating false documents or lying or helping others avoid paying taxes. It was not necessary to make judgments or choices. Part of one's job was to do what one was told to do, and to do it well. Not only did normal moral principles become inoperative, but the morality that is part of the duty to obey superiors became ascendant. As long as they accepted the legitimacy of those they worked for, employees feel obliged to obey orders. Personal preferences could be left at home or abandoned.

Moreover, with authorization in play, employees may not see themselves as personally responsible for the consequences of their actions. They are able to rationalize to themselves that because they were not personal agents, but simply extensions of the authority, they had no choice in doing what they did, and it was not necessary to feel responsible to those who were duped. Beyond the obligatory and formal statements, perhaps in many cases dictated by their attorneys, made in court, they seemed relatively free of guilt.

Authorization processes created a situation in which individuals became involved in activities without making a decision and without considering implications. After the initial step, once the threshold was crossed, the pressures to continue were powerful. In fact, that which may have inhibited individuals from following a path into white collar crime may have led to deeper involvement in efforts to justify their crimes and to avoid negative consequences.

With routinization, activities are so organized that raising ethical questions seem inappropriate. The work of the backstage accomplices at BLMIS became routine, mechanical—programmed. There was little opportunity for raising any questions when one is occupied daily backdating stock prices, fabricating records, and manufacturing monthly statements. It became less imperative to make decisions, minimizing the occasions in which questions, moral and otherwise, might arise. Moreover, focusing on the details of various tasks that needed to be completed—"it is all in a day's work"—it was relatively easy to avoid thinking about the implications of what one was doing. The details of the job became paramount.

> Routinization operates both at the level of the individual actor and at the organizational level. Individual job performance is broken down into a series of discrete steps, most of them carried out in automatic, regularized fashion. It becomes easy to forget the nature of the product that emerges from the process . . . . Organizationally, the task is divided among different offices, each of which has responsibility for a small portion of it. This arrangement diffuses responsibility and limits the amount and scope of decision making that is necessary. There is no expectation that the moral implications will be considered at any of these points, nor is there any opportunity to do so. The organizational processes also help further legitimize the actions of each participant. By proceeding in routine fashion—processing papers, exchanging memos, diligently carrying out assigned tasks—the different units mutually reinforce each other in the view that what is going on must be perfectly normal, correct, and legitimate. The shared illusion that they are engaged in a legitimate enterprise helps the participants assimilate their activities to

other purposes, such as the efficiency of performance, the productivity of their unit, or the cohesiveness of their group.[7]

This theoretical passage from Kelman and Hamilton is a perfect description of what went on backstage at BLMIS.

Next, Chapter 6 looks at how other employees at BLMIS worked to further Madoff's crime. The material examined enables us to reach a new level of understanding of the thinking and actions of those perpetrating a con game, or at least the Madoff con game. Most striking is the disregard by participants in the criminal activity for the truth and for most anyone outside their circle other than family and those clients that Madoff directed them to enrich.

CHAPTER 6

Madoff and the 17th Floor Ensemble

This chapter looks at more of the activities of the BLMIS IA employees who were Madoff's accomplices. Not surprisingly, deception was rampant at the BLMIS IA business, where criminal activity continued for decades. An examination of other con games clearly shows that pretending, misrepresenting, and dissembling were hardly unique to Madoff's con.

Once the Madoff con game was set in motion, it steadily gained enough momentum to continue without end. There was little to prevent it from running smoothly in perpetuity, that is, as long as the United States and much of the developed world economies remained vibrant. However, with regularity, economies sputter. When they do, con games often sputter. Even greatly increasing the layering of secrecy and deception necessary to keep a con game flourishing cannot make it otherwise, regardless of the dauntlessness of the inside man, outside men, ropers, and others backstage working the con.

Getting Started

It has not been, and perhaps never will be, established when the Madoff con game began. Some evidence suggests that it was under way in the 1960s, not long after Madoff began trading securities. It is known that in 1962 he had hidden losses from clients after he had invested too much of their money in risky stocks. Then he inflated profits to enhance his reputation as a sure-footed and high-reaching young investor, someone whose future seemed especially promising. Yet, these suspect actions are just as much a sign of what he might do at some future time than a clear indication of an embryonic con man.

There is more evidence that indicates that Madoff's big con began somewhat later, in the early 1970s, when BLMIS purportedly began using its widely touted arbitrage strategy, a strategy that seeks to profit from pricing errors in the stock market, for its IA client accounts. It is likely that as an eager but not particularly talented or lucky investor, Madoff probably blundered into his con. It would appear that not as an investor, but as a con man, Madoff turned out to be very lucky; regulators who might have exposed him were unlucky, unskilled, or clearly not much interested in discovering if he was operating within or outside of the ambiguous rules of Wall Street.

There was nothing exceptional about Madoff. The origins of his con were likely colorless, although in the end his con turned out to be considerably more florid. He was not in the mold of the imaginative and self-possessed Victor Lustig sitting in the sidewalk cafes of Paris carefully planning how to get a bid from a nouveaux riche French businessman to buy the Eiffel Tower. (Lustig not only received and cashed a certified check for one-fourth of a businessman's offering price for the landmark, but also received a bribe of thousands of francs.) Most big cons involve preparation and rehearsal. The evidence suggests that, unlike the clever Victor Lustig, Madoff largely stumbled into his career as a con man, and learned to prepare and rehearse over the years, becoming somewhat skilled with practice.

However Madoff's con got started, the arbitrage trades almost from the beginning were most likely a fiction; there is no reliable record that actual IA trades were made or executed by BLMIS in the early 1970s. Instead, at Madoff's direction, some of his employees were given the responsibility of creating fake, back-dated documents. During the later years at BLMIS, these employees were located on the 17th floor largely out of sight from most of Madoff's other employees. The back-dated materials were then passed on to other 17th floor employees, enabling them to create documents reflecting the fictitious trades, which were in turn used to deceive clients, and also regulators. A paper trail of false trade confirmation slips and erroneous entries on account statements worked to create an appearance of trading, of nearly uninterrupted profitable trading. Given his growing reputation as an uncanny investor, it is hardly surprising how readily Madoff began to play the role of a financial wizard, sagacious in all matters, noticeably imperious.

At a minimum, for at least two decades, Madoff's con was made possible by a limited circle of 17th floor employees. Yet, those who helped him were more than simply "company men (or women)," individuals who put their allegiance to Madoff or BLMIS above all else. Many were reasonably well rewarded for their assistance, accumulating a great deal more money and possessions than routinely come to office workers.[1] Using the money Madoff was stealing and passing to them enabled them also to live the American Dream. They did not need inherited money or privilege or an academic credential given by some joint-degree program from the Wharton School. All each needed was to be an unquestioning functionary in a con game. Deceived by others or by themselves, many had become convinced that what they were doing was at most simply bending the rules. It was not even clear that anyone was being harmed by their legerdemain.

By the early 1990s, Madoff's IA business was marketed by assuring clients and perspective clients that his then investment strategy—a split-strike options strategy—which involved buying a basket of stocks and writing call options (the right to buy securities at a specified price) against those stocks, and then using the proceeds from the call options to purchase put options (the right to sell securities at a specified price), was fail-safe. By purchasing options and not the stocks themselves, investors would be placing less money at risk in betting that stock prices would rise or that they would fall. His clients apparently did not believe there was any risk in placing money in Madoff's hands.

With the BLMIS investment strategy, clients were promised that their funds would be invested in between 35 and 50 common stocks selected from the Standard & Poor's (S&P) 100 Index—the expectation being that the price movement of these stocks would fairly closely reflect the price movement of the larger number of stocks in the S&P 100 Index. Some victims were told that money not invested in stocks would be temporarily invested in money-market accounts or government-issued securities. The funds would be hedged—an investment made as a balance against the risk of another investment—a strategy intended to offset substantial losses caused by unpredictable fluctuations in stock prices. It was up to Madoff, who was steadily gaining a reputation as a highly skilled investor, to time with great accuracy the buying and selling of his clients' investments, ignoring one of the oldest stock market adages: "Never try to time the market; it can't be done. Winners invest for the long run." Of course, some storied investors have made fortunes timing the market. Madoff's IA account holder found out too late that he was not one of them.

Because Madoff was not actually investing the money of BLMIS IA customers—individuals, charitable organizations, trusts, pension funds, master funds, feeder funds, hedge funds, family, friends, and even those assisting him in his con—whose money was in his own bank account, he essentially never lost; he always appeared to be successful. Madoff proved to be as successful as horseplayers able to pick winners after races had been run. The purported trades he was reporting were priced from market activity that had occurred from a day to months prior to when his backdated documents reported they had been completed. This gave him the benefit of hindsight for what was believed by his investors to be his flawless timing in buying and selling stocks and bonds. Consequently, month in and month out he was in a position to guarantee IA clients that he had at least achieved their expected returns, for most accounts between 10 and 17 percent a year. He appeared, with his technique of hedging, to be proving the adage about trying to time the market decidedly false, at least for someone as skilled as he had consistently shown himself to be; he was proving himself nearly flawless in his ability to time the market. Year after year, Madoff's IA investors saw their accounts steadily grow; some withdrew money to purchase a new home or to pay college tuition for grandchildren or to live more comfortably in retirement than they had anticipated. Happy about their good luck and Madoff's great skill as an investor, others simply watched their investments effervesce.

For the chief counsel to the SIPC trustee, it was "the lack of transparency," which too few had misgivings about, that enabled Madoff to succeed for so long: "For years and years, people [were] saying to Bernie Madoff: 'Who are the counterparties on all those options you're taking out?' Bernie told them that it was part of the secret sauce; he couldn't give that out." Working in the shade made it much easier for Madoff to continue his con: "He [Madoff] literally would talk to customers and say: 'What are you looking for?' and they would say: 'Eighteen percent'—and he would say: 'You got it.' 'Excuse me,' you wouldn't stop and say: 'How can you guarantee that?' But he did, because he didn't have any investments to worry about. You don't worry about it if you don't have to . . . . Bernie did the market three days from now; he created it." Although oversimplified and slightly exaggerated, as much of what came out of the SIPC's trustees fog machine, this portrait fairly well describes the BLMIS IA operation.

Still, as part of the smoke screen, it was imperative for BLMIS employees to constantly prepare assorted models of baskets of stocks. Information such as the value of each stock included in a basket was fed into a BLMIS computer dedicated to the IA business, multiples of the baskets were then allocated, and clients' accounts were altered on a prorated basis, reflecting what clients were then told were their returns. The clients were never disappointed with their returns. Small investors paid taxes on the funds they withdrew; if they chose to do so, larger investors had to hire more accountants and attorneys to find new tax dodges.

The incontrovertible picture of Madoff as a successful investor, a Wall Street genius, was, of course, completely false. He was nimbly able to steal and spend other people's money, but in fact he was not able to make any money as an investor. He was surely not a successor to the storied titans of Wall Street—Jay Gould, J. P. Morgan, or Cornelius Vanderbilt. Nor was Madoff a successor to the fabled nineteenth- and twentieth-century prominent Jewish financiers, Jacob H. Schiff, Bernard Baruch, or any of the numerous Warburgs. However, he fairly closely resembled the early-twentieth-century financier and market-insider-turned embezzler Richard Whitney, with an added advantage of having access to a computer and fairly competent computer programmers who blindly or half-blindly worked alongside of Madoff cheating clients and unhesitatingly spending the scraps passed to them.

After Madoff was caught, his most noteworthy characteristic—that of a bullying, narcissistic materialist with a greatly diminished sense of the truth and with expensive tastes—finally became evident to many of his clients, a number of whom had been fooled, or claimed to have been fooled, for decades.

Some of Madoff's defrauded former clients, single-mindedly intent on recovering their losses, still believing there were millions of dollars hidden away, did not understand, even after he had been sent to prison, that they were enveloped in a con game, that it was all pretense. He had simply taken their money; spent some, shared some with family, friends, and those who helped him perpetrate his con; and given the rest back to those investors who asked for it to purchase a new home or to pay college tuition for grandchildren or to live more comfortably in retirement than anticipated. He gave some to charities; this was surely a nice touch, as there was no better way to burnish one's prominence and acquire new clients. Given the extensiveness of his con and the number of individuals whose lives he upended, it is difficult to believe that Madoff was an altruist, deeply concerned with bettering the lives of others.

A surprisingly number of investors were unable to understand or to reconcile themselves to the fact that BLMIS's IA business did not make money from investing and that there was less of it at the end of the con than what Madoff had gathered up. Where had it gone? Some had been spent on manicures and at auction houses; some had been spent on basics such as redemptions and inflated salaries for 17th floor employees so that the pretense could continue undetected; some that had been given away could not be readily retrieved and recovered. Many victims failed to comprehend that the figures reported on their statements were fabricated. The figures did not reflect gains that had been made from investing. The money given to Madoff was not invested and could never grow. Over the years, the total could only get smaller, and it did get smaller. Some victims insisted that billions more existed because they had been repeatedly told, by Madoff before his con imploded and then by the media after he was arrested. Madoff told the FBI agent who came to his door to arrest him that the amount he had stolen was $50 billion; the media reported it was a little under $65 billion. The larger the number, the larger than life Madoff appeared to be. The amount stolen was seen as an indicator of how gifted Madoff was as a con man rather than a measure of how many foolish or unlucky investors handed their money over to him. Actually, if the larger figures were true, Madoff would have been managing more money than JPMorgan Chase Bank or Goldman Sachs. It was not enough to be an outsized thief; being a fabled one was much more satisfying to Madoff and the media and, apparently, to his victims.

It is not uncommon for victims of a con game to be the last to realize that they had been living in a world of make-believe. In one egregious example of mass delusion, a large number of the over 70,000 victims defrauded by Oscar Hartzell—who perpetrated the Drake Estate swindle, a scheme to recover the nonexistent riches of the sixteenth-century English naval hero and explorer Sir Francis Drake—remained or were turned into his allies well after his fraud was exposed.[2] Hartzell and his outside men continued to bilk them even after he had been deported from England and arrested in the United States. Together Hartzell and his team were able to convince thousands of victims that government officials were conspiring not only to persecute Hartzell but to cheat them—his investors—as well. The government, they were told and believed, had become their adversaries; it was government interference that was responsible for their being deprived of what was justly theirs—the Drake Estate billions that they were convinced were almost within Hartzell's reach.

Hartzell's con first began in the Midwest after World War I and continued through the 1920s after he settled abroad so that—he told his investors—he could more easily access the Drake fortune and work closely with the courts to have the Drake estate returned to its rightful heir, Colonel Drexel Drake, his fictitious creation.

Hartzell's victims were roped into his con game with his fiction that he had uncovered proof that Sir Francis Drake had an illegitimate son who had been jailed in order to avoid scandal and that he had found Drake's true heir and was in contact with him.

From England Hartzell had extensive correspondence with his outside men in the Midwest—as well as with many of his victims those he was defrauding—detailing the progress he was steadily making and the great expenses he was incurring in his efforts to wrest the fortune from the British government and others involved in the intrigue to illegally hold on to it. A constant theme was how daunting problem it was to raise money to underwrite the legal fight against, among others, the "Secret Courts of England," to restore Drake's legal heir to his rightful place.

Hartzell initially estimated that the value of the estate had grown over the centuries to $22 billion; he then claimed it had increased well beyond that amount.[3] His letters and cables describing the sinister forces he was facing, and the need to mount and continue an expensive legal battle in order to claim the inheritance, brought him at least $150,000 annually for more than a decade. Over the years, he defrauded his investors of approximately $2,000,000. The Hartzell con was made easier by the fact that the faithful signed papers promising "silence, secrecy, and non-disturbance."

Hartzell promised that for every $1 he was able to borrow that would enable him to pursue his and his investors' quest, $500 would be repaid after his efforts were successful, which, he continuously promised, would be imminent. Some individuals mortgaged their homes or farms in order to invest. (In the case of the Madoff victims, they mortgaged homes or condominiums.) The Drake donors not only had an opportunity for a financial windfall, but were being given an up-close glimpse of the global world of conspiracy and skullduggery with cloak-and-dagger agents—a great drama.

Iowa's attorney general, who denounced what Hartzell had been doing as a fraud, was in turn denounced, swamped by letters from thousands of irate investors demanding that he remain silent and end his attacks on the obviously beleaguered Hartzell so as not to undercut what he had already intrepidly accomplished for many Americans against great odds in his years he had sacrificed in England. After Hartzell's arrest, investors set up a defense fund for him to underwrite bail and legal expenses. "Hartzell got $15,000 to send to lawyers in England, $68,000 for his bond, $50,000 for his personal use plus

$2,500 a week [until] the date he claimed the estate would be settled."[4] Some of the duped called to give evidence at his trial refused to break a pledge to remain silent in fear that when the Drake fortune was returned to the rightful heir, they would not be given their promised shares; others insisted that Hartzell had done nothing dishonest, that he had not broken any laws. Many politicians who had remained silent before and after the Hartzell con became public were deluged with demands that the government's persecution of him end. Reinforced by cult-like meetings urging them not to break ranks or their silence, nothing could dampen the conviction of a strikingly large number of Hartzell's investors that he was actually the victim of a vindictive government. They had become ensnared by their own dreams.

When Hartzell was sent to prison, the protest continued, "and in the eighteen months [after] Hartzell's conviction, at least $350,000 had been contributed to [those continuing the con]"[5] victims not wavering from the rock-solid belief that he and the still-not-publicly-acknowledged Drake heir were the real victims of a plot.

Likewise, after Charles Ponzi's assurance of quick riches from his expansive investment scheme fell apart in 1920 and he was arrested and charged with 86 counts of mail fraud, some investors continued to hold fast to their belief that he had discovered the secret to abundant wealth for all, that he would be able to make good on his promise. As his biographer wrote: "Still others refused to give up. 'You bet he's all right,' said one man in a North End [Boston] grocery store."

There are, as would be expected, many similarities between these earlier con games and Madoff's. Some Madoff victims and employees—surely less impaired than those who readily gave money to Hartzell and could not be dissuaded that there was no, and had never been, Drake billions—were nonetheless as closely tethered to the pretense that enveloped them as to reality. They (as was the case with Ponzi's investors) continued to believe that they were merely part of an audience, not dramatis personae. As a result, nearly as many bilked Madoff investors directed their anger at government regulatory agencies—for not overtaking Madoff before his con became massive—as at him for the theft of their money. Here is yet another parallel between the Hartzell con and the Madoff con.

More on Deception

With unremitting deception, con men build a fantasy world that those inside have great difficulty detecting and breaking loose from, and this is true of all cons. Victims who were at first deceived become deluded. Those who deceive also become deluded.

Deception is at the heart of all con games. Like a haze it is engulfing, enveloping. The world is not always what it seems to be or what it is said to be. This is surely the case inside a con game.

Two of the more widely read biographies of Bernard Madoff written in the wake of his arrest and conviction use the word "lies" in their titles, *The Wizard of Lies* by Diana B. Henriques and *Betrayal: The Life and Lies of Bernie Madoff* by Andrew Kirtzman.[6] Obviously, Madoff often lied; in fact, as these two biographies make apparent, his entire life was a lie. In light of a greater penchant to deceive others than most individuals, it is hardly surprising that he was untruthful even to those actively engaged in helping him to further his crime. This would be expected, however, as con men routinely deceive their closest accomplices.

For example, as a first step to convince a British banknote printing contactor to manufacture Portuguese currency for him, it was necessary for the con man "who stole Portugal" with "a crime for which in the ingenuity and audacity of its conception it would be difficult to find a parallel," Artur Alves Reis, to provide an authorization for such an unusual request from the Banco de Portugal. He, of course, had to forge the document, a fact he kept from the "men he had selected to help him in his great scheme." What has been accepted as the most accurate account of this truly original twentieth-century con describes the first stage of Alves Reis's artifice.

> That night after his employees left Alves got the signatures—by tracing them. He appended the signatures of Francisco da Cunha Rego Chaves, the High Commissioner of Angola; Daniel Rodriguez, the Minister of Finance; and Delfim Costa, a technical representative of the Angola government. He didn't have to worry how accurate the forgeries were—after all, the consular stamps would vouch for their authenticity. He carefully cut off the two pages of notarization from the original *papel selado* and bound it with the new one with tape and sealing wax. On the soft wax he carefully pressed a signet ring with the Portuguese coat of arms. Then as a final touch he appended two new Portuguese banknotes—one for 1,000 escudos (then about $50) and another for 500 escudos. Presumably these were the banknotes that the agreement would permit the [truly nonexistent] international financial group to have duplicated in return for its loan of $5,000,000 to poor Angola.

Now Alves Reis was ready to present the impressive contract to [his accomplices who] had been patiently awaiting a look at the magic contract Alves Reis had been talking about for several weeks.

As he drove to the Avenida Palace [Hotel], Alves Reis rehearsed his little talk about how difficult it had been to secure the contract from the government, how few were in on the secret, [and] how confidential everything must be kept. A pity, he mused, he couldn't tell them how clever he had been in preparing the contract for unless they believed the contract was genuine he would not be able to get their cooperation.[7]

Oscar Hartzell also deceived those with whom he worked as readily as those from whom he stole. In a letter to the Des Moines attorney handling his legal affairs, Hartzell described the process of presenting his genealogy confirming Colonel Dexter Drake as the rightful heir to the baronetcy and, therefore, the Drake Estate, to the King & Crown's Commission, although neither Colonel Dexter Drake nor the King & Crown's Commission existed. Moreover, he had never made such an application to any court. In another letter, he promised the attorney that the British government would be delivering the Drake Estate money in the summer after an audit was completed. Among other things, this involved assessing the value of gems, adding the value of numerous properties, transferring titles, counting every gold coin, and even figuring the value of "all rock quarries, brickyards, pottery clay, mineral ores, such as tin, etc., fishing rights in rivers, income off railroad land, and all rents from properties, which have been accumulating all these years."[8]

Moreover, here is how his friend Alma Shepard, an "apostle," describes what ended as a contentious encounter she and Hartzell had during her visit to London: "But he wouldn't show me what I wanted to see—Colonel Drake. Nor did he show me any evidence that there was a Drake Estate. He did take me into the vaults of the Bank of England and showed me big bags, like potato sacks, filled with coins, which, he said, were Spanish doubloons and pieces-of-eight which Drake had captured and that belonged to the Drake Estate."

The fact that inside men can be less than forthright with shills, backup men, outside men, those backstage, or ropers lends some credence to the assertions of many who worked to further Madoff's con that they were not fully aware of what he was up to.

Jerome O'Hara and George Perez

Jerome O'Hara and George Perez were the two technicians who developed and maintained programs for the House 17 computer used to create the false and fraudulent books, records, and monthly statements for BLMIS's IA business. According to an FBI agent in a sealed Complaint, here are some specifics of how O'Hara and Perez went about their work:

> For split-strike clients: (i) information about a basket of purported trades (purchases when entering the market, and sales when exiting) was entered into House 17 and was used to generate data-reflecting purported trades; (ii) the data describing the purported trades was stored in several files including the "Settled Trade File"; (iii) trade data and other information stored on House 17 was merged with information contained in a file titled "A. Name File," which contained certain information on an account-by-account basis about all of the IA clients, including, but not limited to, its unique BLMIS account number, in whose name the account was held and the mailing address to which account statements and other documents were to be sent; (iv) the merged information was formatted for presentation on BLMIS account statements and confirmation slips; and (v) account statements and confirmation slips were printed and distributed to IA clients, primarily through the U.S. mails.
>
> For non-split-strike clients, the process was similar. However, because basket trades generally were not executed for those clients, all trades were individually entered into House 17 based on instruction provided by BLMIS employees on an account-by-account basis.
>
> . . .
>
> Beginning at least as early as in or about January 2004 . . ., Madoff and DiPascali directed O'Hara and Perez to further falsify BLMIS's books and records. Madoff's goals . . . were to among other things: (a) reveal information about as few of BLMIS's IA clients as possible, thereby concealing the scale of the business; (b) present explanations of BLMIS's operations that would make it more difficult for the SEC . . . to corroborate with third parties the information provided by BLMIS; and (c) produce documents containing detailed information that appeared to be genuine and from which no unrealistic looking patterns could easily be detected.

In an effort to achieve those goals, Madoff: ... (iii) ... directed DiPascali, and through DiPascali, O'Hara and Perez, to create, retrospectively, different "special" versions of historical BLMIS books and records to meet the actual and/or anticipated requests of the SEC ... ; and (iv) directed DiPascali, and through DiPascali, O'Hara and Perez, to create false documents purportedly obtained from third parties in the ordinary course of BLMIS's business.

In connection with this further deception, O'Hara and Perez ... developed and maintained special House 17 programs that, among other things, retrospectively: (i) created new sets of historical BLMIS books and records for certain subsets of IA clients; (ii) changed information about the identities of IA clients; (iii) added trading counterparties to historical transactions, and changed the identities of those counterparties depending on whether the books and records were being prepared for the SEC (in which case the counterparties were randomly selected from a list of European financial firms) or [others, Europeans] (in which case the counterparties were randomly selected from US financial firms); (iv) created new versions of client account statements designed to mislead the SEC about whether BLMIS had custody of IA clients' assets; (v) incorporated randomization algorithms to create fake records reflecting securities transactions that appeared to be realistic in terms of their size and timing; (vi) generated documents that looked like the output of reliable third parties such as DTC.[9]

In sum, and in addition, to all of this, O'Hara and Perez:

Changed the Identities of Certain IA Clients on the Special Blotters;
Changed Details about the Number of Shares, Execution Times, and Transaction Numbers for Trades Reported on the Special Blotters;
Changed the Counterparties on the Special Blotters;
Created False and Fraudulent Order Entry and Execution Reports;
[O'Hara] Created False and Fraudulent Records about BLMIS Commissions;
Created False and Fraudulent IA Client Account Statements;
Created False and Fraudulent DTC Reports;

Created False and Fraudulent London Stock Exchange Trade Reporting Files[10]

According to the FBI sealed Complaint, in April 2006, after working for BLMIS for almost 16 years, O'Hara closed his BLMIS IA accounts "in which he had an interest and received nearly $1 million," and Perez, after working for BLMIS for almost 15 years, closed a BLMIS IA account "in which he had an interest and received approximately $289,000." And, according to government investigators, in November 2006, both received one-time net bonuses of "more than approximately $60,000." In addition, both "received pay increases of approximately 25 percent at or about the same time."[11]

Madoff as Top Banana

Madoff set the tone of deception at BLMIS. He would endlessly strut and preen about the 17th floor like a matinee idol boasting and dissembling. Court testimony exemplifies his continuous performance.

Q: All right. And you held this belief that everybody someday was going to get their money back because Mr. Madoff consistently lied to you about the extent of his assets and holdings; did he not?

A: He did.

Q: And you believed those lies, did you not?

A: I did.

Q: All right. You—He told you that he was a multi-billionaire, in essence?

A: He led me along so that that would be the conclusion that I would draw, yes.

Q: He led you to believe, in a lot different ways, that he had the assets to pay everyone?

A: Yes.

Q: And one of the ways I think you testified to was leaving, various fancy prospectuses and documents on his couch so that people would walk in and think about all the money that he had?

A: My understanding is, or my belief at this date, that that was left there for my personal use.

Q: And he also told you about what a bigshot he was, for lack of a better term; how he owned PJ Clarke's, for instance?

A: Yes.

Q: Things like that?

A: Things like that.

Q: And PJ Clarke's, it's a hamburger place that was right next to the Lipstick Building?

A: It was 55th Street and 3rd.

Q: In fact, Mr. Madoff told you that the returns he was paying his customers was the cost of him getting the use of their capital, right?

A: That was what I understood the concept to be, yes.

Q: That he was taking the IA money in and investing it in other, better investments, correct?

A: That was my understanding.

Q: That was making—that were making more than 15% right?

A: In essence, yes.

. . .

Q: So whatever the customer return was, Bernie was making more?

A: That's what I was led to believe.

Q: And you did believe it?

A: I did.

Q: All right. Did you believe that he was really doing these IA customers a favor by taking their money?

A: At times, yes.

Q: Right. Because he was sharing these amazing returns with them and taking less, as a result, yes?

A: I found the whole thing to—at the time, to be remarkably advantageous to all sides, yes.

Q: A win-win?

A: A win-win.

. . .

Q: Did he ever tell you, in word or in essence, that the trading room at BLMIS was just one piece?

A: Oh, yes.

Q: And by that, you took it just one piece of all the other things that he owned?

A: Of a complex puzzle of investments, yes.

Q: Of a complex financial empire that he owned?

A: That's what he was trying to portray, yes.

Q: And you believed him?

A: I did.

Q: Did he ever tell you that he had, and I'm quoting, a "lot of plates" he was working from?

A: Yes.

Q: And by that, did you understand that he was again talking about all his wide and varied holdings across not only the country but across the world?

A: That is correct.

Q: Did he ever tell you he owned a bank in France?

A: He did.

Q: That he had different kinds of partnerships and limited partnerships and investments all across the globe?

A: He did.

...

Q: Did he ever tell you he had interests with somebody named Donnie Rechler?

A: Yes. My understanding of Mr. Rechler's business was that he was a major player in the Long Island real estate market.

Q: And Mr. Madoff told you he was in business with Mr. Rechler?

A: Often.

Q: And he told you also that he was in business with Carl Shapiro?

A: Yes.

Q: Tell us who Mr. Shapiro is?

A: He's about a hundred years old today, and he is or was the chairman of a company called Kay Windsor.

Q: So you understood that he's a billionaire?

A: That is my understanding.

Q: All right. And these things that Mr. Madoff said about his financial empire, he didn't just tell you these things, did he?

A: He often said some of things out loud.

Q: On the 17th floor?

A: And other places.

Q: But on the 17th floor?

A: Yes.

Q: In front of staff?

A: Yes.

Q: And Ms. Crupi?

A: Yes.

Q: Did Mr. Madoff ever tell you that he had access to other banks in Europe?

A: Yes.

Q: That he traded in all kinds of foreign currencies?
A: Yes.
Q: That he owned real estate in Europe, Florida, and New York?
A: Yes.
      . . .
Q: You heard him say them within general earshot of others at the company from time to time.
A: He often boasted in public, about his holdings; but he did do that.
Q: Okay. But he would generally boast about his holdings, without asking you for a specific date?
A: Yeah, yes.
Q: Okay. Did you ever hear Mr. Madoff say in public, within the earshot of others, words to the effect of: "We hit a home run today?"
A: Yes.
Q: What did that mean?
A: Some investment he had paid handsomely.
Q: And that statement was made in a public area at the office?
A: I never recall him sitting me down and closing the door and say: "Frank, I hit a home run today." So the answer would be generally, yes.
      . . .
Q: Did you, at any time, tell Ms. Crupi about all the big deals that BLMIS was supposedly doing in Europe?
A: I did.
Q: And you told her this, and were you present when Mr. Madoff told her, more or less, the same thing?
A: Yes.
Q: Because I think as we discussed, Mr. Madoff regularly would sort of walk around the office and announce bits of corporate news to no one in particular?
A: Correct.
Q: That was just a habit he had, for whatever reason he did it?
A: Yes.
Q: Do you believe that Mr. Madoff did this because he was trying to create a certain impression about the IA business among the employees on the 17th floor?
A: Yes.
      . . .

Q: Okay. Thank you. Now, did you ever have a conversation with Ms. Crupi about why it was all right for her to backdate trades and find prices for today's trades in yesterday's newspapers?

A: Yes.

Q: And you told her it was all right, did you not, because the trades were happening in the trading room upstairs?

A: In substance, yes.

Q: Or sometimes you told her they were happening in Europe?

A: Yes.

Q: And did you or someone also tell Ms. Crupi that Madoff did 20% of the volume in the markets on any given day?

A: Not necessarily by me, yes.[12]

Madoff's grandiosity seems for the most part successful. And he surely enjoyed performing. He clearly did not know or chose not to live by Spinoza's proverb that "the world would be happier if men had the same capacity to be silent that they had to speak."

Madoff's Deception

The following seven excerpts from Frank DiPascali's statements to the FBI capture Madoff's deception, his repeated attempts to intimidate his two 17th floor computer programmers, George Perez and Jerome O'Hara. There are also examples of how he worked to deceive two other employees, Annette Bongiorno and Jo Ann Crupi, both of whom managed IA customer accounts in addition to creating false documents. The excerpts also again show that Madoff was eager to deceive others who happened to be within earshot; he was also happy and eager to perform even when not required. Perhaps he was simply rehearsing.

Lies: Seven Examples of Madoff's Deception

According to DiPascali, Madoff never strayed from the paramount falsehood that his IA business was busy investing and making money.

1. Volume [of trading] was not an issue because Madoff told people he was doing the trading in Europe and trading was not included in the domestic exchanges.

2. ... Perez, O'Hara, DiPascali, and Madoff met in Madoff's office.

During the meeting DiPascali sat on the couch, Madoff sat at his desk, and Perez and O'Hara sat in the chairs. Perez and O'Hara told Madoff that what he was doing was illegal and if he closed the [illegal] accounts they would continue to work for him . . . . Madoff raised his voice and told Perez and O'Hara that closing the accounts would never happen and asked them who they thought they were telling him how to run his business. Madoff gave the impression he was not doing anything wrong.

(Another recounting of this meeting adds: "Madoff began by politely reminding them that he been doing this for forty years, that they were computer programmers, for an obsolete system no less, and they did not understand what they were talking about. Madoff then went off into an array of tangential stories about his experiences in the industry, including how he had written most of the rules." A third account of the encounter states: "Madoff did not try to refute their points directly, but instead he tried to bully them into believing there was nothing wrong with the way he was doing business.")

3. O'Hara and Perez confronted Madoff in Daniel Bonventre's office in the presence of DiPascali. Madoff told O'Hara and Perez: "You don't see trades. Trades occur overseas." Madoff then said: "You are not going to tell me how to run my business."[13]

4. DiPascali surmised that Madoff may have fed [Jo Ann] Crupi the same tidbits of information that Madoff had fed to him over the years, giving both of them the impression that Madoff had things under control. Crupi had convinced herself over the years that Madoff had a vast array of assets all over the world to cover his billions of dollars of "liabilities" that were in fact his customers' investment accounts.

5. When Crupi first began to work with [DiPascali] doing IA related projects, [DiPascali] repeated stories to her that he had heard from Madoff. Over the years, Crupi heard of big deals Madoff had just made in Europe many times. She also heard these things from Madoff himself, as he liked to announce such things to no one in particular when on the 17th floor. These stories were part of an overall impression Madoff was giving to his IA employees. He was trying to plant seeds in their minds and let their imaginations fill in the details about the nature of the IA business and how it was run. He wanted to convince them the IA business, despite its noticeable "irregularities," was somehow okay because it was backed up by Madoff's vast worldwide assets.

6. Since DiPascali started working for Madoff, [he] heard Madoff tell Bongiorno about deals he had going on in Europe ... . Madoff made statements aloud in front of Bongiorno and the others in the small room where they all worked in the early days of the firm at 110 Wall Street. Madoff would say aloud things like: "Hey, did you know we do 21% of the NASDAQ volume in a day?" Madoff was planting the seeds in Bongiorno's head to help her legitimize the rules [e.g., "never pretend to trade more than 20% of the volume of NASDAQ for the day"] she had been given by him.

7. In the early 1970s and through the early 1980s ... Madoff would very vocally proclaim he had just achieved great financial success with a deal he had been arranging in Europe or somewhere else overseas .... [DiPascali] eventually realized those pronouncements were calculated ... [to allow listeners] to draw their own conclusion: the idea that Madoff's IA trading activity was somehow backed up by his deals and investments overseas.

To be sure, fooling employees was important for Madoff to continue his fraud undetected, but even more critical was that his primary audience of clients and regulators had no reason to doubt the immensity of his pretense. Two and a half years after Madoff's arrest, Cotellessa-Pitz told the FBI:

Approximately a day after Madoff's arrest, [she] and Bongiorno had a conversation in Bongiorno's office on the 17th floor regarding where they believed trades for the IA business were executed. At that time, [she] and Bongiorno were both devastated at the news of Madoff's arrest. [She] told Bongiorno she believed the trades were executed overseas. Bongiorno seemed surprised at [Cotellessa-Pitz's] statement. Bongiorno told [Cotellessa-Pitz] she believed the trades were executed upstairs in the trading room. Bongiorno incredulously asked why the trades would be executed overseas if they had a trading room upstairs. Bongiorno then stated that if she and [Cotellessa-Pitz] had talked more about their work and had not been so concerned about confidentiality, they could have "blown the lid off the whole thing." ...

On one occasion after Madoff's arrest, David Kugel came into [Cotellessa-Pitz's] office to "shoot the breeze," and they also discussed where they believed the IA trades were executed. Kugel said he believed the IA trades were executed overseas, which matched [Cotellessa-Pitz's] view. This view was also held by Bonventre, Crupi, Margaret Gavlik, and Ed Coughlin. [Cotellessa-Pitz] gathered this information from different conversations she had with these individuals.

Given the culture of crime and deception centered on the 17th floor of BLMIS, it is hardly surprising that others knee deep in the quagmire also showed a great capacity for deception. DiPascali, himself, seemed particularly active as a conjuror. On the 15 different days between April 16, 2009, and February 16, 2012, in which he met with investigators attempting to untangle the Madoff fraud, he told of several instances when he deceived his coworkers. Here are seven:

Lies: Seven (More) Examples at BLMIS

1. DiPascali, Perez, and O'Hara used to socialize, and at one of those dinners Perez and O'Hara asked DiPascali if the entire business was a scam and would blow up in their faces. DiPascali lied and told them the stocks were being held in the books … as a liability. DiPascali had numerous dinners with Perez and O'Hara and over time he opened up to Perez and O'Hara and told them Madoff had assets to cover the books …. DiPascali was not surprised by their questions since they were so involved in the systems. He was surprised it took them so long to ask.
2. Perez and O'Hara worked on making reports for the "special" clients. He [DiPascali] told them the reports were for the SEC and that Madoff did not want all the clients to go to the SEC.
3. DiPascali told some of his employees that Madoff was trading in Europe; he was trading as a principal, not as an agent. Because Madoff was trading out of his own inventory, which he kept in various places overseas, he was able to do things a broker simply acting as an agent would not be able to do, such as allocate these trades to customers after the fact, and backdate them.
4. DiPascali concocted a story that there was an upcoming investor advisory audit and they would be asking Madoff if he was an IA for his employees. If Madoff had to say "yes," the audit would last for two weeks. If he could say "no," it would cut the audit to two days. DiPascali explained that Bongiorno needed to temporarily

cash out all the employee accounts she had, including her own, so this audit would go away quicker.

5. When asked if Crupi was fed any stories to make her think this was legitimate, [DiPascali] recalled initially telling her something Madoff used to say to [him] and others on the 17th floor about a stock "having hit a home run upstairs." He also told her that she was able to do trades using a prior day's price because successful trades were being conducted in the market making and proprietary businesses of BLMIS.

6. Very early on, when teaching [Crupi] the [Stanley] Chais [investment] work, DiPascali repeated the Madoff line about "having the positions upstairs."

7. O'Hara and Perez were running programs they knew involved only a small portion of the IA accounts. [DiPascali] told O'Hara and Perez that Madoff had assured [him] the regulators were only entitled to a more limited set of documents than the auditors had requested. Providing the regulators with information about every little account would just confuse them and waste their time. It was standard industry practice to not show regulators the entire business when they did not ask specifically for that and it did not need it to do the audit.

BLMIS was certainly not the first workplace where employees routinely encountered the curious and unexpected. That fact, however, does not make them any more comfortable or enjoyable places to be. As C. S. Lewis observed, "Hence, naturally enough, my symbol for Hell is something like ... the offices of a thoroughly nasty business concern." The 17th floor at BLMIS was easily within hailing distance of there.

Great Expectations

Customers gave their money to BLMIS because they believed it would earn a higher rate of return than could be found elsewhere. And when they read their monthly, quarterly, or annual statements, they saw that what was earned was clearly in line with what they had been promised. They were getting a good return on their investments; Madoff was earning them a considerable amount of money. It all appeared to be so easy.

It would be expected that if they were disappointed with their returns, Madoff's clients would withdraw their money and invest it elsewhere. By offering a higher and always consistent rate of return, Madoff could feel pretty confident that investors would not be unhappy and would not withdraw their funds in order to place them with another broker. This meant that the earnings credited to accounts largely depended on a client's expectation. All that Madoff needed to know was the expectation of each client. He could readily meet any expectation because he was fabricating earnings, and he could have his 17th floor employees record whatever numbers served his purposes. Because not every account earned the same rate of return, it was constantly necessary for the 17th floor employees to give select or preferred accounts very special attention. Many accounts shepherded by Bongiorno, in particular, showed gains (and, for the purposes of evading paying income tax, losses)—sometimes extraordinary gains—that were barely believable.

For example, a BLMIS account opened in late April 2006 by Jeffry Picower with a deposit of $125 million was given a value at the end of the month at $164 million, an increase in value of one-third in less than two weeks. This extraordinary gain of $39 million was the result of a long series (a total of 57) of back-dated purchases of securities fabricated by Bongiorno, who was responsible for monitoring these faux transactions, are all recorded as having been made during a two-week period in January 2006. This was almost three months prior to the account having been opened or funded. As directed by Madoff, Bongiorno promptly went to work making sure that Picower's expectations were met. Her handwritten notes plainly describe her modus operandi: "Use $125 mil[lion] to set up trading with $51 mil[lion] in gains." The plan specifies: "Go back to Jan 06 [January 2006] [and] increase $50 [*sic*] mil[lion] net in equity." Other documents uncovered by the SEC show that Madoff promised, and had instructed Bongiorno, to fabricate at least a 40 percent annual return for the account. The net effect of her juggling was a profit of $74.5 million for Picower by the end of May and a profit of approximately $81 million by the end of September. In September, Picower withdrew his original $125 million, and the following April he withdrew an additional $55 million from the account. Given such results, it is hardly surprising that in the end Picower pocketed more money from BLMIS than Madoff and all of his relatives taken together. According to one set of financial records, between 1995 and 2008 Picower made 670 withdrawals totaling $6.746 billion from 15 BLMIS IA accounts. (For more on the record of Picower's withdrawals from BLMIS, see Chapter 9.)

The juggling of this Picower account was, of course, not the only time Madoff depended on Bongiorno to help him avert a crisis that might have promptly shut down BLMIS, and surely would have sent him to prison long before 2009. As early as 1992 she and other Madoff employees made use of a range of knowledge and skills of BLMIS backroom procedures honed over the years to be of considerable assistance to prevent his entire scheme from unraveling. Unexpectedly, one of Madoff's longstanding and reliable ropers, A&B, was directed by the SEC to close down its investment business and repay its customers the money it had been collecting and forwarding for Madoff for more than two decades.

A&B was an accounting firm founded by Madoff's father-in-law. Initially it collected small and over the years ever larger amounts of cash from friends, relatives, and clients to funnel directly to Madoff. (Actually, Madoff's father-in-law had earlier encouraged his clients to invest with Madoff, and began operating the first feeder fund to provide capital to his son-in-law for his investment operations.) Labeling what it took in as loans in order to avoid scrutiny from regulators, A&B promised to pay its investors a return of between 13.5 percent and up to 20 percent a year, while Madoff paid a return up to 20 percent (or whatever was necessary) a year on the money forwarded to him. Being able to keep the difference between the interest that Madoff paid and what customers were promised, Frank Avellino and Michael Bienes were soon piling up a great deal of money; they soon became wealthy beyond, according to Bienes, what they had believed possible.

The SEC eventually discovered what A&B had for so long been doing, and because the firm was not licensed to act as an investment advisor and was dealing in unregistered securities, it was immediately shut down by the government. Since it was obviously recruiting investors illegally, A&B was ordered to promptly provide full refunds, a total of $441 million. It also had to pay substantial civil fines totaling about $350,000. BLMIS was told not only to liquidate its A&B accounts, but, much more difficult to do, also to provide account records substantiating the values and trading in those accounts.

Madoff was immediately able to get DiPascali, Bongiorno, and Crupi to recreate the A&B statements to reflect what had been represented to A&B investors.

Over several months Bongiorno worked with others to create reams of historical records and account statements that purportedly reflected profitable trading in the A&B accounts. She was able to make revisions to the account statements to hide the existence of and transactions in some IA accounts from the SEC. For example, an IA account in which Avellino was a principal had periodically transferred funds to and from an A&B IA account. A 1989 A&B statement showed such a transfer, and in order to hide this fact Bongiorno created revised statements to reflect this inflow of funds as a dividend from General Motors, instead of simply a transfer between accounts. These fabricated account statements were then submitted to the regulators.

In his Complaint, the SIPC trustee sums up one challenge facing Madoff's 17th floor employees, and clearly shows the work they did to enable Madoff to get a second wind and longevity:

In and after late June 1992, at Madoff's direction, BLMIS employees scrambled to create the phony A&B IA account with a large enough equity balance to cover the shortfall in the existing A&B IA accounts and to provide a purported cushion. BLMIS [employees] generated fictitious and back-dated customer account statements for the phony A&B IA account going back to at least November 1989. BLMIS filled these fraudulent account statements with dozens of fictitious transactions designed to show realized and unrealized gains from securities and options transactions totaling approximately $65.9 million, the amount necessary to hide the shortfall and provide a cushion .... [For example], the back-dated January 1991 statement reflects the purchase of 5,950 "S&P 100 Index-April 335 call" contracts which were therefore reported on the April 1991 statement to have been sold for an approximate gain of $ 18,019,575 ... [and] the back-dated December 1991 statement also reflected the purchase of 550,000 shares of Ford [Motor Company] stock, all on margin for approximately $13,181,250. On June 30, 1992, the 550,000 shares had a fair market value of $25,231,250 translating into an unrealized gain of $12,050,000.[14]

To cover the cash outflow for the investments of the A&B clients that was due and needed immediately, Madoff simply used securities from other BLMIS clients as collateral for loans, the total of which was added to his cash reserves. He was then able to readily reimburse the A&B clients.

The depleted Madoff reserves were soon replenished when the heretofore A&B clients, confident with how quickly their money had been refunded, and with an undiminished devotion to Madoff, directly reinvested in BLMIS what had been returned by them through A&B. With these new direct investors, Madoff was thereafter spared the bother of having to work through A&B, although he continued to add funds to the various A&B IA accounts. If nothing else, the results of the SEC's action against A&B and, indirectly, Madoff offered a textbook example of unanticipated consequences.[15] (Frank DiPascali, Jr. remembrance of what happened backstage in the effort to provide documentation of the A&B IA account can be found in Appendix 6-B. There is more about A&B in the next chapter.)

In another instance, in 2004 Bongiorno was told to generate millions of dollars of fraudulent gains for the IA accounts of Madoff's sons, Mark and Andrew. "Bernie said make $6 mil[lion] [in gains] + [20] % for taxes + whatever mrgn [margin] int [interest] it should be," her notes read. An adding machine tape attached to her notes calculates that each son was due $7.38 million. Additional notes handwritten by her specify the fraudulent terms—dates, share volume, purchase, and sale prices—of a number of fictitious trades in order to reach the total of $7.38 million for each account. In April, she directed that 2.9 million shares of Lucent Technologies be "purchased" for the account of each son and that the fictitious transaction be back-dated more than a year, to March 2003. The 2.9 million shares were recorded as having been sold the same month showing a gain of over $7.5 million for each account. All that was necessary to complete the deception was for Bongiorno to see to it that Mark and Andrew Madoff's IA customer statements for March 2003 through April 2004 were amended and recreated.

Bongiorno helped other BLMIS employees besides members of Madoff's family. In one instance, in December 2002, Irwin Lipkin (see Chapter 2) wrote to Bongiorno, asking her to "set up losses" in specific dollar amounts in his own account and in the accounts of other family members, presumably for tax purposes. The transactions occurred as follows:

- Irwin requested losses in the amounts of $125,000 for his account (adjusted by Bongiorno's handwritten notes to $143,000), $40,000 for his son Marc, and $30,000 for his son Russell and daughter-in-law Karen. The . . . December 2002 account statements each reflect short-term trades in Micron Technology, Inc. ("Micron") stock, purchasing the stock near the monthly high price and selling near the low price less than three weeks later, resulting in losses neatly and implausibly corresponding to those Irwin had specifically requested: $145,770 for Irwin, $41,925 for Marc, and $31,605 for Russell and Karen.

- Moreover, the Micron shares were purportedly purchased on November 29, 2002 (December 4, 2002 settlement date)—three days prior to Irwin's written request—making it clear that these fictitious trades were back-dated based on historical information.
- Further, the transaction reference numbers on each of these ... account statements were sequential in date order, suggesting that the purchase and sale of each short-term Micron trade took place consecutively—despite the three-week lag reported between the purported purchase and sale and the existence of purported trading activity between the purchase and sale dates . . . .

In the spring of 2007, with the assistance of Bongiorno, Eric Lipkin (see Chapter 2) approved the purported purchase of NVIDIA (a global technology company) shares in the custodial accounts of his daughters. The fictitious purchase was recorded with hindsight, having been purportedly bought near the lowest share price for the entire month of April 2007. With the benefit of that same hindsight, the shares' appreciation during that month generated thousands of dollars of value in the accounts.[16]

Secrecy and More Deception

Surely those who pursue a calling—farmers or dentists or masons—must adopt attitudes and behaviors that will help them make a go of it. Farmers have specific attitudes and behaviors that delineate them from dentists or masons, and putting these to use can help them succeed as farmers. This principle obviously applies to con men whatever the time and whatever the place, whether it is Bernard Madoff, an unexceptional man with an unexceptional background who stole a great deal of money, or Ivar Kreuger, a criminal held in awe decades after his death, a man John Kenneth Galbraith described as having "commanding talents, ... the Leonardo of [his] craft," an exceptional man who stole a great deal of money. Regardless of their obvious differences, Madoff and Kreuger needed to keep their con games secret. There was always the need to pretend, misrepresent, and dissemble. This enabled Kreuger to claim great profitability and grossly inflate the holdings of his financial empire of match factories, banks, real estate, utilities, heavy industries, and mines, as many as 400 companies.

If con men do not spend an inordinate of time pretending, misrepresenting, and dissembling, money will not continue to flow and the crime cannot continue to remain viable. The more they are enclosed in secrecy, the more successful their pretending, misrepresenting, and dissembling. In a con game, speech can often be silver, but silence is always golden. The fewer people who know con men are stealing, the longer their stealing can continue. When asked by a reporter in 1929 about the key to his success, Ivar Kreuger, the epitome of the cosmopolitan swindler, replied: "My success can be attributed to three things. One is silence. The second is more silence. The third is even more silence." It was a silence allowing him "a dimensional existence only in the unpopulated distances of his inner world that was [Krueger's] catalyzer. He moved through life smiling, calm, with his lips sealed. His very silence gave him an air of serenity, until the lesser money minds became convinced he possessed some key to profits that was beyond them,"[17] proving again: the more silence, the more secrecy, the greater the likelihood that a con might continue uninterrupted: "Silence, secrecy, mystification, those were his [Kreuger's] means."[18] As for Madoff, with some regularity, he would brag, bluster, and explode, but never to the extent of jeopardizing his secret and his con.

For many years after what at the time seemed Kreuger's inexplicable suicide, his tangled, convoluted financial dealings were still largely incomprehensible. As one biographer put it: "All [of it was] a jumble, and a very rotten jumble at that. There was too much to remember, [there were] too many immensities, too many crafty foreshortenings . . . . He had had to keep it all in his head; all the clues at any rate. That was his one chance. He had bilked the entire world only by allowing no one in the world to his confidence. It had been a one-man show all the way; or better, [it was] a one-man puzzle . . . . The key pieces he had always kept hidden."

There were hundreds of associates in his worldwide Kreuger & Toll Company structure, directors, managers, lieutenants, pawns. There were figureheads everywhere, but not one intimate, not even a partner. None of the associates understood more than a fraction of the far-flung traffic. Ivar Kreuger had seen to that. Nor in any books anywhere was there more than a hint of what he had done exactly in half a hundred lands. All [of] that was in his head.[19]

Kreuger was able to survive the 1929 crash, but could only weather the economic instability in Europe and America until early 1932. The duration that Madoff was able to weather the worldwide economic downturn, which began in 2007, was not quite as long.

Kreuger, like Madoff, also became a master of deception as the following two examples show. First, on his office floor there was a button he could depress with his foot to cause a telephone to ring so that he could "hold imaginary conversations with important heads of state, financiers, and even kings." Second, at one time during a transatlantic voyage, in order to convince potential American investors that he was much more than an important international financier, "for a period of twenty-four hours at a time" he took over the complete wireless facilities of the ship preventing their use by other passengers. This was much like the unflagging secrecy and deception that allowed Madoff to keep the scope of his thefts hidden from associates, even from some who, it would seem, were close enough to have participated and to have seen some of the juggling firsthand.

There are additional striking parallels at the center of the Madoff and Kreuger con games that help understand their durability. Some will be taken up in Chapter 8. First, however, it is necessary to consider others who fueled the Madoff con game—the ropers.

Appendix 6-A

Excerpts from the Testimony of Bernard L. Madoff before a Committee of the Securities and Exchange Commission, May, 19, 2006

A: Now, that's a fact of life, and you have to understand I'm not saying trust me. I'm saying I've been in business for 46 years. I have a relationship with the regulators and the firms in general in "the street" and I have never, ever—I know the rules and regulations better than most people because I drafted most of them.

The bad news is if I violated them, I can't say: "I didn't know. I was ignorant. I know what the rules are. I go to great pains to stay within those. There's plenty of ways that you can make money in the business doing the right thing. You don't have to look to do the wrong thing.

We document our trades all the time, and that's why in 46 years we've never had any sort of regulatory issue at our firm. We do the best quality activity executions out there. And it's not—you can ask whoever you like—as to whether or not any of the information I have or I am getting is something that could benefit somebody else or information that I have could benefit me, and I'm saying absolutely not. I'd be curious to find out if there's any information out there that I'm missing, but I don't know what that is.

Q: So, I guess the answer to the question—the question was what makes you a good trader—and you said experience. Is that pretty much it?

A: It's experience, and using what tools are available to me which are perfectly open, [and] legal tools to use.

Q: The questions we're asking are not designed to imply that you are front-running.

A: I know. Please, I understand [what] you have to do. I understand your job and I appreciate that. I am not taking anything personally. I am trying to [understand]. I'm not sure I understand, and I know that you not going to tell me anything that this whole issue is about. I never understood it, quite frankly. Quite frankly, when I got a call when this thing [inquiry] first started and they told me: "You got a letter from the commission," they said, "do you know what this is about." And I said: "I have no idea," and I didn't.

   I understand there's a tremendous interest in this as there should be. I participated in all of this stuff from the very beginning, and I don't know the answers to a lot of things. I understand it's not a personal issue. I'm just trying to cut through to give you the information that you want.

   . . .

   The advantage I have and the reason I don't need to be represented by lawyers is I'm not doing anything wrong, so I'm not interpreting. I believe that when you say the fact you're asking me [about], these questions, doesn't mean [that you're accusing me]. I've never been involved in an enforcement inquiry before that I can remember. I haven't determined anything and I'm not taking it personally. I'm trying to answer the questions . . . . To help what you are trying to find out.

   . . .

Q: Is it correct, then, that the equities are traded in Europe?

A: That's right.

Q: What is the rational for executing the equity?

A: Well, first of all, I know I have a conflict of interest with my market making operation that operates during the day. So if

I would do that during the New York hours, I would run into an issue where I now have orders coming in from my domestic customers over here. And how do I separate the two of them so that I'm not sitting with the customer orders that I have here that would have to be crossed with these orders.

So ... there is less market impact if you do them in Europe than if you do them here. And I've developed a network of foreign broker-dealers over the years that are very interested in trading U.S. equities during their time zone, their hours. So it was something that, to me, was a sensible thing to do rather than try to do it during the hours in the U.S.—that I would really have, in my mind, a difficult time with potential conflicts—even though I could.

Q: Are there any other advantages besides eliminating the conflict and minimizing market impact to do it in Europe rather than here?

A: Uh-huh.

Q: You mentioned it you did it after U.S. markets closed, is that correct?

A: Before the U.S. markets open, yes.

      . . .

Q: Who are the counterparties to the option contracts?

A: They're basically European banks.

      . . .

Q: We discussed the equities, but the same question with options. Why foreign dealers rather than U.S.?

A: Because I'm dealing with their time zone, and that's where my contracts are. Most of them happen to be big derivative dealers anyhow.

Q: You said you were dealing in their time zone?

A: I'm dealing before U.S. markets open.

      . . .

Q: Have you spoken with anyone regarding this investigation?

A: No.

Q: Have you spoken with anyone regarding your appearance here today?

A: I mentioned it to Frank DiPascali that I was going to be here.

Q: Other than you would be here, what did you tell him?

A: That I was coming here regarding all the documentation we've been getting.

Q: Did you discuss with Mr. DiPascali or anyone else, the substance of what you would say here today?

A: No.

[**Later: Q:** In fact, Mr. DiPascali, you and Mr. Madoff had discussions about the substance of this testimony?

A: Yes.]

Q: You mentioned that you were aware that Mr. DiPascali has testified here. Did you discuss with him the substance of his testimony?

A: He told me he wasn't allowed to. I asked him how it went, and he said: "It wasn't my favorite way to spend the day." He said: "I'm not supposed to discuss it, and I said: "don't." I don't know who you interviewed other than Frank DiPascali, and he said he wasn't able to talk about it. I felt bad the poor guy had got put through this thing. I said: "Don't talk about it."

Appendix 6-B

Testimony by Frank DiPascali, Jr. Regarding BLMIS's Efforts to Provide Documentation about the A&B Account to the Securities and Exchange Commission[20]

Q: When did you first learn of A&B or its predecessor firms?

A: I heard the name bandied around the office. Annette talking to Bernie about A&B. Annette talking to her girls: "Get me the A&B document such and such, get me this A&B statement from July."

. . .

Q: So who managed their accounts?

A: Annette.

. . .

Q: And how did you come to learn that A&B was being investigated?

A: Because Bernie was throwing himself around the office like a lunatic.

Q: When you say that Bernie was throwing himself around the office, can you describe in more detail what that means?

A: He was, out loud, saying: "These f'ing guys are the dumbest f'ing"—f'ing this and f'ing that. I know that they got themselves into this "S," in respectable terms. He was being crazed.

Q: And was he saying this openly in the office?

A: The 18th floor of 885[Third Avenue] at the time, in 1992, I think it was the only floor we had. I had an office next to what was the kitchen. Then there was a series of empty office, and then there was Annette's department. The trading room was room to my right.

. . .

Q: All right, continue.

A: If you walk in the corridor between my office and Annette's office that is the area where Bernie was ranting and raving when he was discussing it to himself: "The idiocy of these two fellas."

Q: And what specifically did Mr. Madoff say the people and A&B had done that was dumb?

A: Well, what A&B was doing was they were raising money in the public marketplace from investors, and they were issuing promissory notes or IOUs to these people at a specific rate of return. They were then taking those funds that they raised, and they were giving them to BLMIS who had them in brokerage account.

. . .

Q: And you learned that from Mr. Madoff?

A: Absolutely.

Q: So just to be clear, A&B went out and got its own clients, right?

A: They had their own clients, correct.

. . .

Q: And then they were taking that money, A&B was, and giving it to BLMIS?

A: Correct.

Q: And that money was then being placed in an IA account at BLMIS?

A: Correct.

. . .

Q: Was any of the trading real in that account?

A: Not to my knowledge.

Q: And what concerns did Madoff discuss relating to the SEC, [that was] now looking at A&B?

A: He wanted to keep that episode in A&B's office. He did not want the SEC to look any further than the minor violation of failing to register the notes that they were issuing. He could not afford for the investigation to dig any deeper because, as you kept peeling away the onion that would start with A&B, the fraud would have been disclosed.

Q: Now, what steps were then taken to deal with the situation internally at BLMIS?

A: We basically "circled the wagons" and pitched in in any way we could, depending on what abilities you had, to bail Bernie out of a problem.

Q: Who were some of the people that were involved in "circling the wagons?"

A: Annette's department. Annette, myself, clearly Bernie, and then there were some fringe players that dropped what they were doing and ran some tapes for us to balance things out. I was a fringe player myself. I didn't have a lot of expertise in what they were trying to do. I certainly didn't understand all the nuts and bolts of how the computer system worked because what they were basically trying to do was create an entirely new set of books and records that they could give to A&B, that Avellino could then give to SEC and, hopefully, this whole problem would go away.

Q: Now, was Ms. Crupi involved at all in this process?

A: Everyone in Annette's department was involved.

Q: Now, as part of the process, were the account statements that had been generated over the years by BLMIS reviewed by Bernie Madoff and the other people that were working on this project?

A: Yes.

Q: And what did Mr. Madoff say about the state of those statements?

A: He was very uncomfortable turning that over or having Mr. Avellino turn those same statements over to the SEC.

Q: What did he say his concerns were?

A: Well, to a certain amount of the clients that Avellino had been dealing with for many, many years, he was explaining to them that they were doing some sort of hedged arbitrage. Well, quite frankly, the accounts had morphed into something completely different than hedged arbitrage for whatever reason. So Bernie couldn't afford for Frank Avellino to be accused of, basically, a securities fraud by lying to clients.

So they needed to change the complexion of what was previously issued to Avellino because if you looked at the Avellino accounts, like when the music stopped on the date that the SEC would get them, they were very problematic to Bernie. They did not indicate in any way, shape, or form that there was a whole configuration of various securities with no rhyme or investment reason that could be argued to anyone.

And they weren't worth nearly what the liabilities that A&B had to their clients, or if you added up, or the SEC added up or anyone added up, this is what's out there in terms of IOUs and these Madoff statements are the assets that are backing that liability, it didn't add up. There wasn't enough "cushion" there to cover what was out here. Very problematic for Frank Avellino, but anything that's problematic for Frank Avellino at that point is extremely problematic to Bernie Madoff.

So it was "circle the wagons" and let's redo all of this stuff so that Frank Avellino can give the SEC a more cohesive investment picture that is worth considerably more money, that is clearly hedged, and all of that is now consistent with what he's been telling his clients.

Q: Now, stepping back, I want to pick that apart a little bit. The statement that had already been done, the trading on those, was all fake, right?

A: Yes.

Q: The fake trading that those statements had on them did not appear to match up with the strategy that you understood Mr. Avellino to be telling his clients he was engaged in?

A: They were, in essence, the wrong fake trades.

Q: And who had been in charge of putting in those securities to— those fake securities into those accounts?

A: Annette.

Q: So the way to fix that was to redo those statements with the fake trades and replace them with new fake trades?

A: Yes.
   . . .

Q: As Mr. Madoff looked at these statements, the original statements, did he discuss their condition with Ms. Bongiorno?

A: Yes.

Q: What did he express to her?

A: He was illustrating to her that these are unacceptable to him. This is why this had to change. This is why that had to change. This is what we need to do. We need to do this. We need to do that, and we need to do this now because he's got this boiling investigation six blocks away, or whatever.

Q: Now, did you participate in redoing the statements?

A: Yes.

   . . .

Q: Were there actually any assets in these accounts?

A: No.

Q: There were liabilities, right?

A: On Frank [Avellino] and Mike [Bienes'] side, yes.

Q: Because people paid money?

A: That's correct.

Q: But these accounts had no assets?

A: That is correct.

Q: Is the trading real?

A: No.

Q: Did Mr. Madoff have concerns about what the SEC might do with respect to the A&B accounts in terms of appointing someone to oversee them?

A: He was very concerned.

Q: What was his concern?

CHAPTER 7

Of Ropers and Roping

This chapter is about the arrangements between some ropers, those who solicited money for Madoff, and BLMIS. Ropers lure victims/marks/clients/investors into a con game. They were BLMIS's sales force or marketeers. The focus is on what began as an accounting firm, A&B; Madoff's own roping operation, Cohmad Securities; Robert M. Jaffe, a well-connected competitive golfer, and the financier and a resident of "the world's richest apartment building"; and J. Ezra Merkin, vain, overbearing, a pettifogger and sharing other characteristics of Falstaff.

Ropers are salesmen. In a con game they are middlemen, go-betweens, or feeders who solicit money for inside men. They sell victims, marks, clients, or investors the promise of increased wealth. Johnny Hooker, the character played by Robert Redford in *The Sting*, is the roper in that con game. It will be recalled that the task of a roper is to find likely victims/marks/clients/investors and gain their confidence to lure them into a con game. Ropers can be used by inside men without them knowing that they—much like victims—are part of a con. Pitching Madoff's murky investing strategy and earning goodly fees, an assortment of ropers, each with the shared interest in making money, kept the cash stream flowing to BLMIS. Here a handful of Madoff's ropers and their participation in his con game—specifically, how they went about their work—are examined.

A roper is particularly central to a Ponzi scheme, which in order not to wither away needs a steady infusion of new money to meet the expectations of investors who wish to withdraw their profits or some or all of their capital. The brisk activity at BLMIS in 1992 to put together at least $441 million to refund investors—described in the previous chapter—after the accounting firm A&B that had been collecting money for Madoff was forced by the SEC to shut down and its roping activities were abruptly curtailed clearly demonstrates how pivotal ropers are to a con game. When ropers stumble, a con is quickly put in jeopardy of a complete collapse. In 2008, Madoff actually stumbled before his ropers did. Many remained busy into December when Madoff was arrested. However the economy was sour and had begun backsliding into a deep recession. Although it appeared that Madoff was still able to make money, the well of potential investors to keep money flowing to him so that he could meet growing redemptions was rapidly running dry.

This chapter on ropers and roping begins by again focusing on the business practices of A&B, some having been known well before 1992, the year when its centrality to Madoff's con game can begin to be fully chronicled.

A&B

A&B's roping operation took roots in a scheme developed by Madoff and his father-in-law Saul Alpern to lure money to BLMIS. Alpern, acting as a go-between, took money mostly from the retirement savings of family members and friends, promised them an interest rate of 16 or 18 or 20 percent, and bundled and forwarded the money to BLMIS. Madoff was able to use a substantial portion of what was being handed over to pay the interest promise to earlier investors. Ruth Madoff's father was clearly instrumental in the inauguration of Madoff's incipient Ponzi scheme. How much of BLMIS was caught up in the con in the 1960s and 1970s is in dispute.

Alpern and his firm first hired Frank Avellino and Michael Bienes as junior accountants. After Alpern's retirement, Avellino and Bienes became sole partners and renamed the firm; it became much more active investing clients' money with Madoff, "since the late 1960s," according to Bienes. Like their predecessor(s) when Ruth Madoff's father, Saul Alpern, owned the firm and began roping for his son-in-law, Avellino, Bienes, and A&B remained unlicensed, but after two decades of being ropers for BLMIS, A&B eventually came to the attention of the SEC, and its business immediately became the subject of a government investigation.

Even before its investigation was formally complete, it was clear to the SEC that A&B had been, at least beginning about 1984, selling unregistered securities to the public. This conclusion by the SEC, coming after all its time and effort investigating A&B, was both trivial and surely partially incorrect.

The SEC's conclusion was actually widely known long before the SEC began its investigation of A&B. More importantly, SEC investigators were told by Frank Avellino that A&B had been acting as a roper for Madoff "as far back as 1962." This was not too different from Bienes's recollection. (See Appendix 7-A for excerpts of testimony primarily from Avellino—some informative, some double-talk—before an SEC committee investigating A&B's business practices.)

Long before it caught the attention of the SEC, A&B had been assuring its customers at the time loans were offered and accepted that they would receive interest—generally between 13.5 and 20 percent—annually. The amount of interest to be paid to most investors was not negotiated, but was fixed by A&B. A&B credited the interest quarterly.

What A&B paid investors was not contingent on what it earned from investing the money it collected; from the beginning its profits were derived from the difference between what it was paid by BLMIS and the interest it promised to pay customers.

As a rule, customers were not told that all of the money put in the hands of A&B was being sent directly to BLMIS. The SEC found out about this arrangement during the course of its A&B inquiry, but this fact barely caught the attention of investigators. It never occurred to them that BLMIS or Madoff, who was the recipient of a great deal of money being collected illegally, could possibly be at the center of something more nefarious than a simple technical violation. On the first page of the summary of the SEC investigation, it is noted as an aside: "Madoff has been registered as a broker-dealer with the [Securities and Exchange] Commission since January 9, 1960, and is a major third-market participant specializing in computer guided trading strategies." That Madoff was a prominent investment professional was enough to lead SEC officials to conclude that the money being sent to him was being invested as promised—as any unsuspecting observer might assume would be the case. The SEC investigators were both trusting and lacking in imagination.

It is well understood that the first phase and an essential of a con game is the set-up: the assembly and arrangement of the apparatus, properties, tools, and scenery required for the performance. Madoff had an ideal set-up for a massive, far-reaching, and long-lasting financial con. BLMIS, the company he founded, owned, and ran, had since the 1960s moved closer and closer to the center of the American investment world. With his large and well-appointed offices on three floors at a prestigious Manhattan address, it seemed evident that Madoff was successful, very successful. He had clearly reached the pinnacle of American high finance. He led a large family-operated business that employed, among others, his law school–educated brother and two sons, both of whom had gone to college to study finance, as well as other members of his extended family. Moreover, his lifestyle was that of a successful and extremely wealthy man; indeed, he was even costumed for this role as much of his wardrobe was custom-made in Europe. His set-up was clearly convincing to all whom he met and conned. He readily fooled the SEC investigators, which, in truth, did not seem much of a strain.

It was thus beyond the SEC investigators' ken to imagine that Madoff could be involved in criminal activity. It never occurred to them that there might be an offense graver than the very public, but not inconsequential, failure on the part of A&B to comply with the unambiguous and well-understood law forbidding the peddling of securities without SEC approval. The SEC was not primarily looking for fraud. It was simply and narrowly interested in ending an unregistered company's practice of selling unregistered securities, of violating SEC rules. The SEC decided to undertake what it believed was a comprehensive investigation after it came to its attention that A&B was not a licensed broker-dealer, or investment company. A&B no longer provided accounting services; its business consisted solely of investing in the securities market. Its work in finance was not a side business simply to hold customers who wanted additional services: it was what it did. It marketed securities. One might think that this fact alone, that A&B had not accidentally crossed a line, had not wandered into marketing securities, would have caught someone's eye; it apparently had not.

Notwithstanding that A&B was operating outside the law, the SEC quickly learned that the number of clients it was roping for BLMIS, as well as the amount of money it was able to bring in, had steadily and substantially increased between 1984 and 1992 and, as it turned out, many years prior to that time.

Frank Avellino estimated in testimony that by October 1992 A&B had more than 1,000 clients, and that the total amount of money it had at that time placed at BLMIS was in excess of the $441 million outstanding. Actually, according to the SEC, after its investigation was completed, over the years, A&B had borrowed money from "over 3200 individuals and entities" to invest with Madoff.

Moreover, the SEC investigation uncovered the fact that to supplement its securities trading business, A&B by 1980—four years prior to when its investigators determined its business with Madoff began—was already borrowing money, on an unsecured basis, from Chemical Bank. Between 1980 and 1988, when it fully paid off the loan, the amount of money it had borrowed from the bank had reached $2.25 million. From what BLMIS had been paying on the funds it was receiving from A&B over the years, A&B could readily discharge the loan when it decided there was some risk that Chemical Bank could discover more about its activities than it wanted the bank to know. A&B had simply been adding the money Chemical Bank had advanced it to the customers' money it was feeding to Madoff. By 1988 A&B was earning enough from BLMIS from the money flowing into customer accounts that it could readily discharge its Chemical Bank loan. Before that time, A&B had earned considerable profits from the money it had borrowed from the bank. Money from BLMIS had paid the bank the interest on the loan, and considerably more to A&B. A&B had borrowed the money and repaid its debt to the bank without having to reveal much about what the loan was for, and, having itself profited, the bank seemed hardly to care.

New customers found their way to A&B through existing customers. There was no program for solicitation. Referrals and recommendations were verified by the A&B office staff before individuals were accepted as customers. Additional customers also came to A&B and then to BLMIS through other ropers, who received a commission from BLMIS for their referrals from money passed through A&B.

Some at the SEC did think it noteworthy that A&B did not provide a prospectus or any type of information to its customers regarding the specific use of their funds. A&B did not think this unusual; it held that this was consistent with the policy not to actively seek out clients. It claimed that it was simply acting prudently. It did not want money that might appear to be tainted; it did not want to appear to be tainted. In response to occasional queries about specifics, it was repeated to customers by A&B that their money was being invested in the securities market, and they were reminded once more of the fixed rate they would receive in interest. Customers were assured that their money would be safe because of the types of securities that would be purchased and the strategy being used to protect their investments. In one letter to a prospective customer, A&B wrote: "A&B invests with one particular Wall Street broker (the same company since we first started doing business over 25 years ago) who buys and sells stocks and bonds in the name of A&B. The list of securities being traded are top corporations such as IBM, AT&T, etc. It's the mechanics being used to protect the portfolio that makes our business successful. . . . [T]his is a very private group and no financial statements, prospectus, or brochures have been printed or are available. . . . The money that is sent to A&B is a loan to A&B who in turn invests it on behalf of A&B for which our clients receive quarterly interest payments."

A West Coast roper—a Madoff roper once removed who sent money to Madoff through A&B—produced a fact sheet stating, among other things, that customers investing through him were routinely paid 13.5 percent interest compounded quarterly. He added: "When the combined account size is $2 million, the rate will increase to 14 percent." Potential clients were also assured: "At no time is a trade made that puts your money at risk. In over twenty years there has never been a losing transaction."

The fact sheet ended by asking and answering two questions:

How does it work?

The funds you send to A&B are treated as a "loan" by them. All of these funds are sent to a New York broker who invests them on behalf of A&B. The underlying trades, made for the account of A&B are, in general, made as simultaneous purchases of convertible securities and its short sale of the common stock, locking in a profit. Other forms of riskless [*sic*] trading are also used. The brokerage firm that makes these trades is a wholesale dealer that makes the market in [the] Big Board 250 highest volume trading stocks. In practice, the trades are handled by computer for speed and accuracy.

Who handles this account?

A&B of New York City. Over twenty years ago A&B, a CPA firm, started using this form of trading for themselves and a select group of clients. Eventually the arbitrage became so successful that they concentrated all of their efforts on this venture and gave up their accounting practice. They are classified as an "Institutional Client" of the brokerage firm that makes the trade.

A&B discouraged such very public boasting, believing it resulted in needless and undue attention, most particularly from government regulators.

A&B maintained that the investment strategy employed by Madoff made it impossible to lose more than 4 percent of the money invested in any one transaction. Making its point with an array of figures, A&B assured the SEC investigators that if all trades simultaneously lost the maximum 4 percent and at the same time all its investors decided to liquidate their accounts, it had more than an adequate cushion to cover all losses.

The confirmation A&B sent to customers after processing an investment was a form letter that simply stated A&B had received the money and confirmed the customers' instruction about what to do with the earned interest—either pay the money directly to a client or add it to an account balance. It also reminded customers that it would calculate interest quarterly at the previously agreed-upon rate. It repeated the promise that accounts could be closed out by customers at any time and that money would be returned to them within two weeks. In addition, statements were sent to customers every three months.

Not only were individuals and organizations comfortable enough with the information—and assurances—abroad about A&B to place money in its hands, but after its investigation to learn more about A&B, the SEC, seeing no evidence that it was part of a criminal enterprise (although it is unclear whether it was looking for such evidence), was satisfied that it was simply what it said it was.

The Complaint the SEC filed against A&B merely charged it with operating "an unregistered investment company and [having] engaged in the unlawful sale of unregistered securities." The SEC concluded that "many investors view the A&B investments as being similar to an investment in a mutual fund. Many investors purchased A&B notes with their IRA monies and monies obtained from certificates of deposit, because the rate of return was much higher." However, it was never suggested that A&B deliberately misled anyone. Ironically, from comments by two SEC investigators years after its investigation, it would appear that Madoff's reputation as a respected Wall Street trader could have been a restraint, deterring them from looking for malfeasance on the part of A&B.

The SEC simply wanted A&B to be closed down immediately, and it asked the court to appoint a trustee "to direct the dissolution of A&B, to dispose of A&B's assets, [and to] return all investor funds to the investors." In addition, it wanted A&B "to disgorge all unjust enrichment' and "to pay civil penalties." Although the Complaint specified that A&B invested the customer funds at a single broker-dealer who managed the accounts, it did not name BLMIS as the broker-dealer.

Almost two decades after these events, a report by the SEC's inspector general details some of what happened in the wake of the A&B investigation and court order to close out its accounts. First, a staff attorney involved "recalled in the investigation, they found that there was more money at the broker-dealer than was owed to the investors. . . . He indicated that if it was the other way around, then they would have been more concerned that it was a Ponzi scheme." Second, "former New York Enforcement Staff Attorney #2 said: 'When Madoff was approached about liquidating the investments and returning the funds, [he said] that he was able to do so' [and that] 'he was able indeed to liquidate the investments and get the cash available within a very short period of time . . . which would suggest that the money was where we would expect it to be.'" Prior to the court order to liquidate the A&B customer securities, Madoff returned "approximately $113 million" to A&B, and this was promptly distributed to "certain large accounts;" the balance of a $329 million soon followed.

Most clients immediately reinvested what was returned directly with BLMIS. Moreover, as is evident from the material in Appendix 7-B, A&B continued as a roper for BLMIS.

It was not because the SEC badly bungled its A&B investigation that Madoff escaped detection in 1992. After all, the SEC's focus was narrow; it was attempting to determine whether A&B was selling unregistered securities, and it found this to be the case. As it has already been pointed out, in its work the SEC's staff concluded wrongly, very wrongly, that Madoff's ability to return the money A&B had funneled to him so quickly as proof that his business was legitimate. Thus, as is abundantly clear, poor judgment or ineptitude may not always be behind a misstep, even one that may lead to large-scale, long-lasting, and dismaying consequences.

The relationship between A&B and BLMIS did not end in 1992. A&B, Frank Avellino, and Michael Bienes had multiple investment advisory (IA) accounts for themselves and their extended families with BLMIS that were steadily increasing their wealth. Periodically they monitored their balances to make sure that money continued to flow to them on schedule and that the interest and supplementary side payments were deposited as promised. For example, in May 1996, Avellino sent a letter and spreadsheet to BLMIS detailing the amount of money he was owed for 1993, 1994, and 1995. He reminded BLMIS: "I checked the information you sent me. The only correction I have is the adjustment for the distribution of $1,216,000 for 1993 and $1,016,000 for 1994. . . . The net affect on the computation shows a difference of $434,000 in my favor." In another letter in December 1998, he wrote: "*Yes, it's that time of year again.* Just a note to touch base about the accounts: Please make necessary trades in all of the accounts. . . . I believe the total base of the three accounts will be enough to even-up the balance due. My calculations show that BLMIS was *short* (for 12/31/97) approximately *$2,500,000*. Please send me the calculations you have for 1997 and 1998." In summing up how BLMIS continually enriched Avellino and Bienes, SIPC trustee wrote: "Year in and year out, Madoff waved his magic wand and the fictitious gains [from fictitious security trades] found their way into Avellino and Bienes' IA accounts and ultimately their pockets." Avellino may have given up his accounting practice, but he clearly had not lost the ability to determine what he was owed and what his assets were.

Avellino and Bienes are not the only ones who became wealthy from an enduring relationship with Madoff. By keeping the IA accounts of so many others—in addition to that of Avellino and Bienes long after A&B was out of business and the relationship no longer seemed to be benefiting him—overflowing with money year after year, Madoff gave the impression of someone very appreciative. It, of course, cannot be said that goodwill or fulfilling commitments were truly what made him so apparently generous. After all, the IA accounts were being filled with pretend or make-believe money. Madoff also gave the impression of a man who might have felt threatened by blackmail. However, it is not known whether he was concerned about a shakedown or whether he was attempting to reduce the possibility someone might unmask him. Making others who could reveal that he was engaged in a con game rich, unless and until it was discovered that their wealth came from fictitious gains from fictitious security trades and that they would be rich only as long as he fed their IA accounts, was essentially costless and could act as a deterrent to recipients talking out of turn. Because Madoff's con game lasted decade after decade, eventually Avellino and Bienes began to collect winter homes, summer homes, and art, and became philanthropists.

A Roper's Roper

A&B also used other ropers. One that funneled money to Madoff through A&B was Telfran Associates. A&B and Telfran Associates had shared offices at three different locations for over 20 years. Like A&B, Telfran Associates initially collected notes from family, friends, and accounting clients, and like A&B, it began finding lenders from across the United States. It found clients almost entirely through referrals by existing investors.

Telfran Associates paid lenders an average fixed interest rate of 15 percent, and paid interest quarterly. It then lent this money to A&B, who in turn passed it to BLMIS. In November 1992, Telfran Associates owned almost $89 million of A&B notes. Lenders who asked were generally told little beyond that their funds were used to purchase these notes. Some investors were also told that A&B invested with one specific broker-dealer (in New York) who bought securities using arbitrage and hedging strategies. During the three years, from 1989 to 1992, in which this arrangement was in effect, A&B paid Telfran Associates approximately 19 percent interest, which, of course, means that it was unlikely that A&B could settle with BLMIS for less than 20 percent.

On receipt of money from clients, Telfran Associates issued notes and sent letters confirming receipt and the agreed-upon interest to be paid. Clients were also assured that loans would be returned upon written request within 30 days.

In one interview almost two decades after the 1992 SEC investigation, Michael Bienes, perhaps the most Runyonesque of all of Madoff ropers, was still being asked about the relationship between A&B and Telfran Associates:

Q: Now, you had these [other] accountants [Edward] Glantz and [Steven] Mendelow involved in this other sort of feeder fund that's feeding money [to A&B]. How did that work? How did Telfran Associates work?

A: Telfran Associates was formed by Glantz & Levey, the accounting firm. When I first met Alpern, the two firms were in a suite at 10 East 40th Street. Then we went over to the Young & Rubicam building. Again, we shared a suite. Then we moved to 535 Fifth Avenue, and we shared a suite.

Q: With?

A: Glantz & Levey. In fact, we were very clever. We never had firm names on the door. We always had the names of the partners in alphabetical order, so when people walked in, they saw a suite twice as big as what we were occupying. We shared common areas and common expenses, and we were always eating out of each other's pot. You know how that is.

Q: So they got involved. You brought them on the ...

A: Well, they were watching, and they said: "Oh"—they were very bright guys—"Oh, hey. What is this?" And my partner said:

"Let me tell you something. You want to do this? You don't go to Bernie. You come to us."

Q: So that's Frank [Avellino] talking?

A: "Work through us." Yeah. "You work through us," because Bernie was the well. If you have a well that's supplying cool, clear water, you don't want everybody to come and feed their cattle there. So they said: "Okay." Frank says: "I'll show you how to set it up accounting-wise. But god damn it, you've got to be perfect. You cause any problems [and] we'll throw you the hell out. You've got to—no nonsense, no crap, and no bad money. . . . No question about this now. This is the rule we always follow." "No, no, no—no problems. No problems." "You don't do favors for any investor. They get 1099 [IRS forms]. No cash better be floating around. You've gotta be. . . ." And they did. And I remember that.

Q: What were you worried about, Mob-Money?

A: No. No; not Mob-Money. The mob wouldn't go in for that kind of stuff; bad news people; the bad news people who get in trouble.

Q: So you were sending money off to Madoff?

A: Yeah.

. . .

Q: You were issuing notes to people?

A: Yeah.

Q: And then you were giving these people, depending on what they put in, 18, 17, or 16 percent returns?

A: Correct.

Q: And you were getting a little bit of the spread, because Bernie was making a bit more?

A: Yes, so just a little bit.

Q: So he would give you a little piece of the action for bringing him the investments?

A: No. He was giving us a rate of return. No, no piece of the action—a rate of return. And we were offering people less. I mean, you don't have to be a rocket scientist to figure that out. If Bernie is giving us 20 or 19 percent, I'm not going to give you 22 [percent]. I'm going to give you a couple of points less.

Q: So, how did it work with Telfran Associates?

A: Telfran Associates, we took a little piece of their piece, and it worked its way down. We took a fraction of their give. They went through us. We sent it in. They were a client of ours.

Q: So, they were giving their investors less?

A: Oh, yeah. Their investors were getting less than ours was [*sic*], because they had come in later, and they wanted a little more than they should have had, I think. I never asked them, but I always felt they were taking a titch too much, a titch too much.

   So they were like an associate of ours, and we used to have to reconcile their accounts to our accounts.

Q: And then Richard [Glantz], the son of Edward?

A: See, he was a lawyer in California.

Q: And he got involved?

A: He got involved.

Q: So his clients were getting even less?

A: Yes, of course.

Q: Or is he dealing directly with you? Or is he dealing directly with. . . .

A: No, Richard was dealing through us.

Q: So, he's given the same return that Telfran Associates are getting?

A: Yeah. Yeah. Yeah.

Q: So, now you've expanded the base?

A: Right.

   Like A&B, Telfran Associates was an unregistered investment company engaged in the unlawful sale of unregistered securities.

   The additional interest that it was necessary to pay on the money that came to him from a roper's roper could hardly have been more than a passing concern to Madoff. His most important need after making sure he could keep his con hidden was the continuous need for money; his con game had an insatiable appetite for increasing amounts of it. It should be noted again that whatever the seeming expenses to his business, there were in actuality no increased costs for Madoff for the money he was settling on others; the money he paid out was not his, but stolen and imaginary unless used. The balance sheet or bottom-line calculations for businesses in general are not applicable to a con game as long as money to steal can be found. In exchange for legal tender, Madoff was giving something that had an expiration date; it had value only until his con game was unearthed. The money and possessions derived from Madoff's con still in someone's hands after he was caught (which were eventually gathered up by the SIPC trustee through what were referred to as "clawbacks," or the Department of Justice) can also be considered little more than the con game's assets.

Cohmad Securities

Ropers who brought money to Madoff were generously compensated in commissions and fees. The arrangements Madoff made with his many ropers varied considerably and seemed haphazard although they truly were not; what ropers received was at least what was needed to keep them looking for additional investors or other ropers. It bears repetition that BLMIS could be generous because the money it was paying ropers or ropers' ropers was either stolen from investors or was fictitious profits from investments never made.

Some of Madoff's roping also was done through the broker-dealer Cohmad Securities (Cohmad), which he and Maurice J. Cohn, a former neighbor, had established in 1985 with the express purpose of finding more clients for BLMIS. Before partnering with Madoff, Cohn had been an American Stock Exchange trader whose firm, Cohn, Delaire, & Kaufman, had been purchased by a London Stock Exchange trading firm. Cohmad is, of course, a contraction of Cohn and Madoff.

Cohmad leased office space from Madoff and was located within BLMIS's offices. It had a core staff of six. The two businesses shared a reception area, office equipment, administrative costs, and a telephone lease and services. Cohmad even utilized BLMIS's computer network and its payroll facilities. The Cohmad employee benefit program, including the dental plan, life insurance, and the collection of FICA (Federal Insurance Contributions Act) payroll taxes for its registered representatives and other employees, was administered for many years through BLMIS. All of this, of course, also suggests an uncommonly close relationship. With Cohmad, Madoff had, in effect, become his own roper of high-net-worth clients.

Maurice J. Cohn and his daughter, Marcia B. Cohn, who together owned almost three-quarters of Cohmad Securities (almost all the rest was owned by Bernard and Peter Madoff), together with other Cohmad employees, were paid well over $100 million in commissions for the $1 billion their company collected for BLMIS from over 800 accounts between 1985 and 2008. Starting in 1996 through 2008, the total Cohmad was paid ("known payments") was $98,449,000 million—for example, 1996: $4,789,000; 1999: $9,874,000; 2002: $10,905,000; 2005: $7,240,000; 2008: $2,615,000. Between June 2003 and June 2007, Cohmad received almost $37.5 million in fees for referring customers to BLMIS.

The commissions paid to Cohmad were calculated on the amount invested in BLMIS, minus withdrawals, not on the amount under management. For example, if an investor's initial investment had been $100,000, Cohmad stopped receiving any fees from the account if the investor withdrew the $100,000 (or more) from it, even if under BLMIS's management it had, on paper, grown to $500,000. Clearly, BLMIS was primarily interested in the money brought in from new accounts. If ropers received compensation for account totals beyond that, BLMIS would essentially be giving them a fee from fictitious profits from investments that were in actuality never made. Madoff would not be fair and unselfish doing so, but profligate, paying a commission on money generated by the computer on the 17th floor, where his con game operated.

A very significant percentage of Cohmad's total income was from fees it received from BLMIS. Of Cohmad's total income of $80,115,000 between 2000 and 2008, $67,430,000 or a little over 84 percent was fees paid by BLMIS for "account supervision." Cohmad's (including Maurice J. Cohn's) total income for the seven-year period 2002 through 2008 was $68,544,000; of that $61,724,000 or 90 percent was from fees from BLMIS. For the 12-month period ending June 30, 2008, Cohmad's revenue from BLMIS totaled $3,737,000, while its total revenue for the same period was $3,748,000. Moreover, "limited documents produced [for Massachusetts regulators] indicate that from January 3, 2007 to December 2, 2008 Cohmad received approximately $7,046,678.96 from [BLMIS]."[1] Cohmad kept a portion of the payments it received from BLMIS for itself and then distributed the majority of money to its registered representatives based on the amount of money under management.

In the three years prior to Bernard Madoff's December 2008 arrest, Maurice J. Cohn was paid a flat fee of $2 million a year from BLMIS. Between 2002 through 2008 he received $14.6 million ("known payments") from BLMIS—for example, 2002: $2,437,000; 2005: $1,931,000. As the SIPC trustee put it: Cohmad "had little other business or purpose apart from steering customers" to BLMIS.

One would think that the fact that Cohmad's registered representatives were rewarded only for what they brought in and not from what was withdrawn from this amount—along with the fact that it was necessary for Madoff to pay so much money in referral fees to rope investors in the first place—might have suggested to someone that this was because he was not earning money as an investor, and it was therefore necessary to find it elsewhere. Apparently, no one was paying that close attention; regulators certainly did not notice.

Of course, ropers, as they watched their and their family members' BLMIS IA accounts steadily grow, did not look beyond the immediate challenge of continually finding and cultivating clients for long-term investment with BLMIS. It is possible that at least some ropers knew that the amount of money in the clients' IA accounts was actually considerably less than what clients were being told was there. In his Complaint against Cohmad, the SIPC trustee wrote: "Cohmad and the Cohmad representatives were not deceived by the BLMIS customer statements or the fictitious profits. In fact, Cohmad and BLMIS set up a database whereby Cohmad monitored the actual cash value of a BLMIS customer's account without considering the fictitious profits. This database was developed by a BLMIS employee, and the technical support was provided by BLMIS."

While many of the SIPC's trustee's assertions should be treated with skepticism, the contention that some at Cohmad knew more about Madoff's con game than they acknowledged may well be true. With press releases and other methods to manipulate the media the SIPC trustee and the federal prosecutor were adept in convincing those paying attention that they were keenly interested in rounding up the money Madoff had stolen and those who had helped him do it. However, in spite of their bluster, they fell wildly short in both efforts, particularly the latter—and particularly in the case of Cohmad.

Beyond what was obvious in the simple amalgam of Cohn and Madoff in the name, Cohmad trumpeted its association with Madoff. The connection with Madoff was most evident in how it marketed itself:

COHMAD SECURITIES was founded in 1985 by two professionals with more than fifty years experience in stock brokerage, market making, and personal service to wealthy individuals and small institutions.

Maurice J. Cohn received his "basic training" at Salomon Brothers. In 1967, he founded the New York Stock Exchange member firm Cohn, Delaire and Kaufman, a small but highly respected specialist firm. ...

Bernard L. Madoff founded the firm Bernard L. Madoff Investment Securities in 1960. He has been the guiding force in the growth and development of one of the most prestigious broker-dealers on Wall Street. He is an industry leader, past Governor of the National Association of Securities Dealers, Chairman of the NASD International Committee, and presently serves as a director of other industry associations.

Cohmad Securities, a small brokerage firm, offers its clients something special—old-fashioned service! As a correspondent of Bear, Stearns & Company, Inc., Cohmad combines the advantages of a large firm—financial soundness, SIPC insurance, discounted commissions, and direct phone lines to the floors of major exchanges—with those of a small firm—personal service, access to the firm's experts and unique investment ideas. As a result of the firm's association with Bernard L. Madoff Investment Securities and the expertise of Cohmad's professional staff, we are able to offer our clients—wealthy individuals and small institutions—the type of service they deserve.[2]

Cohmad seemed to take every opportunity to remind clients and potential clients that Bernard Madoff was fully in charge of their investments. In a 1991 letter to a prospective client, for example, Maurice J. Cohn begins: "At the suggestion of your brother . . ., I am enclosing some information and new account forms to open a managed account at Bernard L. Madoff Investment Securities . . ."

After finding clients for Madoff and taking their money, it was necessary for Cohmad's registered representatives to help BLMIS keep the money. This was best done by reminding clients of the value of having their money invested where it was and keeping it there. In one instance of promotion and promise, Maurice J. Cohn wrote to a client:

Your portfolio management report as of June 30, 1992 is enclosed. The results, in my opinion, are satisfactory, with our average account up approximately 17 percent, from January 1 to June 30. For those of you who like comparisons, during this same period the Standard & Poor's 100 Index was down about 2.1 percent and the Dow Jones Industrials were up 3.9 percent. Our "mission" is to protect your investment (and mine!). To accomplish this, we maintain our discipline and stick with the same strategy, by buying a portfolio of "blue chip" equities, selling call (index) options on your portfolio, and buying put (index) options to protect your portfolio against violent bear markets. Once again, we are not economists or security analysts. We are risk managers and our associates are very good at what they know best—namely, trading.[3]

In short, clients were repeatedly assured by Cohmad that their money was safe and would continue to grow steadily. In fact, according to Cohmad, "certain BLMIS-related individuals maintained Cohmad brokerage accounts, including Elaine Solomon, Jo Ann Crupi, and Ruth Madoff."[4]

Finally, the interconnection of Cohmad and BLMIS was reflected in the fact that both Maurice J. Cohn and Marcia B. Cohn had access to BLMIS's offices. Marcia B. Cohn had a master key, which granted her access to the 17th floor, the hub of the Madoff con game, as a rule, off-limits to unsuspecting BLMIS employees. Her door access card indicated that it was used with regularity to enter the 17th floor even on the day Madoff was arrested.

Robert M. Jaffe

Robert M. Jaffe owned 1 percent of Cohmad Securities, and served as a vice president. A registered representative for Cohmad and an unregistered representative for BLMIS, Jaffe, described by a small team of journalists as someone with "impeccably coiffed hair, a golf game to envy, and a $17 million waterfront mansion . . . a man to be seen," was married to the daughter of Carl J. Shapiro, who with the many millions that had come to him after he sold his New Bedford, Massachusetts-based women's apparel company, parlayed his great wealth, investing through Madoff, into a considerable fortune exceeding $1 billion. Jaffe was also a "man to see if you wanted in on a sure thing—Bernard L Madoff's investment funds."

Jaffe went to work for Cohmad in 1985, putting him in position to be the nexus between Shapiro and Madoff. He worked out of Cohmad's Boston office, which he managed for almost two decades. Partly contributing to Jaffe's success as a roper was the fact that not only he was an excellent amateur golfer, but also he was intimate with Madoff; he was his "debonair middleman." "Jaffe had access to Madoff, and that made him a superstar," one friend from Palm Beach who knew them both observed. "He was bigger than life." Moreover, Jaffe's connection to Shapiro, who resided in Florida as well as Boston, attracted many investors from South Florida, particularly members of the exclusive Palm Beach Country Club, along with clients he had cultivated with both his championship golf game and his salesmanship in the Boston area and the Northeast.

What is known about Jaffe's work at Cohmad's Boston office is more incomplete than might be hoped; according to court testimony by a Cohmad office clerk he routinely had many of its records shredded. Moreover, when asked by Massachusetts officials to respond to questions about his business activities, Jaffe invoked his Fifth Amendment right not to give testimony, and that phase of the investigation was left unfinished. In his effort to avoid giving testimony to Massachusetts officials, Jaffe first engaged in a series of delaying tactics: requesting additional time due to his attorney's vacation schedule, requesting additional time in order to obtain a new attorney, requesting additional time because of illness, requesting additional time because of plans to seek another attorney, requesting more time because of illness, requesting additional time after hiring another attorney, and finally challenging the subpoena to testify as unconstitutional. It was after a court ordered him to appear and testify that Jaffe invoked his Fifth Amendment right (and Article XII of the Massachusetts Declaration of Rights), and refused to testify. Still, it is plainly known that, at least in Massachusetts, Jaffe arranged for BLMIS personnel to send company account-opening documents directly to clients, and in turn received fees for his referrals.

From about 1989 through 2009, Jaffe brought in more than 160 accounts and more than $1 billion for investments from clients he introduced to BLMIS. Although he ostensibly worked for Cohmad, he directed clients to BLMIS as the following excerpts from a 2001 letter to a new client makes evident:

> On Wednesday I requested that account papers be sent to you for establishing an account with Bernard L. Madoff Investment [Securities] for yourself. . . .
>
> The envelope from Madoff should also include the following wire instructions [for depositing funds]: . . .
>
> When you have completed the documents please send them to Bernard L. Madoff Investment [Securities] . . .
>
> Please either mail a copy to me at the above address or fax a copy . . . so I can follow the progress of the account. . . .[5]

Jaffe seemed to operate almost like an independent contractor for BLMIS. In fact, he was compensated by BLMIS, not by Cohmad. He was paid a commission of at least 1 percent, sometimes more,[6] for each account he signed up. More importantly, year in, year out outsized returns found their way to his BLMIS IA account, with annual returns of up to 46 percent, although they mostly varied from over 30 percent when it was first opened to 20 percent in later years.

Jaffe's work brought him close to $150 million between 1996 and 2008. Over the years he withdrew at least $150 million from his BLMIS IA account. According to the SEC, Jaffe would periodically make requests to Madoff for his compensation "seeking a specific dollar amount of gains for a given period." It was then necessary for a 17th floor employee to backdate trades to fabricate transactions as cover for payments to him.

It was arranged by Madoff that Jaffe would receive his transaction-based compensation from profits from the purported trades of securities. What was due was, with regularity, added to his IA BLMIS account. However, according to the BLMIS records recovered by the SIPC trustee, before he requested the amount he wished to withdraw from his account, that amount was added to the account from purported trades of securities. Clearly the trades were backdated. Some examples from five different years:

> 1998: For the second quarter of 1998, he requested a "figure" of $360,632 in a letter dated July 6. The transaction that purportedly accomplished this gain (Microsoft securities) occurred on July 1.
>
> 2001: For the first quarter of 2001, he requested a "figure" of $472,913 in a letter dated March 29. The transaction that purportedly accomplished this gain occurred on March 12.
>
> 2003: For the second quarter of 2003, he requested a "figure" of $605,287 in a letter dated June 24. However, "since the last quarter the gain that was taken was $167,692 more than the amount requested," Jaffe was asking only for "a gain in the amount of $437,595." The transaction that purportedly accomplished this gain (Delta Airlines and Xilink securities) occurred on June 5.
>
> 2006: For the first quarter of 2006, he requested a "figure" of $600,815 in a letter dated April 5. The transaction that purportedly accomplished this gain (Aetna securities) occurred on April 4.
>
> 2007: For the third quarter of 2007, he requested a "figure" of $600,538 in a letter dated October 28. The transaction that purportedly accomplished this gain (Aetna securities) occurred on September 14.

(See Appendix 7-C for the perspective of a counsel to the SIPC trustee on the involvement of Jaffe and Cohmad in the Madoff con game.)

With a pleasant appearance and an extremely wealthy father-in-law, and little more, Robert Jaffe effortlessly funneled a great deal of other people's money to Madoff and in return Madoff funneled a great deal of other people's money to Jaffe.

In court proceedings in Massachusetts in a regulatory investigation of Cohmad for unethical or dishonest conduct or practices, an attorney for the Enforcement Section of the Office of the Secretary of the Commonwealth summed up what was found out about Jaffe's roping for BLMIS:

> Mr. Jaffe's business, as conducted on Cohmad letterhead, in a Cohmad branch office, was to refer client accounts to BLMIS and facilitate the opening of those accounts. It can also be inferred from Mr. Jaffe's on-the-record testimony taken on February 4, 2009, before the Enforcement Section, that Mr. Jaffe was compensated for referring clients to BLMIS. ...
>
> Jaffe also monitored the status of those accounts he referred. Ms. Swigar testified that the branch office at 29 Commonwealth Avenue received incoming correspondence in the form of BLMIS monthly statements sent by clients Mr. Jaffe referred to BLMIS.
>
> Ms. Swigar also testified that she would input the long balances and the short balances from those documents into a database. After Ms. Swigar provided the statements to Mr. Jaffe, she would ... shred them upon Mr. Jaffe's direction. Ms. Swigar also testified that she did not believe that any of those statements was over three years old.
>
> Ms. Swigar testified that Cohmad received those referenced statements as incoming correspondence. The books and records requirement ... requires that Cohmad preserve for a period of not less than three years. ...
>
> As the facts establish and the books and records violation indicate, Mr. Robert Jaffe, a Cohmad registered representative, referred investors to BLMIS and subsequently monitored those investments through those accounts maintained in the database by Ms. Swigar. Absent ... are any documents or information relating to the referrals Mr. Jaffe made to Cohmad.[7]

In the same hearing, this picture of Jaffe is affirmed and complemented by an attorney for Cohmad:

> A Complaint that was filed by the SEC ... charged: "In fact, Madoff paid Jaffe directly, and none of the millions of dollars of compensation that Jaffe received from BLMIS flowed through Cohmad.".... [At most, it would appear] that Mr. Jaffe received, at an office where Cohmad was located but where several other businesses were located, BLMIS account statements. ... The evidence does not show that those were Cohmad documents. The evidence shows that they were Mr. Jaffe's documents relating to individuals that ... he suggested make investments in BLMIS.[8]

J. Ezra Merkin

J. Ezra Merkin was another prodigious roper for Madoff. Unlike Robert Jaffe, Merkin, the managing partner of hedge funds (Gabriel Capital LP, founded in 1988) with assets valued at approximately $4.5 billion, was a recognized money manager and financier prior to becoming a roper for Madoff. He was a partner in a large private equity firm, Cerberus Capital Management. Cerberus, after acquiring 51 percent of General Motors' financial arm GMAC (General Motors Acceptance Corporation), installed Merkin as its nonexecutive chairman. Merkin was characterized in one magazine as "an intellectual showman, a marvel of erudition ... in a community that values intellect, piety, generosity, and the wealth that is their indispensable underpinning ..., [and as] one of the wisest men on Wall Street."[9]

The son of a successful and wealthy investment banker and owner of transatlantic oil tankers, Merkin was obviously successful and wealthy in his own right well before he and Madoff met. He became even more so in the years that he roped for Madoff; in close to two decades he collected $2.4 billion for BLMIS's IA business. For doing little else but handing over money from three of his hedge funds to Madoff, Merkin collected annual management fees of 1 percent and in 2003 raising the management fee for one of the three to 1.5 percent, and for some of the investments, he also collected an annual incentive fee of 20 percent of their appreciation.

The people and institutions Merkin brought to BLMIS were described as "a kind of Jewish social register." He also brought in many charities, many with a Jewish affiliation. Merkin was particularly adept at roping money from nonprofit organizations on whose boards he sat. For example, as head of the investment committee of the Yeshiva University board, and in violation of tenets regarding conflict of interest, he directed part of its endowment, $14.5 million, to BLMIS, all of which yielded him management fees, at first 1 percent and later 1.5 percent. In a 2003 disclosure to the Yeshiva University board, it was reported that he was managing 10 percent of the school's endowment. Merkin made at least $10 million from his investing for Yeshiva University, primarily with BLMIS, over the years. Moreover, and not of insignificance, Madoff was also on the board of Yeshiva University.

Until December 2008, Merkin and Madoff, working together, made a good deal of money. Notwithstanding his well-advertised and putative wisdom, Merkin seemed to have a blind spot about how Madoff was consistently successful as an investor. In fact, beginning in December 2008, Merkin has repeatedly pled ignorance about what Madoff was doing with the treasure he assiduously roped for BLMIS.

In an April 2009 Complaint, filed under state charity and security and charity laws, against Merkin, the New York Attorney General, Andrew Cuomo, asserts and fairly well demonstrates that, from the beginning, the foundation and explanation of his roping for Madoff are a succession of damning half-truths (and whole lies). In a 54-page document, the Attorney General appears to be interested in more than simply compelling Merkin to return the estimated $470 million in fees that he improperly collected from BLMIS, but in exposing Merkin's enterprise as a shallow fraud, something that other legal actions involving BLMIS seem less interested in achieving. From the Complaint:

> Merkin created Ascot Partners and the Ascot funds, an offshore fund in 1992 for the sole, but undisclosed, purpose of serving as a feeder to Madoff. ... In his testimony before the Attorney General, Merkin stated that he formed Ascot "largely" for the purpose of investing with Madoff, and that, from the beginning: "Substantially all" of Ascot's assets were tendered to Madoff. As of the end of the third quarter of 2008, Ascot had over 300 investors with a total of $1.7 billion under management. During the course of its investigation, the office of attorney general interviewed over half of Ascot's U.S. investors. Approximately 85% of them did not know until after Madoff's arrest that Madoff managed and had custody of virtually all of Ascot's assets.
>
>   . . .

Although Merkin entrusted billions of his investors' money to Madoff, and told one investor that Ascot was so safe he "would put his own mother in it," Merkin's confidence in Madoff does not appear to have extended to his own investments. Merkin's Ascot management fees for the years 1995 to 2007, which totaled more than $169 million, were paid directly to him, not reinvested in Ascot. Aside from these fees, Merkin invested, personally and through family trusts and foundations, approximately $7 million in Ascot in its first six years, but less than $2 million over the following decade. Merkin therefore realized cash earnings from Ascot of approximately $169 million, and, through Ascot, lost only a small fraction of that amount to Madoff's Ponzi scheme.

As of May 2008, over $215 million of the $1.7 billion reportedly under management in Ascot, or approximately 12%, consisted of the appreciated investments of approximately 35 non-profit organizations.

Merkin was therefore receiving annual income of over $3.2 million in management fees from these organizations Of the non-profits' investments, over $115 million (nearly 7% of Ascot assets under management) consisted of investments held by organizations to which Merkin had a fiduciary duty on account of his positions as director, trustee, advisor, or member of the investment committee. These investments were yielding over $1.7 million in annual management fees for Merkin.

Merkin hid Madoff's involvement from most of his investors by creating offering documents, reports, and other material that failed to disclose Madoff's management of the fund and falsely conveyed that Merkin personally managed Ascot's assets on a day-to-day basis.

Madoff's role as the manager of Ascot's assets is concealed in all of the Ascot Memoranda. They falsely state that ... the success of the fund depended on Merkin's abilities as a money manager: "All decisions with respect to the management of the capital of the Partnership are made exclusively by J. Ezra Merkin. Consequently, the partnership's success depends to a great degree on the skill and experience of Mr. Merkin."

Merkin was evasive when asked, in testimony before the Attorney General, whether the language in the Ascot memoranda was consistent with the fact that Madoff actually had control of Ascot's assets:

Q: I'll finish the paragraph which ends on page thirteen: "Consequently, the partnership's success depends to a great degree on the skill and [experience] of Mr. Merkin."... Do you see that?

A: I do.

Q: Isn't it the skill and experience of Mr. Madoff that is important to the success of Ascot?

A: That's not what this says. It doesn't say it does and it doesn't say it doesn't.

Merkin's personal attention to individual trades is also repeatedly touted in the risk disclosures that take up a large portion of each memorandum:

- "The Partnership also may take positions ... in options on stock of companies which may, in the judgment of the managing partner, be potential acquisition candidates. ..."
- "Such purchases may include securities which the managing partner believes to undervalued."
- "Investments in debt claims and the securities of companies that have filed for bankruptcy ... may be made at various stages in the bankruptcy process based on the managing partner's judgment that there is sufficient profit potential."
- Merkin has "ultimate responsibility for the management, operations and investment decisions made on behalf of the partnership."

The Ascot memoranda further concealed the fact that Ascot was a Madoff feeder by representing to investors that Merkin would spend much of his time managing Ascot's assets. The 1992 memorandum states that "The managing partner is required to devote substantially his entire time and effort during normal business hours to his money management activities, including (but not limited to) the affairs of the partnership." Later memoranda make similar representations. In fact, Merkin devoted very little time to the management of Ascot. In testimony before the attorney general, Merkin admitted that his "monitoring" of Ascot consisted of, at best, general conversations with Madoff approximately once per month:

It was monitoring. It was talking to [Madoff]. It was a very long relationship. I spoke to him ten or 15 time[s] a year. I spoke to or saw him 10 or 12 times a year. It might have been as often as once a month depending on what was going on. It wasn't so much second guessing. ... Fifteen would be high in a given year, ten could be low in a given year, and my guess it was more in the beginning, then a bit less, and then it developed back up again.

The Ascot memoranda disclosed that Ascot might make use of outside money managers. But the plural is always used in discussing such "other investment entities":

The partnership will make investments through third-party managers, using managed accounts, mutual funds, private investment partnerships, closed-end funds, and other pooled investment vehicles (including special purpose vehicles), each of which is intended to engage in investment strategies similar to the partnership's (collectively, "other investment entities").

Beginning with the 1996 Ascot memorandum, Merkin underscored that multiple money managers would be used, stating that the "independent money managers and 'other investment entities' will trade wholly independently of one another and may at times hold economically offsetting positions." Such statements were false and misleading because, in fact, all funds were entrusted to a single manager, Madoff.

In the Ascot memoranda there is no warning about the largest risk that Merkin took in his management of Ascot, and the one that ultimately caused Ascot to be a total loss to Merkin's investors: entrusting a single third-party manager with custody and trading discretion for the entire capital of the fund.

Only beginning with the March 2006 offering memorandum did Merkin mention the name Madoff at all—and there, he mischaracterized Madoff's role, stating that Madoff was one of Ascot's two prime brokers and suggesting that Ascot traded using an even larger number of brokers: "Morgan Stanley & Co., and BLMIS currently serve as the principal prime brokers and custodians for the partnership, and clear ... the partnership's securities transactions that are effected through other brokerage firms." In fact, in 2006, approximately 98 percent of Ascot's transactions were both affected and cleared by Madoff, and Madoff had custody of over 99 percent of Ascot's purported securities holdings.

Further, Merkin misrepresented the role of Morgan Stanley & Co. by referring to it as Ascot's "principal prime broker." From at least 1999 through 2008, Madoff, not Morgan Stanley & Co., held virtually all securities purportedly acquired by Ascot. The account statements for Ascot's Morgan Stanley & Co. accounts show that the Morgan Stanley & Co.'s role was almost entirely limited to acting as a bank to transfer cash between Ascot and investors, and between Ascot and Madoff's JPMorgan Chase Bank account. By asking investors to wire their funds to the Morgan Stanley & Co. account, and describing Morgan Stanley & Co. as a prime broker, Merkin further concealed Madoff's role in Ascot, and misleadingly gave comfort to investors by claiming that some or all of Ascot's assets were held at a major brokerage firm.

When asked during testimony before the attorney general whether the Ascot memoranda disclosed Madoff's role in Ascot, Merkin pointed to the 2006 disclosure that Madoff was one of Ascot's two "principal prime brokers," but strained to explain how that disclosure was adequate:

Q: And is there a discussion of . . . the relationship you have with Bernie where he is doing the six to eight trades a year?

A: I'm sure the six to eight trades is not in the document. I'm sure the basic strategy, that is the split-strike . . ., whether in those words or other words are in the document.

. . .

Q: Describing Mr. Madoff as a prime broker wouldn't fully describe the relationship you had with him that Ascot had with Mr. Madoff; is that fair?

A: I'm not sure. Describing Mr. Madoff as the prime broker would certainly convey some sense that the accounts were custodied [*sic*] there or could be custodied [*sic*] there which I would think of as a fairly important risk factor.

Q: Mr. Madoff, his trading was absolutely central to what Ascot did; is that fair?

A: Yes.

None of the written materials sent to investors or prospective investors properly disclosed the fact that Ascot was a conduit to Madoff, and that Madoff had complete custody and control of Ascot's assets.

1. Merkin concealed Madoff's role when speaking to investors:
   Many investors invested with Merkin because they knew him personally, through family, or through one of the nonprofit

organizations with which Merkin was affiliated. For example, Merkin's investors include 5 of the 16 members of the investment committee of a nonprofit organization which he chaired.

Merkin generally failed to disclose Madoff's role, but he also led investors to believe that he, with the help of his staff, personally managed Ascot's assets on a day-to-day basis. If investors asked who carried out Ascot's trading activity, Merkin would sometimes deceive them by explicitly indicating that he and his employees did so. Merkin told one investor that his staff "right here" was doing the trading, and pointed to the trading area outside a glass partition in his office. Similarly, when a representative of a nonprofit organization met with Merkin prior to an investment in Ascot in 2006, Merkin falsely answered the question with words to the effect that "it's all done by them," pointing toward two employees visible through the glass partition. The traders seated in this area, however, were involved only in managing Ariel's and Gabriel's assets, not Ascot's.

When an investor explicitly asked about Madoff's role, Merkin or his employees would regularly deny that Ascot was managed by Madoff, or minimize Madoff's role. For example:

In approximately 2007, Merkin told two investors during a meeting they requested after hearing rumors that Madoff managed Ascot, that all but an insubstantial portion of Ascot was managed directly by Merkin and that he had not given Madoff any Ascot assets to invest.

A member of an investment committee of a non-profit organization noticed that Ascot's returns were similar to those reported by another hedge fund that was widely known to be a feeder to Madoff. After being told by a Merkin employee that Ascot assets were "held" at Madoff's firm and that Madoff had some management role, the committee member directly asked Merkin if he was investing Ascot funds with Madoff. Merkin responded that he was not, but that Ascot used a strategy similar to Madoff's. . . .

Merkin at times concealed the fact that Ascot engaged in the split-strike conversion strategy by misrepresenting Ascot's investment strategy as well as its management. For example: An investor met with Merkin in approximately 2001 to discuss investments by his family in Merkin's funds. Merkin falsely told the investor that both Ascot and Gabriel invested in distressed debt. . . .

2. Merkin made misrepresentations concerning the safety of Ascot:

Merkin made false and misleading statements to investors to foster the impression that Ascot's funds were held with a sound, credit-worthy broker. After the failure of Bear Stearns in early 2008, a member of the investment committee of a non-profit organization, concerned about the potential loss of Ascot assets, asked Merkin about counterparty risk. Merkin falsely told the committee member that Morgan Stanley & Co. held Ascot's assets. Similarly, when a representative of a non-profit organization, just after the collapse of Lehman Brothers in September 2008, asked in an email about counterparty risk that Ascot and Ariel might be exposed to, an employee falsely responded: "We try to maintain multiple banking and brokerage relationships which allows for flexibility during times of market turmoil." In fact, Ascot had only one brokerage relationship, with Madoff. The employee also stated, falsely: "We . . . monitor the credit-worthiness of all counterparties."
. . .

Merkin told an investor that Merkin required Ascot's auditor, [the worldwide accountancy firm] BDO Seidman, to visit Madoff's offices two or three times a year to perform standard operational due diligence. The manager took comfort in this fact. However, this representation was false. BDO Seidman did not perform standard operational due diligence. . . .

3. Merkin made misrepresentations concerning the 2003 increase in Ascot fees:

In 2002, Merkin decided to raise the management fee he received from Ascot, as of January 1, 2003, from 1% to 1.5% (a difference of $5.3 million per year based on the $1.06 billion under management in 2003). This change required investor approval. To obtain approval, Merkin gave different justifications to different investors, and made false or misleading statements to justify the increase. In a letter to investors seeking approval of the increase, Merkin vaguely cited "rising expenses." In testimony before the attorney general, Merkin similarly claimed that the fee increase was due to increased general operating costs, but could not give specifics:

Q: What was the specific cost that went up?

A: I'm not sure of the specific cost. Broadly speaking, it was the back-office cost of monitoring the portfolio, constructing a profit and loss, watching the strategy, and communicating with investors. I can't remember off-the-top-of-my-head what was covered or not, so I don't want to say for sure.

Because Merkin did not actually manage Ascot, there were no Ascot expenses that would have remotely justified a fee increase of this magnitude.[10]

From answers to other questions about his relationship with Madoff and BLMIS, it will soon become even more apparent that Merkin was an integral part of the con.

Many who invested with Merkin, not imagining that he was simply passing their money to BLMIS, were, of course, pleased to find out that their accounts immediately showed "Madoff-like" returns.

Somewhat surprisingly, however, like Robert Jaffe, Merkin was not curious about how such a seemingly ordinary individual like Madoff had developed his Midas touch. It is readily understandable that someone mostly unremarkable like Jaffe would imagine that Madoff was remarkable. On the other hand, Merkin was both erudite and an experienced investor. His father, the prominent banker and philanthropist, was often described as scholarly. The younger Merkin had graduated with honors from Columbia College and had a law degree, again with honors, from Harvard University. As was his father, he was a philanthropist and patron of the arts. He had become the nonexecutive chairman of GMAC as a relatively young man.

Being well-ensconced on the boards and fund-raising networks of many charitable, educational, and nonprofit organizations put Merkin in a singular position to rope the endowments of New York Law School, New York University, Yeshiva University, Bard College, Keren Matana [an Israel-based foundation], Harlem Children's Zone, Homes for the Homeless, and the Metropolitan Council on Jewish Poverty. (It is worth reiterating that in May 2008, over $215 million of the $1.7 billion under management in Ascot—or approximately 12 percent—consisted of the appreciated investments of 35 nonprofit organizations.) As a money manager and roper, Merkin was able to use his wide and various philanthropic activities for his own financial advantage.

There are at least six possible explanations of why Merkin unhesitatingly became a roper for BLMIS, and with seemingly indifference funneled so much of his clients' money into the Madoff swindle; the six are not mutually exclusive. First, his reputation as a well-grounded investor was grossly inaccurate and vastly inflated; second, he knew that BLMIS was involved in fraud[11] and, hoping, in the words of his sister, "to get in on a piece of the Madoff action";[12] third, he was indolent and irresponsible in overseeing his clients' investments; fourth, he was too preoccupied with his various business and charitable enterprises to give his BLMIS investments the attention they obviously needed; fifth, the $470 million BLMIS paid him in fees over the years overpowered his judgment; sixth, he was simply a dupe. Merkin's testimony to regulators, beginning less than two months after Madoff was arrested, suggests that all six were at play. Was he a dishonest, busy, and greedy fool, and more? In his testimony, Merkin describes a number of aspects of his relationship with Madoff, first how he went to Madoff not long after he founded Gabriel Capital, and how quickly he became dependent on Madoff.

Meeting Madoff

Q: [Describe how you met Bernard Madoff?]
A: I don't remember how or what circumstances caused me to come to his office ... I knew of Mr. Madoff. I knew of his reputation on Wall Street. He was an acquaintance of my father's.
     My father had a very favorable opinion of him, and at some point or other, I found myself in his office discussing, broadly speaking, his activities in market making and money management.
Q: When did that occur; when did you first meet him?
A: I don't know for sure. I just don't know for sure, very late 1980s, maybe 1990, something like that.
Q: About when did it come about when you started to have financial dealings with Mr. Madoff?
A: Early 1990s.

Skepticism Regarding Madoff

A: There were over time persons who expressed skepticism about one or another aspect of the Madoff strategy or the Madoff return.

Q: Who are these people?

A: I'm not sure I know specific names of specific people. They may have been. . . .

Q: Let me jump in. Who, sitting here today, can you specifically recall that made such a concern to you?

[**Attorney:** skepticism was the word he used.]

A: Right. Almost, let me start again. A person who expressed skepticism about the Madoff return was Jack Nash [deceased former president of Oppenheimer & Company and hedge fund manager].

. . .

Merkin's Ascot Partners, L. P. with Ascot Fund[13]

Q: With respect to, and I just sort of want to take this on a fairly high level for starting, starting with Ascot, when was Ascot formed?

A: Early 1990s.

Q: And when did Ascot start to invest with Mr. Madoff?

A: I would guess something like 1992 or 1993.

Q: Did it do anything before investing with Madoff?

A: I didn't have—virtually nothing.

Q: Was Ascot created for the purpose of investing with Mr. Madoff?

A: Ascot was created largely but not entirely for that purpose.

Q: Did you have discussions with Mr. Madoff about creating a fund that would effectively [feed] assets to his operation?

A: I'm not sure we had a discussion along those lines, but we certainly opened up managed accounts and got managed account documentation from the Madoff office in the name of Ascot, or else we never would have been able to invest with him through those accounts.

Q: And from the time that Ascot started to invest with Mr. Madoff, or was substantially all of the assets of Ascot with Mr. Madoff?

A: Substantially all, yes.[14]

Q: And did that change from 1992 up until Mr. Madoff's arrest?

A: It went up a little bit, but substantially remained the same all the way through with small variations.[15]

. . .

Q: How did you, given sort of your understanding of the business as someone who runs one, how did you understand Mr. Madoff to make money just on charging commissions?

A: I'm not sure what the question is, but Mr. Madoff charged commissions, was paid the commissions and like any other broker-dealer made money off of those trades, off of the execution of those trades.

Put differently, I've had numerous, maybe too many, several conversations with Mr. Madoff over a long period of time as to how profitable the business was to him given the way he had structured it.

Now, going back to what I had said before, quite awhile before, the basic Madoff strategy that we were involved with meant catching, and this changed, it evolved over time. . . .

You remember when I was referring to that before that meant we were coming in six times or seven, coming out six or seven or eight times with the stocks and option. So it's basically when we moved to the OEX [Standard & Poor's 100 Index] baskets, 50 stocks at a time that have to be bought and sold on the OEX, the puts and calls, and for what you pay for buying treasuries; the commission on that is not anywhere near that.

In other words, those are not high commission businesses.[16]

. . .

Oversight

Q: So you weren't doing, based on that, you weren't doing a lot of second guessing, is that right?

A: I wasn't sure that's what you were asking. It wasn't second guessing, it was fiduciary responsibilities for oversight of the portfolio, and we were entrusting, we were giving money to Bernie because we believed in the combination of his executions and his calls.

And our job was to make sure that, number one: He wasn't varying from the strategy, and number two: In other words: If he said we were going to lose 2 percent and the ticker turned up and we were [actually] going to lose 2.5 percent, but we were never in a position [when] we were going to lose 5 percent or 10 percent if he said we were going to lose 2 percent.

. . .

Q: The 10 to 15 times a year approximation, [of speaking a year to Madoff] about how far back does that go?

A: I don't remember. Fifteen would be high in a given year, 10 could be low in a given year, and my guess it would be more in the beginning than a bit less, and then it developed back up again.

. . .

Concealing the Centrality of Madoff

Q: Wouldn't that be important for investors to know [that Madoff was your prime broker]?

A: Well, I think there's a description of the trading strategy in the document, and if I'm mistaken, I'm mistaken. There's a description of where the accounts are custodied [*sic*]. There were lots of conversations with lots of investors about Mr. Madoff's role, and I'm not sure there's anything I'm missing.

   . . .

Q: [Was it ever suggested] that you not disclose your relationship with Madoff to others?

A: I don't think Bernie ever said to me: "Don't disclose our relationship."

Q: Even if he didn't use those words, did you have that understanding that he would prefer you not disclose your relationship?

A: I think Bernie felt that as appropriate you disclose the relationship, and, by and large, respect privacy.

Q: Did you take steps to conceal your relationship with Mr. Madoff?

A: From whom?

Q: From investors in Ascot.

A: Such as?

Q: Any investors.

A: No—such as what steps?

Q: Like not telling them that Ascot is affiliated with Mr. Madoff.

A: I did not have a policy of not disclosing a relationship with Mr. Madoff or not, I think that's the question you asked. I certainly had a policy of answering all questions about Ascot as fully as I possibly could. There were investors who came through, who breezed through in a very short period of time and may have [not] gotten to ask questions.

   . . .

Q: The bottom of the page, "Dependence on the Managing Partner. All decisions with respect to the management of the capital of the Partnership are made exclusively by J. Ezra Merkin." Do you see that?

A: Yes.

Q: Is that accurate?

A: I just want to say one thing; the risk factor is something else entirely.[17]

Although he was not as direct, even at times more evasive, with his interrogators than what they would have preferred in order to understand what he did for Madoff and what Madoff did for him, there is nonetheless a good deal of revelatory material in Merkin's answers here. Not least in importance is that Madoff had more control over their business relationship than did Merkin. At least, Merkin's testimony suggests that conclusion.

Like Madoff, these ropers had made a Faustian bargain. Like Madoff, they were magicians who promised and produced—with the incantations of Wall Street gibberish—steadily increasing wealth. Unlike Faust however, few, if any, were interested in gaining infinite knowledge. All seemed only to want money and possessions. In fact, ropers did not appear interested at all in knowing how Madoff could consistently be so successful year in, year out. As they saw it, that it was an advantageous arrangement for them was all they needed to know. By finding clients and money for BLMIS they were realizing a substantial windfall of millions and millions of dollars. However, there was a catch; indeed, it would not be a Faustian bargain without one. In the end almost as much ruin came to many of the ropers who furthered the con as to its victims. First of all, they brought in real money and, in part, were paid with fictitious money. When the Madoff con had run its course, the savings in all BLMIS accounts— those of nonropers and ropers alike—were gone. Moreover, the SIPC trustee had begun his search for clawbacks. He and the courts wanted "unjust enrichments" returned so that they might be given to those from whom they were stolen.

Still while it may be true that "almost as much ruin came to many of the ropers," this was not the case for all. Most ropers continued to own much of what their fictitious money had purchased. They continued to claim that this was fair as they were merely pursuing their careers—selling equities. It was not easy even for those whose IA accounts at BLMIS had suddenly evaporated—and who were convinced that those who played some part in taking their money and who knew all along what was happening—to counter the latter's contention that they were simply "selling equities." Almost six years after Madoff was arrested, many ropers had still managed to hold on to their money that had not vanished when BLMIS went bankrupt. In spite of a staff of scores and scores of investigators, accountants, and attorneys and a budget of hundreds of millions of dollars, with notable exceptions, the SIPC trustee, through a lack of effort or incompetence, had not made much progress to hold ropers to account.

In his review of Arthur Miller's *Death of a Salesman*, the theater director and drama critic Harold Clurman pointed out that the art of salesmanship as practiced in America had mostly produced alienation. "Salesmanship," he wrote, "implies a certain element of fraud: the ability to put over or sell a commodity regardless of its intrinsic usefulness." This, of course, impoverishes the individuals involved in a transaction; they are "rendered secondary to the deal." In effect, a salesman sells his personality, an imitation of his true self, artificial, which has "now become a means to an end—namely, the consummated sale."[18] The salesman is described by Miller's Willy Loman's friend as "a man out there in the blue, riding on a smile and a shoeshine."

Surely, Madoff's ropers may have been riding on a little more. Yet, all, Willy and the ropers, have become commodities, what Clurman called "a spiritual cipher."[19] Miller never tells his audience what his everyman, Willy Loman, sells, what is in the two valises that he carries from customer to customer. What the product is seems unimportant.

Appendix 7-A

Excerpts from the Testimony of Frank Avellino and Michael Bienes before a Committee of the Securities and Exchange Commission, July 7, 1992

Q: You say you make money investing; is that correct?
A: [Avellino] Yes.
Q: How do you do that?
A: A&B primarily invests in securities through a brokerage house on behalf of A&B, and the securities, like all other securities, are bought and sold and create profits and losses, and at the end of a given year we were fortunate enough to have profits.
Q: First of all, who do you invest through, what brokerage firm?
A: Bernard Madoff.
    . . .
Q: Who do you primarily deal with at this entity?
A: Bernard L. Madoff.
    . . .
Q: How many accounts do you have there, at this firm?
A: As of now, five.
Q: Why do you have five accounts?
    . . .

Q: These five accounts are all entitled "A&B"?
A: Yes.
. . .

Q: So A&B does solely invest money in Bernard L. Madoff, through Bernard L. Madoff, buying securities through them?
. . .

Q: Mr. Avellino, who determines how the monies will be invested?
A: Mr. Madoff.
Q: Is this a discretionary account . . . with all five accounts?
A: Yes.
. . .

Q: Do you ever make a decision on what securities to purchase?
A: Never.
. . .

Q: Are you aware of the strategy that Mr. Madoff utilizes?
A: Oh, yes. . . . What [A&B] basically has are, of course, long positions. He buys securities for the accounts of A&B, and the strategies that have been highly successful over the years. . . . Mr. Madoff uses the hedges basically as Standard & Poor's, puts and calls. Every security that we have in the long position has a hedge, every single one of them.
Q: Do you have any input into how to employ these strategies at all?
A: None at all.
. . .

Q: Do you recall the date that A&B started investing with Mr. Madoff?
. . .

A: 1963, [19]64 [*sic*].
. . .

Q: Since 1983–84, that time period, do you know how A&B has done investing with Mr. Madoff? . . . Financially, has A&B made money each year?
A: Yes. . . .. But from an economic point of view, every single year has a profit . . ., as far back as 1962 [*sic*].
Q: Mr. Avellino, when you started investing with Mr. Madoff, where did these monies come from?
A: Loans.
Q: Loans from whom?
A: Individuals.
Q: Could you tell us how these loans work?

A: Yes. ... I borrow money from a Mr. Smith for which I pay interest. The proceeds of the loan are put into my checking account. I now write a check from my checking account, send it to Bernard L. Madoff on behalf of A&B. Like any other brokerage account, he takes the cash, gives me credit for it, and goes out and executes whatever positions he has to do. We, A&B, borrow money. We put it—as we receive the checks—we put it in one checking account at Chemical Bank, which reads "A&B," and it sits there. ... We borrow money and we also return money on the loans. ... Let's assume that we have $100,000 in a checking account. We have requests for returns of loans and it's a periodic thing, it's a revolving thing, it's in and out, in and out. We know that at any certain time that if I take $100,000 on Monday, should I send it to the broker, that invariably somebody will call us up within a week and say: "We need money back. We want some money back." So rather than send it to the broker and treat him as my bank—which is not what he likes; we are the bank—we absorb whatever interest we pay out because it's a non-interest-bearing account, by the way.

But the operation is such that as we get requests to return money, we have the money in the checking account. So we invariably make up lists from day-to-day of the monies that we have to return; so at any given day I know what the requests are. I have a procedure, and the procedure, again, has evolved over all these years. Every Wednesday of every single week we make up the returns-list of checks for the loans that have been requested for return. We know how much the amounts are; we make up those checks; we always have capital in our accounts. A&B has a capital account, so the monies sitting there at any one time is capital that A&B has. It could be $1 million; it could be $4 million. We don't bother the broker with that. We have a revolving cash-checking fund balance at all times.

Now, when two weeks go by, and I have $10 million in the account, and I know from experience I've never sent back more than $2 million in any high week, I look at the balance and I say: "Well, this money is not going to sit here; I have to put it to work for myself, ourselves." I make out a check to Bernard L. Madoff for the excess of what I don't think I'm going to need, and he now takes the check and goes out and does this security [buying] and selling, et cetera, et cetera.

...

Q: How much do you usually have in this account?
A: Depending on the season; it depends on the time of year. Come April 15th, that cushion has to be very big because we have clients that call us up between April 5th and April 15 that need money tomorrow because their tax returns are due. So the cushion could be $5 million. The smallest amount in the bank could be $800,000. The most I've ever had at any given period is probably $6 million. That's the average on a yearly, month-to-month basis.

. . .

Q: Mr. Bienes, do you recall the time, the date, when A&B borrowed money from Chemical Bank on an unsecured basis to do investing?

. . .

A: It was over a period of years. It would have to go back to 1980 or 1979, 1980.
Q: That was initially when it started?
A: I think. I can only say: "I think." I remember meeting with the gentlemen from the bank around 1980. It could have been a little sooner, but let me give you a rough estimate. . . . I can give you the end of it. We repaid the final loan in October of 1988.

. . .

Q: When did A&B start borrowing money from individuals?
A: [Avellino] Probably in 1962.
Q: At some point in time, did borrowing from individuals increase?

. . .

A: Yes.
Q: When?
A: Since 1962.

. . .

Q: How did you come about to borrow these funds?
A: [Avellino] Let's go back to 1962. This was something that was only done on my behalf—whatever the company was at that time—by word of mouth, and it was a nucleus of, and still is, friends, relatives, ex-clients, if you will, of A&B, cousins of my friends and relatives, nephews of my friends and relatives, and it evolved and evolved. So it's all by word of mouth and reputation, by integrity, by performance, by paying interest, never ever skipping an interest payment to anyone. Our word was our bond and it's basically the same thing today. It has not changed.

. . .

Q: Can you describe what would happen if someone called to lend money?

A: If somebody would call my office . . . [he or she would be asked]: "Who are you," of course, if they haven't identified themselves already. They would say they are Mr. So and So, who was told by their brother, cousin, whatever, to call up because they have a loan that they are receiving X amount of interest on and it sounds good and they have been with this loan for about 20 years plus, which is the average, and could they, in turn, lend us some money and would we take it.

We don't stop at that. We follow it through. We make sure this person is telling the truth, number one. Number two, every party that is in there is related to someone that started this thing or lent money originally, and the phone call that would come in would say: "I am Mr. Jones and I hear you have a good thing going," or "program," or whatever, and is immediately answered with: "We don't tell you anything. We will tell you nothing. We are a private company; we invest for ourselves, so wherever you got this information from, please go back and check your sources again."

And basically, this is the response you get at all times and will get at all times. This is probably, and I'm anticipating what precipitated this call, that somebody called, and we invariably say: "We are not going to give you anything," because the questions—when I answer the questions: "Do you have a brochure?" or: "Do you have a prospectus?" or: "Do you have a financial?" And my answer is: "We have none of those things because we are not in that business. We don't do any of those things that you are anticipating. We don't advertise; we don't solicit; we don't promote. We are a private investment company, and we only deal with relatives, friends, clients, and people who are associated with friends, relatives, and clients."

. . .

Q: Is that also the case that people write in to inquire about A&B?

. . .

A: There are times when we get a check with a letter that says: "We are aware of your" whatever they call it "enclosed, please find a check. . . . [P]lease open up an account, a loan account." And in every instance, if there is no [personal] relationship to that letter and that check, it immediately goes back. There's no "ands, ifs, or buts." [We respond]: "We are sorry that we are not able to accommodate you. We will not take your check." That is also part of this process.

. . .

A: If the person is a legitimate person, et cetera, et cetera, et cetera, she'll say: "You will get." Most of the time, by the way, they call and say: "We know you pay X amount," and most of the time they are wrong because if we paid X amount to Mr. Smith, it doesn't mean I'm going to pay the same amount to Mr. Jones. It depends on the economic conditions of our times, [on the prime interest rate]. We have old-timers sitting there for many years and we don't disturb them [by changing the interest rate]. They are our loyal lenders.

. . .

Q: Are there investors that you have that are getting 13 percent or 13.1 percent?

A: The lowest that we had ever was getting 13.5 percent, and that's, by the way, the Copperman group.

. . .

Q: Do you ever mention arbitrages . . .?

A: I could honestly say, and you could check any record that you want with me from 1962 to today, in thousands of transactions, of what I call arbitrage, which is bona fide convertible buying and selling, there has never been a loss.

Q: A&B?

A: A&B.

. . .

Attorney: Could you explain what you mean by "hedge" and what impact that hedge would have on the approximately $400 million that was loaned to A&B in investments?

A: If you look at the $400 million that we owe to lenders and you looked at my portfolio and, by the way, all of the $400 million plus are with Bernard L. Madoff, every single dollar, it is invested in long-term Fortune 500 securities. It is, to use the word, "protected" with hedges of Standard & Poor's Index. . . .

Appendix 7-B

Testimony That A&B Continued as a Roper for BLMIS after 1993

Q: How did you come to learn that certain of these accounts had a rate of return that was targeted?

A: As it pertained to me in the basket split-strike strategy?

Q: Yes.

A: I was called into a meeting that was about to break up between Bernie and Frank Avellino.

. . .

Q: When, approximately, did this occur?

A: The winter of 1993.

Q: What happened in that meeting?

A: Bernie introduced me to Frank Avellino, who I don't think I had met him up to that point. They basically gave me a quick synopsis of what their meeting was about and handed me a document that had figures on it that illustrated the meat and potatoes of their meeting.

Q: What was your understanding of the figures that were on there?

A: It was funds that needed to be put into various client accounts that had split-strike strategy as a method of paying these individuals for bringing in money.

Q: Who were some of the individuals that were going to get this credit?

A: Stephen Mendelow, Ed Glantz, Richard Glantz, a trust for Aaron Levy controlled by his son Joel. That's all I can remember off the top of my head.

Q: These accounts were of individuals that were bringing additional customers in to BLMIS?

A: Yes.

Q: As part of bringing in new customers, what was given to them?

A: In essence, a commission.

Q: The commission for bringing in those customers?

A: Correct.

. . .

Q: Do you recognize this document?

A: I do.

Q: What is it?

A: The typewritten information on the document is what was given to me at the tail end of the Bernie Madoff-Frank Avellino meeting explaining who and in what quantities we were given to [put money into] these accounts, put funds into these accounts.

Q: Is that the credit for bringing in the clients that you just discussed?

A: It is.

. . .

Q: As part of these people coming back in, did these folks bring in additional customers to BLMIS?

A: These entities were clients of A&B. A&B, being closed down by the
      SEC, had no vehicle to pay them any longer. The purpose of this
      was illustrated to me and explained to me that since Frank
      [Avellino] can't pay these guys anymore for the money they
      originally brought in to A&B and now those very same clients are
      going to be transferred, if you will, to BLMIS, if you will, and
      have direct accounts, the only vehicle that Frank and therefore
      now, Bernie would have to pay these managers of other people's
      money would be [add money] their personal accounts.
      . . .
Q: What were they getting that extra money for?
A: For originally bringing in the clients to A&B and then
      subsequently those clients became clients of BLMIS.
Q: Did those payments continue after this and into the 1990s and
      beyond?
A: Yes.

Appendix 7-C

**Comments by Oren J. Warshavsky, a Counsel to the SIPC Trustee
(International Law Practicum [Spring 2012]), Regarding Robert M.
Jaffe ("One of the People That Marketed Madoff") and Cohmad
Securities[20]**

We would start to see the people who marketed Madoff from the
very beginning. For some of them, we couldn't figure out how they
got paid—what was happening.

The first person we started to look into was a guy from Boston,
Robert M. Jaffe. You may have heard the name. His father-in-law—just
for some background—was Bernard Madoff's first big customer. . . .

Then we have this fellow Robert Jaffe. Different people are writing
to us: "Hey, Robert Jaffe put my money into Madoff." We didn't see
any record. We couldn't figure out how this guy got paid. Where
was all the money going? And the accounts led up to close to $1 billion
of money funneled in by just this one individual. With Robert Jaffe, we
then found out that he had set up a company—and we pled this in our
case—that he would actually write to Bernie every quarter and say:
"Bernie, my number for this period is . . ."—and then he'd pick a number, say, $500,000—and he would take it as a long-term capital gain.
He would take it by telling Bernie the number. A few days after Bernie
received the letter showing the number, there would be a securities

transaction showing up on Mr. Jaffe's statement; there would be a purchase of securities from a year [sic] or two earlier, and then a sale of securities. And that would somehow always come to the exact number, which would be the referral fee.

So Robert Jaffe: We looked at him and we asked ourselves: "What else could he be involved in? Where was he?" It turned out that he was an officer in a company called Cohmad. Cohmad, as it turns out, was a broker-dealer that was housed inside BLMIS. . . . So we started to take a look at who Cohmad was. Cohmad actually referred over fourteen hundred of Madoff's accounts.

. . . So we wanted to figure out: Who is Cohmad? How did they get paid? Where did that money go? We found out that Cohmad actually kept something that we call the Cohmad cash database, which tracked the principal in everybody's account. . . . Cohmad knew the precise amount of principal that was invested, and it knew it for every customer. It also knew when the customers actually took out more than their principal. And Cohmad had that running total; that's how it calculated its cash and commissions. . . .

. . . We plugged these numbers into the database; we would look through it and run the database, and, sure enough, we could pretty closely correlate to the amount of commissions we saw being paid out.

. . . Ultimately, we had thousands of cases and there were about a hundred cases where there are what we call bad faith cases and dozens of feeder funds that we are suing. Each one had a story just like that, where it started out looking like one unusual person in Boston, and it turned into a loose network of people who are affiliated with each other who were all somehow profiting on the back end of Madoff. . . .

CHAPTER 8

Roping in a Globalized World

This chapter examines the international money collecting activities by ropers for BLMIS that made the globalization of the Madoff con game possible, and for 15 years, remarkably successful. Before globalization, Madoff's con game brought him millions of dollars; after globalization, it began bringing him billions, bringing BLMIS remarkable success until Madoff's run of luck was brought to a sudden halt by the worldwide economic downturn.

Globalization

The first known use of the term *globalization*—international trade, the movement of people hither and yon, the diffusion of capital and investments, and the dissemination of culture—was in 1951. Obviously, the process of globalization existed well before then, indeed, well before recorded history. It is known that the prosperity of the Sumerians of Ur around 2000 BCE was in large part based on their active and far-flung trade in textiles and metals.

Globalization: Adam Smith and Karl Marx

The seemingly increased pace of globalization is not even a twentieth-century phenomenon. As Adam Smith pointed out, "the Venetians, during the fourteenth and fifteenth centuries, carried on a very advantageous commerce in spiceries, and other East India goods, which they distributed among the other nations in Europe. They purchased them chiefly in Egypt. ..." Then, "the great profits of the Venetians tempted the avidity of the Portuguese. ..."[1] By the early decades of the sixteenth century, the ascendancy of international trade was already apparent. Its catalyst was the exploration and increased trade with the New World, creating "a new and inexhaustible market to all the commodities of Europe [giving] occasion to new divisions of labor and improvements in art." This, in turn, unleashed "productive powers" and increased revenues and wealth throughout Europe.[2]

Settled trade with the New World quickly developed: "In the disposal of their surplus produce, or of what is over and above their own consumption, the English colonies have been more favored, and have been allowed a more extensive market. ..."[3]

> The general advantages which Europe, considered as one great country, has derived from the discovery and colonization of America, consists, first, in the increase of its enjoyments; and secondly, in the augmentation of its industry.
>
> The surplus produce of America, imported into Europe, furnishes the inhabitants of this great continent with a variety of commodities which they could not otherwise have possessed, some for conveniency and use, some for pleasure, and some for ornament, and thereby contributes to increase their enjoyments.[4]

In 1848, Karl Marx more directly addressed the continuous, relentless momentum of globalization:

> The discovery of America, the rounding of the Cape, opened up fresh ground for the rising bourgeoisie [for the ascending capitalists]. The East Indian and Chinese markets, the colonization of America, trade with the colonies ... gave to commerce, to navigation, to industry, an impulse never before known ... a rapid development. ... Meantime the markets kept ever growing, the demand ever rising. ... Modern industry has established the world market. ... This market has given an immense development to commerce, to navigation, to communication by land.[5]

Marx added that "in place of the numberless indefeasible chartered freedoms" capitalists (the grand bourgeoisie) have "set up that single, unconscionable freedom—Free Trade"[6] (a shibboleth still used today). The end product is globalization as we see and presently experience it, and how it is justified.

Marx also wrote: "The need of a constantly expanding market for its products chases the bourgeoisie over the whole surface of the globe. It must nestle everywhere, settle everywhere, [and] establish connections everywhere."[7]

As his con game grew, Bernard Madoff was constantly in need of new capital, and he chased it everywhere. (It also chased him.) Early in the con, Madoff and his ropers tapped local money, first from relatives and friends, largely through word of mouth. Ropers then moved across the United States—to California, Colorado, Florida, Massachusetts, and Minnesota—and then to Europe.[8] It was not too long before Madoff was stealing billions of dollars instead of millions.

BLMIS raked in much new money through the widely popular late twentieth-century phenomenon, international feeder funds. The money collected in feeder funds was sent by ropers, who located and gained the confidence of investors, to BLMIS where it was erroneously assumed, at least by those investors who knew of its destination, that it was being invested.

Walter M. Noel, Jr. and the FGG

Walter M. Noel, Jr., the money manager and founding partner of a U.S.-based investment company, FGG, with his cosmopolitan family and global connections, was an important asset for the globalization of the Madoff con game. Before he founded his firm in 1983, Noel had worked as a senior vice president for Chemical Bank in Switzerland where he headed the International Private Banking Department; before then he held a similar position at Citibank. Noel's Brazilian-born wife was from a prominent Swiss family. Three of his sons-in-law who worked for FGG were born outside of the United States—Switzerland (Philip Toub), Colombia (Andrés Piedrahita), and Italy (Yanko Della Schiava)—and sought out investors from Europe, Asia, Latin America, and the Middle East whose money found its way through FGG to BLMIS. Foreign investors, primarily from Europe, provided FGG with much of its managed assets.

With offices that stretched from London, Lugano, and Madrid in Europe to Beijing and Singapore in the Far East and with Noel's kinship ties—not only his sons-in-law, but also a niece, brother-in-law, and cousin operating from Brazil—in place to help, FGG quickly became an indispensable roper—a combine of inside men (at first, little more than an extended family) in the business of collecting money in a con game—for the globalization of BLMIS.

In an interview with the Massachusetts Securities Division regulators, Noel detailed the, at first, tentative and then quickly flourishing relationship between BLMIS and FGG.[9]

Q: When was the first time you communicated with him [Bernard Madoff]?
A: In 1989, spring, early summer of 1989.
       . . .
Q: Did he try to—was he trying to seek some sort of investment in his fund?
A: Well, when we went to him, we didn't know if he would accept money or not. We didn't know if we thought we'd give him some money or not, but he was introduced and we heard him out as to what he was doing and so forth.
       . . .
Q: When you met him in 1989, was it your impression that he was operating under the Cohmad [Securities] entity?
A: That was the first name on the door.
Q: When was the first time you had a serious conversation with Mr. Madoff in regard to potentially investing with his funds?
A: I don't recall how many conversations we had, but we decided to give him $1.5 million, I believe it was that amount of money, and I think the date was July 1st 1989, and that had been following probably one, two, or three meetings with him. . . .
Q: What was the next amount that was managed by Mr. Madoff?
A.   We added another $1 million to it, I think it was January 1st 1990 or six months later. . . .
Q: Okay, and then after that?
A: The next money managed by Madoff that we provided was in December 1st 1990, eleven months later from that. . . . But, anyway . . . we gave him, and again, just an estimate, about $4 million for Fairfield Sentry, which was a totally Madoff managed fund.
       . . .
Q: How much money was contributed through the years to that fund?
A: I don't know how much was contributed, but it was in the order of $7 billion in the fall of 2008. . . .

Q: And was all that money under the control of [Bernard L.] Madoff Investment [Securities]?

A: Yes, that was all in an account with [Bernard L.] Madoff [Investment] Securities, I think is what he called his business.

Q: Who would be in charge of adding capital to that fund, adding investments? Would that be something Mr. Madoff would do or was that something that Fairfield [Greenwich Group] would engage in?

A: We provided, that was money we brought to the fund, through our group of partners and agents and all.

Q: How did you grow the number of investors throughout the years? What sort of tools and mechanisms did you use?

A: We traveled the world widely and built on contacts. It [was] started by me, virtually, and we were up to 140 [employees] probably mid-2008, and maybe 20% of those people were involved in raising money for it. We have many funds, though, so Madoff was one of a number of funds.

Q: As new investors, as you committed new investors in the Fairfield Sentry Fund, were they told that their investment was going to be managed by Mr. Madoff?

A: Yes. . . .

Q: Did you keep constant contact with Mr. Madoff throughout the years? Let's say, for example, 2005, did you have constant contact with Mr. Madoff?

A: I had quite frequent, maybe once, twice a month, largely bringing in prospects and clients because he was open to—so, when you ask: "Did they know?" Yes, we always told them: "We could introduce you if you want to come." As a person very active, and particularly active in the early days, one of the few bringing in clients, I saw him once or twice a month. . . .[10]

Madoff worked to convince FGG that its proprietary and confidential split-strike strategy—creating a portfolio by buying representative shares of the S&P 500, selling call options at a strike price above the current index, and buying put options at or close to the current index using the cash from the call options—would yield returns on investments that could not be matched elsewhere.[11] Actually, Madoff's strategy was simply in his imagination; it was not applied to actual FGG trades. Madoff gained FGG's confidence and succeeded in convincing its executives that the split-strike conversion strategy was a surety, although it seems that perhaps, at most, one or two FGG executives had any idea of how it worked.[12] By December 2008, well over 90 percent of the FGG's Sentry Funds, which comprised about half of FGG funds, were invested with BLMIS, not quite, as Noel believed, 100 percent.

FGG charged clients an annual fee of 1 percent for overseeing assets invested with it—for providing access to exclusive hedge funds and for its work in performing due diligence on investments and on the ongoing monitoring of accounts. It also charged clients an annual performance fee of 20 percent on year-to-year investment gains. The bulk of the fees FGG earned were performance fees generated from the investment gains derived from BLMIS's purported returns.

In October 2008, the Fairfield Sentry Limited Fund had assets of over $7.2 billion. According to its records, on December 1, 2008, FGG had invested $6,061,508,679 (Fairfield Sentry Limited: $5,704,321,487; Greenwich Sentry LP: $280,939,058; Greenwich Sentry Partners: $10,248,134; BBHF Emerald: $51,200,000; Greenwich Emerald: $14,800,000) with BLMIS. On the final entry of its 16-page September 30, 2008, BLMIS statement for the Fairfield Sentry Limited account, it is credited with a balance of $15,608,244,354.04. FGG was told that for the first nine months of the year its investment had increased by 4.5 percent, although the index the Sentry Fund tracked, the S&P 100 DRI, was down 30.84 percent for the year.

The Sentry accounts at BLMIS generated approximately $500 million in management and performance fees for FGG between 2003 and 2008. In testimony, the controller of Fairfield Greenwich-Bermuda, Mark McKeefry, estimated that the Sentry Fund earned over $100 million for each of the years 2008, 2007, 2006, and 2005. According to the Fairfield Sentry directors' reports, the total performance fees from 2002 through June 2008 were over $547,000,000 and the management fees were over $200,000,000. Whatever figures are used, it is clear that FGG was roping a great deal of money for Madoff to steal and that it was charging large fees from the fictitious earnings, while its account balance steadily increased.[13] Making each other quite wealthy was a good arrangement for BLMIS and for FGG—not so much for investors.

FGG was clearly not just another roper for BLMIS. It was a key roper in spite of the fact that neither Noel nor any of its other top executives knew much about BLMIS, and how it was consistently able to earn money quarter after quarter, year after year.[14] When Madoff was pressed for details about his IA business, he occasionally responded, but as often he simply declined, or he replied with a cliché, or he was general or evasive, conveying little information. (He, of course, lied, and the evidence suggests that the FGG executives were for the most part unaware of these instances until after his arrest.) In a meeting between FGG executives and Madoff in October 2008, when he was asked for "a list of key personnel involved in the split-strike conversion strategy," and to "provide a brief description of their roles," the recorded response was vague—and proved useless: "The people involved in the split-strike conversion strategy are traders, systems analysts, programmers, and operations people. No names given."[15]

The more FGG tried to learn about BLMIS, the more it became evident that it had not learned much, and that it would not learn what BLMIS did not want it to know. No FGG executive ever managed to learn the names of any of BLMIS's counterparties, those with whom it traded securities. All that they were told was that there were a number of them, and that they were located in Europe. Asked by the Massachusetts Securities Division regulators about this particular curtain, about BLMIS's unwillingness to identify counterparties—with whom they were transacting business on behalf of FGG—in spite of repeated requests, Amit Vijayvergiya summarized the problem from his perspective as head of FGG risk management:

Q: Who were some of his options counterparties?

A: Well, we'd asked a number of times and he did not disclose to us who the counterparties were. In fact, I recall in 2008 at least one example when counterparties were coming under some stress that we, perhaps on two occasions, ... went to him and asked if the counterparties he used included Bear Stearns [& Company]. His response was: "no." [We asked] if they included Lehman Brothers, and his response was: "no." When I say "his" I'm talking about either Frank [DiPascali] or Bernie [Madoff]. I don't recall specifically with who the conversation was.

But he did ... say that he would not be able to provide us with a list of the counterparties for reasons of confidentiality; he did not want to jeopardize the fidelity of the strategy or his ability to place the put hedge by revealing who the counterparties were; but he provided us with a lot of other information that brought us to a level of comfort. ...

It wasn't unusual ... for players in the hedge fund role to be protective about their positions. Nonetheless the information that Bernie or Frank provided about the limits ... attached to the selection of counterparties seemed quite reasonable. ... They used a number of counterparties, OTC [over-the-counter] options counterparties, international banks, and derivative dealers. In 2003, when I first joined the firm, I recall hearing that they used anywhere from 8 to 12 counterparties, but as markets became more stressed in the 2008 time frame they had extended that to 15 or upwards counterparties to diversify the counterparty exposure risk.

So that was the first element of his explanation of why he really couldn't give us the names for the reasons I outlined. He could provide us with a general description of the counterparty credit risk limits that were applied, a diversification across a number.

Two—and this seemed really sensible to us—he said there was maximum exposure to any single counterparty of 10%. .... And so that made sense.

Q: I understand that he doesn't want to tell you in advance what he's buying and selling; he's worried about front-running and such. But why couldn't he tell you who his counterparties were? How was that explained? Why was that a breach of confidentiality, just who the parties were? I mean obviously they were big parties, presumably reputable financial institutions. Why couldn't he tell you just who some of them were?

A: The widespread or general knowledge of those counterparties would compromise the ability of a hedge, in fact, to be put on if it was widely known that [they] ... were perhaps engaging in a transaction to sell puts and purchase calls. ... My understanding was that the general knowledge of that information might impair the ability of the hedge to be constructed at a fair and reasonable price.

Q: Wasn't the information he was giving you in your [due] diligence [investigation or analysis to confirm material facts about a potential investment] meeting, wasn't that confidential? Wasn't that sort of assumed that if he told you it was for purposes of FGG's due diligence, and it wouldn't go out into the general public?

A: I don't know why or what he thought about that. I can tell you what my understanding was.

. . .

Q: Were options reviewed with the counterparties?

A: Correct. It was a boilerplate master options agreement which, by the way, also disclosed that there was performance assurance that was demanded which is a form of collateral as I understand it. So in addition to the 10% limit—my understanding from Madoff or Frank—[was] that they [the counterparties] would have to post performance assurance in the form of U.S. Treasury bills. All of those things made sense.

Q: Did you ever receive the evidence that they actually did post performance assurance?

A: I don't recall receiving evidence of that.[16]

In essence, as to whether the names of counterparties should be disclosed, Madoff (or DiPascali) was able to convince FGG executives that they could only benefit from his withholding information from them. The argument, as understood by FGG executives, was obviously compelling; they quite readily were persuaded by the thin rationale offered by Madoff.

At the same time, FGG did not appear inclined to make much of an effort to protect itself from the risk of being victimized by Madoff. This is apparent from the responses to a series of questions about its process of conducting due diligence from the Massachusetts Security Division regulators by one of its founding partners, Jeffrey Tucker.

Q: And what checking did FGG do, to go kind of behind these returns to make sure that sure that Madoff had, in fact, obtained these returns?

A: I'm not aware of any.

Q: Okay. Is there any due diligence that FGG did with respect to— prior to FGG individuals investing in the Emerald Fund and FGG offering the BBHF Fund to some investors? Is there any due diligence that FGG undertook with respect to the fund other than having received Madoff's list of returns that he provided?

A: For me just the conversation I had with him about the strategy. I'm not aware of what anybody else did.

Q: Madoff gave you a list of returns and it sounds like he had a conversation with you about it. Approximately how long was the conversation?

A: The initial conversation?

Q: Yes.

A: Five minutes; ten minutes maybe.

Q: You had a 5/10 minute conversation, [and] you received a list of returns. I'm trying to understand what other due diligence FGG did with respect to this modified split-strike conversion strategy prior to FGG individuals investing in it and prior to BBHF offering it to other investors. . . .

A: Nothing that I did. . . . I'm not aware of what anyone else might
     have done. . . .

Q: But if anyone had done something it is likely you would have been
     aware. . . .Weren't you . . . a central member of the Emerald [Fund]
     team, the team at FGG that put this Emerald Fund together?

A: Yes.

Q: Okay, so as a central member of the Emerald [Fund] team, if
     someone at FGG had done some due diligence into this
     modified split-strike conversion strategy would you likely have
     been aware of what they were doing?

A: Yes.

Q: And you weren't aware of anyone having done due diligence?

A: I was not.[17]

Tucker's testimony is surprising in light of its repeated contention
that due diligence was at the core of what made FGG successful and
special. A marketing brochure titled "Fairfield Greenwich Group:
The Firm and Its Capabilities," addressing the selection and oversight
of those with whom it chooses to work with distributed months before
Madoff's arrest, boasted:

> FGG carefully assesses the controls and procedures that manag-
> ers have in place and seeks to determine actual compliance with
> those procedures.
>   . . .
>   Once FGG begins a relationship with a manager and brings the
> fund to market, FGG's due diligence process evolves into a simi-
> larly multi-faceted risk monitoring function. FGG's deep,
> ongoing joint venture relationship with its managers greatly
> facilitates communication and a continuing dialogue with its
> managers, and thereby enhances the effectiveness of FGG's man-
> ager review process. . . .

The testimony of the FGG executives shows how short they all fell
in even approaching these standards, particularly those that assure
transparency.

As the Massachusetts Security Division regulators saw it, FGG "violated its fiduciary duties to its investors in myriad ways. It, in essence,
served as an outside marketing agent for Madoff." In short, it worked
as a roper instead of "an independent investment advisor. . . ."[18]
As Walter Noel put it: "We were not involved in executing any part of

the strategy or doing anything but turning money over to [BLMIS]." Finally, FGG's "lack of meaningful due diligence into Madoff's operations was so glaring that it comes as no surprise that FGG did not discover that Madoff's operation was no more than a Ponzi scheme."[19]

In spite of FGG's 18-year history with Madoff, it also had not been told and had not found out the names of the traders working its accounts. Moreover, its executives were kept from the trading floor where BLMIS was allegedly buying and selling securities for FGG investors. Clearly, it would appear that not only Noel, but also, generally, FGG was strikingly uninvolved in its purported business, unless that business is narrowly defined as roping for Madoff. (For additional examples of Madoff's evasiveness, see Appendix 8-A, and for additional examples of how little information FGG executives were given by BLMIS about its operations, see Appendixes 8-B and 8-C.) FGG appeared only to want enough information about BLMIS to keep clients content; its executives were content as long as the management and performance fees continued uninterrupted.

Of course, a coherent description of how BLMIS went about the work of making money for its IA clients was not feasible because it was simply keeping it, not actually investing. What was clear to the FGG leadership was how successful BLMIS had seemingly become and, as a result, how successful FGG had subsequently become. It appears that the understanding of FGG executives of Madoff's con did not go much beyond that. Months after Madoff had been arrested and sent to prison, some FGG executives were still having difficulty grasping the fact that while they were roping for Madoff, they were being victimized by him.

As important as Walter M. Noel, Jr. and his FGG colleagues were as ropers for Madoff, they were not more important than Sonja Kohn for shepherding clients and their money from around the world to BLMIS.[20]

Sonja Kohn[21]

Except for the fact of her gender, of all of Madoff's ropers, Sonja Kohn fits the archetype described by Maurer:

> The outside man travels on railroads and steamship lines. . . . He "roots out" the mark, makes the initial contact, decides whether or not he is worth playing for, makes a tentative estimate of the game he will respond to best, puts him in touch with

the inside man, is tied up with him during the play, and generally assists with the play in the big store.

Upon the roper falls the responsibility of ferreting out marks to be trimmed. . . . Without a slow and steady stream of marks coming in, the big store cannot show enough profit to operate in the face of high overhead. . . . Hence ropers are just as essential to the prosperity of a big store as salesmen are to the success of a legitimate business. . . .

Comments one inside man: "You can always spot a good roper by the fact that he is out railroading continually for marks."[22]

Kohn moved from Italy to New York City in the early 1980s but did not meet Bernard Madoff until near the end of the decade. Kohn, who was initially in the import-export business, wholesaling and manufacturing accessories and watches, began her career in finance working as a retail stock broker for Merrill Lynch. She quickly began developing an interest in what she characterized as "the institutional side of finance." In addition, as she put it: "given my background, I was able to apply being multilingual and multicultural in my business dealings."

In 1987, with others, Kohn founded a broker-dealer firm, but soon resigned to "create an international investment program with a central hub, but where each country had local managers to sell the investment program." In 1990, she "set up Eurovaleur," with offices in New York and operations throughout Europe; Eurovaleur traded European funds in 14 stock markets, and was overseen by a Swiss money manager. It soon developed into a commodity and securities broker that also offered a broad range of legal and financial services as well as investment services. As Kohn put it, "in the 1990s . . . most finance companies were offering products which invested only in their own countries, dominated by local currencies. This created a market opportunity for American companies to penetrate European markets by offering their products and to compete with the local institutions." Kohn's work at Eurovaleur "involved extensive traveling to meet various European financial institutions to find suitable local managers and to find good partners for the local investment business." She was able to develop a number of contacts, mostly in Europe, with those with access to investors or to money.

Kohn met Madoff's business associate Maurice Cohn, who as a principal of Cohmad was in the business of primarily soliciting accounts (e.g., roping) for BLMIS, and it was Cohn who introduced

Kohn to Madoff, "which," Kohn said, "I believe took place in around 1987 or 1988. . . . So far as I can recall, the first meeting took place in Mr. Madoff's office in New York. . . . It was clear he was interested in seeing how I could assist him with the international growth of his business." Even before they met, it was evident that both Madoff and Kohn saw globalization as a great opportunity to gain access to vast pools of money. As much money as there was to be roped between Palm Beach and Beverly Hills, there was a good deal more that could be tapped in the European Common Market. In fact, in 1983 Madoff had set up London offices, MSIL, as an additional step to increase its presence in the international financial world. (BLMIS promoted its MSIL affiliate as a venture that "enabled the firm to develop an increasingly important position in the global securities marketplace. MSIL has quickly become the largest market maker in listed U.S. equities in London.")

The ostensible purpose for MSIL was to hold a seat on the London International Financial Futures Exchange. However, its primary function was to facilitate the concealment of Madoff's con and to distribute its proceeds. Although over the years MSIL conducted some legitimate business, it was used in large part to pay for goods and services for Madoff family members—including money for Bernard Madoff's yacht and home in the south of France and Peter Madoff's Aston Martin automobile—and to launder money diverted from the United States. As noted earlier, some of the money stolen from IA customers was sent from BLMIS to MSIL and then returned and credited as profits to BLMIS's market making and proprietary businesses.[23]

Here is Kohn's account of her first meeting with Madoff:

> He told me that BLMIS was becoming more international, [and that] knowledge of international markets and trends was essential as the international activities of U.S.-quoted firms increased. He said that traders needed to have information about international trends, developments, and activities since the percentage of income generated outside the US was continuously increasing in size and importance. In this context, Madoff mentioned his company in the UK, MSIL—which is the first time I had heard about this company—through which he said he carried out the same business as BLMIS but [which was] targeted at European clients and investors. It became clear to me that Madoff was particularly interested in my contacts internationally and my knowledge of international markets. I remember telling

him that I knew a number of institutions in the financial services industry where there might be synergies.

Throughout the meeting Madoff spoke almost exclusively about his market making business. Although he did mention that he also managed accounts that were set up with him, he emphasized that BLMIS was not a money managing firm and that he did this for a small group of people he liked.[24]

Subsequently, Madoff and Kohn worked out an agreement wherein she was able to tell prospective clients interested in meeting Madoff that she had a singular relationship and access to him, and that an introduction from her would yield superior returns to their investments. Kohn describes her contacts and work for Madoff as follows:

As a result of this initial discussion, I introduced a number of senior executives of financial institutions and other contacts to Madoff when I believed that strategically they could work well together. ... I did not ever seek or need to "sell" Madoff to potential investors: he was so highly regarded and it was so difficult to get an appointment that getting this opportunity to see Madoff was a highly prized opportunity.

The majority of the introductions that I made were potential clients for the market making business. ...

However, I did not normally know which specific aspect of Madoff's business (if any) my contacts would invest in ... I generally had no follow-up with either Madoff or the contact and so had no idea what business arrangements (if any) had been entered into, which aspect of Madoff's business had been invested in or what returns were generated.

I do not remember in total how many people I introduced to Madoff over the twenty-year period that I knew him. ... I probably introduced him [to] more than twenty-one, [more than one a year]. The meetings [most of which I attended] would normally last between forty-five minutes and an hour. I found that those who visited Madoff were usually amazed at the efficient and high-tech facilities available at his offices which were, at that time, probably unique even on Wall Street. Madoff would never make sales speeches about his business or discuss in any detail anything other than his market making business. In fact, he spent most of the time with clients showing them around the offices, discussing the evolution of Wall Street after World War II, and debating different aspects of electronic trading.[25]

Elsewhere, Kohn describes how she became the nexus between Madoff and some high-net-worth investors:

Back then the few "lucky ones" could only get a managed account by agreement of Mr. Madoff himself, which usually would be given only after a personal meeting. However, getting to meet Mr. Madoff was itself difficult since he was one of "the great and the good" of Wall Street. He cultivated a reputation of inaccessibility. The fact that I personally later became known as someone who could get [others] an introduction to Mr. Madoff, resulted in many people and institutions approaching me. In fact, I turned many of them away because I knew that unless I only introduced major and important potential clients to Mr. Madoff he might become fed up with me and that would undermine my relationship with him.

. . .

I developed a reputation in Europe for having both the knowledge of who did what on Wall Street and the ability to get meetings with those people. Thus, Europeans approached me to assist them with introductions when they were coming to New York. . . .

Following my first meeting with Mr. Madoff, my subsequent meetings with him began to develop a pattern. We would meet in his office in New York in the Lipstick Building, which was itself an impressive tower block. If I was with contacts from Europe, he would normally walk us all through his trading floor, showing off the electronic trading capability which included the use of double flat screen set ups, touted by Mr. Madoff as unique on Wall Street at that time. If I was meeting him by myself, I would not walk around the trading floor. Mr. Madoff's offices in the Lipstick Building were made totally out of glass. All of the employees sitting in this part of the office could see my meetings with Mr. Madoff and the guests I was introducing to him. My introductions to Mr. Madoff were made in full view of the employees in the most visible way. I do not understand why it is suggested . . . that any part of the process was secret.

Our meetings were held during normal working hours and would typically last about an hour. If I was with guests then they would tend to ask a variety of general questions about Wall Street; about the stock market in the USA; and the development of electronic trading and many other topics. Mr. Madoff would speak extensively about his market making operation, his dedication to the latest technology, and his international office in London. He would not speak about his "money management," or about "assets under management," or about "investment performance." He would be focused instead on discussing trends in international markets; in finding out about the businesses of the people I was introducing him to; and he would usually offer his services for the execution of stock purchases and sales orders.

Arrangements for meetings were generally made at my instigation and would normally involve one of my staff telephoning Mr. Madoff's secretary to agree on a date and a time to meet. . . .

Mr. Madoff was always my primary contact within his organization . . . I viewed [him] as my business partner. . . .

I would occasionally receive requests from the people whom I had introduced, particularly if my contacts wanted me to smooth over any problems that had developed in their relationship with Mr. Madoff. . . .

The [SIPC trustee] claimant has tried to paint my activities as secretive and lacking transparency. My interactions with Mr. Madoff and his companies were in fact the opposite. There was no attempt to make the appointments over cellular phones and directly with Mr. Madoff. Appointments were always scheduled with secretaries and employees and not directly between Mr. Madoff and me. All the appointments were (to my best recollection, excluding one in an Italian hotel) in the New York office and a few times in the London office. . . .

Most of my discussions with Mr. Madoff were oral. However, the exchange of ideas is also evidenced to some extent in . . . correspondence: "It was, as always, a pleasure to spend time with you and brainstorm ideas and opportunities. . . . Enclosed information [is] about *HypoVereinsbank* and *Direkt Anlagebank*. As mentioned, *HypoVereinsbank* is # 2 in Germany, # 3 in Europe, and # 4 worldwide. . . ." This fax epitomizes my approach to the services I was providing—a range of services. . . . There was no clear distinction between the various services when they were supplied, when they were invoiced, and when they were paid for. . . . Often, I would follow up on the ideas discussed by providing ad hoc pieces of written research or extracts of relevant documents, addressing the issues which we had discussed. ... Mr. Madoff would also encourage me to discuss my ideas with his colleagues in the UK ...[26]

These Kohn-arranged meetings resulted not only in the Madoff con game becoming altogether globalized, but it also brought what was to become a new major roper to BLMIS, one who was to become so involved in such a wide array of activities that she became indispensable to the success of Madoff's con.

The Madoff-Kohn Financial Arrangements

Here is how Kohn describes her financial arrangements with Madoff:

Once I had effected introductions to Madoff, if the institutions I had introduced used Madoff for their execution business or made investments with Madoff, I would receive a commission from Madoff based on the amounts that they had invested.[27] The payment of commissions for the making of introductions is ... an extremely common practice in the financial services industry where contacts are key and highly prized.

I do not recall the initial discussions with Madoff about commissions, but I do remember that it started at one % of the sums invested and later dropped down to one-half %. This operated on a fairly informal basis whereby each quarter my offices would be informed by Madoff's offices of the sum that would be paid as commission and then money would be paid by check or by wire transfer. Although Madoff provided me early on with breakdowns of the sums invested over the relevant period, I was not able to verify the calculations objectively because after an introduction was made I did not receive any follow-up information from Madoff or from those I introduced on what amounts had been invested or what kind of business they were doing. The payments were, therefore, based on trust, which I had no objection to because this is how European private banks also operated at the time because they were unable to disclose information about their clients. ...

In around 2000, Madoff told me that the calculations for the commissions were getting cumbersome because it required keeping track of whom I had introduced, which area of the business they had invested in, and what redemptions had been made. He told me instead [that] he would pay me a flat fee per year, payable in quarterly installments, in place of having to provide me with detailed breakdowns of the business that those I had introduced were undertaking. Then he told me that the total amount invested with him by institutions I had introduced by then was $1.3 billion, which amounted to a flat rate payment of $6.5 million per year (being one-half % of $1.3 billion). ....[28]

Two years after this explanation of how the financial arrangements between her and Madoff had evolved, Kohn added the following:

Ms. Jones would communicate to me on a quarterly basis some figures which she said represented amounts attributable to my introductions. There was no way for me to verify the information provided, even though these figures were used to calculate the sums to put on the invoices. After the calculations were made, I would not keep the figures Ms. Jones had provided. After 2001, I was no longer presented with these figures. ...

He [Madoff] told me that this fee [of $6.6 (*sic*) million] should be paid annually in four quarterly payments. He also directed that the payments should be split, with $775,000 being billed quarterly to MSIL and $875,000 being billed quarterly to BLMIS. ....[29]

The Madoff–Kohn relationship blossomed. In the not very many years she was in the United States, before returning to Europe, she became "the reference for many European professionals in the United States with whom I had contact in assisting them to understand the workings of Wall Street. As I had strong contacts in Austria and elsewhere in Europe, I was often involved in arranging schedules for high ranking representatives of European banks and other financial services providers when they visited the United States. I would introduce some such visitors to Madoff if requested, but also to other entities I had established relationships with on Wall Street. These included representatives of clearing houses, banks, brokerage firms, asset management firms, and other third market makers." Her work promoting investors and investment opportunities and acting as an emissary and making introductions brought Kohn only occasional compensation from some who benefited from her services. On the other hand, payments from Madoff, grateful for the influx of new money that found its way to him through the work of his assiduous and foremost roper, were generous and continuous until his arrest.

Kohn did more for BLMIS than help it find prospective clients:

> In addition to being paid for the introductions, Madoff told me that he wanted me to provide him with more of the sort of research and analysis of international financial markets that I had been sending him on an informal basis and that the payments would be intended also to cover this research. I do not recall when this conversation happened, but I was happy for the provision of research to be on a more regular basis given that I had the infrastructure to produce the research already in place. This also confirmed in my mind that Madoff valued the research I was already providing and was committed to expanding his business interests internationally.

Kohn contends that after a time Madoff asked that her research and analysis of various global economic trends be provided more formally in the form of written research. For her "corporate communication and research," as well as consultancy, activities, Kohn had founded Infovaleur in 1996 to provide Madoff and others with "research and analysis on international financial markets." Infovaleur or Tecno, another one of her companies, completed or outsourced numerous research reports that were sent to, paid for, but mostly ignored, by BLMIS and MSIL.[30]

To facilitate her roping activities for BLMIS, and to focus more attention on marketing a mix of funds, in 2003 Kohn founded Bank Medici ["to create a strong investment bank with European partners for foreign investment"]. Bank Medici obtained a full banking license which allowed it to carry out investment banking services, and it established a number of feeder funds, much of the money from which found its way to BLMIS. These feeder funds generated hundreds of millions of dollars in management and distribution fees for Kohn and her colleagues. The funds did invest not only with BLMIS, but also with each other. This fostered an illusion of diversification and helped to hide the fact that most of the invested money was destined for BLMIS.

During the 1990s, even before Bank Medici was established, Kohn's operation grew exponentially. She continued to rope billions in dollars and euros to BLMIS. Two accounts in which over $1 billion was invested were: Thema International Fund ($1,043,697,424), which opened its BLMIS account in 1996, and Herald Fund SPC ($1,533,741,975), which opened its BLMIS account in 2004. (Of course, some of this money had been withdrawn well before BLMIS's bankruptcy. For example, the Herald Fund withdrew a total of $578,033,847 of its total investment between September 2004 and December 2008.)

In return for the funds she solicited, Kohn earned a considerable amount of money, variously described as, among other things, "payment for services," "commissions," payments for "consulting," payments for "research services," and payments for "strategies and strategic alliances." In a witness statement, Kohn stated: "I was happy to provide the research to Madoff as part of my client management. . . ." However, "payments were not primarily for research, but were commissions for introductions made."[31] Kohn set up a network of companies in the United States, Europe, and elsewhere to help her collect and distribute the money that was flowing from Madoff—from roping clients, from commissions she charged funds that found their way to BLMIS, and from the research reports she sent to BLMIS and MSIL—to her family, friends, and associates.

In 2013, after a six-week trial, a London High Court judge dismissed a civil lawsuit (to recover $50 million) against Kohn, Madoff's sons, and a number of MSIL directors that, among other things, alleged $6.8 million had been subverted to Kohn. Although the liquidators of MSIL technically brought the case, they worked closely with the SIPC trustee who financed it and was the interested party. In his written decision, the judge not only cleared Kohn—and all the other defendants—but was expansive in extolling her career and character. (See Appendix 8-D for excerpts from the judge's 188-page opinion.)

Ivar Kreuger

It is clearly not the case that con games were first introduced as a diversion or entertainment at carnivals or fairgrounds; they have existed and have been global as long as people have traveled to barter and trade. In a globalized world, it is surely not surprising that con games, as with much criminal activity, are international in scope; they have become globalized. National borders may be a particular challenge to those trafficking in people, weapons, and drugs or who are stealing money. Generally, however, all enterprises that are part of the globalized economy find themselves operating in a similar connected world as multinational corporations—for example, petro-leum companies, pharmaceutical manufacturers, media conglomer-ates, automakers, technology giants, and banks.

The industrial empire of Ivar Kreuger, the early twentieth-century con man, is a model of how up-to-date, the latest, technology can be used to advance the practice of the globalized con. Of course, unlike Bernard Madoff, Kreuger did not have a team of computer technicians or a staff member who "used data from the Internet to create fake trade blotters" as accomplices, but his con became globalized as he began to rely more heavily on the railroad, telegraph, and ocean liner—the modern technology of the early twentieth century—in his con that depended on readily channeling large sums of money mostly from investors in the United States to Europe. Kreuger frequently crossed the Atlantic to beguile American financiers, and they fre-quently crossed the Atlantic to be beguiled.

BLMIS was among the first on Wall Street to introduce automated trading, making it possible to buy and sell securities over the Internet. With the exception of its IA business, BLMIS employed the most advanced computer equipment. This, it said, enabled it to cut down on costs, so that it could ostensibly be competitive with other brokers. The innovate technologies, however, were largely stage props, as BLMIS was involved in much less trading than its clients believed.

In Europe, some of the money Kreuger collected from American investors was then loaned to governments that were financially stag-gering in the wake of World War I. The governments received the money in exchange for interest payments and arrangements wherein Kreuger's match manufacturing companies would be given monopo-lies. Here is one account summarizing the core of Kreuger's globalized con game:

> His plan was to obtain the money from American bankers plus the public by the flotation of a completely new company called the International Match Corporation. The company would invest the money in the following way: (1) all proceeds would be paid over to individual national governments in the form of loans, (2) these loans would, of course, command interest, (3) in return for the loans, the country would grant to the International Match Corporation a monopoly for making matches within that country, (4) the combination of the interest payable on the loans and the guaranteed profits from a monopoly situation would enable the

International Match Corporation to pay out higher than average dividends. Moreover, and here was the sucker bait, the whole operation would be "gilt-edged" because not only were profits assured from a monopoly situation, but the only people with whom the International Match Corporation would be dealing would be reputable and accredited national governments. The scheme appeared totally foolproof and secure.[32]

The money siphoned off from IMCO [the International Match Corporation] into the Zurich corporations often, as not, ended up in a shell company rejoicing in the unlikely name of A. B. Russia (in practice Mr. Kreuger's personal bank account) or in one of several banks [he owned or controlled]. ...[33]

As soon as he acquired a specific and tangible asset he would borrow on the security of that asset, thereby acquiring more funds to acquire yet more assets on which he could borrow more funds ... etc, etc. Where Kreuger undoubtedly overstepped the mark ... was that he would not borrow just *once* on the security of each asset but often two or three times and would pledge the same asset to several banks![34]

By the 1920s, the International Match Corporation had "monopoly-for-loans *quid pro quo*"[35] arrangements with over a dozen European and Latin American countries for the production, distribution, or sale of safety matches.

In the decade before he came to ruin, Kreuger raised $150 million from American investors, almost all of which was transferred abroad to finance his government-loan program, expand his business empire, and pay interest and dividends on outstanding debts. With a sleight of hand that even bewildered his closest associates, he would shuffle it from one bank and country to another where it eventually appeared to evaporate. He kept his con game (a complicated Ponzi scheme in which not all of the dividends paid to investors came exclusively from new investors) going by securing more and more money by overwhelming American financiers predisposed to invest with mounds of charm and promises of even greater riches. Eventually, when he began paying out more than he was bringing in, he quickly began exhausting his resources. However, before the capital he controlled totally disappeared and his con game was exposed or his business empire collapsed, he committed suicide.

After having clearly become globalized, what was described as Ivar Kreuger's "merry money-go-round" continued to accelerate "at ever faster and [move into] more stratospheric levels." He had been "sucked into the funny money paper cyclone"[36] as other con men in the world of global finance later in the twentieth century would be. This is precisely what happened to Bernard Madoff.

More on Kreuger and Madoff

Ivar Kreuger, like Bernard Madoff, enticed investors from around the world with large dividends from greatly exaggerated or nonexistent earnings: Artfully, Kreuger "produced profits that became the talk of all counting rooms, 11%, 15%, [or] 30%." He also looted the assets of some of the companies he controlled. Moreover, both Kreuger and Madoff were eventually upended by a credit crunch; redemptions began to outpace investments. Unlike Madoff, Kreuger actually had capital in businesses. His assets were unsustainably overleveraged and he had also greatly overvalued them. Madoff was more successful defrauding than at legitimately making money through investing; he had not been a successful businessman. As his con game came to an end, Kreuger—crossing the Atlantic yet again—worked diligently to stave off its collapse. Madoff, who over the years, seemed only to be riding a wave, unraveled more quickly. Yet, although almost paralyzed, he continued to threaten,[37] beg, and barter. With egregious deception that entrapped long-standing business associates, he drifted toward the inevitable.

It has been said of Ivar Kreuger that he had contempt for those from whom he stole, believing that they were badly flawed. "I've built my enterprise on the firmest ground that can be found," he once remarked, "the foolishness of people."[38] In a number of interviews from his prison cell, Bernard Madoff also denigrated those from whom he stole. He told one journalist: "Everyone was greedy. ... Look, there was complicity, in my view. ... Believe me, if you don't think they had doubts, they had doubts." In an exchange with another journalist he complained about the "willful blindness" of banks and hedge funds: "They had to know, but the attitude was sort of 'if you're doing something wrong, we don't want to know.'"

"It is a fact," one of his biographer wrote, "that what Kreuger fashioned became a kind of fantasy, such a mixture of real and unreal, with the line between increasingly difficult to distinguish, that he would no longer know where truth left off and fiction began."[39] Even after his admission of guilt, without the burden of no longer having to act, to continue his pretense, the same might also be said of Bernard Madoff.

Kreuger was a dreamer. However, his pursuit of the American Dream never allowed Madoff to dream. Perhaps as a result, despite similarities, there was something Brobdingnagian about Kreuger. Not so for Madoff.

In the end, con games seem to succeed for as long as they do on a mixture of covert actions, greed, willful blindness ("there's none so blind as those who will not see"), hubris and humbug, human folly, and a run of luck.

Appendix 8-A

Excerpts from the Minutes of a Meeting at BLMIS between Bernard Madoff and Frank DiPascali, Jr. and Four FGG Executives, October 2, 2008[40]

"Describe procedures for trade entry and trade processing." "Not answered."

"What back-office system is used? Describe the capabilities and any known limitations." "Hardware is IBM; software is proprietary."

"Describe the process and controls for the settlement of option trades." "Electronic settlement."

"Are dual signatories required? Please provide the names of people on the authorized signatory list." "Yes. Names not provided."

"Please describe the experience and tenure of the team responsible for developing the models/algorithms used by the split-strike conversion strategy." "Between 15 and 47 years. Frank [DiPascali] has thirty-two years with BLMIS."

"Have there been any changes to these models/algorithms in the past three years? If yes, please describe." "Yes, they are always looking at the models and fine-tuning them."

"What is the maximum capacity for the split-strike conversion strategy?" "Not answered."

And, of course, Madoff dodged the paramount question about counterparties, about those with whom he purportedly traded: "[Madoff] will not disclose the names of the counterparties 'for obvious reasons', (i.e., confidentiality). . . ." [The FGG executives] were only assured: "All the counterparties are large institutions."

Appendix 8-B

Testimony of Two FGG Executives[41] Regarding Familiarity with BLMIS Operations

Q: Who are some of the key personnel at Madoff Investments who were involved in the split-strike conversion strategy [BLMIS's method for investing that putatively enabled Bernard Madoff to be such a successful investor] in 2008?

A: Bernard L. Madoff and Frank DiPascali, Jr., are the two names that I know of who are the key people involved in the split-strike conversion strategy.

Q: Who else? Do you know the names of any other people?

A: I don't.

Q: Did you guys push and try to get some names?

A: Well, we certainly asked the question.

. . .

Q: So you asked and didn't get any names. Did you push the issue or just leave it at that?

A: I don't recall.

Q: How would you know these people actually existed and were conducting the strategy?

A: Well, in the first case, Madoff had described that to us. Madoff after, you know, eighteen years of a very lengthy and trusted relationship, an individual who had a stellar reputation and great credibility in the industry provided us with this information so we had every reason to believe it was true.

In the second case, at some point in the last couple of years, I don't remember exactly when, I was present for an on-site [visit]—maybe the last two or three years—with Madoff where Madoff took us for a tour of his market making [where securities were bought and sold] floor. I believe Jeffrey Tucker [a founding partner of FGG] was at that meeting and I think Mark McKeefry [the controller of Fairfield Greenwich-Bermuda] might have been at that meeting.

Q: When did you go on that tour?

A: It would have been either two or three years ago. It feels in that time frame. I'm not entirely sure.

Q: Is that the same floor that did the [Fairfield] Sentry [Group] trades?

A: No, it was the market making floor and we saw in the market making business that there were dozens of trades.

Q: But did you take an analogous tour that was trading the split-strike conversion for Sentry [Funds]?

A: I did not.

Q: Did you ask to?

A: I had not asked as I recall. I don't recall asking Madoff.
           . . .
Q: So as far as you know you just don't know who anybody . . . other
           than Frank DiPascali and Bernard Madoff . . . that were executing
           the split-strike conversion strategy? Is that correct?
A: I'm saying I did not know, correct.
Q: Who ran the algorithmic trading platform?
A: I know that I heard from Madoff that he had a number of quants
           [quantitative analysts], MIT PhDs, certainly PhDs and quants—
           who, as Madoff described, built the algorithm systems and
           models to produce the signals to activate the entry and exits
           [from the market].
Q: But you don't know the names of any of these people, is that
           correct?
A: No, I did not.
           . . .
Q: So on the split-strike conversion strategy there are algorithms;
           I'm assuming there are computers, people presumably typing in
           inputs and receiving outputs. Where was that all occurring?
A: I have not seen those systems. Where they were occurring we
           understood—I understood from hearing Madoff say this and
           from hearing Jeffrey [Tucker] and others describe this—they
           were, I think, it was on the 17th floor of his offices.
Q: But you never actually saw that portion of his offices?
A: No, I did not.
Q: Do you know if anyone else at FGG did?
A: I don't know if anyone else at FGG did.
           . . .
Q: Have you ever had a tour of the part of Madoff's offices where he
           engaged in the split-strike conversion strategy?
A: No.
Q: Do you know of anyone else at FGG who has had a tour of the
           portion of Madoff's offices where he engages in the split-strike
           conversion strategy?
A: I don't know.
Q: You don't know of anybody?
A: I'm not aware of anybody that had access to it.
           . . .
Q: And at this point of time in October 2008, how did you know
           that these people [Madoff's split-strike conversion strategy team]
           actually existed and were conducting the strategy?

A: Well, again, we continued to get trade confirmations, monthly statements, you know, an operating relationship.

Q: Anything else that comes to mind?

A: Frankly, we—the SEC had done its investigation in 2005/2006—drew comfort from the fact that it had not taken any action; probably all I can think of now. [Here it is not mentioned that FGG executives were coached by Madoff on how to help him to deceive the SEC.[42]]

. . .

Q: What checking did FGG do to go kind of behind these returns to make sure that he had—that Madoff had—in fact, obtained these returns?

A: I'm not sure of any.

Q: Okay, is there any due diligence that FGG did with respect . . . to the fund other than having received Madoff's list of returns that he provided [to] you?

A: For me, just the conversation I had with him about the strategy. I'm not aware of what anybody else did.

Appendix 8-C

FGG Testimony Regarding Information or Knowledge about BLMIS Trades[43]

Amit Vijayvergiya

Q: A trade occurs on day T; when would FGG receive the trade confirmation from BLMIS?

A: It would typically be received T plus three, T plus two or T plus three.

Q: T plus two or T plus three, and how would it be received?

A: In paper form. Madoff would send those trade slips to CITCO [a custodian] as the primary recipient. A duplicate would be sent to FGG's New York office and also to Fairfield Greenwich-Bermuda's office.

Q: How would they be sent?

A: By mail.

. . .

Q: Did you ever want to ask to get the information sent more quickly or by fax or by e-mail or something to get it in a little less time?

A: Yes. I recall asking if it was possible for FGG to receive a fax on the trade day. ... The response was that for reasons of confidentiality and protecting their positions that the fax would need to be, could not be sent. ... My recollection is somewhat vague on this. I don't want to describe this as a definitive recollection, but that technologically they were equipped to send us the information on a month-end basis electronically.

Q: (by Vijayvergiya's attorney): Do you recall a discussion of front running?

A: Correct. Thank you. I do recall a conversation of front running on this topic where the description or the reason that was given was that in order to avoid any possibility of front running the trades that the trades themselves would be sent so that it could be received on a T plus two or T plus three basis after the trade itself had occurred.

Q: So the reason for not sending it by fax, well initially you said it was confidentiality; you're saying a separate reason is to make sure no one received the confirmation knowledge of what happened until two or three days later so there would be no possibility of front running.

A: Again, my recollections of both of those are general at this point so I won't be able to give you a definitive answer.

Q: Going back to front running; the trade has already occurred. What difference would it make if you get it T plus one or T plus three in terms of front running? ...

A: The way the split-strike conversion strategy would be implemented. I'll give you my understanding here. The way it would be implemented would be over the course of several days, so on each of what may be three trade days a basket of stocks and option collars would be constructed as evidenced by the trade ticket information that we received and from conversations we had with Madoff. So by the time a full implementation occurred it would be three days.
      ...

Q: How would that have occurred?

A: It's not frequent, but to my general recollection, as I was describing earlier, we received information from BLMIS—these trade tickets, month-end statements, paper copies, the electronic files. There was another way, and that is that we would receive some information about the asset value in the accounts on Friday mornings, so meaning the prior Thursday night's close. ... It had been going on for years before I joined the firm where someone from BLMIS—generally it was Erin, Eric, or Rob, the names I described earlier. There would be a discussion with one of the three people from BLMIS and someone from FGG where those account values were communicated.

Appendix 8-D

Excerpts from London High Court Opinion of Justice Andrew J. Popplewell, October 18, 2013[44]

19. MSIL's case against Mrs. Kohn can be summarized as follows. The true reason for the MSIL-Kohn payments was for introductions to Bernard Madoff's IA business. The written research provided to MSIL was, as she knew, valueless per se and worthless to MSIL in its trading business. It was provided merely as a pretext for the payments. The pretext was maintained by false invoicing purporting to justify the payments as being for such research. This dressing up of the payments by the provision of worthless research and false invoicing reflected Mrs. Kohn's knowledge that the payments were not for MSIL's benefit or in MSIL's interests.

20. Mrs. Kohn disputes this analysis. Her case is that the payments were for a range of services which she provided, and for which she was paid a proportionate amount pursuant to an agreement reached with the chief executive and owner of MSIL; it was a matter of indifference to her whether the payments were made by BLMIS or MSIL, which she regarded simple as parts of Bernard Madoff's single global business.

. . .

108. Mrs. Kohn's case was that that there were three strands to the services she agreed to provided and for which she was paid, namely (1) introductions of people, (2) advice, information and ideas about global financial and economic matters, communicated at face-to-face meetings with Bernard Madoff, and (3) written research. She regarded the first of these as the most significant.

. . .

354. The following elements of the evidence are important to an assessment of Mrs. Kohn's honesty:

(1) Until December 2008, Mrs. Kohn had no reason to questions the integrity of Bernard Madoff. . . .

(2) Mrs. Kohn knew that MSIL (through Bernard Madoff) had made an agreement for the provision of her services which included introductions, information and research. . . .

(3) The sums paid to her in respect of those services, including the MSIL-Kohn payments, were no more than reasonable remuneration for the value of the services provided. . . .

(4) She made no secret about the provision of those services. The face-to-face meetings were made in Bernard Madoff's glass fronted office for all his fellow directors and staff to see. The written research was openly provided and discussed with the London directors. . . .

(5) She made no secret of the invoicing for the services, or of the payments themselves. The invoices were sent by post. She or her husband collected the checks making no secret of their visits for that purpose. The electronic payments were, she correctly assumed, paid through the company's usual facilities and recorded openly in its books. . . .

(9) She believed that the services she provided conferred substantial benefits on MSIL. This was true of introductions as well as information, advice and research. . . . She regarded her introductions as valuable to MSIL as well as BLMIS; they were introductions of people, not money, and, so she believed, useful to any proprietary trading business which she understood to be operated by BLMIS in New York and MSIL in London.

. . .

469. I cannot forbear from recording the commendable dignity and restraint which I have observed in each of Mr. Raven, Mr. Flax, Mr. Toop and Mrs. Kohn throughout the trial. Bernard Madoff's fraud itself blighted their lives and tainted their good names simply by association. . . . To this was added the burden of this unfounded claim, making serious allegations of dishonesty, which threatened financial ruin and personal humiliation. It was commenced without forewarning—some discovered they were the subject of the claim by reading of it in the newspapers—and has been pursued aggressively and relentlessly over several years, on occasion with an unfair degree of hyperbole (for example referring to the MSIL-Kohn payments as "secret kickbacks" when there was nothing secret about them and on MSIL's own case they were introductory commissions which were not excessive). Mrs. Kohn's has suffered poisonous press releases by the SIPC trustee (for example, referring to her as Bernard Madoff's "criminal soul mate, whose greed and dishonest inventiveness equaled his own") and been subject to a worldwide freezing order and extensive disclosure of her family's assets and affairs.

CHAPTER 9

Steerers

In a con game, steerers are those who stand out as winners, sometimes big winners. They are proof that success is possible and easy. They become a con game's boosters.

Because the wealth of all of Madoff's clients—scattered at first around the United States and then around the world—steadily increased, he had no end of steerers, from many modest winners to several big winners, but all winners and all potential steerers to extol the wizardry of Madoff and BLMIS. In a short con, steerers are often merely posing as satisfied participants. In a long con, there are some individuals who make a great deal of money before it collapses, and, as a matter of course, they become obvious steerers.

Some BLMIS investment advisory (IA) clients were instructed not to broadcast too widely where their money was invested. To the degree that those individuals did not tell others about their increasing wealth, this would curtail their effectiveness as steerers. However, as the steady growth of the BLMIS IA business shows, reticence was not a rule commonly practiced by BLMIS IA investors. The word got around, and money continued to pour into the BLMIS 703 Account day after day, week after week, and year after year. BLMIS was in business for almost 50 years.

In Madoff's con, a larger percentage of ropers could readily be classified as steerers than the reverse.

Charles Ponzi—who promised investors a 50 percent profit within 45 days and a 100 percent profit within 90 days with a scheme to buy discounted postal reply coupons in Europe and redeem them at face value in the United States (a form of arbitrage)—figured out an unparalleled way to bring those who were making money from his con, that is, potential steerers, to the attention of prospective clients. He made it possible and easy for those claiming their newly found wealth to encounter those investing in his scam. They were simply given an opportunity to mingle together in his Securities Exchange Company offices.

> Meanwhile, the outer office began to resemble an illegal betting parlor, or a corner of the stock exchange. Always it was filled with a dozen or more people of all ages, sexes, and descriptions, who waited to invest, waited to collect, or merely stood discussing the wondrous ease with which money could be made these days if one knew how to do it. Several times a day the crowd would separate to leave a path from the front door to the door of the inner office, and a momentary silence would fall while Ponzi made his entrance or exit and the people stared at him in awe. As the days passed, the crowd grew larger, and Ponzi's passage was greeted with a smattering of applause.[1]

What likely investor would not be impressed? What likely investor would not be persuaded that there was very little risk? Ponzi and his audiences never tired of the performance.

Madoff's Steerers

The con man Bernard L. Madoff had a number of obvious steerers—many practiced investors, male, Jewish, and long-time associates and friends—whose IA accounts made a great deal of money—able to bear witness to his acuity as someone who could easily make anyone richer, much richer. Here is a synopsis of how three of them, all dead two years after Madoff's arrest—Jeffry M. Picower, Norman F. Levy, and Stanley Chais—worked with Madoff to become steerers. It is likely that the three caught the attention of many potential BLMIS investors, although it is not possible to estimate the number. Their success as BLMIS investors surely caught the attention of the SIPC trustee who forced forfeiture of some of their money stolen and given to them with indifference by Madoff.

Jeffry M. Picower

The accountant, attorney, and entrepreneur, Jeffry M. Picower was by far Madoff's most conspicuous steerer, having made more money than anyone else, including Madoff, from the con. He met Madoff through Saul Alpern, Madoff's father-in-law; he was the brother-in-law of the roper Michael Bienes, who worked for Alpern and had been married to and later divorced from Picower's older sister. Picower also had an MBA from Columbia University, and worked for the large accounting firm Laventhol & Horwath.

Picower set out to make a great deal of money; he marketed tax shelters and invested in merger and acquisitions, and was convinced that Madoff could help him do so. Thus, it is obviously not by mere chance that Picower found himself in Madoff's orbit and began an IA account at BLMIS, probably in the mid-1970s, perhaps even earlier.[2] The Madoff–Picower relationship was not based on friendship, but was strictly a business arrangement.

Beginning in the 1970s, and over the course of more than 30 years, Picower invested large sums of money[3] with BLMIS on behalf of himself, his businesses, his family, and numerous charitable organizations he established.[4] He was an aggressive investor willing to take big risks for high returns.[5] The regular account statements he received from BLMIS indicated that BLMIS was pursuing a buy-and-hold strategy, purchasing blue-chip corporate equities and low-risk securities and holding them for extended periods of time, rather than moving in and out of the market as was Madoff supposedly preferred investment strategy. Picower claimed, as did another of the three steerers, Stanley Chais, as well as others, that he came to believe his "account returns were generally consistent with movements in the broader markets and with returns achieved by other large and distinguished investment managers, such as Warren Buffett. ..."[6] This led him, he explained, "to be taken in by the professional, timely, and superior services BLMIS provided its customers, and the strong returns it reported. ..."

Over time, BLMIS in fact provided Picower with "strong returns." According to the SIPC trustee's records, between 1996 and 2007, a number of Picower's trading accounts had annual returns of more than 100 percent. On about two dozen occasions, the annual return exceeded 50 percent. During the same period, the biggest annual gain in either the Dow Jones Industrial Average or the S&P 500 was 31 percent; this was for the S&P 500 in 1997. The S&P 500's annual average for the period was slightly under 9 percent.

According to the SIPC trustee and as Figure 9.1 shows, from 1996 and continuing until 2005, Picower withdrew large sums of money from his BLMIS accounts. In 2001, he withdrew $821,000,950; in 2002, he withdrew $922,221,107; and in 2003, he withdrew $1,025,301,463.

Figure 9.1   Picower's Withdrawals from BLMIS Account.

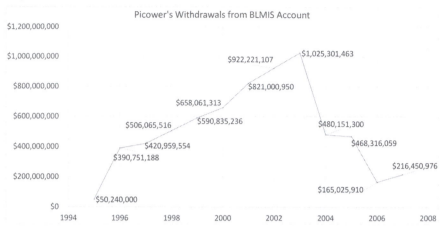

Picower's Withdrawals from BLMIS Account

Adapted from Dan Nguyen and Jake Bernstein, "Chart: The Picower-Madoff Transfers, from 1995–2008," *ProPublica*, June 23, 2009.

Beginning in 1995 until BLMIS went into bankruptcy, Picower made 670 withdrawals totaling $6,746,066,548. Well before 2005, the steady and continuing schedule of large withdrawals became a serious problem for BLMIS; on occasion it was simply overwhelmed.

In December 2008, Picower had 15 different accounts at BLMIS, the largest of which was Decisions Incorporated and through which he transacted his investment business. Over the years, he was able to withdraw either directly or from his accounts more than $7.2 billion.

Between 1995 and 2008, of Picower's 670 withdrawals, $5,771,339,795 was from his Decisions Incorporated account. In 2003, he made 52 withdrawals from his various accounts. By 2009, Picower was on a list published by *Forbes Magazine* of Americans worth at least $1 billion.[7] Although often described as somewhat secretive and even reclusive, someone who preferred to stay out of the public spotlight, Picower's great wealth, much of it coming from his investments at BLMIS,[8] was by itself enough to make others take notice. Whether or not he may have been reluctant to become one, he was surely a steerer for BLMIS.

Even before Madoff's trial and imprisonment, the SIPC trustee, contending that Picower was a party to the fraud, filed a Complaint against him seeking the "payment and turnover . . . of any or all" of his multibillion dollar investment returns through him to other

BLMIS customers. Not surprisingly, Picower countered that he was not "a party to the fraud," not liable for the return of what he considered his earnings, legal earnings from his BLMIS accounts. In response to Picower's Motion to Dismiss the Complaint filed at the end of July 2009, the SIPC trustee filed an Opposition to the Motion to Dismiss, reiterating a number of allegations:

> Picower wired $125 million to BLMIS. . . . This deposit constituted more than ¼ of the total cash that Picower ever invested in BLMIS. Within two weeks, the $125 million deposit had purportedly grown to $164 million because of a dramatic "gain" on the securities held in the account. . . . So . . . that within two weeks after he opened his account, he had made almost $40 million from trading that supposedly occurred months before the account was opened or funded.[9]
>
> . . .
>
> In May 2007 Picower and [April] Freilich [a Picower employee] asked BLMIS employees to change the trading activity that had supposedly occurred in the Picower Foundation account for January and February 2006 in order to generate additional gains. After some discussion about the exact amount of gain Picower wanted, and clarification that the gain should be for 2007, Freilich directed BLMIS to generate $12.3 million in gains for January and February. Although it was several months too late to make any actual trades in January or February, BLMIS created statements that reported new transactions in January and February 2007 resulting in a purported gain of $12.6 million. . . . The Picower Foundation's May 2007 statement reflected different holdings than had been reflected in its account statements from January through April 2007. The total value of the account was $54.6 million higher on May 31, 2007 than it had been in April 2007 largely because of these newly fabricated holdings and new history.[10]
>
> . . .
>
> Picower faxed a letter dated December 1, 2005 directing various sales across various accounts. BLMIS reported the sales having settled on December 2. This alone is suspicious, as settlement is typically three business days after the trade date, and the sales would have had to take place before December 1. But the letter was not

actually faxed to BLMIS on December 1—it was faxed on December 22 and backdated by Picower to December 1. . . . Picower's own independently maintained records reflect the stock that was supposedly sold before December 2 was still held by the accounts as of December 16.[11]

. . .

In December 2005, BLMIS created back-dated "purchases" of stock in certain accounts, recording them as having settled almost a full year earlier. . . . Along with an unrealized gain of about $79 million, the accounts were instantly credited, in December 2005, with quarterly dividends for March, June, and September 2005. . . . Neither the dividends nor the purchases appear on Picower's 2005 account statements for the months from January 2005 through November 2005 from BLMIS. Nor do the stock positions, which supposedly would have been held since January, appear on the portfolio appraisal system that Picower maintained as of November 30, 2005.[12]

Clearly from his investigation, the SIPC trustee was convinced that he had enough evidence to compel Picower to return all, most, or some of the money that he had withdrawn from his BLMIS accounts. Apparently, Picower's attorneys were also convinced that the SIPC trustee had amassed enough compelling evidence to place Picower in legal jeopardy.

By September 2009, the SIPC trustee was no longer alleging that Picower was a co-conspirator of Madoff, and negotiations to settle the SIPC claim against Picower began. (According to Picower's attorney at that time, "the Picowers in good faith have initiated discussions with the trustee to reach a settlement in order to avoid years of extensive litigation.")

On October 15, 2009, Picower initialed or signed each of the 36 pages of his last will and testament.

On October 25, 2009, at the age of 67, Picower was found drowned at the bottom of his swimming pool in Palm Beach, Florida, calling to mind the death of another self-made, mysterious, and somewhat shady stalker after the American Dream, Jay Gatsby, as he too was at home swimming.

On December 17, 2010, Picower's estate announced a forfeiture settlement with the government for money "derived from proceeds traceable to offenses orchestrated by Bernard L. Madoff that were part of a scheme to defraud investors." Barbara Picower agreed to return $7,206,157,717 that her husband had withdrawn from BLMIS.[13]

This total is over 40 percent of the estimated principal lost—or the money stolen—in the Madoff con. (Since the interest-earnings of this money were not returned, the BLMIS's $7.2 billion that Picower had use of for years before his estate agreed to forfeiture can be seen as a decidedly large zero-interest margin loan.) From the total that in the end the Picower estate wrote off, the SIPC trustee was immediately able to put aside $5 billion to return to defrauded BLMIS clients.

Norman F. Levy

Norman F. Levy was already a highly successful New York commercial real estate broker when Madoff was still in public school. By the time Madoff started BLMIS, Levy was president of Cross & Brown, one of America's largest real estate firms. At one point he had ownership in 70 properties, including the Seagram Building, and almost two dozen shopping centers. Levy began investing in BLMIS in 1975, and at the time of his death in September 2005 at 93, there were 39 accounts in his name and the names of his children and family and charitable trusts, a significant amount of Levy's total assets. One SIPC trustee document estimated that Levy's investments in BLMIS "helped [in increasing] his wealth from $180 million in 1986 to $1.5 billion in 1998."[14] Levy gave Madoff more than his money to invest; he gave him credibility with and unusual access to bankers, most notably, JPMorgan Chase Bank.

In spite of the great difference in age between them, Levy and Madoff became close friends, as close as possible in the secretive and competitive world of Wall Street. In fact, Levy designated Madoff as an executor of his estate, vesting in Madoff the power to make unilateral investment decisions regarding the estate's non–real estate assets.

As described to a journalist by the American model (and actress) Carmen Dell'Orefice, the Levy–Madoff relationship was not only intimate but also genuine. What she participated in and observed is a window into how a steerer can further a con, as well as how the long-running Madoff con flourished seemingly without plan or direction, at least from Madoff.

Dell'Orefice began her interview by describing how Levy, whom she had been dating for four months, first introduced her to Madoff after giving her the initial $100,000—a substantial gratuity for a recently acquired companion—to begin a BLMIS IA account, and how immediately she and Levy, as a couple, became friends of Bernard and Ruth Madoff.

On Valentine's Day, 1994, Levy asked her to meet him at Madoff's office. She arrived early, and remembered: "And there was a little man sitting behind a very big desk. 'Are you Mr. Madoff?' I asked." She found little about him impressive except for his wealth. After the meeting and the opening of her IA account, she, through her relationship with Levy, was accepted as part of Madoff's inner social circle. Soon after, Dell'Orefice, Levy, and Bernard and Ruth Madoff took their first of many trips together to London. "Bernie arranged for the honeymoon suite at the Lanesborough," she explained. "It was the suite Bernie usually stayed in, but he gave it up to Norman. Bernie and Ruth ... had a suite upstairs."

As the friendship of the four blossomed, Dell'Orefice's initial investment of $100,000 grew into millions. She recalled that the four were together for many dinners, family gatherings, charity balls, and BLMIS picnics. Dell'Orefice detailed trips on yachts and outings in New York and evenings at the Madoff house in Palm Beach—an uninterrupted dozen years of Norman, Carmen, and Bernie and Ruth. They celebrated birthdays together. She told of how Madoff built a yacht for Levy in the last years of his life. Dell'Orefice shared a picture of Madoff aboard the yacht at sea kissing Levy on the cheek. Many times Levy said of Madoff: "He is my son."

Dell'Orefice noted that Madoff always deferred to Levy, and often and readily did him favors. In France, he found Levy his favorite ice cream, and brought it to him. Although Madoff consumed little alcohol, he planned wine-tasting tours for Levy. He arranged other excursions. To relax, Levy and Madoff spent their time watching television and movies and listening to music. (It is unclear whether Dell'Orefice recollection that Madoff's "taste leaned to the likes of Neil Diamond" is true or said to malign.)

Levy was a large and gregarious man, someone who could readily become the center of attention. The Madoff Dell'Orefice remembers was not only "little," but "shy," at least in the shadow of Levy, whose wealth and putative ability as an investor was what drew the attention of others.[15] Levy was a perfect steerer, a front man who lent respectability to Madoff's con. However, Levy was much more than a figurehead.

Dell'Orefice never saw Levy and Madoff talking business "except on the telephone." Yet, Levy conducted a great deal of business with BLMIS. Table 9.1 taken from a letter from the president of the SIPC to the chair of the House of Representatives Subcommittee on Capital Markets shows the extensiveness of that business between 1992 and 2005.

There is no need to belabor what this table makes evident—the Levy–Madoff business relationship was as robust as their social relationship.

Table 9.1   Norman Levy's BLMIS IA Account, 1992–2005

Year	Cash In	Cash Out
1992	$1,108,364,660	$994,048,201
1993	$1,387,358,368	$1,517,903,726
1994	$2,279,645,611	$2,128,805,955
1995	$3,542,773,369	$3,453,047,453
1996	$5,372,928,546	$5,471,231,206
1997	$7,067,467,981	$7,377,869,833
1998	$10,102,787,010	$10,039,234,425
1999	$15,316,343,975	$15,227,808,969
2000	$23,044,584,696	$23,103,627,635
2001	$35,095,634,103	$35,154,090,159
2002	$862,232,070	$898,796,993
2003	$307,000,000	$246,934,119
2004	$161,511	$49,478,915
2005	$137,576	$35,629,433

Source: Letter from Stephen P. Harbeck, president of SIPC to Congressman Scott Garrett, op. cit. 14–15.

Levy's BLMIS IA account over many years was extraordinarily active. In 1997, Levy transferred $7 billion to the 703 Account and the 703 Account transferred $7 billion back to Levy; in 1998, Levy transferred $10 billion to the 703 Account and the 703 Account transferred $10 billion back to Levy; in 1999, Levy transferred $15 billion to the 703 Account and the 703 Account transferred $15 billion back to Levy; in 2000, Levy transferred $23 billion to the 703 Account and the 703 Account transferred $23 billion back to Levy; in 2001, Levy transferred $35 billion to the 703 Account and the 703 Account transferred $35 billion back to Levy. These amounts are many times greater than the combined transfers of all other BLMIS IA investors, who put in a total of $10.2 billion and took out $8.5 billion in the 703 Account, during this period.

What the following paragraph, summarizing court submissions by the SIPC trustee, shows is consistent, although not identical, with these not quite believable figures.

Levy received almost $76 billion from the BLMIS 703 Account at JPMorgan Chase Bank between December 1998 and September 2005. This total, by itself, might have caught the attention of someone at the bank; the pattern of transactions is precisely what financial institutions are cautioned to look for in order to detect money laundering or other fraud: repetitiveness and not readily explained spikes in activity. Repetitiveness and spikes in Levy's account are most evident. For example, during 2002, BLMIS initiated outgoing transactions to Levy in the precise amount of $986,301 on 318 separate occasions, sometimes multiple times on a single day, and from December 2001 to March 2003, the total monthly dollar amounts coming into the 703 Account from Levy were almost always equal to the total monthly dollar amounts being withdrawn from the 703 Account by him. Further, there was a downward spike in activity between Levy and the 703 Account after December 2001. In December 2001, a total of approximately $6.8 billion was moved in and out of Levy's BLMIS IA account and shortly thereafter Levy's activity with the 703 Account decreased significantly. Many of Levy's transactions with the 703 Account were conducted by check, which is something also somewhat unusual on its face. In December 2001, Levy deposited checks daily in the amount of $90 million. This unusual blizzard of Levy–Madoff transactions, the rapid-fire flow of checks or "round-trip" checks, suggests money laundering and/or check kiting (taking advantage of the float to make use of nonexistent funds).[16]

The account of these Levy–Madoff transactions, as put together from bank records and as accepted by both the government and JPMorgan Chase Bank as factual, found in Appendix 9-A, shows in as much detail the closeness of the Levy–Madoff business relationship. More importantly, what these excerpts also show is how executives at JPMorgan Chase Bank—just as at least the vast majority of BLMIS investors, SEC investigators, FGG executives, and many BLMIS 17th floor employees—did not understand that they were at the center of a con game.[17] A key passage in a memorandum referred to in the appendix quotes a senior investment officer at JPMorgan Chase Bank, working with a quantitative analyst, as stating that he was "very comfortable" with Madoff, "his operation," and "the conservative, risk-adverse investment approach." It eventually occurred to the bank executive that perhaps Madoff may have been fudging the numbers, but it obviously did not occur to him that Madoff was committing a crime.

In short, what is patently clear about the Levy–Madoff business relationship is that billions of dollars were routinely transferred in and out of the 703 Account by Levy and Madoff. Sometimes daily, they wrote checks back and forth to each other to, among other things, take advantage of normal delays in the check-clearing process and make it seem as though the accounts had more money in them than they did. Interest was paid on the inflated amount. When Levy was informed about the scheme by a bank official, he reportedly responded:

"If Bernie is using the float, it is fine with me; he makes a lot of money for my account."[18] It is unclear, with all of the checks swirling around, whether or not Levy thought that Madoff was committing a crime.

Finally, Levy was given bank loans which were used to fund his investments with BLMIS. In 1996, he had $188 million in outstanding loans from JPMorgan Chase Bank, and he was not only able to use this money to continue to greatly increase his wealth by earning much more from his IA accounts at BLMIS than the cost of the loans, but he was able to provide BLMIS a large amount of cash to perpetuate the con. JPMorgan Chase Bank continued extending loans to Levy year after year, making him ever wealthier and helping Madoff to extend his con.

The treasure Levy amassed demonstrated for many in the world of finance and beyond that a social or professional (or social and professional) relationship with Madoff could be quite beneficial. It is no wonder that a half dozen years after his father's death, and even after hearing that Madoff had illegally taken $250 million out of his father's estate, Levy's son, Francis, was able to tell an interviewer: "My father believed in Bernie Madoff. He would say: 'If there was one honorable person, it is Bernie.'" Francis Levy added: "I'm not angry at him [Madoff]." What Levy heir would be?

Stanley Chais

Stanley Chais was almost as much a roper as a steerer for BLMIS. He was described by the California Attorney General as merely serving as a "Madoff middleman." However, he was much more than that. He is best classified as a steerer as he seemed much more interested in increasing his own family wealth through BLMIS than the wealth of others including friends or his feeder funds he used to pass money to BLMIS.

Chais began investing in BLMIS in the 1970s, and over the years he held 60 or more entity and/or personal accounts at BLMIS. By the time Madoff was arrested in 2008, Chais had withdrawn over $1 billion from his BLMIS accounts, funneling much of it to his children and their spouses, and to various entities he created in great part for the benefit of his extended family. He also established, and was the general partner for, three feeder funds begun in the 1970s—the Popham (1975), Lambeth (1970), and Brighton (1973) Funds—feeder funds that raised money from others to pass to BLMIS. The three were limited partnerships, but took in money from additional subfunds. Chais told investors in these feeder funds that he achieved unusually strong and steady returns using a complex combination of investing in stocks and currency, along with derivative and futures trading. Much like the practice at BLMIS, with the assistance of his account- ant, Chais "distributed periodic reports to the Chais Funds investors, representing each investor's purported balance and returns based upon the BLMIS reports that were provided to Chais. Madoff pro- vided Chais the account statements that Chais in turn provided to the Chais Funds investors." According to the account statements, the Chais Funds consistently yielded purported annual returns between 20 and 25 percent, and supposedly did not have returns of less than 10 percent since at least 1995.[19]

A backstage 17th floor employee succinctly described in court how Chais account was able to steadily continue to grow.

Q: When do you recall first becoming familiar with Mr. Chais?
A: I've heard the name as far back as certainly the 1980s; early 1980s. I heard that name in 1977.
Q: Okay. Do you recall how you heard that in 1977?
A: Bernie said: "I have a client named Stanley Chais. His wife is a writer. She wrote a screenplay." He threw it at me. He said: "go read it, kid. Tell me if it's any good." Her name is Pamela Chais, and I remember where I read the screenplay, which was Ralph Madoff's office; so it had to be 1976 or 1977.
Q: Did Mr. Chais have accounts with BLMIS?
A: Yes.
Q: Do you recall what types of accounts they were?
A: They were Annette[Bongiorno's] accounts.
          . . .
Q: Now, did there come a time that you were assigned respon- sibilities with connections to Mr. Chais' accounts?
A: Yes.
          . . .
Q: And what were you tasked with doing?
A: To create a strategy for him that would be hedged using stocks and individual stock options for five of his accounts, three of which were funds that he managed and one was an offshore or foreign philanthropy trust and the other was trust for one of his children.
Q: And as part of your involvement with Mr. Chais' accounts did you learn about requirements he had for the trading in his accounts?
A: For the account that I managed?
Q: Yes.

A: He was never allowed to take a loss. ... He wanted to either break even or make money on all three legs, which was insane. So Bernie switched gear, and he could not put him back in this arbitrage, but Stan claimed he couldn't—didn't know how to account for a loss was all about. Losses were just not part of his universe. So he forced Bernie to redirect the trading strategy within the same strategy but never write a ticket that has a loss. It was insanity.

...

Q: Now, after the conversation you testified about in which Mr. Chais said his accounts were not permitted to lose money, was a new trading strategy implemented in which there would never be a loss for any of his accounts?

A: What Bernie decided to do was to—in order to ensure that the strategy would never result in a loss he stopped charging him commissions because there was one time where we actually put on a strategy and took it off and the net of the three legs was zero, and Stanley still complained that he lost money.

We, quite frankly, were baffled at where, we don't see it, and it turned out it was the $100 or $200 or $300 [dollars] in commission on the option transactions that was posted that caused him to go into the red slightly. So Bernie put down a mandate never charge him a commission, and this way it ensured that even if you bought stock at 10 or bought an option at two and sold it at two, where you would on paper break even, you wouldn't be in the red because you weren't even charging commissions.

...

Q: Now, was that option strategy something that could be implemented in the real world, in the manner it was with Mr. Chais?

A: No.

Q: And was any of the trading in Mr. Chais' account real?

A: No.

...

Q: Briefly describe, from a high level, how the fake trading that was going on in Chais accounts occurred?

A: She [JoAnn Crupi] would have a list of securities that were fairly well known stocks that were very volatile, typically. She maintained that list, and then occasionally when it was necessary to put Mr. Chais' money to work in the five accounts that she and I were responsible for, she would take what's known as a Bloomberg sheet.

When you punch up a security symbol on screen, there are certain parameters you can request that will give you historical pricing. I think the first page goes back about 20 trading days. It shows you the high, the low, the last sale, maybe it shows you the opening, but it's historical pricing data of a security.

So she would typically look to her list, print out an array of historical stock prices and, based on the level of the stock price, she would choose which options would most likely work. So she would print a put option spreadsheet, and a call option spreadsheet, and then she would lay them out on the table and look for the pricing movement and the days where the stock was—had the widest range, and she would literally build a little puzzle.

. . .

Q: And were you able to see how she was working on these documents?

A: Initially I taught her how to do it; so I would see every move she made.

. . .

Q: Now, you said that there is an expected rate of return of 19½%, which we see on the top right-hand side?

A: Yes, sir.

Q: What was your understating of the return—of what that expected rate of return was?

A: It was an amount that was dictated by Bernie.

. . .

Q: And what is the expected rate of return?

A: It is how much money something should earn over a period of time.

Q: So in this case, Mr. Chais' account, this Brighton account, should earn 19½%. Do you know over what time period that would be?

A: Annualized for the second quarter of 2006.

Q: So—

A: So it's approximately 5% per quarter.

Q: 19½%?[20]

From 1995 through 2008, the Chais Funds withdrew more money from BLMIS than they contributed. The funds' investors, excluding Chais, made the following contributions and received the following distributions:

Popham's Limited Partners made total contributions of approximately $9,541,000 into the Fund and made total withdrawals of approximately $95,978,000 from the Fund, for total net profits of approximately $86,437,000.

Lambeth's Limited Partners made total contributions of approximately $105,761,000 into the Fund and made total withdrawals of approximately $326,439,000 from the Fund, for total net profits of approximately $220,678,000.

Brighton's Limited Partners made total contributions of approximately $45,729,000 into the Fund and made total withdrawals of approximately $148,877,000 from the Fund, for total net profits of approximately $103,148,000.[21]

Chais, on his own behalf (and on behalf of the 1991Family Trust from 2004 onwards), made the following contributions and received the following distributions:

Made approximately $12,087,000 in contributions to the Funds and took total withdrawals of approximately $355,779,000 from the Funds for total net profits of approximately $343,692,000.

The Chais Family Accounts and Chais Entity Accounts received total distributions of approximately $202,300,000 from Madoff in excess in total contributions.

Chais, on his own behalf, as well as on behalf of his family members and entities related to him and his family members withdrew at least $545,992,000 more than they invested with Madoff.[22]

The money invested in the three Chais Funds was sent directly to BLMIS. From directly passing money invested in the Chais Funds to BLMIS, Chais received management fees of 25% of annual reported earnings of more than 10%, which occurred almost always. The commissions, totaling $269,608,000, paid to Chais were returned to BLMIS and paid into one of his IA accounts.[23] In their final monthly statements before BLMIS's bankruptcy, Popham's account balance, with over 110 investors, was approximately $130 million; Lambeth's account balance, with over 260 investors, was approximately $400 million; and Brighton's account balance, with over 90 investors, was approximately $380 million, a total of $910 million (actually closer to 1 percent more) that was lost with the collapse of Madoff's con. In light of these facts, the SIPC trustee came to believe that the Chais Funds were "dominated and used merely as an instrument of Chais to benefit the interests of Chais and those of his family."[24]

Table 9.2 is a listing of the 24 Chais BLMIS IA accounts with total withdrawals of at least $5 million between 1996 and 2008.

As would be expected, most of the money from the total withdrawals of $1,152,597,634 from these 60 Chais BLMIS IA accounts was for investors of the Popham, Lambeth, and Brighton funds. However, a substantial amount was withdrawn for the use of Chais, his wife, his children, his grandchildren, and the other entities created for the benefit of his family. In fact, the accounts of Chais's extended family members "received drastically higher rates of returns than those reported for [other accounts Stanley Chais putatively managed] during the same periods."[25]

Between 1996 and 2007, the returns for the Chais Family Accounts at BLMIS were impressive. There were 125 instances of returns exceeding 50 percent and more than 35 instances of returns of at least 100 percent. (These substantial returns often followed manufactured losses in accounts for the purpose of evading the payment of taxes.) While the S&P 500 Index saw annual average returns of 10.7 percent and 52 months of negative returns during this period, Chais's accounts at BLMIS, according to the SIPC trustee, had an annual rate of return of over 39 percent.[26]

According to the SIPC trustee, Chais's exceptional returns beyond what most BLMIS IA customers generally expected was largely due to an uninterrupted stratagem of creating fictitious purchases and sales of equities. One example:

Defendant Appleby's [in which Pamela Chais (his wife) is an officer and/or director and/or principal] account as of December 1997 purportedly included 43,600 shares of Dell Computer Corp. Among the "trades" reported in Appleby's March 1998 statement

Table 9.2 Chais's Withdrawals from BLMIS Accounts

Account Name	Amount
Appleby Productions Ltd. Defined Contribution Plan	$369,204
Appleby Productions Ltd. Money Purchase Plan	$14,116,741
Appleby Productions Ltd. Profit Sharing Plan	$2,672,832
The Brighton Company	$246,125,569
Chais Family Foundation	$53,448,000
Chais 1991 Family Trust 1	$30,900,000
Chais 1991 Family Trust 2	$2,000,000
Chais 1991 Family Trust 3	$5,000,000
Emily Chais	$8,943,000
Emily Chais Trust 1	$1,447,682
Emily Chais Trust 2	$4,382,503
Emily Chais Trust 3	$6,085,765
Emily Chais Issue Trust 1	$2,808,282
Emily Chais Issue Trust 2	$3,019,701
Emily Chais 1983 Trust	$383,394
Mark Hugh Chais & Mirie Chais Jt Wros	$13,545,000
Mark Hugh Chais Trust 1	$1,411,832
Mark Hugh Chais Trust 2	$4,212,295
Mark Hugh Chais Trust 3	$6,058,938
Mark Hugh Chais Issue Trust 1	$2,822,804
Mark Hugh Chais Issue Trust 2	$3,250,855
Mark Hugh Chais 1983 Trust	$369,970
William Chais	$3,757,500
William Frederick Chais Trust 1	$1,649,870
William Frederick Chais Trust 2	$4,188,650
William Frederick Chais Trust 3	$5,811,512
William F. Chais Issue Trust 1	$2,796,770
William F. Chais Issue Trust 2	$2,942,089
William Frederick Chais 1983 Trust	$379,194
Madeline Celia Chais 1992 Trust	$1,539,368
Chloe Francis Chais 1994 Trust	$1,076,800
The 1994 Trust for the Children of Stanley & Pamela Chais	$3,931,052
The 1996 Trust for the Children of Pamela Chais & Stanley Chais	$35,841
Jonathan Wolf Chais Trust	$1,178,883
The 1996 Trust for the Children of Pamela & Stanley Chais	$20,578,301
Tali Chais 1997 Trust	$578,614
Ari Chais 1999 Trust	$328,277
Chais Investments	$10,400,000
Justin Robert Chasalow 1999 Trust c/o Stanley Chais	$336,949

(**Continued**)

Table 9.2   (Continued)

Account Name	Amount
Rachel Allison Chasalow 1999 Trust c/o Stanley Chais	$336,710
Benjamin Paul Chasalow 1999 Trust c/o Stanley Chais	$336,105
Al Angel Trustee of the 1999 Trust for the Grandchildren of Stanley and Pamela Chais	$4,070,177
Mirie Chais Te'Ena 12	$350,000
William Chais & Wrenn Chais 1994 Family Trust Dated 4/25/95	$5,750,000
Ari Chais Transferee # 1	$7,492,494
Tali Chais Transferee #1	$7,490,647
Madeline Chais Transferee #1	$5,832,056
Chloe Chais Transferee #1	$5,751,489
Jonathan Chais Transferee #1	$5,752,047
Benjamin Paul Chasalow Transferee #1	$5,925,998
Justin Robert Chasalow Transferee #1	$5,923,037
Rachel Allison Chasalow Transferee #1	$5,923,908
Chais Family Foundation	$3,000,000
The Lambeth Company c/o Stanley Chais	$451,944,399
Onondaga Inc. Money Purchase Plan	$23,404
Onondaga Inc. Defined Benefit Pension Plan c/o Stanley Chais	$6,911
The Popham Company	$144,037,543
The Unicycle Trading Company c/o Stanley Chais	$541,483
The Unicycle Trading Company c/o William Chais	$16,796,000
Unicycle Corp. Money Purchase Plan	$429,189
TOTAL	$1,152,597,634

was the fictitious sale of 21,800 shares of Dell on June 17, 1997, for a total of $2,357,125. The statement reflected a securities position of 21,800 shares of Dell valued $1,476,950, and a total market value of all securities of $4,152,213.13. But Dell stock had a 2:1 split in July 1997: Appleby's 43,600 shares in Dell had been, back in June 1997, only 21,800 shares. So, if Appleby really had sold 21,800 shares on June 17, 1997 (instead of nine months later when the "transaction" was being created) the Dell position would have been fully liquidated and the remaining balance for these securities would have been zero. Accordingly, the sale of Dell securities on the March 1998 statement was clearly fabricated, a fact which should have been obvious to Chais. The following month, the April 1998 Appleby statement reversed the fictitious entry, reflecting [an adjustment] of 21,800 shares of Dell with no corresponding value, and a reduction of the total market value of securities for the account of $2,806,566,50. [This was an] inexplicable disappearance of holdings that represent about one third of the account value.[27]

It is emphasized that Chais's success investing the Chais Family Accounts in BLMIS resulted, for the period 1995 through 2008, in "Chais and his family members [withdrawing] approximately a half a billion dollars more than they invested with Madoff."[28]

A Complaint against Chais filed by the California Attorney General includes additional information regarding the Chais–Madoff relationship.[29] Notably, some of Chais's California investors claimed that they had no knowledge that the two had even worked together; in fact, they "had never heard of Madoff before his downfall." The Complaint alleges that, in fact, "Chais instructed his accountant that neither Madoff nor Chais wanted Madoff's name or involvement disclosed to Chais Funds investors." After Madoff's arrest, of course, Chais was forced to disclose to these investors "that the man actually handling all of their funds was Madoff." If this not knowing that Chais was simply passing their investments to BLMIS was generally true and not isolated or rare, Chais would not have been a Madoff steerer to this set of investor or to their friends with whom they discussed financial matters. Chais could not have been a Madoff steerer to the many he told in detail that he was directing the investments employing a complex, effective and reliable, strategy.

By not acknowledging that he was simply shuffling money to Madoff, by conveying the false impression that he was actively and personally managing money handed over to him, Chais was able to substantiate his investment-savant image "by appearing to provide unfailing large returns to his investors. [This would be the case after] the mid-1990s, after Chais told Madoff that he could not tolerate losses and that he did not want there to be any losses in any of the Chais Funds' trades. Madoff apparently accommodated Chais's request and seems to have produced 'made-to-order' returns for him [including occasional, 'made-for-order' losses]. Between 1999 and 2008, despite supposedly executing thousands of trades on behalf of the Chais Funds, Madoff did not report a loss on a single equities trade. ... Madoff appears to have generated losses for the Chais Family Accounts on demand."[30]

In court, an attorney for the SIPC trustee familiar with the Chais–Madoff relationship outlined his understanding of how BLMIS IA money was passed to Chais.

The money would come out of Madoff, and it would go to the City National Bank in California.

City National Bank in California would then have two buckets, or, at least, it was essentially two buckets.

One bucket was for [the] Chais family, all the entities that are Stanley Chais, his wife, his children, all those entities.

The second bucket was called the arbitrage. That was what it was called by Madoff. But that is three entities: Popham, Lambeth, and Brighton Funds. They are entities in California where investors, people come into these entities and for 30 years, or more than that perhaps. Stanley Chais [acting here as a roper] was the one that these investors gave their money to. He, Your Honor, would give the money to Madoff. . . .

Money would go from City National Bank to an account that Mr. Chais had at Goldman Sachs and that is in two parts. One I will call the liquid account; it has the liquid assets. The other is partnerships, real estate partnerships. . . . There were millions of dollars potentially owed on those real estate investments. And what has been happening over time, as Madoff gave the money to Chais, Chais was able to use that money to make his capital calls to Goldman Sachs.[31]

Eleven months and a day after Picower's heart attack and drowning in Florida, Chais, who had been suffering a rare blood disease, died at age 84 in New York.

There were countless other Madoff steerers, who, unlike Picower, Levy, and Chais, survived and who also escaped the threat of entanglement with the legal system.

Appendix 9

Transactions between BLMIS and Norman F. Levy at JPMorgan Chase Bank (Beginning in the Mid-1990s until 2005, the Year of Levy's Death)

Beginning in the mid-1990s, employees in the Private Bank for Chemical Bank, a predecessor of JPMorgan Chase Bank, identified a series of transactions between the account of a Private Bank client [Norman F. Levy] and accounts held by BLMIS, including the 703 Account. As one of the bank's largest individual clients, with a portfolio valued (as of the mid-1990s) at approximately $2.3 billion, Levy was highly valued by JPMorgan Chase Bank and its predecessors and was provided with his own office within the JPMorgan Chase Bank's offices. In addition, the bank's Global Trust & Fiduciary Services business line served (along with Bernard L. Madoff) as co-executor and co-trustee of Levy's will, and stood to earn approximately $15 million in fee income upon his death.

The transactions between Madoff and Levy consisted of "round-trip" transactions which would typically begin with Madoff writing checks from an account at another bank ("Madoff Bank 2") to one of Levy's accounts at JPMorgan Chase Bank and its predecessors. Later the same day, Madoff would transfer money from his 703 Account to his account at Madoff Bank 2 to cover the earlier check from Madoff Bank 2 to Levy at JPMorgan Chase Bank. And, in the final leg of the transaction, as known to JPMorgan Chase Bank, Levy would transfer funds from his JPMorgan Chase Bank account to the 703 Account in an amount sufficient to cover the original check he had received from Madoff at Madoff Bank 2. These "round-trip" transactions occurred on a virtually daily basis for a period of years, and were each in the amount of tens of millions of dollars. Because of the delay between when the transactions were credited and when they were cleared (referred to as the "float") the effect of these transactions was to make BLMIS's balances at JPMorgan Chase Bank appear to be larger than they otherwise were, resulting in inflated interest payments to BLMIS by JPMorgan Chase Bank. . . .

In or about 1996, personnel from Madoff Bank 2 investigated the "round-trip" transactions between Madoff and Levy. As a result of that investigation, which included meetings with representatives of BLMIS, Madoff Bank 2 concluded that there was no legitimate business purpose for these transactions, which appeared to be a check kiting scheme, and terminated its banking relationship with BLMIS. . . .

JPMorgan Chase Bank allowed Levy's transactions to continue, although JPMorgan Chase Bank did require Levy to reimburse JPMorgan Chase Bank for the interest payments that these transactions had cost the bank.

After Madoff Bank 2 closed the BLMIS account in or about 1996, Levy and BLMIS continued to engage in "round-trip" transactions, the sizes of which increased, entirely through JPMorgan Chase Bank accounts. In December 2001, Levy engaged in approximately $6.8 billion worth of transactions with BLMIS—all between Levy's account at JPMorgan Chase Bank and the BLMIS 703 Account—in a series of usually $90 million transactions. These transactions continued through 2003.

JPMorgan Chase Bank Private Bankers did not report the "round-trip" transactions between Levy and BLMIS to JPMorgan Chase Bank anti-money laundering personnel. After Madoff's arrest in 2008, JPMorgan Chase Bank anti-money laundering personnel reviewed the activity and filed a suspicious activity report concerning the above transactions.

QUESTIONS ABOUT BLMIS'S INVESTMENT RETURNS

In or about 1993, Levy requested that a senior investment officer of the Private Bank of Chemical Bank, a predecessor of JPMorgan Chase Bank, meet with Madoff so that Levy could better understand how Madoff regularly generated consistent returns. Along with a quantitative analyst, the senior investment officer met with Madoff. A memorandum from around the time of the visit reports that the senior investment officer was "very comfortable" with Madoff, "his operation," and "the conservative, risk-adverse investment approach" for Levy, and that the analyst said that "it is quite possible for top-notch investment advisors to make 20–30% annual returns through such short-term programs." However, the senior investment officer later explained that he and the analyst could not understand how BLMIS was able to generate such consistent quarterly returns for Levy despite historic volatility in the market, and therefore concluded that BLMIS "might be smoothing out the returns" by sharing trading spreads and profits from BLMIS market making business with Levy.

In or about 1998, the JPMorgan Chase Bank Private Bank conducted a review of BLMIS because it had been extending credit to Levy to invest in BLMIS. The review reflected that, according to BLMIS account statements, Levy's reported investments, the substantial majority of which were invested through BLMIS, had increased from $183 million at the end of 1986 to $1.7 billion in early 1998—an increase of 830% in 12 years. The JPMorgan Chase Bank Private Bank also learned that BLMIS reported consistently positive returns for Levy at all times, including through the 1987 stock market crash and subsequent stock market corrections.[32]

CHAPTER 10

JPMorgan Chase Bank

With approximately $2.4 trillion in total assets as of December 31, 2013, JPMorgan Chase Bank is the largest banking institution in the United States. The bank has six business segments and is registered both as a provider of investment advisory services and as a brokerage firm. Basically, only one of JPMorgan Chase Bank's six business segments, Investment Banking, did business with BLMIS. JPMorgan Chase Bank Investment Banking was responsible for servicing and maintaining the BLMIS bank accounts, issuing investment-related advising and assistance to BLMIS feeder funds, and assessing the market and credit risks associated with BLMIS and BLMIS feeder funds. JPMorgan Chase Bank was BLMIS's primary bank for more than two decades.

Although it would be expected that JPMorgan Chase Bank and BLMIS would do a great deal of work together, the bank did not fully carry out its oversight responsibilities. In effect, it tolerated BLMIS's lawlessness, and over many years it was tangentially—unhappily for many of Madoff's victims—"working *for* BLMIS," as much as "working *with* BLMIS." It is estimated by the SIPC trustee and reported often in the press that by working with and for BLMIS, by not stopping the Madoff con when it readily could have done so, JPMorgan Chase Bank made at least half a billion dollars in fees and profits from BLMIS. JPMorgan Chase Bank did not dispute this estimate.

As was evident in the previous chapter, JPMorgan Chase Bank allowed the Levy–Madoff business relationship to flourish. In fact, soon after it began, with considerable help from the bank, the Levy–Madoff business relationship became one of Madoff's principal business relationships. At the same time, Levy was instrumental in facilitating the JPMorgan Chase Bank–BLMIS relationship which became increasingly central to the Madoff con.

Moreover, as has been documented in previous chapters (see particularly Appendix 1-B), the BLMIS 703 Account at JPMorgan Chase Bank was the keystone of the Madoff con.[1] The fact that the 703 Account was at a JPMorgan Chase Bank provided the bank with a unique window into BLMIS and the con. As the U.S. Attorney leading an inquiry into the JPMorgan Chase Bank–Madoff relationship put it: "From ... October 1986 through Madoff's arrest ... the Madoff Ponzi scheme was conducted almost exclusively through ... accounts held by JPMorgan Chase Bank ... collectively the 703 Account. During that time period, virtually all client investments were deposited into the primary BLMIS account ... and virtually all client 'redemptions' were paid from a linked disbursement account, also held by BLMIS at JPMorgan Chase Bank." Billions of dollars flowed through the 703 Account at JPMorgan Chase Bank.

A number of JPMorgan Chase Bank executives who had the opportunity, and obligation, to look through the window into the BLMIS operations and could have readily seen and perhaps forestalled the con failed to do so, or, if they did see or suspect BLMIS of bending or breaking the rules, failed to act on what they saw. In the months prior to Madoff's arrest, some JP Morgan Chase Bank executives began to see and became alarmed about the possibility that BLMIS was at least in part involved in fraud. The fraud was not becoming apparent to enough of them, and to those to whom it was becoming apparent, too few did much to try to end it.

In a court document, the SIPC trustee specified a number of irregular aspects of the 703 Account that should have caught the attention of JPMorgan Chase Bank executives.

The 703 Account reflected a pattern of large dollar transactions. Between 1998 and 2008, BLMIS transferred $84 billion out of the 703 Account to just four customers. These transactions represented over 75% of the wires and checks that flowed out of the 703 Account.

. . .

The 703 Account showed occasional spikes in overall activity, which should have prompted further investigation by the JPMorgan Chase Bank. Shortly before the beginning of the credit crisis, over the period beginning in the first quarter of 2006 and ending in the first quarter of 2007, there was a significant increase in the total dollar amount[s] transacted in the 703 Account. This increase in activity included a significant increase not only in third-party wires, but also in book transfer activity. During this period, the average dollar amount of each transaction increased by over $60 million, from $17 million to $78 million.

. . .

There was also a downward spike in activity between the 703 Account and [Norman] Levy's account at the Private Bank after December 2001. In December 2001 alone, BLMIS engaged in approximately $6.8 billion worth of transactions with Levy. Shortly thereafter, Levy's activity with the 703 Account decreased dramatically.

. . .

Incredible spikes in the 703 Account's overall activity were accompanied by incredible spikes in offshore activity as well. Between 2004 and 2008, the dollar amount and volume of the 703 Account's international wire transfers with high and medium risk jurisdictions increased 83% and 67%, respectively.

. . .

In addition, many transactions in the 703 Account involved handwritten checks totaling hundreds of millions of dollars in a single day.[2]

Perhaps without setting out to do so, JPMorgan Chase Bank—like so many institutions and individuals—was in slow time lured into Madoff's con. Before realizing that it was entangled, the bank became an indispensable part of the con's machinery. Surely, not by design, the bank became as central to enabling the con to continue as were those who handed over their money to Madoff, or those who worked on the 17th floor at BLMIS, or Madoff's close associates and ropers who set out to find and fleece his victims.

Thus, knowing the nature of the relationship between BLMIS and JPMorgan Chase Bank—how BLMIS used JPMorgan Chase Bank and how JPMorgan Chase Bank used BLMIS—is indispensable to understanding fully how the Madoff con game worked.

JPMorgan Chase Bank Investments through BLMIS

By 2006, JPMorgan Chase Bank began considering issuing financial products based on BLMIS-related feeder funds. In February, after visiting FGG, Chen Yang, who worked in JPMorgan Chase Bank Market Risk Management, wrote:

> I do have a few concerns and questions: 1: All trades are generated by Madoff's black box trading model and executed by Madoff. It's not clear whether FGG has any discretion or control over the auto-pilot trading program. ... 2: Is it possible to get some clarification as to how the fund made money during the market distress? ... How did they manage to get better than 3M T-Bill returns? ... For example, from April to September 2002, the S&P 100 Index is down 30%, cash yielded 1%, and the [FGG] fund [handled by BLMIS] was able to generate over 6% returns.[3]

Mostly what Yang received during his visit to FGG were verbal descriptions of the investment guidelines and restrictions FGG had agreed upon contractually with BLMIS, making him uneasy. Other bank employees had other concerns. About another BLMIS feeder fund, a JPMorgan Bank management employee expressed "surprise" that after "their 14 years in the business," the bank was the first "investor" that spotted a lack of documentation, and another responded: "they have position-level transparency once a month with a one week delay, but they don't run risk analysis and don't have the know-how of how to do this. ... It doesn't look pretty." Nonetheless, in the months following these concerns from one of its employees, JPMorgan Chase Bank markedly increased its investments of BLMIS-related feeder funds.

Unlike JPMorgan Chase Bank, others doing business with BLMIS did act on growing, inchoate suspicions. At least one other bank (Deutsche Bank) ended its business ties with BLMIS and filed a suspicious-activity report with regulators in 1996 after the flurry of daily round-trip transactions between Levy and Madoff came to light and was incompletely and inadequately explained. Madoff's account was quickly closed and his deposits were turned over to JPMorgan Chase Bank.

It was not until a dozen years later that the London office of JPMorgan Chase Bank filed a suspicious-activity report with the UK Serious Organised Crime Agency. There were a number of disturbing aspects about BLMIS's business that precipitated Rebecca Smith, a JPMorgan Chase Bank assistant general counsel in the London office, to share her "reason for suspicion." She reported to British regulators:

JPMorgan Chase Bank has sold several million dollars worth of structured investment products to clients ... in London. The products reference various underlying funds which are advised and ultimately controlled by BLMIS in New York, into which funds the sale proceeds are invested, either directly or via funds of funds. ...

JPMorgan Chase Bank's concerns around Madoff securities are based (1) on the investment performance achieved by the funds which is so consistently and significantly ahead of its peers, year-on-year, even in the prevailing market conditions, as to appear too good to be true—meaning that it probably is; and (2) the lack of transparency around Madoff securities trading techniques, the implementation of its investment strategy, and the identity of its over-the-counter option counterparties; and (3) its unwillingness to provide helpful information. As a result JPMorgan Chase Bank has sent out redemption notices in respect of one fund, and is preparing similar notices for two more funds. ...

BLMIS acts as sub-advisor, sub-custodian, and broker/dealer to the funds in question, as noted above. ... Fund managers appear to know very little about how BLMIS strategy and systems work, and seem unconcerned in view of its consistent profitability. JPMorgan Chase Bank is also concerned about the conflict of interests which the three combined roles of BLMIS could represent, as noted above. ...

Of further concern to JPMorgan Chase Bank [is] the following:

(1) The BLMIS auditors, Friehling and Horowitz, are relatively small and unknown, and probably more dependent than is appropriate on retention by BLMIS.[4]

It appears that JPMorgan Chase Bank filed the suspicious-activity report only after representatives of a Swiss company selling and distributing the BLMIS-controlled funds were threatened in a telephone conversation that "Colombia interests ... will not be happy with JPMorgan Chase Bank's" redemption action, accompanied with "thinly veiled threats to the security of bank staff involved, e.g., 'we know where you are and where you live/work.'"

Smith's concerns were not communicated to her American colleagues (who typically file between 150,000 and 200,000 suspicious-activity reports a year).

Actually, the picture of what JPMorgan Chase Bank employees knew, and understood, about what was going on at BLMIS is somewhat clouded. After Madoff's arrest, the bank's attorneys interviewed dozens (perhaps at least 90) bank employees who may have known something about the JPMorgan Chase Bank–BLMIS relationship, but the bank refused to share the interview notes and other material with regulators from the U.S. Office of the Comptroller of the Currency. Although working with the regulators and investigators might have opened a window into the JPMorgan Chase Bank–BLMIS relationship, JPMorgan Chase Bank executives decided not to cooperate and declined to provide the material, claiming attorney–client privilege. The U.S. Office of the Comptroller of the Currency argued that the notes were germane to its inquiry particularly since when it had conducted its own interviews with JPMorgan Chase Bank employees it had found a "pattern of forgetfulness." Suspicious that some claimed memory lapses from those it interviewed were feigned, it pressed to no avail for the bank's interview materials.

The U.S. Office of the Comptroller of the Currency referred the matter to the Department of Treasury's Office of Inspector General requesting it issue a subpoena for the interview materials and other documents. The Office of Inspector General issued a subpoena, but it was ignored by the bank. The Department of Justice was then asked to enforce it. However, the Department of Justice denied the request: "On September 19, 2013, the Office of [the Department of Treasury] Inspector General's counsel met with the U.S. Office of the Comptroller of the Currency's counsel regarding the Department of Justice's decision, and the U.S. Office of the Comptroller of the Currency agreed that the Office of Inspector General could not undertake any further actions regarding the matter. ... The matter was accordingly [closed]."[5]

What is not in doubt about the JPMorgan Chase Bank–BLMIS relationship is that the bank did numerous things for BLMIS. It held its money. It loaned it money. It helped it launder money. It offered BLMIS an umbrella of legitimacy. In return, BLMIS, like all institutions and individuals who do business with banks, made money for JPMorgan Chase Bank.

It should also be added that JPMorgan Chase Bank Equity Exotics even began working as a BLMIS feeder fund, selling notes linked to BLMIS's performance and hedging the notes by investing its own money into BLMIS feeder funds. After more of the bank's customers wanted to invest in these BLMIS-linked notes, Equity Exotics sought permission to increase its exposure, and that triggered a JPMorgan

Chase Bank internal investigation in 2007 in which one executive concluded: "The main risk this trade poses is systemic fraud at the BLMIS level," and in which the head of due diligence responded that they should visit the BLMIS accountant's office "to make sure it is not a 'car wash.'" Was this a joke that happened to hit the mark or had the head of due diligence revealed that he knew a good deal more than most of his colleagues?

The considerable evidence, almost all collected by government investigators, in the January 2014 "Deferred Prosecution Agreement" between the U.S. Department of Justice and JPMorgan Chase Bank shows the bank's collaboration with BLMIS.[6] JPMorgan Chase Bank did not disavow the long list of allegations of how it enabled the BLMIS con to continue, how, in many years of working with BLMIS, it continued to break the law: It "admit[ed] and stipulate[d] that the facts set forth in the Statement of Facts [of the Deferred Prosecution Agreement] ... are true and accurate." Because the "Deferred Prosecution Agreement" illuminates what may be close to the most complete analysis of the JPMorgan Chase Bank–BLMIS relationship, in an attempt to more fully and accurately describe this relationship, the essence of a number (18 from a total of 85) of particularly germane excerpts from the 19-page Statement of Facts is reviewed.

Overview of JPMorgan Chase Bank-BLMIS Banking Relationship

8. BLMIS maintained a continuous banking relationship with JPMorgan Chase Bank and its predecessor institutions ... between at least approximately 1986 and Madoff's arrest. ...

9. BLMIS held a series of linked direct deposit and custodial accounts at JPMorgan Chase Bank organized under the umbrella of a centralized "concentration account" ... the 703 Account. The 703 Account was the bank account that received and remitted ... the overwhelming majority of funds that Madoff's victims "invested" with BLMIS. In addition, BLMIS maintained linked accounts at JPMorgan Chase Bank through which Madoff held the funds obtained through his Ponzi scheme in, among other things, government securities and commercial paper.

10. Between approximately 1986 and Madoff's arrest, the 703 Account received deposits and transfers of approximately $150 billion, almost exclusively from BLMIS investors. The 703 Account was not a securities settlement account and the funds

deposited by Madoff's victims into the 703 Account were not used for the purchase and sale of stocks, corporate bonds, or options, as Madoff had promised his customers he would invest their money. Nor were the funds deposited into the 703 Account transferred to other broker-dealers for the purchase and sale of securities.

11. The balance in the 703 Account increased over time, peaking at approximately $5.6 billion in August 2008. Between August 2008 and Madoff's arrest ... billions were transferred from the 703 Account to customers of BLMIS. ...

12. At various times between the late 1990s and 2008, employees of various divisions of JPMorgan Chase Bank and its predecessor entities raised questions about BLMIS, including questions about the validity of BLMIS's investment returns.

The Use of JPMorgan Chase Bank's Anti-Money-Laundering Tools

19. A JPMorgan Chase Bank banker signed the periodic certification [that BLMIS complied with all "legal and regulatory-based policies"] beginning in or about the mid-1990s through his retirement in early 2008, when the client relationship was assigned to a second individual. In March 2009—three months after Madoff's arrest—[the second individual] received a form letter from JPMorgan Chase Bank's compliance function asking him to certify the client relationship again.

20. During his tenure at JPMorgan Chase Bank, Richard Cassa periodically visited Madoff's offices and obtained financial documents from BLMIS in connection with periodic loans JPMorgan Chase Bank made to the firm. Despite those visits and financial documents, and despite the fact that Cassa was aware of Madoff's standing in the industry, he had a limited and inaccurate understanding of both Madoff's business, as well as the purpose and balance of the demand deposit accounts maintained by BLMIS at JPMorgan Chase Bank. Cassa believed that the 703 Account was primarily a BLMIS broker-dealer operating account, used to pay rent and other routine expenses. Cassa also believed that the average balance in BLMIS's demand deposit account was "probably [in the] tens of millions." He did not understand that the 703 Account was, in fact, the account used by BLMIS's IA business, and achieved balances of more than $1 billion

beginning in approximately 2005, and up to $5.6 billion by 2008. Cassa stated that he recertified his sponsorship of the BLMIS relationship each year because no adverse information about BLMIS was brought to his attention.[7] [For Cassa's description of his work with BLMIS as the JPMorgan Chase Bank relationship manager at BLMIS, see Appendix 10-A.]

21. With respect to the computerized anti-money laundering system, on two occasions the system generated "alerts" with respect to potentially suspicious activity at BLMIS. In January 2007, the 703 Account [was] "alerted" because of unusual third party wire activity. On the day of the alert, January 3, 2007, the 703 Account received $757.2 million in customer wires and transfers, 27 times the average daily value of incoming wires and transfers over the prior 90 days of activity, virtually all of which came from Madoff "feeder funds" that offered to invest funds from their own customers in BLMIS. In July 2008, the system [was] "alerted" due to activity associated with Treasury bond redemptions. In both cases, the anti-money laundering investigators closed the alerts with a notation that the transactions did not appear to be unusual for the account in comparison to the account's prior activity. In both cases, prior to closing the alerts, the investigators attempted to review the KYC (Know Your Customer) file for BLMIS but, upon receiving error messages to the effect that no file was available, did not conduct further investigation into the business of BLMIS beyond a review of the company's website. . . .

Concerns at JPMorgan Chase Bank about BLMIS

32. One Chase Alternative Asset Management fund manager commented on approximately December 10, 1998, that BLMIS returns were "possibly too good to be true. . . ." In 2007, JPMorgan Chase Bank's fund of funds again considered a BLMIS investment, and also discontinued the due diligence early on because the first stages of the process provided "little additional insight as to the source of the BLMIS returns" and because JPMorgan Chase Bank learned that Madoff would not meet with JPMorgan Chase Bank personnel to answer their questions. . . .

45. Shortly after a committee meeting ended [on June 15, 2007], John Hogan, the bank's Chief Risk Officer had lunch with Matt Zames, who headed Interest Rate Trading, Global Foreign Exchange, Public Finance, Global Mortgages, Tax-Oriented

Investments, and Global Fixed Income at JPMorgan Chase Bank's Investment Bank. During the lunch, he sent an email stating: "For whatever it is worth, I am sitting at lunch with Matt Zames who just told me that there is a well-known cloud over the head of Madoff and that his returns are speculated to be part of a Ponzi scheme. He said if we Google the guy we can see the articles for ourselves—please do that and let us know what you find." In follow-up correspondence with Hogan, Zames provided more specifics about the article and offered to find it if Hogan had any difficulty locating it. . . .

46. In response to Hogan's email about the Madoff Ponzi scheme rumors, Carlos Hernandez, the Head of Global Equities at JPMorgan Chase Bank's Investment Bank, wrote that JPMorgan Chase Bank should "seriously look into it" as the bank had lent BLMIS money through its Broker-Dealer Banking Group. . . . And in another email several days later, Hogan wrote: [Another bank executive] "told me Madoff has a very shady reputation in the market."

52. On June 23, 2008, after reviewing emails about the failure of one of the feeder funds to provide information to JPMorgan Chase Bank, including how the money sent to BLMIS was invested, and the departure of various feeder fund employees, a senior Equity Exotics banker emailed the head of the Equity Exotics desk: "How much do we have in BLMIS at this moment? To be honest, the more I think about it, the more concerned I am."

53. In or around September 2008 . . . , JPMorgan Chase Bank began to consider redeeming its positions in the BLMIS feeder funds.

54. In mid-September 2008, following the collapse of Lehman Brothers and growing concerns about counterparty risk . . . , JPMorgan Chase Bank's Head of Global Equities, Carlos Hernandez, directed Investment Bank personnel to substantially reduce JPMorgan Chase Bank's exposure to hedge funds. . . .

56. [An October 16, 2008, JP Morgan Chase Bank memo concluded]: "I could go on, but we seem to be relying on Madoff's integrity (or the [feeder funds'] belief in Madoff's integrity) and the quality of the due diligence work (initial and ongoing) done by the custodians . . . to ensure that the assets actually exist and are properly custodied [sic].

80. Whereas the balance in the 703 Account reached approximately $5.6 billion in August 2008, by October 16, 2008—the

date of the memo [from the London-based Equity Exotics desk]—the account balance had fallen to $3.7 billion. Thirteen days later, when the U.K. suspicious-activity report was filed, the balance had fallen another $700 million, to approximately $3 billion. And in the five business days after the U.K. suspicious-activity report was filed, approximately $2.45 billion more was withdrawn from the 703 Account, leaving a balance of approximately $550 million, some 90% less than it had been in August of the same year.

81. Most of the funds withdrawn during this period went to the same two feeder fund groups in which JPMorgan Chase Bank had invested—and then redeemed—JPMorgan Chase Bank's own funds. Between October 1 and October 28, 2008, JPMorgan Chase Bank placed redemption orders for approximately $276 million from two particular feeder funds. On November 4, 2008, approximately $1.3 billion was paid from the 703 Account to those two feeder fund groups in four transactions. Later in November 2008, JPMorgan Chase Bank placed redemption orders for an additional approximately $23.1 million from one of the funds; Madoff was arrested before the funds were ever received, however.

82. ... Between October 16, 2008, and Madoff's arrest, approximately $3.5 billion of the $3.7 billion in the BLMIS accounts at JPMorgan Chase Bank had been withdrawn to pay customer redemptions.

To be sure, employees at JPMorgan Chase Bank [and its predecessor entities] raised concerns "at various times" between the late 1990s and 2008 about Madoff, including some questions about the validity of his purported investment returns. For example, the chief investment officer of JPMorgan Chase Bank Global Wealth group had long refused to do business with BLMIS. His group had conducted due diligence and after "seeing all the red flags, chose not to invest with any BLMIS feeder funds." A number of months after Madoff's arrest, he wrote that his staff was never able "to reverse engineer how [BLMIS] made money, and because BLMIS did not satisfy [the bank's] requirement for administrative oversight" he decided that it would be imprudent to do business with it.

Generally, JPMorgan Chase Bank clearly became suspicious about BLMIS's operations before most others. However, the concerns on the part of some JPMorgan Chase Bank employees about the bank's "inability to validate Madoff's trading activity or even custody of assets" and their questions about his "odd choice" of using a small, unknown accounting firm to do its books did not fully surface until just a few months before BLMIS imploded. There was insufficient time for the bank to fully unwind its relationship with Madoff, to protect its financial interests, and as a consequence it was much too slow to report to regulators and others what had been slowly becoming evident only after many years of working for and with BLMIS.

After working uneventfully with Madoff for many years and contributing much to keeping his con afloat, in the early fall of 2008, executives at JPMorgan Chase Bank became uneasy doing business with him. Subsequently, the bank's many and large withdrawals from BLMIS late in the fall contributed much to the Madoff con's final and rapid unraveling. Hardly unexpectedly, it would seem on the bank's part, it had simply made the best of an inviting business opportunity, and bailed out when the opportunity seemed to be less inviting.

Appendix 10-A

Richard Cassa's Description of His Work at BLMIS as JPMorgan Chase Bank's Relationship Manager

Q: You worked at JPMorgan Chase Bank, is that correct?

A: That's correct.

Q: When did you work there?

A: I worked at JP Morgan Chase Bank from 1968 through March of 2008.

Q: Are you currently employed?

A: No, I am not.

Q: Retired?

A: Yes.

. . .

Q: What sort of jobs did you have?

A: What sort of job? Most recently I was a relationship manager in what was called the broker-dealer division. I spent some time in private banking. Prior to that time probably half of my career was on the retail side.

. . .

Q: BLMIS was one of your clients beginning in about the mid-1990s?

A: One of my clients, yes.

Q: It was a JPMorgan Chase Bank client even before that?

A: Yes ...

Q: Until when was BLMIS one of your clients?

A: Until I retired in March of 2008.

Q: During that 15 or so years that BLMIS was your client, was there a point of contact that you had at BLMIS that you dealt with?

A: Yes.

Q: Who was that?

A: Dan Bonventre.

Q: Over those 15 or so years, how often did you speak to or meet with Mr. Bonventre?

A: Probably a couple of times a year, three or four.

Q: For what kind of reasons?

A: Just to maintain a relationship. They weren't a very big client of the bank. We would go over, say hello, see if there was any other services or business we could do with them.

Q: Over those 15 or so years that BLMIS was your client, did you ever have occasion to meet with or talk to anyone else that worked at BLMIS?

A: The only other name I remember—well, it would have been Bernie Madoff. I spoke to Bernie a couple of times on the phone, and Jeff Ferraro was an operations manager there.

Q: How many times would you estimate you spoke to Jeff Ferraro over those 15 or so years?

A: Maybe two or three.

Q: How many times in your life have you talked to Bernie Madoff?

A: I can recall three times.

Q: When you met with Dan Bonventre or talk to him a few times a year, was that in person or by phone or both?

A: Mostly in person. I did talk to him occasionally on the phone.

Q: When you met in person, where did you typically meet with him?

A: At his office.

   ...

Q: When did BLMIS, to your knowledge, seek or obtain loans from JPMorgan Chase Bank?

A: At one time I know they had a line of credit, probably back in the early 1990s. They stopped using it, and I don't remember the exact date. Because they stopped using it, the credit facilities were cancelled. Then they did come in for a loan; I guess, in 2005.

   ...

Q: Mr. Cassa, did you have an understanding, prior to Mr. Madoff's arrest, of what that 703 Account was used for?

A: Yes. It was a basic checking account. Checks would come in and out, payments would be made, and wire transfers would go in and out. It was pretty normal checking account for that type of firm.

Q: Do you know what part of BLMIS business that checking account was associated with?

A: Well, we always knew them as a market maker, basically a company that traded securities.

Q: So was it your understanding that the 703 Account was associated with the market making business?

A: That's correct.

Q: Did you have an understanding, prior to Mr. Madoff's arrest, of the size of the 703 Account?

A: Well, not really. We didn't see—if you're referring to size—the activity that goes in and out of the account?

Q: What was the average balance?

A: Well,—I don't recall.

Q: I mean did you have a sense, prior to Mr. Madoff's arrest of whether that account held millions or tens of millions or billions of dollars?

A: Probably tens of millions [of dollars].

Q: Now, prior to Mr. Madoff's arrest, did you know that BLMIS had an IA business, a business of advising customers?

A: Yes. Yes, most broker-dealers did.

Q: What was your understanding of—I'll call it—the IA business at BLMIS?

A: We really didn't know much about it. Again, we knew them as market makers.

Q: Did you and Mr. Bonventre ever discuss the IA business?

A: No.

Q: Where did you gain your understanding that there was an IA business?

A: I don't recall.

Q: Mr. Cassa, did you have an understanding, prior to Mr. Madoff's arrest, that the 703 Account was associated with BLMIS IA business?

A: It's hard to answer. He had one account with us. We assumed he ran all his business, both parts, both sides of his business through it.

Q: Is that because you understood there was only one firm, BLMIS?

A: That's correct.

. . .

Q: Mr. Cassa, what was your understanding of what assets are reported in BLMIS audited financials and FOCUS reports?

A: All their assets.

Q: To include the cash in the 703 Account?

A: Yes.

Q: And what was your understanding of the liabilities that were listed in BLMIS audited financials and FOCUS reports?

A: They were the basic liabilities of the firm.

Q: All their liabilities?

A: Yes, if they were on their FOCUS report and their audited statement, yes.

Q: To include, for example, the loans that JPMorgan Chase Bank had extended to BLMIS?

A: Correct. If there would have been loans outstanding as of the date of the audited statement, they would be, they should be on there.

CHAPTER 11

Revisiting the Crime Scene

M ost big cons closely follow a script, progressing through the same stages, although from con game to con game the stages may vary in detail.

Typically, the first eight steps of a big con are:

1. Locating and learning about a well-to-do victim.[1] (*Putting the mark up.*)
2. Gaining the victim's confidence. (*Playing the con.*)
3. Steering the victim to meet the inside man. (*Roping the mark.*)
4. Permitting the inside man to show the victim how to make a large amount of money. (*Telling the tale.*)
5. Allowing the victim to make a goodly profit. (*Giving the convincer.*)
6. Determining how much more the victim will invest. (*Giving the breakdown.*)
7. Sending the victim for more money. (*Putting the mark on the send.*)
8. Fleecing the victim. (*Taking off the touch.*)[2]

This was the template followed by the Madoff team.[3]

The numerous cons within cons spawned within BLMIS were like scattershot. Returning to the dramaturgic metaphor, a single play was not mounted at BLMIS; instead a number of overlapping improvisations were concurrently performed. It seemed to be, to use C. Wright Mills's term, "a network of rackets."[4] Much of the time there was direction by Madoff, but not always. Once direction was given on one matter, exigencies often demanded that attention immediately be drawn to another.[5] The constantly shifting focus—most importantly, keeping the roping operation going, keeping the books and records up-to-date, keeping regulators at bay, producing and mailing account statements to clients—and continual crisis management allowed the con game to succeed month after month, year after year. The theater sometimes almost became vaudeville, but it continued to flourish until just months before Madoff's arrest when it could no longer even stumble along. The longer the con game continued, the longer, Madoff and his accomplices could "live large"—pay for and enjoy an expensive life style—and for some, bask in the ego-nourishing rays of the limelight, if only of family, friends, or neighbors.

What criminologists call lure—"arrangements or situations that turn heads" and, when there is little credible oversight, provide an opportunity to commit crime[6]—enabled Madoff's promise of consistent and substantial returns for IA accounts to appear to be particularly attractive, and for the con to succeed for as long as he did. In their discussion of the financial services industry revolution and lure, Shover and Hochstetler have written: "The rapid infusion of money into stocks along with widespread demand for speculative opportunities is a profound economic change, because eager but naïve investors are lure. Just as street hustlers target those who seem out of place or confused, investment counselors and firms look to attract these 'under-informed investor(s).'"[7]

O. Henry once observed that "truly great swindles are ... beautiful and simple." Having no overriding design or sharp focus, Madoff's con was neither beautiful nor truly simple. It looked more like a juggling act, a muddle of movement and disjunction. In the end it did little else but create an illusion for thousands that they were steadily getting wealthier. However, Madoff's con surely had an overriding theme. The theme of each ad hoc tableau was to take investor's money, a great deal of money, enough money to keep the con viable and to satisfy the insiders' appetite for a wide range of material possessions and expense accounts and vacations for the many involved backstage or as ropers and steerers. All members of Madoff's cast—even seemingly bit players in the overall con, but more central to one or more subplots—after learning what they needed to do in order to keep the con going, were, with some degree of autonomy, set to work to enrich Madoff, his family, his friends, and themselves, and to sustain the beliefs of investors that their material lives were also improving while actually diminishing.

A great deal of attention in the early chapters in *Bernard Madoff and His Accomplices* was given to examining the criminal acts of 15 BLMIS employees, including Bernard and Peter Madoff, charged with and convicted of committing a variety of felonies. Ten worked exclusively in the BLMIS IA business. Some of the 15 told of stealing money. Others told of repeatedly failing to pay taxes. Some of the 15 told of submitting false information and documents to the government and to other financial institutions. Others told of helping to launder money globally, and of assisting Madoff, Madoff family members, and BLMIS to avoid paying taxes and to avoid other financial obligations. Some committed all of these crimes and more. Others were involved in crime for decades. Some were involved for shorter periods of time. All drifted—"the gradual process of movement, unperceived by the actor, in which the first stage may be accidental or unpredictable"[8]—into becoming Madoff's accomplices. As is the case with most corporate crime, most escaped public notice because they were not persons of significance and were engaged in routine activities—as ropers keeping the spigot open, finding new customers and convincing them to invest or, as backstage accomplices, manufacturing, preparing, and distributing false trade confirmations and account statements. In short, they were busy mechanically keeping the enterprise going.

There seemed to be little to deter them. The costs of working to further Madoff's con seemed trifling or infinitesimal, especially if not employed by BLMIS. The SIPC trustee and others formally investigating the con seemed not very interested in finding larger beneficiaries of the Madoff con criminally liable; a large number appeared to have been given a pass. Generally, formal sanctions against the white collar crime of defrauding investors are relatively lax—they often are not even part of the criminal code—as are negative social sanctions. Criminalization and stigmatization (from family, friends, and neighbors) were obviously not expected by most Madoff's accomplices after the con was widely reported in the media. For example, dozens wrote testimonials on behalf of Peter Madoff, commending his character, after he acknowledged in court of committing a bundle of felonies; Robert M. Jaffe, with his smooth backswing and fashionable attire, was still welcome at the country clubs to which he continued to belong.

No evidence could be found that Bernard or Peter Madoff or any of the 13 other offenders (except perhaps Frank DiPascali, Jr.) ever regarded himself or herself as a criminal, although in court the 10 who agreed to a plea bargain were required to admit that they were just that.

This form of denial has been found in other studies of white collar crime—and of individuals convicted of a number of other crimes such as drunken driving and nonviolent sex offenses. From prison, Bernard Madoff repeatedly maintained that he was backed into crime by economic forces beyond his control and by greedy clients—some formerly his friends—who took advantage of him. Even in the face of overwhelming evidence to the contrary, some backstage accomplices maintained they had no idea that they had been involved in a criminal enterprise. (This matter is discussed again later in this chapter.)

The Madoff con game needed to draw in many others besides his backstage accomplices. Madoff's ropers—particularly Frank Avellino, Michael Bienes, Marcia B. Cohn, Maurice J. Cohn, Sonja Kohn, Robert M. Jaffe, J. Ezra Merkin, Walter M. Noel, Jr., and Jeffrey Tucker—although not ultimately labeled as criminals, were entangled in the BLMIS IA business. They were instrumental in helping to make the con viable. Indeed, not only Madoff and his felonious accomplices, but also many of these long-standing friends and intimates appear to be lawless.[9] It was as if rules guiding most Americans most of the time were simply irrelevant to the Madoff brothers and to a number of their employees and friends. They stole at every opportunity. The overarching concern of wealthy friends[10] who worked with Madoff to perpetrate the con was simply to become wealthier. Not only among the backstage accomplices, but also among those whose BLMIS IA accounts were continually manipulated and that continued to swell, there appeared to be little curiosity about how Madoff could so easily and steadily make so much money. Hundreds of heedless and greedy investors helped make the con successful, and, in effect, they were an essential part of the con. The money kept accumulating, and little else seemed to matter to those on both sides of the con.

Madoff's con was shaped by what Madoff was. The con was not colorful or intricate because Madoff was a man with an average mind, indifferent to much else except to keep his con thriving, and who, in addition, was somewhat vacuous. He often bullied others, and did seem gifted at that. As someone with a passion for material things, and for little else, he clearly understood that to procure the services of his accomplices it was simply necessary to keep doling out money in all directions. He appeared unnecessarily generous; however, it was not his money he was spreading about. The following brief exchange between Daniel Bonventre and an Assistant U.S. Attorney shows Madoff's lavishness in order to hold his accomplices' loyalty.

Q: You do acknowledge that during the years in question, you were receiving payments on your behalf for the Richmond Country Club?

A: Yes.

Q: And were you also receiving payments for your personal American Express Card?

A: Correct.

Q: And the Dalton School (an elite and sheltered Manhattan preparatory school)?

A: Correct.

Q: And Chemical Bank, Chase Manhattan Bank for your home equity line of credit?

A: Correct.

Q: And the 79th Street Owners' Association?

A: Yes.

From reading court documents and reviewing additional court testimony describing years backstage at BLMIS, it seemed at times as if those associated with Madoff may have come from a parallel or alternate universe with few guiding principles beyond taking others' property or helping someone else take others' property. Although it obviously had many characteristics of other groups, from its earliest years, the BLMIS team began to develop its own subculture of identifiable and distinctive motives, drives, rationalizations, and attitudes—a number of learned behaviors—a subculture (but, still abiding the American Dream of Success, far from being a fully developed counterculture) of professional criminals.[11] The IA business was kept isolated from the rest of BLMIS both to prevent those employees who were not knowingly involved in the con from learning about it and to allow the 17th floor criminal subculture to more easily take root. The arrangement also simplified tutelage to the BLMIS IA business culture.[12] By the early 1990s, it was readily apparent that how the BLMIS IA business operated was unlike other investment companies.

What is less clear is whether the BLMIS criminal management was able to recruit so many people whose values and behavior were outside generally accepted ethical behavior or whether it was able to socialize them to unhesitatingly commit crimes on a regular basis. How many fathers have their sons follow them into careers of lawbreaking? Although "parental Fagins" are not unheard of, it will strike many as unusual, as something from an unusual subculture. However, BLMIS had at least two long-time employees who did so, and the four ended up pleading guilty to various felonies. In addition, what did family members and friends think about BLMIS employees, with ordinary jobs and careers, who were becoming extraordinarily wealthy? Even if the crime wave on Wall Street in recent decades is real, and not a media-driven exaggeration, it is unlikely that federal prosecutors could unearth as many criminals—with as many uncurious family members and friends—at similar organizations the size of the BLMIS IA business. (Some of the criminal management, for example, Bernard Madoff, Peter Madoff, Daniel Bonventre, and Frank DiPascali, Jr., recruited family members who were not implicated in the Madoff con.) It would appear that BLMIS was able to readily recruit accomplices not averse to engaging in criminal activity in order to help the Madoff con to succeed.

It is the extralegality at BLMIS that is noteworthy and significant. Those charged with returning the stolen money to BLMIS investors and with prosecuting Madoff and his most obvious accomplices gave a good deal of attention to who may or may not have known that Madoff was operating a Ponzi scheme. Basically, however, this is truly a trivial matter. Yet, the SIPC trustee and many in the criminal justice system spent too much time pursuing the question. It would seem discovering who knew or did not know the full extent of Madoff's con[13] is a great deal less important than knowing who did what to facilitate it, and what it is they precisely did.

From the record, it is evident that many more than those who ended up in court knowingly and repeatedly were participants in the Madoff con. From their testimony (see Appendix 7-A), there is little question that Frank Avellino and Michael Bienes repeatedly lied to regulators. So did J. Ezra Merkin (see Chapter 7). Merkin's reaction to the investigation looking into his relationship with Madoff was to appear mostly bothered by the unwanted attention. He was very good at feigning nonchalance; it is unclear if he understood what all of the fuss was about. (Was it all a show, something a devout and educated personage, a philanthropist and patron of the arts, need concern himself about? Was he simply involved in performance art, believing it was serious drama?) There would appear to be sufficient evidence to indict Maurice J. and Marcia B. Cohn and Robert M. Jaffe. The Cohns' (partners in and managers of one of Madoff's side businesses) outright refusal to cooperate with those attempting to recover money lost by BLMIS victims may have been a simple and successful legal tactic, but there are too many incriminating facts that were surprisingly ignored by the authorities, most obviously, Marcia B. Cohn's close work with some

BLMIS 17th floor employees. Apparently it seemed easier for the SIPC trustee and federal prosecutors to pursue the BLMIS 17th floor back-stage employees than the Cohns after, simply by stonewalling, they won the early round. Jaffe's father-in-law may have paid the trustee $38 million on Jaffe's behalf to placate the SIPC trustee, but that does not make Jaffe any less guilty of assisting BLMIS employees of playing a double game with his IA account and of unlawfully shredding documents. It may have been difficult to press criminal charges against the estates of Madoff's sons after both had died, although, for example, the youngest, Andrew, could not have been unaware that his BLMIS IA account was being manipulated to enable him to commit fraud in a divorce settlement and to add additional unearned money to his wealth at the expense of the family he was shedding. The authorities did not believe it unusual that millions of dollars were deposited into the IA accounts of Madoff's sons with the pretext that these were loans. At the same time, it may have been difficult to press criminal charges against Walter M. Noel, Jr. who embodied the WASP ideal, as widely understood, it is not against the law to be vacuous. Not enough attention was given to these questions. Surely, one consequence of this fact is that six years into the Madoff-con inquiry only 15 individuals had been charged and prosecuted with a crime in which obviously there were many more participants.

The SIPC trustee's office was stunningly wasteful and inept, almost feeble in its work. It failed to find out very much beyond what forensic investigators had learned in the months immediately following Madoff's arrest about what went on backstage at BLMIS, and it largely failed to understand what had been found.

Further, the SIPC trustee's office was primarily interested in recovering and returning as much of the money still recoverable that Madoff had taken for his own use. Its work here was far from being successful. As Table 11.1 shows, at the end of the summer of 2014, nearly six years after Madoff's con game imploded, almost all of the money the SIPC trustee's office had collected to redistribute to Madoff's victims had come from very few settlements with insiders who had made millions of dollars more than they were asked to return. Moreover, the SIPC trustee's office expenses were close to $1 billion, which greatly enriched him and many attorneys on his staff.

Table 11.1 leaves little doubt that the SIPC trustee's work was a labor in vain: Of the less than $10 billion in forfeitures claimed by his office, $8.5 billion came from four settlements—three of Madoff's large investors and the bank that was looking the other way when he was

Table 11.1   SIPC Trustee's Recovery from Madoff Con (August 2014)*

Recovery	$9.825 billion
Trustee's fees	$927.8 million
Four large forfeitures:	
JPMorgan Chase Bank	$543 million
Carl Shapiro	$550 million
Jeffry Picower (estate)	$7.2 billion (forfeiture)
Norman Levy (estate)	$220 million
Total: four large forfeitures	**$8.5 billion**

* A little over a year later, the SIPC trustee reported that his office had recovered a total of $10.9 billion and on his website he further reported that the "cumulated total paid" in the recovery was $1.25 billion.

defrauding his clients and laundering money. It is also important to note again that through their IA accounts at BLMIS, these three large individual investors made a good deal more money than was forfeited on their behalf.

In short, in six years, the SIPC trustee and other authorities, charged with disinfecting the mess Madoff had made, had done little more than to intermittently dole out a handful of slaps on the wrist, most of them to the con's bit players.

There may or may not have been a predisposition on the part of many of the BLMIS employees to defraud others or to commit other crimes. What is clear is that they were drawn into crime through their long-term associations with BLMIS coworkers—Bernard Madoff recruiting his younger brother; neighbors recruiting neighbors; senior employees recruiting junior employees; fathers recruiting sons.[14] These felons were taught and learned criminality in the BLMIS criminogenic environment just as they, as children, were taught and learned how to speak and read at home and in nursery school. The precepts of the BLMIS 17th floor criminogenic subculture were relatively easy to infer, although some of the clerical staff were apparently never given cues and suspected nothing unusual. Much of the time, however, the criminogenic environment was so pervasive at BLMIS that it was sometimes difficult for those involved in the fraud to forget that there were others close by who might be oblivious that the IA business was a fraud. Frank DiPascali, Jr. describes how Madoff, himself, would forget.

A: He was never, ever, ever, except on few occasions, private about it. . . . It was an open environment. And at times he didn't know when to shut the hell up, in my opinion.

Q: What do mean by "he didn't know when to shut the hell up, in [your] opinion?"

A: There were times when I cringed over things that came out of his mouth regarding this fraud, things I know that people I believed had no clue there was a fraud would now be tipped off that there possibly was. I literally told him "shut up" or walked out in the hallway and said "would you please stop. You cannot continue to talk out loud like this. This is not right." And he'd go: "Oh. Okay. Okay. I got you. I got you, but I need to do this, this, and this." He was a frantic lunatic sometimes. ... He talked out loud a lot.[15]

If nothing else, this indicates that Madoff surely felt at ease on the 17th floor, in the partially imaginary world he had created.

Shover and Hochstetler believe the number of individual who might be predisposed and tempted to engage in white collar crime greatly increased in twentieth-century America, and that they largely came from middle class homes with an educational attainment "beyond what is true of street criminals."[16]

The backgrounds of white collar criminals are tilted conspicuously toward the middle and upper classes. Children of these worlds have less material need, yet many appear as ready recruits to white collar crime. Products of privilege and location in the class structure where personal respect is granted routinely and rarely disputed openly, they also exploit positions of organizational power. The ease with which the products of privilege turn to crime suggests there may be qualities and pathologies in their *generative worlds* that are functional equivalents of family conflict and deprivation that figure prominently in the early lives of street criminals. Whether at home, at school, or engaged in leisure activities, social and cultural conditions of middle class life appear to generate ample and probably increasing numbers of individuals prepared to commit white collar crime.[17]

Clearly, BLMIS did not need to look far to find sufficient backstage accomplices. It was not for lack of sufficient backstage accomplices that his con game unraveled.

Imitation: Tarde and Sutherland

Many sociologists have posited that criminal behavior can be rooted in what Gabriel Tarde called the "tendency towards imitation." In his

1890 "explanation of the criminal side of societies," Tarde emphasizes that "all the important acts of social life are carried out under the domination of example. ... After this how can we doubt that one steals or does not steal, one assassinates or does not assassinate, because of imitation?"[18] In fact, Tarde's formulation that deviance is learned is based on his more general theory that commonplace psychological interactions among individuals are at the foundation of social life: "And now my readers will realize, perhaps, that the social being, to the degree that he is social, is essentially imitative."[19]

Although Tarde was not a dominant influence on twentieth-century American sociological theorizing, for over 70 years American criminologists have labeled and referred to this process of learning criminal behavior formulated by him as differential association.

Most notably, in summarizing his theory of the origins of white collar crime—"defined approximately as a crime committed by a person of respectability and high social status in the course of his occupation" (and what was practiced at BLMIS)—Sutherland[20] contended that differential association has its genesis in the same general process as other criminal (and noncriminal) behavior. "The hypothesis of differential association," Sutherland wrote, "is that criminal behavior is learned in association with those who define such behavior favorably and in isolation from those who define it unfavorably, and that a person in an appropriate situation engages in such criminal behavior if, and only if, the weight of the favorable definitions exceeds the weight of the unfavorable definitions."[21] To be sure, for Sutherland, learning criminal behavior is not restricted to imitation; it includes other forms of learning as well.

For over half a century, the basic tenets of differential association, which posits that criminal behavior is learned in and regulated by social groups where individuals are embedded has been in the ascendancy in criminological theory.[22] In fact, that criminal behavior is culturally transmitted through social interaction is consistent with a great deal of current sociological thinking, and with common sense.

These tenets advanced by Tarde and Sutherland still largely shape the thinking of criminologists. Indeed, Simon, writing about corporate executives, has spoken directly to and highlighted them: "Corporate criminal behavior, like any other type of behavior, is learned. ... It is the corporate environment, not the street gang or the college education, that teaches and sometimes demands the learning of such behavior."[23]

The process of learning within BLMIS was consistent with Tarde's second law of imitation, namely, that it spreads from the top down.

This law suggests that lower status individuals will follow the lead of higher status individuals in hopes their imitative behavior will result in their receiving the rewards accorded the latter. Those at BLMIS who emulated Madoff were substantially better rewarded than those who did not. However, not all who were generously rewarded, for example, Madoff's sons, Ruth Madoff, and Peter Madoff's daughter, were legally implicated in the con.

It is worth reiterating Tarde and Sutherland's central contention that criminal behavior is learned, and it is learned under the same conditions and in the same way as conforming behavior in association with like-minded individuals. From this perspective, in the sense that it is social, criminal behavior is normal. We know, particularly from Chapters 3, 4, and 5, how 17th floor employees at BLMIS acquired the necessary skills to become accomplices. Employees at BLMIS learned to launder money or to cheat the IRS, just as they learned to answer the telephones or to trade equities. We do not know, however, how and where Bernard Madoff acquired the skills that set him off on the path to becoming a con man. It is suggestive that his mother once had a business that traded equities before she was shut down by government regulators and that his father-in-law appears to have been his first roper. It is clearer that Madoff's brother was also a felon and his wife surely knew more about the con than she publicly admitted. (She withdrew $5.5 million from her Cohmad Securities account two weeks before Madoff was arrested and another $10 million from her Cohmad Securities account the day their sons turned him into the authorities.) The Madoff con may well have been a family business.

A decade before expounding on differential association in *White Collar Crime,* Sutherland described the process germane to what occurred at BLMIS. He wrote that those who become white collar criminals may come from "good neighborhoods and good homes" (the point made by Shover and Hochstetler decades later). Moreover, after completing their education, they may be idealistic, but after finding employment in "business situations in which criminality is practically a folkway," they are "inducted into that system of behavior just as into any other folkway."[24] Criminality was not "practically a folkway" on the 17th floor at BLMIS; it was clearly one. The excerpts from DiPascali's testimony in Appendixes 1-E and 2-A, as well as in Appendixes 2-C and 6-B, show this quite well, as does Cotellessa-Pitz's and David L. Kugel's testimonies found in Chapters 3 and 4.

After years of interviewing a number of prisoners who had been convicted of embezzlement and criminal violation of financial trust,

Cressey concluded "even criminal practices in a more obvious sense, are sometimes presented to persons just beginning employment or enterprise in a business, and the individual's success or continued employment in such business is dependent upon his acceptance of them. The individual either accepts the definitions which sanction criminal behavior or he is eliminated from the business by competition from men [*sic*] who have accepted them."[25] The 17th floor backstage accomplices obviously readily accepted and adopted BLMIS IA business folkways.

What occurred backstage at BLMIS is fully consistent with ideas put forth by Tarde and Sutherland about the genesis of criminality. Today, some are still skeptical of the explanatory value of the concept of differential association, contending that, although plausible and perhaps correct, it is more a set of principles than a theory and consequently is difficult to test. Some go further, asserting that it cannot be adequately scientifically tested. From his study of embezzlers and violators of financial trust, Cressey, one of Sutherland's foremost students, concluded still "it is doubtful that it can be shown empirically that the differential association theory applies or does not apply to crimes of financial trust violations or even to other kinds of criminal behavior."[26]

Bernard Madoff and His Accomplices certainly does not come close to reaching the threshold of a natural experiment, but it is a persuasive observational study of the robustness of the differential association theory. By themselves, the accounts of those committing felonies, particularly in Chapters 3, 4, and 5, are convincing evidence that criminal behavior was taught and learned at BLMIS. These accounts are complemented by what was discovered about the activities of Madoff's ropers and steerers, and other BLMIS business associates, who were able to elude criminal charges, but whose questionable business relationships with the BLMIS IA business were reviewed by various governmental authorities and have become part of the public record. That criminal charges had still not been, and may never be, brought against some of the BLMIS ropers and steerers six years after Madoff's con had come to light, is less a reflection of what they did to further the con than of the reality of the world of high finance and the American criminal justice system as experienced by the wealthy and well connected.[27] What Walter M. Noel, Jr., had to say about investing in BLMIS shows beyond any doubt—notwithstanding his gentlemanly breeding and good looks, patrician manner, degrees from prestigious American institutions of higher learning, impeccable family connections, and daughters with husbands who were able to advance his business prospects—that he was a dullard or simply an effective dissembler. (Some might find the fact that investors would entrust millions and millions of dollars to Noel and his team of mediocrities to pirate, in itself, perplexing.)

The JPMorgan Chase Bank employee, Richard Cassa, whose responsibility it was, as relationship manager, to understand something about the BLMIS IA business could also be described as dim. It is difficult to believe that so many with successful careers who in the end worked to further the Madoff con appear to be only somewhat average. Frank DiPascali, Jr. with little education and regard for the truth, might be an exception. His various and contradictory accounts of what went on backstage at BLMIS make a great deal of what he says suspect;[28] his evolving account of the IA business was in the end not always useful. However, he was at least as knowledgeable about the con as Madoff. Because of him it was sustained longer than if Madoff, whose limited abilities were evident before[29] and during the con, had had to manage without him. In fact, many entangled in the Madoff con seem to have no special genius (other than nerve), certainly as far as knowing how to invest. When thinking about the oft-repeated narrative of their having exceptional skills as investors, one is reminded of Elizabeth Bowen's description of Aldous Huxley as "the stupid person's idea as a clever person."

On Justifications and Rationalizations

One striking finding of this study of the BLMIS IA business is that in the many pages of court testimony and in other documents describing the variety and extensive criminal activities therein, such as FBI reports and materials submitted to the courts, lacking are acknowledgments by the accomplices that what was done were in any way the acts of common criminals. Some might not have expected this finding. However, Sutherland, with his observation that not only is criminal behavior learned through differential association but so are "motives, drives, rationalizations, and attitudes,"[30] provides the obvious explanation for it. Quite simply, the BLMIS accomplices were most interested in justifying—that is, defending—what they did. Much of their efforts in their accounts were directed to protecting themselves from blame in order to not only stay out of prison but also minimize possible stigma from family, friends, neighbors, BLMIS clients, and the public. The rationalizations learned through differential

association provided them with useful justifications to distance themselves from blame. Just as they learned to help steal money, so too they
learned how to deflect subsequent blame.

Justifications and rationalizations of criminal acts have long been
observed and commented on by others. Even when individuals have
not done something they would rather not have others know about,
they repackage and embellish stories, making them more logical and
palatable than life itself. In their study of juvenile delinquency over
50 years ago, Gresham M. Sykes and David Matza referred to these
as "techniques of neutralization,"[31] by which "disapproval flowing
from internalized norms and conforming others in the social environment is neutralized, turned back, or deflected. ... Social controls that
served to check or inhibit deviant motivational patterns are rendered
inoperative. ... [One is] something more like an apologetic failure,
often more sinned against than sinning in his [or her] own eyes."[32]

In their discussion of these techniques of neutralization Sykes and
Matza divide them into five major types:[33]

1. The denial of responsibility, or lacking responsibility. Here the
    contention is that the harm to the BLMIS IA business clients
    was unintentional, an accident. In fact, actions may even have
    been due to forces outside the individual and thus beyond con-
    trol. Criminal acts were committed because he or she was some-
    one "helplessly propelled into new situations"; he or she was
    more acted upon than acting. In short, he or she was a victim of
    circumstance.
2. The denial of harm. Here the contention is that most of the
    BLMIS IA business clients from whom money was stolen could
    well afford it, and, in addition they would have eventually gotten
    it back had there not been a worldwide economic downturn.
3. The denial of the victim. Here the contention is that the harm was
    not wrong in light of the circumstances, that others were trans-
    gressors. (There are no examples of this technique of neutralization
    being invoked by the BLMIS IA employees. Although after
    Madoff's arrest many expressed the view that his clients got what
    they deserved, and Madoff also suggested precisely that to me
    and to others in prison interviews. Moreover, defrauding his clients
    seemed to enhance Madoff's sense of power and self-esteem while
    at the same time diminishing their stature in his eyes.)
4. The condemnation of the condemners. This is an attempt to
    change the subject. Here the contention is that those critical of

what was done at BLMIS did not fully understand or appreciate how the business could best operate. Moreover, everyone at times cuts corners a little. The rationalization is that the blame for the Madoff con was unfairly shifted to those merely doing what they were directed to do.

5. The appeal to higher loyalties. Here the contention is that the demands of the larger society were sacrificed for the demands of family, friends, and colleagues who had other needs and expectations. In short, there was at times a higher loyalty that was pressing Madoff's accomplices.

Put generally, in their accounts and defense, Madoff, his brother, and members of his retinue of accomplices alternately expressed the beliefs that: It was not their fault; After being asked to become involved, what was one to do?; It was expected, it was part of the job; There was an understanding that that was how things were done; They did not understand; They should do what was asked; They did not steal anyone's money; What they were doing was for the benefit of others, not themselves.

To the degree that their accounts were believed, a perfect crime was committed. Not perfect in the sense that no one was caught, but perfect because obviously no crime had been committed.

Finally here, using the threefold typology of business owners—(a) amoral calculators who willfully violate the rules, (b) organizational incompetents who do not understand the rules, and (c) political citizen who because of principled disagreement violate the rules—developed by Kagan and Scholz in their research on compliance with regulatory rules, Madoff is without question the first type.[34]

The American Dream of Success and Madoff's Dream

In a chapter titled "The North Begins to Hustle," the great American historian James Truslow Adams places the dawn of the American Dream of Success in the decades before the middle of the nineteenth century: "The fact that opportunity appeared at least to be open to everyone kept alive the belief in the American Dream. After Andrew Jackson [whose presidential term was from 1829 until 1837], every boy was being told he might be President of the United States. ... [John Jacob] Astor [1763–1848] had been a foreign immigrant, scarcely able to read and write, yet there he was, rich as Croesus, and dictating to the government. Native or foreigner, rich or poor, learned or unlearned, the race was free for all, and the prizes beyond the imaginations of the preceding generation or of European magnates."[35]

Durkheim, among others, has pointed out that not only in America, but wherever there has been rapid industrialization, "greed is aroused without knowing where to find ultimate foothold. Nothing can calm it, since its goal is far beyond all it can attain. Reality seems valueless by comparison with all the dreams of fevered imaginations; reality is therefore abandoned, but so too is possibility abandoned when it in turn becomes reality. A thirst arises for novelties, unfamiliar pleasures, nameless sensations."[36] This has been particularly true—since at least the mid-1850s—against the backdrop "when everything that man had considered as inalienable became, [Marx noted], an object of exchange. ... This is the time when the very things which to then had been communicated, but never exchanged; given, but never sold; acquired, but never bought—virtue, love, conviction, knowledge, conscience, etc.—when everything, in short, passed into commerce. It is the time of general corruption, of universal venality ... the time when everything, moral or physical, having become a marketable value, is brought to the market to be assessed at its truest value."[37]

One tenet that precipitated the early development of the American Dream of Success was the hope of opening all avenues of opportunity to as many citizens and immigrants as possible. Two conditions that greatly animated this cultural ethos were the country's seemingly limitless potential wealth and the lack of social barriers, particularly the circumstance of birth, to hamper or frustrate ability and ambition. The American Dream of Success produced young men of vitality, devotion, and resolve, and in the end self-made men. It framed rags-to-riches successes. It came to embody society's basic values, most particularly, achievement, individualism, and overwhelming materialism (the fetishism of money). And as Robert K. Merton observed: "Moreover, in the American Dream of Success there is no final stopping point. The measure of 'monetary success' is conveniently relative. ... There is no stable resting point, or rather, it is a point which manages to be 'just ahead.'"[38] There is widespread agreement that the goal of monetary success enjoys a position of prominence in America, that it has largely become the benchmark of achievement.

The earliest idea that the American Dream of Success would allow all Americans to lead the "good life"—as the ancient Greeks saw it—was slowly recast that the principal and perhaps singular measure of fully attaining the American Dream of Success was accumulating money and material possessions. Possessing money evolved from being a means to an end to becoming an end in itself. In what it has become, the American Dream of Success can be characterized both as a national virtue and as a national vice.

The increased centrality of the American Dream of Success in the twentieth century was to generate exceptionally strong pressures to succeed by any possible and necessary means, almost at any costs. There were few limits on unadorned competitiveness—in education, in sports, in leisure-time pursuits. For businesses, there were pressures from all directions to maximize profits. In the demanding world, there was an unrelenting fear of falling behind. Considerable flexibility in selecting the means to obtain success was permitted. Principally, it was necessary to get out front and to stay there. Since industrialization, Durkheim has also pointed out, "the longing for infinity [for an indefinite goal] is daily represented as a mark of moral distinction, whereas it can only appear within unregulated consciences which elevate to a rule the lack of rule from which they suffer. The doctrine of the most ruthless and swift progress has become an article of faith."[39]

According to Merton, the American Dream of Success "enjoins the acceptance of three cultural axioms: First, all should strive for the same lofty goals since these are open to all; second, present seeming failure is but a way-station to ultimate success; and third, genuine failure consists only in the lessening or withdrawal of ambition."[40] In the face of the American Dream of Success, individuals may pursue the cultural goal using institutional means, that is, they may "conform," or they may react by rejecting the goal and/or the means of reaching it.

Adaptation that is not conformity, that is, accepting both the goal and institutionalized means of moving toward it, can take the form of "innovation," "ritualism," "retreatism," or "rebellion."[41]

The ascendance of the American Dream of Success has helped create a culture of tolerance for those millions in its pursuit. The result was the accommodation to economic claims and a devaluation of noneconomic institutions, functions, statuses, and roles. On this point Messner and Rosenfeld have written: "In American society the economy is an institution that by design is much less constraining than other institutions. It is a free-market economy, governed by the principle of laissez faire. Ironically, then, Americans tend to be strongly attached to the institution with the least restraining qualities—the economy. ... The relative impotence of non-economic institutions also implies that they are limited in the incentives, penalties, and social support that they can offer for socially prescribed or proscribed behavior."[42]

Thus, there are obvious costs to this societal imbalance of weakened social institutions, except, of course, economic institutions. As individuals have pressed ahead decade after decade America's social problems—its poverty rate, its urban decay, its suicide rate, its international military adventures, and its crime rate, both street crime and white collar crime—have become intractable in spite of the public and government's commitment to alleviate them.

Madoff's life was dominated by the altered interpretation of the American Dream of Success. However, he was not actually part of the theatrics. His was the American Dream of Success to make his mark at any cost. He was truly an innovator; in every respect he abandoned the institutional means to success. He did not bother to engage in competition, a requisite in the pursuit of the American Dream of Success. He did not follow the established rules or even bend them. He was not testing his ability as an investor. For decades, he lied and defrauded readily and constantly. Obviously, and as Merton cautioned: "Many procedures which from the standpoint of particular individuals would be most efficient in securing desired values—the exercise of force, fraud, power—are ruled out of the institutional area of permitted conduct."[43]

In the typology of modes of individual adaptation to the American Dream of Success developed by Merton, Madoff was the consummate innovator. "Great cultural emphasis upon the success-goal invites this mode of adaptation through the use of institutionally proscribed but often effective means of attaining at least the simulacrum of success—wealth and power." Madoff had "assimilated the cultural emphasis upon the goal without equally internalizing the institutional norms governing ways and means for its attainment."[44]

In many respects, Madoff's narrative is a standard and familiar American Dream story. Like the central character in many of these stories he is ambitious not only for himself, but also for his extended family. Almost from its beginning he becomes its undisputed paterfamilias as do most central characters in such sagas, in real life and in fiction.

Like other famous paterfamilias—John D. Rockefeller or Joseph P. Kennedy, Sr., or Vito Corleone—in building his family business Madoff's movements were guarded and his relationships carefully managed, enabling him to steadily create and sustain an empire, all the while protecting his family. There is also a great deal of support here for the aphorism attributed to Balzac: "Behind every great fortune there is a great crime." There is also evident an essential part of the narrative: excessive secrecy, great success, the appearance of entrepreneurship, and emphasis on keeping a tightly knit family tightly knit. In the end, Madoff, Rockefeller, Kennedy, and Corleone became surrounded by mystery, mystique, and myth, as do some of their closest associates. (In Madoff's case, the most obvious examples are Sonja Kohn and Jeffry Picower.)

Madoff's limitless and aggressive ambition in the pursuit of wealth was evident long before his immoral ethic of success at any cost. Through BLMIS he created a fantasy world of great wealth, power, and self-indulgence. The finale seemed to be little more than a narcissistic and hedonistic pursuit of an extraordinary cache of money and philistine material possessions.

Notes

Introduction

1. Edwin M. Schur, "Sociological Analysis of Confidence Swindling," *Journal of Criminal Law and Criminology*, 48, Number 3, 1957, 298. Schur also notes: "Perhaps too little attention has been paid to the interesting fact that confidence rackets are called 'games', while most other criminal offenses receive (even from their practitioners) far less playful appellations." At the same time, relating their lifework, many con men tell of periodically enjoying a sense of play.

2. What is meant by *deception* here and throughout the book is intentionally to cause others to have false beliefs or intentionally to cause others to persist in false beliefs that the deceiver believes to be false.

3. In his comprehensive 1940 study of American con men and con games, Maurer wrote: "A con mob ... consists of a minimum of two—the roper and the inside man. When the mark is played against the [big] store [an 'establishment against which big-con men play their victims'] ... the mob also includes the personnel of the big store—the manager or bookmaker who has charge of the impressive-looking shills, and the minor employees such as ... clerks." David W. Maurer, *The Big Con: The Story of the Confidence Man* (Indianapolis: Bobbs-Merrill, 1940) (Reprinted: Anchor Books, 1999, Introduction by Luc Sante), 134. Later Maurer adds: "The roper and the inside man are the principals of any mob. Upon them depends the success of the big store, for, however elaborate a set-up is provided, and however secure the fix, all is useless without the services of a man who can bring in marks, and one who can give them a convincing play gaining a mark's confidence," 137.

4. Alva Johnston, "The Legendary Mizners," in Alexander Klein, editor, *Grand Deception* (London: Faber and Faber, n.d.), 218.

5. This is but one of the many abbreviations of proper nouns used throughout the book. Others are:

Proper Nouns	Abbreviations
Avellino & Bienes	A & B
Bernard L. Madoff Investment Securities	BLMIS
Depository Trust Company	DTC
Fairfield Greenwich Group	FGG
Federal Bureau of Investigation	FBI
Investment Advisory accounts	IA accounts
Internal Revenue Service	IRS
Madoff Securities International Limited	MSIL
Security and Exchange Commission	SEC
Securites Investment Protection Act	SIPA
Securites Investment Protection Corporation	SIPC
Standard & Poor's	S & P
United States	U.S.

6. This number is significantly smaller than figures often reported in the media. When he was arrested, Madoff estimated the fraud to be $50 billion, surely a boast that would make his theft appear even more epic. Another figure widely reported is $64.8 billion, the combined balance on client statements at the end of November 2008, shortly before BLMIS went into bankruptcy. On the other hand, the total customers who filed claims with the SIPC trustee, charged with returning as much stolen money as possible, reported they lost approximately $17.3 billion.

7. When Madoff was arrested, BLMIS "had only approximately $300 million in assets at the time, including approximately $234 million in cash and cash equivalents" in accounts at JPMorgan Chase Bank. U.S. Department of Justice, "Deferred Prosecution Agreement," JPMorgan Chase Bank, January 6, 2014, Exhibit C/Statement of Facts, 2. Obviously, this was not nearly enough to meet the demand for the billions of dollars that BLMIS customers requested returned in the coming weeks. (The Deferred Prosecution Agreement essentially suspended an indictment for two years, before letting it lapse, as long as JPMorgan Chase Bank admitted its actions and overhauled its controls against money laundering.)

8. A Government Accountability Office document dated September 13, 2012, reported that the SIPC trustee provided the following figures: account holders (individual/family and institution)—7,964; claims filed—16,519; claims filed by direct investors—5,543. (See "Securities Investor Protection Corporation: Customer Outcomes in the Madoff Liquidation Proceedings," GAO-12-991, 10, 14, 15.)

9. R. M. MacIver, *Social Causation* (Originally published by Ginn and Company, 1942), (New York: Harper Torchbook edition, 1964), 88.

10. Georg Simmel, *The Sociology of Georg Simmel*, translated, edited, and with an Introduction by Kurt H. Wolff (Glencoe, IL: The Free Press, 1950), 307–308.

11. Ibid., 312.

12. Erving Goffman, *The Presentation of Self in Everyday Life* (Garden City, New York: Doubleday & Company [Doubleday Anchor Books], 1959), 18 (see footnote 1).

13. Maurer, *The Big Con*, 143–44.

14. Maurer, *The Big Con*, 101.

15. Ever interested in furthering his con, Madoff recruited some of his backstage accomplices as ropers. See Chapter 5.

16. There is an extensive record of Madoff lying, intentionally misleading others meant to make them believe what he did not believe. Sissela Bok defines a lie as "any intentionally deceptive message which is *stated* .... Deception, then, is the larger category, and lying forms part of it." She adds: "I shall use instead a more neutral, and therefore wider, definition of a lie: an intentionally deceptive message in the form of a *statement*." See *Lying: Moral Choices in Public and Private Life* (New York: Random House [Pantheon Books], 1978), 13–15.

17. Many of the investors who Madoff defrauded were also materialistic, greedy, and unconscious. For most victims, however, not enough material has been collected so far that bears on their degree of mediocrity. See Lionel S. Lewis, *Con Game: Bernard Madoff and His Victims* (New Brunswick, NJ: Transaction Publishers, 2012.)

18. Even the U.S. tax laws favor unearned wealth, taxing earned income at a higher rate than that from capital gains.

19. As Table 0.1 shows, for nine years from 1992 to 2008, BLMIS paid out more money than it took in, but for eight of those years, there was not a large difference in what was paid out and paid in. However, this pattern of the cash out not greatly exceeding the cash in dramatically changed in 2008, and Madoff's con game was quickly over.

20. Jarndyce and Jarndyce is the long-term litigation at the center of Charles Dickens's *Bleak House*; it is a legal proceeding that displays the absurdity of the Court of Chancery in England. In the opening pages of the novel, Dickens writes: "Jarndyce and Jarndyce drones on. The scarecrow of a suit has, in course of time, become so complicated, that no man alive knows what it means. The parties to it understand it least; but it has been observed that no two Chancery lawyers can talk about it for five minutes, without coming to a total disagreement as to all the premises. Innumerable children have been born into the cause; innumerable young people have married into it; innumerable old people have died out of it. Scores of persons have deliriously found themselves made parties in Jarndyce and Jarndyce, without knowing how or why; whole families have inherited legendary hatreds with the suit. The little plaintiff or defendant, who was promised a new

Table 0.1   Cash in/Cash out, BLMIS Accounts, 1992–2008

Year	Cash In	Cash Out
1992	$904,272,560	$1,018,689,670
1993	$664,370,878	$609,219,797
1994	$577,959,780	$651,932,259
1995	$884,907,897	$955,450,002
1996	$1,303,802,139	$1,076,280,471
1997	$1,995,752,125	$1,259,163,989
1998	$2,718,098,944	$1,657,646,062
1999	$2,606,597,014	$1,866,578,080
2000	$2,584,913,116	$2,598,132,080
2001	$2,309,389,766	$2,425,894,417
2002	$2,453,094,123	$2,664,015,048
2003	$2,855,614,441	$3,423,072,194
2004	$4,045,208,942	$3,477,761,846
2005	$3,616,547,123	$4,767,292,175
2006	$5,950,968,943	$4,385,862,882
2007	$7,284,217,506	$4,506,919,231
2008	$6,308,498,696	$10,556,646,750

Source: Letter from Stephen P. Harbeck, president of SIPC, to Congressman Scott Garrett, January 24, 2011, 15.

rocking-horse when Jarndyce and Jarndyce should be settled, has grown up, possessed himself a real horse, and trotted away into the other world. Fair wards of the court have faded into mothers and grandmothers; a long procession of Chancellors has come in and gone out; the legion of bills in the suit has been transformed into mere bills of mortality; there are not three Jarndyces left upon the earth perhaps." Near the end of the over 750-page novel, the will is settled, but, not surprisingly, "the whole estate has been found to be absorbed in costs." The ultimate purpose of the case appears to have had no other purpose but to line the pockets of lawyers.

21. See Lewis, *Con Game*.

22. The best, the one most accurate, and containing the least unsubstantiated gossip is Andrew Kirtzman, *Betrayal: The Life and Lies of Bernie Madoff* (New York: HarperCollins Publisher, 2009.)

23. After a trial in England in which she and others were charged with, among other things, receiving illegal payments from the Madoff businesses, the justice hearing the case wrote of Kohn and three others: "Bernard Madoff's fraud itself blighted their lives and tainted their good names simply by association . . . .To this was added the burden of this unfounded claim, making serious allegations of dishonesty, which threatened financial ruin and personal humiliation. It was commenced without forewarning . . . and

has been pursued aggressively and relentlessly over several years, on occasion with an unfair degree of hyperbole .... Mrs. Kohn has suffered poisonous press releases ... and been subject to ... extensive disclosure of her family's assets and affairs." (See Madoff Securities International Limited [in Liquidation] and Stephen Raven et al., The High Court of Justice, Queen's Bench Division, Commercial Court, Case No: 2010 Folio 1468, The Honorable Mr. Justice Popplewell's Judgment, October 8, 2013, "Conclusions and Postscript.")

24. C. Wright Mills, *Images of Man: The Classical Tradition in Sociological Thinking* (New York: George Braziller, 1960), 16.

25. John Kenneth Galbraith, "Introduction," in Robert Shaplen, editor, *Kreuger: Genius and Swindler* (New York: Knopf, 1960), ix–x.

Chapter 1 Of Bernard L. Madoff and Others

1. W. C. Crosby and Edward H. Smith, "Con," *Saturday Evening Post*, January 24, 1920, 8–9.

2. He reportedly confessed to his brother earlier.

3. Madoff propagated the fiction that both were financially successful, although they were not. Indeed, as the table below shows, it was necessary, at least in the later years of his con, to pore in millions of dollars stolen from IA customers to keep the market making and proprietary trading businesses operating in order to hide the fact that they, in actuality, were not viable businesses at all.

4. In a lawsuit filed in 2012, the SIPC trustee asserted: "In [the] fiscal year 2007, approximately $174 million was transferred from the IA business to an MSIL bank account. During this time period, approximately $103 million

Table 1.2 Amounts Transferred from BLMIS IA Business to Market Making and Proprietary Trading Businesses, 2000–2008

Year	Direct Transfers	Indirect Transfers	Total
2000	$42,966,679	$32,500,000	$75,496,679
2001	$12,410,095	$59,993,500	$72,403,595
2002	$8,855,299	$51,628,142	$60,483,441
2003	$4,982,025	$92,384,791	$97,366,815
2004	$6,852,980	$82,113,022	$88,966,002
2005	$5,406,024	$63,901,013	$69,307,037
2006	$0	$73,217,622	$73,217,622
2007	$0	$121,243,288	$121,243,288
2008	$0	$75,459,701	$75,459,701
Total	$81,503,101	$652,441,077	$733,944,178

Source: Letter from Stephen P. Harbeck, president of SIPC, to Congressman Scott Garrett, January 24, 2011, 20.

was transferred back to bank accounts controlled by BLMIS where it was displayed on financial statements prepared for the market making and proprietary trading businesses as commission income.[And again], in [the] fiscal year 2008, approximately $90 million was transferred from the IA business to an MSIL bank account. During this time period, approximately $87 million was transferred back to bank accounts controlled by BLMIS where it was displayed on financial statements prepared for the market making and proprietary trading businesses as commission income." The SIPC trustee continued: "Based on financial statements prepared by BLMIS for [the] fiscal year 2007, this redirected commission income represented approximately 60 percent of the total revenues reported by the market making and proprietary trading businesses. For [the] fiscal year 2008, this redirected commission represented more than 70 percent of the total revenues reported by the market making and proprietary trading businesses." The trustee further concluded: "The financial statements prepared by BLMIS for [the] fiscal years 2000 through 2008 falsely indicated that the market making and proprietary trading businesses generated tens of millions of dollars in net income. In reality, however, the market making and proprietary trading businesses would have generated millions of dollars in *losses* [emphasis in original] had they not been supported by the fraudulent transfers of customer property from the IA business." (*Irving H. Picard, Trustee for the Liquidation of Bernard L. Madoff Investment Securities, LLC, v. Peter B. Madoff*, estate of Mark D. Madoff, Andrew H. Madoff, individually and as executor of the estate of Mark D. Madoff, Susan Elkin, Stephanie S. Mack, Deborah Madoff, and Shana D. Madoff, United States Bankruptcy Court, Southern District of New York, May 4, 2012.)

5. The Madoff fraud has been written about extensively. See in particular: Erin Arvedlund, *Too Good to Be True: The Rise and Fall of Bernie Madoff* (New York: Portfolio, 2010); Diana B. Henriques, *The Wizard of Lies: Bernie Madoff and the Death of Trust* (New York: Times Books, 2011); Andrew Kirtzman, *Betrayal: The Life and Lies of Bernie Madoff* (New York: HarperCollins Publisher, 2009); Lionel S. Lewis, *Con Game: Bernard Madoff and His Victims* (New Brunswick, NJ: Transaction Publishers, 2012). These volumes, and, in fact, as a whole, the books and articles about Madoff that have appeared with regularity have provided mostly biographical detail, as a great deal less was known about BLMIS in the early months and years after his arrest. From numerous newspaper accounts of the court proceedings from a five-month criminal trial in New York City, lasting from October 17, 2013, until March 24, 2014, of five BLMIS former employees—Annette Bongiorno, Daniel Bonventre, Jo Ann Crupi, Jerome O'Hara, and George Perez —some facts about BLMIS's operations were dispersed and more fully understood. Of course, as in any court trial, for obvious reasons, some of the testimony was not completely reliable. The probity of witnesses in this instance seems somewhat greater given that

some had previously pled guilty to having worked with Madoff to further his fraud and had entered agreements with federal prosecutors to testify with the hope of receiving a reduced prison sentence. One witness had met with federal prosecutors dozens of times to prepare him for his court appearance, a reason to doubt his fidelity, and the trustworthiness of his memory.

6. Harry Markopolos, *No One Would Listen: A True Financial Thriller* (Hoboken, NJ: John Wiley, 2010).

7. *"The Sting"* (A Movie), 1973.

8. Excerpted from: Jay Robert Nash, *Hustlers and Con Men* (New York: M. Evans and Company, 1976), 97–106. With his net profit of over $500,000 from the con, Arnold went back to Kentucky, where he purchased livestock and a house on 32 acres. One of the investors in the con filed a lawsuit to recover his money, which Arnold settled out of court with a payment of $150,000. This additional material is from a 1940 account by A. J. Liebling in the *New Yorker Magazine*.

9. Material from: J. R. "Yellow Kid" Weil and W. T. Brannon, *"Yellow Kid" Weil: The Autobiography of America's Master Swindler*, Chapter 3, "A Tip for Mr. Macallister" (Chicago, IL: Ziff-Davis, 1948).

10. John Kenneth Galbraith, "Introduction," in Robert Shaplen, editor, *Kreuger: Genius and Swindler* (New York: Knopf, 1960), x.

11. Allen Churchill, *The Incredible Ivar Kreuger* (New York: Rinehart & Company, 1957), 216–18.

12. O. Henry, "A Tempered Wind," in *The Complete Works of O. Henry* (Garden City, NY: Doubleday & Company, 1960), 324–37.

13. Richard H. Blum, *Deceivers and Deceived* (Springfield, IL: Charles C. Thomas, 1972), 234.

14. Excerpted from Kirtzman, *Betrayal*, 120–21.

15. Throughout the book, all the excerpts from testimony have been edited to remove false starts, obvious typographical errors, repetitions common in speech, and the like that might distract rather than add to a reader's understanding of the Madoff con.

16. Jeffrey Tucker, testimony, Commonwealth of Massachusetts, Office of the Secretary of the Commonwealth, Securities Division, in the Matter of Bernard L. Madoff Investment Securities, March 12, 2009, 97–102. A few months earlier, Tucker had given the same account to the FBI: Q: "In general, did you ever request documentation to substantiate his [Madoff's] response?" A: "I would look at documents. Specifically, in 2001, I had a conversation with Madoff and I told him that I wanted to confirm that our assets were there . . . . So, I was up at Madoff's and he said: 'You pick the dates'. I don't remember the specific dates I picked, but I do remember they were prior to the day I was up there. Frank DiPascali was there and they went to retrieve several ledgers. They showed me the purchases and sales blotters, which included the name of the counterparty, price, amount, etc. I picked AOL, so we got to the AOL page in the stock record. I saw our clients' names

and looked at the total balance for Madoff and made sure it tied to the balance on our account statements, which it did. Then we went to the DTC terminal, entered the name and the balance tied to the stock record. To me it clearly indicated that it was Madoff's account with DTC."

A very similar description of this event from a series of interviews beginning in 2009—almost all with Frank DiPascali, Jr.—can be found in redacted FBI documents: 1. "Soon after, Madoff brought Tucker to the 'cage' on the 17th floor and had DiPascali show Tucker some positions on the computer screen. DiPascali observed Madoff laugh and tell Tucker: 'See, they are there.'" 2. "Madoff provided DTC runs for third-party verification, although these runs were completely fictional. The fictional paper copies of the DTC runs eventually transformed into a fictional DTC screen used to show positions held by Jeffrey Tucker of Fairfield Greenwich Group . . . . Tucker and Madoff came down to the 17th floor and Madoff asked Individual to log into the DTC terminal. Tucker stood over Individual's shoulder as Individual brought up the stock positions for the dates requested." 3. "Then Madoff brought Tucker down to the 17th floor into the room where Individual's desk and computer were located. Madoff casually asked Individual if there was a way to show Tucker his DTC positions right there since Madoff did not want to take Tucker into the 'cage', where DTC positions are normally monitored, since the 'cage' was messy and did not normally entertain visitors. Individual responded that in fact could be done, and Individual asked Madoff what date he wanted to see . . . . By asking the question of Madoff, Individual allowed Madoff to casually respond: 'Oh just bring up the end of the month'. Individual went through the log in procedure that had been set up by . . . using the first numbers of Individual's driver's license as the password, to bring up the screen showing the BLMIS DTC report. The log in procedure was also part of the charade, giving Tucker the impression Individual was logging into an external system, as would have been the case when one logged into the actual DTC system . . . .Madoff asked Tucker to pick whatever security he desired. Tucker viewed the security, believing he was verifying DTC shares segregated in the BLMIS account for the benefit of their Fairfield Greenwich Group customers, and he was satisfied."

17. FBI document.

18. This charge was not challenged by Peter Madoff's attorneys.

19. *United States of America v. Peter Madoff*, United States District Court, Southern District of New York, S7-CR-228 (LTS), (C6T8MAD1), June 29, 2012, 29–43.

20. In 2010, the U.S. Attorney prosecuting the Madoff con game commented: "As we allege again today, others criminally assisted his [Madoff's] epic crime. A house of cards is almost never built by one lone architect." The FBI assistant director-in-charge of the Madoff investigation added: "We knew early on that a fraud of this scale could not have been the work of one person alone." Only days after Madoff's arrest, by mid-December 2008, it was clear that many others had surely assisted Madoff. In February 2009,

Table 1.3 Annual and Monthly Balances in 703 Account, 1999–2008

As of:	703 Account Closing Ledger Balance	Average Monthly Closing Ledger Balance
December 1999	$2,320,237	$5,061,827
December 2000	$20,493,643	$6,707,467
December 2001	$26,581,003	$8,599,687
December 2002	$2,401,631	$1,492,461
December 2003	$4,061,657	$1,369,215
December 2004	$1,084,601	$1,262,028
December 2005	$323,218	$1,238,669
December 2006	$394,700	$498,220
December 2007	$742,309	$633,968
December 2008	$229,407,266	$20,116,566

Source: Letter from Stephen P. Harbeck, president of SIPC, to Congressman Scott Garrett, op. cit., 16.

one forensic accountant began raising some very obvious questions: "In order for him to have done this by himself, he would have had to have been at work night and day, no vacations, and no time off. He would have had to nurture the Ponzi scheme daily. What happened when he was gone? Who handled it when somebody called in while he was on vacation and said: 'I need access to money'?" A litigator prominent in securities matters echoed the growing skepticism about Madoff having acted alone: "Simply from an administrative perspective, the act of putting together the various account statements, which did show trading activity, has to involve a number of people. You would need office and support personnel, people who actually knew what the market were for the securities that were being traded. You would need accountants so that the internal documents reconcile with the documents being sent to customers at least on a superficial level." (See David Glovin, David Voreacos, and David Scheer, "Madoff Must Have Had Help, Lawyers Say, Citing Trustee Report," February 24, 2009, Bloomberg News.)

21. In the final years of the Madoff con, the centrality of the 703 Account is most evident in 2000 and 2001. The annual and monthly average closing ledger balances in the account between 1999 and 2008 are shown in Table 1.3.

22. *United States of America v. Jerome O'Hara, et al.*, United States District Court, Southern District of New York, 10 CR 228 (LTS), testimony of Frank DiPascali, Jr., before the Honorable Laura Taylor Swain, October 17, 2013–March 24, 2014.

Chapter 2 Backstage, the Accomplices

1. David Gelles and Gillian Tett, "From behind Bars: Madoff Spins His Story," *Financial Times*, April 8, 2011; Charlie Gasparino, "I'm a Victim, Too," FOXBusiness, August 25, 2011.

2. Goffman reminds us that while it may "take deep skill, long training, and psychological capacity to become a good stage actor, … almost anyone can quickly learn a script well enough to give a charitable audience some sense of realness in what is being contrived before them …. Scripts even in the hands of unpracticed players can come to life because life itself is a dramatically enacted thing." It is this reality that surely accounted in some part for Madoff's run of luck (Erving Goffman, *The Presentation of Self in Everyday Life* (Garden City, New York: Doubleday & Company [Doubleday Anchor Books], 1959), 71–72.)

3. Ibid., 22.

4. Ibid., 73.

5. *United States of America v. Jerome O'Hara et al.*, United States District Court, Southern District of New York, testimony of Craig Kugel.

6. Erving Goffman, *Strategic Interaction* (Philadelphia: University of Pennsylvania Press, 1969). Goffman defines seduction as "maneuvering a definition of the situation such that the subject is led to believe that the observer is to be treated as something of a teammate to whom strategic information can be voluntarily trusted," 37.

7. *United States of America v. Frank DiPascali, Jr.*, United States District Court, Southern District of New York, 09-CR-764 (RJS), August 11, 2009, 44–51.

8. *United States of America v. Irwin Lipkin*, United States District Court, Southern District of New York, 10-CR-228 (LTS), November 8, 2012, 29–37.

9. *United States of America v. David Friehling*, United States District Court, Southern District of New York, 09-CR-700 (AKH), November 9, 2009, 38–42.

10. *United States of America v. Enrica Cotellessa-Pitz*, United States District Court, Southern District of New York, S5 10-CR-228 (LTS), December 19, 2011, Exhibit 8, 29ff.

11. Cotellessa-Pitz provides a fuller account of what she saw and did backstage at BLMIS in Chapter 3.

12. *United States of America v. Eric S. Lipkin*, United States District Court, Southern District of New York, S3-10-CR 228 (LTS), June 6, 2011, Exhibit 6, 32–35.

13. By way of example, in April 1994, Kugel generated pricing information involving the purported purchase and short sale of Micron Technology. The market volume for Micron when-issued securities on

April 5 was approximately 28,700, but the volume of such securities purportedly sold short by BLMIS that day was 2,195,364.

14. Kugel provides a fuller account of what he saw and did backstage at BLMIS in Chapter 4.

15. *United States of America v. David L. Kugel*, United States District Court, Southern District of New York, S4 10-CR-228 (LTS), November 21, 2011, Exhibit 7, 32–34.

16. *United States of America v. Craig Kugel*, United States District Court, Southern District of New York, 10-CR-238 (LTS), June 5, 2012, 27–30.

17. Stanley Milgram, "Behavioral Study of Obedience," *Journal of Abnormal and Social Psychology*, 67, Number 4, 1963, 371–78.

18. Thomas Blass, *The Man Who Shocked the World: The Life and Legacy of Stanley Milgram* (New York: Basic Books [paper], 2004), 93.

19. Lionel S. Lewis, *Con Game: Bernard Madoff and His Victims* (New Brunswick, NJ: Transaction Publishers, 2012).

20. Ken Auletta, *Greed and Glory on Wall Street: The Fall of the House of Lehman* (New York: Random House, 1986), 138.

21. The family ties—the Kugels, the Lipkins, and the Madoffs—of BLMIS's 17th floor accomplices are not unlike the family ties that held any number of locally based crime networks of the Mafia, the criminal enterprise that was organized crime in the United States for a good part of the twentieth century, together and made them effective for so many years. Members of what was known as the (Stefano) Magaddino Crime Family, for example, included his brothers, Antonino, Giuseppe, and Gaspar, and his son-in-law, James LaDuca. (Joseph "Lead Pipe Joe" Todaro Sr., Joseph "Big Joe" Todaro Jr., and brother, Richard Todaro, also became part of the Magaddino Crime Family.)

22. Goffman, *Presentation of Self*, 79.

23. Ibid., 77–84.

24. Ibid., 104.

25. The judge also instructed the jury: "No one can willfully and knowingly violate the law and excuse himself from the consequences of his conduct simply by pleading that he or she followed someone else's orders. In other words ... it is no defense that the defendant was just following the orders of his or her employer." (*United States of America v. Jerome O'Hara et al.*, United States District Court, Southern District of New York, Preliminary Charge.) See the section "The Response to Authority" in the chapter.

26. Ibid.

27. *United States of America v. Jerome O'Hara et al.*, United States District Court, Southern District of New York, testimony of Winifer Jackson.

28. Goffman, op. cit., 77.

29. *United States of America v. Jerome O'Hara et al.*, United States District Court, Southern District of New York, testimony of Frank DiPascali, Jr.

30. Ibid.
31. *United States of America v. Jerome O'Hara et al.*, United States District Court, Southern District of New York, testimony of Daniel Bonventre.

Chapter 3 Deception: Backstage with Enrica Cotellessa-Pitz

1. *United States of America v. Jerome O'Hara et al.*, United States District Court, Southern District of New York, testimony of Enrica Cotellessa-Pitz.
2. David Shulman, *From Hire to Liar: The Role of Deception in the Workplace* (Ithaca and London: ILR Press [Cornell University Press], 2007), 156.
3. Sissela Bok, *Lying: Moral Choices in Public and Private Life* (New York: Random House, [Pantheon Books], 1978), 22.
4. Georg Simmel, *The Sociology of Georg Simmel*, translated, edited, and with an Introduction by Kurt H. Wolff (Glencoe, IL: The Free Press, 1950), 313.
5. Ibid., 149.

Chapter 4 Deception: Backstage with David L. Kugel

1. *United States of America v. Jerome O'Hara et al.*, United States District Court, Southern District of New York, testimony of David L. Kugel.
2. Marvin B. Scott and Stanford M. Lyman, "Accounts," *American Sociological Review*, 33, Number 1, February 1968, 46–62.
3. Terri L. Orbuch, "People's Account Count: The Sociology of Accounts," *Annual Review of Sociology*, 23, 1997, 455–78.
4. Scott and Lyman, "Accounts," 47.
5. Kenneth Burke, *A Grammar of Motives* (New York: Prentice-Hall, 1945).
6. Michael L. Benson, "Denying the Guilty Mind: Accounting for Involvement in a White Collar Crime," *Criminology*, 23, Number 4, November, 1985, 583–607.
7. Sissela Bok, *Lying: Moral Choices in Public and Private Life* (New York: Random House, [Pantheon Books], 1978), 20.
8. Ibid., 18–19.

Chapter 5 Deception: Backstage with Annette Bongiorno

1. *United States of America v. Jerome O'Hara et al.*, United States District Court, Southern District of New York, testimony of Annette Bongiorno.
2. Not surprisingly, some of the BLMIS backstage accomplices were more obviously marks than were Madoff's intimates, who were long-standing clients.

3. *United States of America v. Paul J. Konigsberg*, United States District Court, Southern District of New York, Information, S12 10 Cr. 228 (LTS), paragraphs 15–21.

4. Herbert C. Kelman and V. Lee Hamilton, *Crimes of Obedience: Toward a Social Psychology of Authority and Responsibility* (New Haven: Yale University Press, 1989). Actually, Kelman and Hamilton first focus on why people engage in mass violence. However, the more general question is what impels individuals to disobedience given the "powerful habit of obeying authorities that seems to manifest itself wherever human groups are found."

5. Kelman and Hamilton are examining the My Lai massacre, a crime of obedience, in Vietnam, involving behavior, the wanton killing of scores of "occupants of the village of My Lai 4," obviously far more pernicious than stealing money. However, what Kelman and Hamilton found and wrote is completely apropos to understanding aspects of the Madoff con, most particularly how some backstage accomplices came to understand and explain their behavior. A third condition discussed by Kelman and Hamilton, which is inappropriate with respect to the Madoff con, is *dehumanization*.

6. Kelman and Hamilton, *Crimes of Obedience*, 20.

7. Ibid., 18.

Chapter 6 Madoff and the 17th Floor Ensemble

1. Not only did Madoff and his family live a "lavish lifestyle", but many backstage accomplices greatly benefited at BLMIS. Their salaries were beyond generous and their IA account balances surged. In his court testimony, Frank DiPascali, Jr. describes how his compensation was determined and his unlimited use of the company credit card:

Q: One of the things I think you testified to at BLMIS was you got to set your own salary?
A: I did.
Q: When you wanted a raise or needed a raise, you would simply tell Eric Lipkin?
A: Yes.
Q: You also said that when you wanted a bonus or needed a bonus you would simple take a bonus?
A: That is correct.
Q: We have covered the meals and private jets and the cars, correct?
A: Yes.
Q: Tickets to the [New Jersey] Devils. Are you a hockey fan?
A: My kids are.
Q: Trips to see your kids at college on a fairly frequent basis?

A: Yes.

   ...

Q: And how long did you maintain the credit card?

A: Until December of 2008.

Q: Can you describe for us some of the charges that you made that were of a personal nature?

A: Almost every meal I ate in a restaurant between 1985 and 2008 was charged on that card. Airline tickets were charged on the card for personal pleasure trips. All sorts of personal expenses that were consistent to the lifestyle that I was leading, which was going out to dinner a lot, traveling a lot, being with my kids a lot, ... flying to Boston to take my daughter and her friends out to dinner when they were at college. So I stayed at the Hotel Commonwealth a lot. Things like that were all put on the corporate card.

Q: And when you made those charges, did you know that they were personal expenses?

A: Sure.

Q: Did you ever declare this as income on your taxes?

A: No, I didn't.

   ...

Q: Did you have and understanding of who reviewed these credit cards?

A: Ruth Madoff.

Q: And from time to time would you hear from Ms. Madoff about the charges that were on your card?

A: Yes.

Q: Did she ever chide you about one of the charges?

A: Yes.

Q: Do you recall which one?

A: I charged some stuff at Toys Я Us.

Q: And what did she say about that charge?

A: She told me that that would jump off the page . . . .

Q: And did you continue to charge stuff at Toys Я Us?

A: Yes.

   ...

Q: And did your use of that credit card grow over time?

A: Exponentially.

Q: Can you tell us some of the ways that it grew and some of the charges you began to put on it?

A: More extravagant vacations. I owned a bigger boat; so we traveled more often and to nicer places. I worked late more often and ate dinner in the city a lot. So the amount of charges and the type of charges all increased in number and in value.

   ...

Q: And how much did those seats cost on an annual basis, approximately?

provided

A: $25,000

Q: And did you use those seats for personal use or for business use?

A: For my kids.

2. One biographer writes: "One State Department official reckoned there were as many as 200,000, although 70,000 to 80,000 is a more likely figure." See Richard Raynor, *Drake's Fortune: The Fabulous True Story of the World's Greatest Confidence Artist* (New York: Doubleday, 2002), 105.

3. According to one source, the amount grew from "$10 billion, [to] $20 billion, [to] $40 billion, [to] $100 billion [as] he ... began steadily to inflate the figure." Ibid., 104.

4. Bill Slocum, "The 70,000 Heirs of Sir Francis Drake," in Alexander Klein, editor, *Grand Deception* (London: Faber and Faber, n.d.), 328.

5. Ibid., 329.

6. For the full citation of both biographies, see Chapter 1.

7. Murray Teigh Bloom, *The Man Who Stole Portugal* (New York: Charles Scribner's Sons, 1966).

8. Rayner, *Drake's Fortune*, 91.

9. Southern District of New York, *United States of America v. Jerome O'Hara and George Perez*, Debra C. Freeman, Magistrate Judge, Sealed Complaint, M. Kathryn Scott, Special Agent with the FBI, November 12, 2009, 16–18.

10. Ibid., 20–28.

11. Ibid., 5, 31–32.

12. *United States of America v. Jerome O'Hara et al.*, United States District Court, Southern District of New York, testimony of Frank DiPascali, Jr.

13. The encounters with Madoff (and DiPascali) clearly unnerved O'Hara and Perez. In a handwritten letter, dated September 13, 2006, that he expected to remain sealed to protect himself from reprisals, Perez wrote: "I have expressed to my boss, Frank DiPascali, Jr. my unwillingness to work on projects which I am uncomfortable with. I don't know how far up the ladder my unwillingness has been communicated, but it is the matter of [a] short time before it hits the top. I fear for my job, my family, my future." The following day, O'Hara typed a similar letter: "I am writing this letter out of fear. Fear for my job, fear for my family, fear for my life as I know it today. We, myself and George Perez, have been told that recent regulatory requirements will require a good deal of new programming to merge data from [one computer] House 17 to the House 05 [computer] system. Based on the preliminary discussions with management about this project, we feel very uncomfortable in doing this work. This has been expressed to one of our managers in no uncertain terms. I will not do it. I have reconciled within myself to try to handle my day-to-day job functions, because I cannot afford to quite [*sic*] my job at this time. I do not know who to turn to; I do not know

whom I can trust. I do not know how Mr. Madoff will take this news when he comes home from Europe. I very well could be out of a job. Kind Regards."

14. *Securities Investor Protection Corporation, Irving H. Picard, Trustee v. Frank J. Avellino, etc.*, United States Bankruptcy Court, Southern District of New York, Adv. Pro. No. 08-01789 (BRL), December 10, 2010, 42–43.

15. See Robert K. Merton, "The Unanticipated Consequences of Purposive Social Action," *American Sociological Review*, 1, number 6, 1936, 894–904.

16. *Securities Investor Protection Corporation, Irving H. Picard, Trustee v. Irwin Lipkin, Carole Lipkin, Eric Lipkin, Erika Lipkin*, United States Bankruptcy Court, Southern District of New York, Adv. Pro. No. 08-01789 (BRL), November 11, 2010, 18–19, 26.

17. Earl Sparling, *Kreuger's Billion Dollar Bubble* (New York: Greenberg Publisher, 1932), 179.

18. Ibid., 183.

19. Ibid., 2.

20. *United States of America v. Jerome O'Hara et al.*, United States District Court, Southern District of New York, testimony of Frank DiPascali, Jr.

Chapter 7 Of Ropers and Roping

1. Commonwealth of Massachusetts, Office of the Secretary of the Commonwealth, Securities Division, Administrative Complaint and Ex Parte Motion, In the Matter of: Cohmad Securities Corporation, February 11, 2009, 15. The figures compiled by the Massachusetts regulators are somewhat different from those found in SIPC documents. For example, the Massachusetts regulators concluded: "Additional documents produced by Cohmad evidence (that from July 1, 2001 through December 2, 2008) Cohmad submitted requests for payment of 'professional services' totaling in excess of $52 million from [BLMIS]," ibid., 16.

2. Client Information: Cohmad Securities Corporation (885 Third Avenue, New York, NY 10022).

3. Letter to clients from Maurice J. Cohn, president, Cohmad Securities Corporation, July 17, 1992.

4. Commonwealth of Massachusetts, Complaint and Ex Parte Motion.

5. Letter to Andrew Chaban from Robert M. Jaffe, Cohmad Securities Corporation, November 3, 2001.

6. In the aftermath of the BLMIS collapse, a number of investors roped by Jaffe expressed surprise that he received any remuneration for helping them move their money there. Some were more suspicious about what he

may have known about Madoff's con, and were as angry at him as they were at Madoff.

7. Commonwealth of Massachusetts, Office of the Secretary of the Commonwealth, Case No. E-2009-0015, In the Matter of: Cohmad Securities Corporation, III, December 10, 2009, 30–39.

8. Ibid., 52–56.

9. Steve Fishman, "The Monster Mensch," *New York Magazine,* February 22, 2009.

10. *Supreme Court of the State of New York, People of the State of New York v. J. Ezra Merkin and Gabriel Capital Corporation*, Complaint, April 6, 2009, 9–24.

11. Merkin, like Madoff, converted investments to cash at the end of each month, which, although not illegal, is clearly a stratagem to avoid regulatory scrutiny.

12. Daphne Merkin, "If Looks Could Steal," *New York Times*, March 22, 2009.

13. It is worth noting that although Merkin had told investors of his other two hedge funds, Gabriel Capital Corp. and Ariel Fund Ltd., that he was investing in distressed assets and bankruptcies, he also, beginning in 1990, handed over one-fourth of those funds to BLMIS in addition to essentially all of the Ascot funds.

14. At the end of the third quarter of 2008, Ascot had over 300 investors with a total of $1.7 billion invested with BLMIS, all of which would be lost by the end of the fourth quarter. According to the Complaint of the New York State's Attorney General "Merkin, however, concealed the fact that Ascot was a Madoff feeder fund from the vast majority of his investors. During the course of its investigation, the office of the Attorney General interviewed over half of Ascot's U.S. investors. Approximately 85% of them did not know until after Madoff's arrest that Madoff managed and had custody of virtually all of Ascot's assets."

15. Actually, Merkin did little investing himself, but used other companies to manage the Gabriel Capital, L.P.'s assets. In December 2001, BLMIS managed 19.8 percent and Cerberus Capital Management managed 45.3 percent of $557,227,424.

16. The day of Madoff's arrest, Merkin sent out a letter to Ascot partners that read in part: "Dear [Limited] Partners. ... Our fund, Ascot Partners, L.P., which has substantially all of its assets invested with Madoff is a victim of this fraud. Bernard Madoff was a prominent member of the securities industry for over 40 years, and we have invested with him for many years. I am shocked, as I know you are, by this fraud. As one of the largest investors in our fund, I have suffered major losses from this catastrophe. At this point, it is impossible to predict what recovery, if any, may be had on these assets."

17. Examination under oath of J. Ezra Merkin, *In the Matter of Madoff Charities Investment*, January 30, 2009.

18. Harold Clurman, *Lies Like Truth* (New York: Macmillan, 1958), 69.

19. Ibid.

20. Presentation at the International Law Practicum, Spring 2012. Transcript reprinted with permission from *International Law Practicum Journal*, Spring 2013, 25, No. 1, published by the New York State Bar Association, One Elk Street, Albany, NY 12207.

Chapter 8 Roping in a Globalized World

1. Adam Smith, *The Wealth of Nations*, 5th edition (New York: Random House, 1937), 525.

2. Ibid., 416.

3. Ibid., 541–42.

4. Ibid., 557.

5. Karl Marx, *The Communist Manifesto*, in *Capital and Other Writings*, ed. Max Eastman (New York: Random House, 1932), 322.

6. Ibid., 323–24.

7. Ibid., 324.

8. One member of the team of SIPC attorneys charged with winding down the Madoff con, many of whom often seemed out of their depths in understanding or completing the task, did correctly conclude that "a Ponzi scheme [of its size and duration] was only possible if he went global. ... International entities became an important component of Madoff's sales pitch, helping convince customers that he was trading overseas. But Madoff didn't just hang a shingle in London as part of a sales ploy. He often covered losses in his trading operation indirectly with funds that were transferred [back-and-forth]." It is unclear how many of the vast number of SIPC attorneys involved fully realized that there was much more to Madoff's globalization—which was the incessant need to raise a great deal of money to keep the con game funded—than simply a sales pitch and money laundering. (See "A Message from the SIPC Trustee's Chief Counsel, David J. Sheehan," November 7, 2012.)

9. It is, of course, possible that the ropers quoted throughout this chapter misremember salient facts or are engaged in a performance, a prominent feature of con games. Some to which these ropers are testifying could help them avoid being indicted for committing a felony; some to which they are testifying makes them look greedy and empty-headed.

10. On-the-record interview of Walter M. Noel, Jr., Office of the Secretary of State, Securities Division, Commonwealth of Massachusetts, February 11, 2009.

11. Of course, Madoff was not the first con man to try to convince his marks that it was necessary to keep details about his money-making scheme from competitors lest they pirate them. For example, John Worrell Keely, who claimed he had developed a revolutionary motor to harness the basic "etheric force" that could convert water to fuel, had made essentially the

same argument over a hundred years earlier. For a quarter of a century, Keely resisted calls from investors to share his secret of "etheric force," contending that he had yet to complete his research, and to reveal what he had already learned would make it possible for others to do so and capitalize on his decades of work. See Alexander Klein, "Atomic Energy, 1892–1899: RIP," in Alexander Klein, ed., *Grand Deception* (London: Faber and Faber, n.d.), 153–159.

12. When asked by regulators to describe the "proprietary models and algorithms" of the split-strike strategy, Jeffrey Tucker replied: "I don't—I'm not familiar with them." The exchange continued: Q: "Do you know anything about them?" A: "No."; Q: "Who at Fairfield would know anything about them?" A: "Amit [Vijayvergiya, the head of risk management and president of Fairfield Greenwich-Bermuda] would—may have some knowledge of this, but the models themselves, I don't think anybody in the firm had access to."

13. According to a May 2009 Complaint filed by the SIPC trustee, while for the S&P 500, 36.1 percent of the months between January 1996 and December 2007 had negative returns, for the same time period only 2.9 percent of the months for four different FGG BLMIS accounts showed negative returns.

14. In an exchange with a journalist in 2013, Madoff made it clear—somewhat bragging—that FGG executives were not alone among his investors in not knowing details of his IA business: "People asked me all of the time how did I do it, and I refused to tell them, and they still invested with me. My investors were sophisticated people, smart enough to know what was going on and how money was made—but still invested with me without any explanation." (See Sital S. Patel, "Madoff: 'Don't Let Wall Street Scam You, Like I Did,'" *Wall Street Journal* [Market Watch], June 5, 2013.)

15. "BLMIS Operational Due Diligence" meeting, at offices of BLMIS, October 2, 2008.

16. On-the-record interview of Amit Vijayvergiya, Office of the Secretary of State, Securities Division, Commonwealth of Massachusetts, March 6, 2009.

17. On-the-record interview of Jeffrey Tucker, Office of the Secretary of State, Securities Division, Commonwealth of Massachusetts, March 12, 2009.

18. Administrative Complaint, Office of the Secretary of State, Securities Division, Commonwealth of Massachusetts, April 1, 2009, Conclusion of Summary.

19. Ibid.

20. After the series of interviews with FGG executives, the Commonwealth of Massachusetts filed a Complaint against the company charging fraud, most particularly, of breaching fiduciary duty to clients. The case

was settled the following September when FGG agreed to provide restitution to Massachusetts investors and pay a civil penalty.

21. Almost all of the following information is from Kohn's pretrial 2nd witness statement and 6th witness statement in Madoff Securities *International Limited and Irving Picard v. Stephen Ernest, John Raven, et al.*, June 6, 2011, and March 1, 2013, in the High Court of Justice, Queen's Bench Division, Commercial Court, a case in which she was a defendant. Kohn states at the beginning of the 6th witness statement: "Unless otherwise stated, the facts and matters to which I refer in this witness statement are within my own knowledge and I believe them to be true."

22. David W. Maurer, *The Big Con: The Story of the Confidence Man* (Indianapolis: Bobbs-Merrill, 1940), 138.

23. It is estimated that between 1983 and 2008 BLMIS paid at least $600 million into MSIL. After the money was sent back, much of it was recorded as trading commissions from London.

24. High Court of Justice, Queen's Bench Division, Commercial Court, *Madoff Securities International Limited and Irving Picard v. Stephen Ernest John Raven et al.*, 2nd witness statement of Sonja Kohn, 26–27.

25. Ibid., 27–29.

26. Op. cit., 6th witness statement of Sonja Kohn, 19–30.

27. Some might think that those so anxious to set an appointment with Madoff that they felt it necessary to ask Kohn to intercede on their behalf to arrange a meeting would pay her the commissions. That Madoff was paying her large sums of money year after year might have suggested to some that his indifference to finding new clients was pretense, part of the con.

28. High Court of Justice, *Madoff Securities International Limited and Irving Picard v. Raven et al.*, 2nd witness statement of Sonja Kohn, 32–33.

29. High Court of Justice, *Madoff Securities International Limited and Irving Picard v. Raven et al.*, 6th witness statement of Sonja Kohn, 31–35.

30. Here are two relevant passages about the Kohn–Madoff relationship found in one journalist's profile of Kohn: "Financial-industry records show that Sonja [Blau] Kohn passed the first two of five securities-licensing exams in November 1984 and joined Merrill Lynch in mid-1985. Kohn was always trying to think of new business schemes, says a person she tried to enlist in Internet ventures: 'She was always looking for the things that were going to make her rich. She was motivated by greed and the power that comes to people who are wealthy. Madoff would have been a dream come true.' . . . People who know Kohn and those investigating her agree on one point: while she is a charming and extremely hardworking saleswoman, her most important distinguishing characteristic—indeed, her No. 1 asset—was her unparalleled access to Madoff. . . . With offices across the street from the opera house in Vienna and three blocks from La Scala in Milan, Kohn cultivated the image of a woman of culture, and of political and economic power. She promoted

herself as 'Austria's woman of Wall Street'—cachet that privately included her offer of entrée to Bernie. One former employee recalls: 'She would tell people she had Bernie's private mobile number.' Her sales pitch included this line: 'Everything I touch turns to gold.'" Allan Dodds Frank, "Bernie's Bag Lady," *Newsweek/The Daily Beast*, February 20, 2011.

31. Kohn's explanation after 2009, when Madoff was sent to prison, of why she received these payments was often met with skepticism. A judge to whom it was offered wrote: "No real explanation is currently put forward by Mrs. Kohn as to why, if, as she contends, the payments were essentially legitimate payments. . . . It seems to me that this is an area which cries out for a proper explanation from Mrs. Kohn which has currently not been forthcoming. . . . For the purposes of these applications, I simply proceed on the basis that the claimants have an arguable case that Mr. Madoff and Mrs. Kohn disguised the true nature and purpose of the payments." Again: "it seems to me that what emerges is a sufficiently arguable case of deliberate wrongdoing, the issuing of sham invoices and the disguising the true nature of the payments of millions of dollars." And elsewhere, with reference to Kohn's credibility, the judge adds: "Making every allowance for the fact that Mrs. Kohn may have been under a lot of stress at the time that she was being questioned in the presence of representatives of the FBI and the SEC, the suggestion that she did not remember or needed to make further enquiries about companies which she has used as vehicles for BLMIS and MSIL payments over a number of years is difficult to accept. In my judgment these answers were thoroughly evasive at best."

32. Elliott J. Mason, "Ivar Kreugar [*sic*]—A Match for Anyone," in Colin Rose, ed., *The World's Greatest Rip-Offs: The Extraordinary Inside Story of the Biggest, Most Inventive Confidence Tricks in Recent Times* (New York: Sterling Publishing, 1978), 153.

33. Ibid., 155.

34. Ibid., 156–157.

35. "Fraud and Financial Innovation: The Match King," *The Economist*, December 17, 2007.

36. Ibid., 149.

37. Even on the Monday of his final week in business, Madoff, who was finding it increasingly difficult in meeting the relentless calls for redemptions and whose Ponzi scheme was near the end of its downward spiral, was actively trying to intimidate his ropers. In an e-mail, Jeffrey Tucker reported to other executives at FGG: "Just got off the phone with a very angry Bernie who said if we can't replace the redemptions for 12/31 he is going to close the account. His traders are 'tired of dealing with these hedge funds,' and there are plenty of institutions who can replace the money. They have been offered this all along, but 'remained loyal to us.' Also feels we will not

raise the $500 [million] for Emerald. Not sure of the next step, but we best talk. I think he is sincere," Letter Jeffrey Tucker to Executive Committee, FGG, and Walter M. Noel, Jr., December 8, 2008.

Clearly, the FGG executives were intimidated. Two days later, Tucker responded to Madoff with an over two-page letter full of explanations, suggestions, and promises. It begins: "We fully understand the frustration of your traders at this unique time," and it ends: "Finally, we apologize for failing to keep you informed of pending redemptions in a timely manner. We will strive to improve communications between our firms through more frequent reporting of redemptions and subscriptions received. Our firm is very dependent on its relationship with your firm. You are our most important business partner and an immensely respected friend. As a firm, we are prepared to commit to dedicating ourselves exclusively to the Sentry and Emerald Funds. Throughout 2009, we will engage in no other fundraising initiatives. Our mission is to remain in business with you and to keep your trust. [We, the senior FGG executives,] would like to speak with you in person. All three of us will be available to meet with you any time next week. If more convenient for you, Walter and I are available to come over this week. I will follow-up by telephone to arrange a meeting," Letter Jeffrey Tucker to Bernard L. Madoff Investment Securities, December 10, 2008.

38. Robert Shaplen, *Kreuger: Genius and Swindler* (New York: Knopf, 1960), 128.

39. Shaplen, *Kreuger*, 43.

40. "BLMIS Operational Due Diligence" meeting at offices of BLMIS, op. cit.

41. Vijayvergiya and Tucker, on-the-record interviews, op. cit.

42. Tucker's contention that FGG relied on SEC oversight is probably untrue. In a telephone conversation in 2005 with Mark McKeefry and Amit Vijayvergiya about an impending SEC investigation, Madoff gave them instructions of what they should say to the regulators. (The call begins: Madoff: "Obviously, first of all, this conversation never took place, Mark, okay?"; Vijayvergiya: "Yes, of course."; Madoff: "The less you know about how we execute, and so on and so forth, the better you are other than, yes, you could—you know, you could, if they asked: 'Do you know that Madoff—do you know if Madoff has Chinese Walls' [information separation or firewalls], and you say,:'Yes.' Look, your position is to just say: 'Listen, Madoff has been in business for 45 years, he executes a huge percentage of the industry's orders. He's a well-known broker. We make the assumption that he's doing everything properly.'"...; Madoff: "What I'm giving you and basically what you should respond to them. Obviously, not that we had—we didn't have a conversation on all of this stuff, but that's basically—that's what they expect to hear and what they want to hear. ...") By answering to the SEC attorneys as they were directed, by tailoring their responses to Madoff's needs, the FGG executives may well have helped him evade SEC detection.

43. Vijayvergiya, on-the-record interview, op. cit.
44. *MSIL v. Stephen Raven et al.* (2010 Folio 1468).

Chapter 9 Steerers

1. Donald H. Dunn, *Ponzi: The Incredible True Story of the King of Financial Cons* (New York: Broadway Books, 2004), (first published as *Ponzi: The Boston Swindler*, 1975), 141.

2. It cannot be ruled out that the Madoff Ponzi scheme began in the 1960s. It also cannot also be ruled out that it began with Madoff's father-in-law, who encouraged his accounting clients to give him their money to invest with Madoff. According to Michael Bienes, he did so, in fact, routinely.

Q: When do you get into investing other people's money with Bernie Madoff?

A: Saul [Alpern], his father-in-law, had been doing it since the late 1960s, I think, if not before. He had, like, a green book. It's a plastic, loose-leaf book. He had these blank sheets printed up, and Nanette, the secretary, would type them in, and he would do the pencil work. You got a transaction, and then the next transaction; you got the check from the previous transaction. And he showed you the new transaction—buy, sell, profit, and check—from [the] previous transaction.

Q: Let me be clear. This was Saul Alpern?

A: Yeah, his father-in-law.

Q: Was taking money?

A: From his clients, family, and friends. He had it when he left.

Q: And giving it to his son-in-law?

A: Yeah, of course.

    (See Interview with Michael Bienes, FRONTLINE/PBS, "The Madoff Affair," posted May 12, 2009, 5–6.)

3. The precise total Picower invested at BLMIS is unclear. Some have estimated that it was as low as 1 or 2% of what he withdrew from his BLMIS accounts over the years. Some newspapers reported that the figure was approximately $620 million, but this figure, although widely accepted, was not confirmed. In any case, the amount invested was surely less than 10% of his total withdrawals.

4. In a legal declaration, Picower and his wife, Barbara, described their philanthropy as "extensive and well-documented." Between 2002 and the end of 2008, over $163.9 million was given to a variety of highly visible organizations—including the American Museum of Natural History, the Educational Broadcasting Company, the Massachusetts Institute of Technology, the New York Public Library, the Metropolitan Museum of Art, the Children's Aid Society, Harlem Children's Zone, Children's Health Fund, Rockefeller

Table 9.3 BLMIS Withdrawals (in millions of dollars)

Year	Gifts to MIT	BLMIS Withdrawals
2001	10.2	821
2002	10.0	922
2003	10.0	1.025
2004	10.2	480
2005	10.2	468
Total	$50.6 million	$3.72 billion

University, Weill Cornell Medical Center, Beth Israel Deaconess (a teaching hospital of Harvard Medical School), and the American Ballet Theatre—by the Picower Foundation. This appears to be quite generous, but is only a small part of what he withdrew from BLMIS. The chart here shows his five-year gift to the Massachusetts Institute of Technology's Picower Institute for Learning and Memory and total withdrawals from his BLMIS accounts.

5. Picower once invested $600,000 in a Broadway production that turned out to be a Ponzi scheme.

6. Picower's returns may have been somewhat less than what the SIPC trustee claimed. In fact, the SIPC trustee's assertions of outlandish returns for many other BLMIS investors often seemed to be exaggerations not later supported by the facts. In a May 12, 2009, court filing, the SIPC trustee wrote: "Picower's Decision Inc. #2 account, for example, [was] purported to earn *over 950%* (emphasis in original) in 1999." (See United States Bankruptcy Court, Southern District of New York, *Bernard L. Madoff Investment Securities, LLC, and Irving H. Picard v. Jeffry M. Picower, etc.,* 19.) A year and a half later, in another court filing, the SIPC trustee wrote: "Informal discovery and further research has confirmed that the 950% return that BLMIS reported to Mr. Picower in certain BLMIS documents was inconsistent with the much lower rate of return that Mr. Picower purportedly received based on the entirety of BLMIS records for that account." (See United States Bankruptcy Court, Southern District of New York, *Securities Investor Protection Corporation v. Bernard L. Madoff Investment Securities, LLC, and Irving H. Picard,* December 17, 2010, 8.) The allegation by the SIPC trustee that Picower had borrowed from his accounts at BLMIS and that he owed the bankrupted BLMIS "a considerable balance" was another of his many exaggerations. The SIPC trustee first claimed: "In the course of the trustee's investigation into the accounts held by the Picower BLMIS account holders, certain margin loans owed by certain BLMIS account holders to BLMIS were identified. The SIPC trustee determined that certain Picower BLMIS account holders borrowed on margin from BLMIS and, when the Ponzi scheme collapsed in December of 2008, there was a considerable balance owed on these margin loans. The SIPC

trustee's investigation disclosed that the margin loans were funded by the investments of other customers in connection with Madoff's Ponzi scheme, and appear to have been the primary vehicle through which transfers were made to the Picower BLMIS account holders." However, in the legal settlement, the SIPC trustee acknowledged that "additional information ... had come to ... [his] attention, including evidence that Mr. Picower had contributed real securities to certain BLMIS accounts ..."[and] largely abandoned his initial claim. (See *United States Bankruptcy Court, Southern District of New York, Securities Investor Protection Corporation v. Bernard L. Madoff Investment Securities, LLC, v. Jeffry M. Picower, Memorandum of Law*, December 17, 2010, 4–7.)

7. As the following paragraphs make apparent, Picower was worth substantially more than the approximately $1 billion fortune that *Forbes Magazine* estimated he had amassed. He kept much of his wealth in personal brokerage accounts at Goldman Sachs, about $4.5 billion in unrealized gains, including $2.2 billion in Apple Computer stock. In a letter a year after his death, Goldman Sachs described him as a "valued client" who had generated returns of more than $2 billion over three decades. Like many others, Picower obviously knew more about investing, and was better at it, than Madoff. After Picower's death, Madoff, apparently bothered by this fact and perhaps other matters, retaliated by indefatigably gossiping to a *New York Times* reporter. Asked who knew of his fraud, Madoff responded: "Picower was the only one that might have. I mean, how could he not?" Madoff then added that Picower was "devious enough to exploit" BLMIS when it was short on funds. In a final thrust, Madoff continued: "Picower had no friends. He was a very strange person."

8. In spite of his substantial withdrawals from his IA accounts, Picower asked BLMIS for, and was the recipient of, tax-loss statements with the apparent purpose to avoid paying taxes.

9. United States Bankruptcy Court, Southern District of New York, *Bernard L. Madoff Investment Securities, LLC, and Irving H. Picard v. Jeffry M. Picower, et al.*, Memorandum of Law in Opposition to Defendants' Partial [*sic*] Motion to Dismiss, September 30, 2009, 5–6.

10. Ibid., 7–8.

11. Ibid., 8.

12. Ibid., 8–9.

13. Apparently, Jeffry Picower had a great deal more money than the $7.2 forfeited from his estate in the civil settlement with the U.S. Attorney. According to a newspaper story at the time of the forfeiture: "In the late 1990s, Mr. Picower's personal brokerage accounts at Goldman [Sachs] were worth about $10 billion, according to two people with direct knowledge of the account. 'It was amazing,' said a former Goldman [Sachs] executive. 'The guy was worth $10 billion, just at Goldman [Sachs]'" (Diana B.

Henriques, "Deal Recovers $7.2 Billion for Madoff Fraud Victims," *New York Times,* December 17, 2010).

14. The figures quoted in Appendix 9-A are slightly different: $183 million and $1.7 billion.

15. Mark Seal, "Madoff's World," in Graydon Carter, ed., *The Great Hangover: 21 Tales of the New Recession* (New York: Harper Perennial, 2010), 338–40.

16. In a brief aside with a bankruptcy judge, an attorney for Levy's children questioned the possibility that Madoff and Levy were simply check kiting:

Attorney: We heard about this exchange of checks. And, Your Honor, I'll frankly say that we'll never know what was behind that exchange. Mr. Levy is dead and Mr. Madoff is a pathological liar. But what we do know or at least what I believe is a reasonable imprint is that Mr. Madoff was somehow manipulating Mr. Levy in connection with those checks that were exchanged. If one looks at the exchanges set forth in the [Stephen P. Harbeck] January 24, [2011] letter and adds them up one would see that Mr. Levy gave Mr. Madoff $211 million— $211 million—more than he received from Mr. Madoff. Again, [it was] Mr. Madoff taking money from Mr. Levy.

Judge: You think he was money laundering?

Attorney: Pardon?

Judge: Do you think Mr. Madoff was money laundering?

Attorney: I don't think it was that, Your Honor. I really don't. I don't think it was money laundering at all. There's a suggestion in the JPMorgan Chase Bank Complaint that maybe it was check kiting. You don't have check kiting if both accounts are in the same bank. You had the Madoff account at JPMorgan Chase Bank. You had the Levy account there [too].

United States Bankruptcy Court, Southern District of New York, In the Matter of *Bernard L. Madoff and Securities Investor Protection Corporation v. Bernard L. Madoff Investment Securities, LLC,* March 30, 2011, 13–14.

17. JPMorgan Chase Bank forfeited $1.7 billion (plus a separate $350 million civil fine to the Comptroller of the Currency and another $543 million in private lawsuit settlements for the benefit of Madoff's victims) for not reporting that it suspected he was laundering money, for not catching him soon enough, and for not reporting its suspicions because it was his bank. Various government regulators, led by the SEC, did not catch Madoff, even though they were his regulators. Moreover, the government had received a suspicious-activity report in 1996 regarding the JPMorgan

Chase Bank–Madoff relationship (see Appendix 9-A), but apparently failed to act on it. JPMorgan Chase Bank might have been guilty of covering up a crime or simply of ineptitude (see Chapter 10). The SIPC trustee and the federal prosecutor were selective in whom to label as being involved in criminal behavior, in choosing whom to investigate and whom to charge with committing a crime. Only some 17th floor employees, of all of those on the 17th floor and beyond who might have been criminally indicted by the prosecutor for aiding and abetting Madoff, found themselves in court, before a judge, and facing prison.

18. JPMorgan Chase Bank eventually asked that the money it had lost in the "float" be repaid.

19. Superior Court of the State of California, County of Los Angeles, *People of the State of California v. Pamela Chais*, First Amended Complaint, September 9, 2011, 6.

20. United States District Court, Southern District of New York, United *States of America v. Jerome O'Hara, et al.*, 10 CR 228 (LTS), testimony of Frank DiPascali, Jr., before the Honorable Laura Taylor Swain, October 17, 2013–March 24, 2014.

21. *Securities and Exchange Commission v. Stanley Chais*, United States District Court, Southern District of New York, Complaint, June 22, 2009, 9.

22. Ibid., 10.

23. See note #29 below.

24. United States Bankruptcy Court, Southern District of New York, *Securities Investor Protection Corporation v. Bernard L. Madoff Investment Securities, LLC*, In re: *Bernard L. Madoff and Irving H. Picard v. Douglas Hall, et al.*, January 4, 2012, 8.

25. United States Bankruptcy Court, Southern District of New York, Burton R. Lifland, Bankruptcy Judge, *Bernard L. Madoff Investment Securities, LLC, and Irving H. Picard v. Estate of Stanley Chais, et al.*, Memorandum Decision and Order, February 24, 2010, 14.

26. The bankruptcy court fully accepted these figures, and much more. In his Decision and Order, the bankruptcy court judge wrote: "While motive and opportunity are sufficient to infer fraudulent intent, the allegations in the Complaint [against Chais] additionally support a finding of 'conscious misbehavior or recklessness.' The allegations in the Complaint, accepted as true, demonstrate that Stanley Chais, who earned substantial fees in connection with his management of [family members'] accounts, was consciously aware of the fraud. Despite his sophisticated knowledge as an investment advisor, Stanley Chais, *inter alia*, (i) instructed Madoff to backdate trades and manufacture account losses for tax purposes; (ii) actively concealed BLMIS's role as [the] money manager; (iii) and failed to investigate numerous indicia of fraud, including consistent and astronomical rates of return and BLMIS's lack of transparency. Through their close familial ties to Stanley Chais, who controlled their accounts, it is plausible that [family

members] were similarly aware that BLMIS was predicated on fraud."
Op. cit., 15–16. Only eight months before this written decision, Chais had
written the judge: "Of course, I want to defend myself and my family. ...
In the past several weeks, I have been accused of some terrible and untrue
things" (Letter from Stanley Chais to Judge Burton R. Lifland, May 18,
2009). Obviously, neither Chais's declaration of innocence nor his defense
in the courtroom worked to soften the judge.

27. United States Bankruptcy Court, Southern District of New York,
*Bernard L. Madoff Investment Securities, LLC, (Debtor), Irving H. Picard
(Plaintiff) v. Stanley Chais, Pamela Chais, Emily [Chais] Chasalow, Mark
Chais, William Chais, etc.*, Complaint, May 1, 2009. 35–36.

28. Op. cit., *Securities and Exchange Commission v. Stanley Chais*,
Complaint, 2.

29. Superior Court of the State of California, County of Los Angeles, *The
People of the State of California v. Stanley Chais*, Complaint, September 17,
2009. (It is asserted twice in this Complaint that "Chais charged the Chais
Funds approximately $269,608,000 in fees" between 1995 and 2008,
enough to make him quite wealthy apart from what he withdrew from his
BLMIS IA accounts.)

30. Ibid., 8–9.

31. United States Bankruptcy Court, Southern District of New York,
*Bernard L. Madoff Investment Securities, LLC, (Debtor) and Irving H.
Picard, Trustee for the Liquidation of Bernard L. Madoff Investment
Securities, LLC, (Plaintiff) v. Stanley Chais, et al.*, Hearing, May 5, 2010,
45–47.

32. U.S. Department of Justice, JPMorgan Chase Bank, "Deferred
Prosecution Agreement," Exhibit C/ Statement of Facts, op. cit., 5–7.

Chapter 10 JPMorgan Chase Bank

1. In 1986, the 703 Account was at Chemical Bank, which acquired and
merged with Chase Manhattan Bank a decade later; Chase then acquired
J.P. Morgan & Co. and together they became JPMorgan Chase Bank in
December 2000.

2. United States Bankruptcy Court, Southern District of New York,
*Securities Investor Protection Corporation v. Bernard L. Madoff Investment
Securities, LLC (Irving H. Picard v. JPMorgan Chase Bank, etc.)*, Complaint
(Second Redacted Version), April 14, 2011 (first filed: December 2, 2010),
61–63.

3. See letter from Representatives Scott Garrett, Peter King, Ileana Ros-
Lehtinen, and Carolyn McCarthy to Gene L. Dodaro, comptroller general
of the United States, June 3, 2011, Appendix H.

4. Serious Organised Crime Agency (UK), SAR Ref: 82270, 1–2.

5. Memorandum for Laura L. McAuliffe, Senior Advisor, U.S. Office of the Comptroller of the Currency, from Jason J. Metrick, Special Agent-in-Charge (Acting), Department of Treasury, Office of Inspector General, Subject: JPMorgan Chase Bank, October 8, 2013. A week before the meeting, the Assistant Attorney General had written the Department of Treasury's Office of the Inspector General: "I have concluded that I must deny the request on the current record, as the referral has not identified a sufficient basis for seeking to pierce the facially-valid claim of privilege that attaches to those records and contemplates confidentiality requirements in litigation that are inconsistent with long-standing government policy. . . . Any litigation seeking to invoke this exception would necessarily demand at the outset 'a showing of a factual basis adequate to support a good faith belief by a reasonable person . . . that *in camera* review of the materials may reveal evidence to establish the claim that the crime-fraud exception applies'" (Letter to Eric M. Thorson, Inspector General, Department of Treasury, from Stuart F. Delery, Assistant Attorney General, Department of Justice, September 12, 2013, 1). Less than four months later, JPMorgan Chase Bank admitted to the facts of the Deferred Prosecution Agreement, including committing crimes, and paid a fine of $2.5 billion.

6. U.S. Department of Justice, JPMorgan Chase Bank, "Deferred Prosecution Agreement" (beginning with the sub-headings "Criminal Information" and "Acceptance of Responsibility" and followed by a two-count Information and Statement of Facts), op. cit.

7. Clearly, Cassa did not understand that the 703 Account was not a small, miscellaneous expense account, but was the main instrument of the Madoff con. Cassa's successor, Mark Doctoroff, the next relationship manager for JPMorgan Chase Bank for BLMIS, did not seem to have a better understanding of his client. In November 2013, Doctoroff testified in court he did not know that BLMIS had a formal IA unit or that the 703 Account was used for that business. Less than a month before BLMIS ran out of money and Madoff's con came to an end, he recommended approval of a request for a loan of $200 million for BLMIS—twice BLMIS's credit limit of $100 million—to JPMorgan Chase Bank's credit department: "They are doing well financially," Doctoroff emailed. "They are looking at the current market as an opportunity to make investments, true to their value investing style." The loan was never made.

Chapter 11 Revisiting the Crime Scene

1. Some con men, for example, Charles Ponzi and William F. Miller, actually sought out those with little money to invest. In fact to attract money, Miller, who promised and paid 10% a week, is said to have related to potential investors in his Bible class that the reason he was helping them increase their wealth was because, as he saw it, it was unfair that "the Morgans and the Goulds and the Vanderbilts are making so many millions

when us little people are making so little—and I've decided to do something about it" (See "The Devious Dodge of 520-Percent Miller," in Alan Hynd, *Professors of Perfidy* [New York: A. S. Barnes and Company, 1963], 121–22).

2. David W. Maurer, *The Big Con: The Story of the Confidence Man* (Indianapolis: Bobbs-Merrill, 1940), 4. Of course, others besides Maurer have long attempted to delineate "the elements which constitute the full-blown technic of confidence gaming." According to the confidence man Crosby's schema, "there are six definite steps or stages ... with [one following] the other with absolute precision": "The fine con has its introduction, development, climax, dénouement, and close, just like any good play." The parts are the FOUNDATION WORK (preparations), APPROACH (getting in touch), BUILD-UP (rousing and sustaining interest), PAY-OFF or CONVINCER, THE HURRAH (sudden crisis or unexpected development), and THE IN-AND-IN (con man also puts some money into the deal) (See W. C. Crosby and Edward H. Smith, "Con," *Saturday Evening Post*, January 24, 1920, 71).

3. The largely unexpected suddenness of the Madoff con's unraveling, of course, precluded the final stage of many cons, cooling the mark out.

4. C. Wright Mills, *Images of Man: The Classical Tradition in Sociological Thinking* (New York: George Braziller, 1960), 17.

5. This is not to say that Madoff was not exacting, quite the opposite. For example, Philip Toop, a director and head of trading at MSIL, who spent some time at BLMIS, described Madoff as carrying "micromanagement to a new level." At his first day at the New York office, Toop says: "I'd brought a pear in for my lunch. Something fell from the pear on to the floor and he came out of his office and said: 'What is this?' And he ripped up the carpet tile that the pear juice had spilt on to, he went to a closet that was right behind where the trader I worked for, Marty Joel, sat, and got a fresh carpet tile out, put it back into the floor, and said: 'Wear it in' and walked back into his office" (Harriet Dennys, "Bernard Madoff: The Inside Story of an Obsessive Control Freak Who Fooled the World," *Telegraph* [Online], UK, August 12, 2013).

6. Neal Shover and Andy Hochstetler, *Choosing White Collar Crime* (New York: Cambridge University Press, 2006), 27–28.

7. Ibid., 35.

8. David Matza, *Delinquency and Drift* (New Brunswick, NJ: Transaction Publishers, 1995), 29. Matza also reminds us here that "the juvenile delinquent as drifter more approximates the substantial majority of juvenile delinquents who do not become adult criminals," and that was surely true of a substantial majority of BLMIS employees who did not become fully committed to its crimogenic subculture.

9. None perhaps was as perfidious as Madoff, who stole money from a long-time paramour. In an attempt to recoup some of her lost money, she

later published a tell-all book about the relationship. It was not commercially successful. See Sheryl Weinstein, *Madoff's Other Secret: Love, Money, Bernie, and Me* (New York: St. Martin's Press, 2009).

10. After his final stumble, Madoff not only was without money, but also seemingly without friends. Peter Madoff's involvement in the crime at BLMIS did not result in his losing his friends. In fact, dozens of individuals—from distant family members to clergy, physicians and other professionals—wrote presentencing victim impact statements, attesting to his goodness and extolling his countless virtues. It was as if they could not grasp the fact that he was waiting to be sent to prison, and that they were not writing to recommend him for membership to a country club. In light of the facts of the Madoff con, it is difficult to imagine that many of them would have been willing to invest with Peter Madoff or someone under a similar legal cloud.

11. "Professional crime" here refers to nonviolent criminal occupations "pursued with a high degree of skill to maximize financial gain and minimize the possibility of apprehension . . . [and] include[s] . . . confidence swindling" (James A. Inciardi, *Careers in Crime* [Chicago: Rand McNally, 1975], 2).

12. Writing about the profession of theft, Sutherland pointed out: "Tutelage by professional thieves is essential for the development of the skills, attitudes, codes, and connections which are required in professional theft." And he adds: "A person can become a professional thief only if he is trained by those who are already professionals. It is ridiculous to imagine an amateur deciding to become a pickpocket, con man, . . . jewelry thief or shake man [extortioner] without professional guidance" (See A Professional Thief [Chic Conwell], Edwin H. Sutherland [annotator and interpreter], *The Professional Thief* [Chicago: University of Chicago Press, 1937], viii, 21.)

13. Given the public outrage after Madoff's arrest, one would hardly expect many who were implicated in the con to fully acknowledge that they were aware of the fact.

14. To be sure, in light of this pattern, it is difficult to believe that at least a few other relatives or friends were not recruited into working to further the Madoff con. It is unlikely, for example, that Peter Madoff's wife, Marion, who was kept on the BLMIS payroll in a no-show job, was unaware that she was committing fraud.

15. United States District Court, Southern District of New York, *United States of America v. Jerome O'Hara, et al.*, 10 CR 228 (LTS), testimony of Frank DiPascali, Jr., before the Honorable Laura Taylor Swain, October 17, 2013–March 24, 2014.

16. Op. cit., 52–53.

17. Ibid., 55.

18. Gabriel Tarde, *Penal Philosophy*, trans. Rapelje Howell (Modern Criminal Science Series), (Boston: Little, Brown, and Company, 1912), 322.

19. Gabriel Tarde, *The Laws of Imitation*, trans. Elsie Clews Parsons (New York: Henry Holt and Company, 1903), 11. Early in his chapter

"The Logical Laws of Imitation," Tarde writes: "Invention and imitation are, as we know, the elementary social acts" 144.

20. Edwin H. Sutherland, *White Collar Crime* (New York: Dryden Press, 1949), 9.

21. Ibid., 234.

22. Throughout his career, Sutherland reformulated his idea of differential association, finally settling on nine axioms, the first four of which are: "criminal behavior is learned"; "criminal behavior is learned in interaction with other persons in a process of communication"; "the principal part of the learning of criminal behavior occurs within intimate personal groups"; "when criminal behavior is learned, the learning includes (a) techniques of committing the crime, which are sometimes very complicated, sometimes very simple, [and] (b) the specific direction of motives, drives, rationalizations, and attitudes." Edwin H. Sutherland and Donald R. Cressey, *Criminology*, 8th ed. (Philadelphia: J. B. Lippincott, 1970), 75–76.

23. David R. Simon, *Elite Deviance* (Boston: Allyn and Bacon, 2002), 72.

24. Edwin H. Sutherland, "White Collar Criminality," *American Sociological Review* 5, no. 1 (February 1940): 11.

25. Donald R. Cressey, "Application and Verification of the Differential Association Theory," *Journal of Criminal Law, Criminality, and Police Science* 43, no. 1 (May–June 1952): 49–50.

26. Ibid., 52.

27. According to some, committing an illegal act makes one a criminal. However, even if individuals are known to have committed illegal acts, they are not designated criminals here as they have not been judged so by a court of law. In short, according to the juristic perspective, one is not a criminal unless having been adjudicated as such by the courts. Here crime is an intentional act in violation of criminal law, committed without defense or excuse, and penalized by the state.

28. Two brief telephone conversations with Bernard Madoff in the fall of 2013 confirmed the impression from the record that he was most ordinary. He did not seem to be someone guided by logic. A few comments he made suggest that he saw himself as exceptional. Unfortunately, the exchanges were not long enough to determine why someone whose only success in life was defrauding investors of money arrived at this conclusion. The impression he left was that of a velvety C+ undergraduate student in an era of grade inflation. From his own experiences, the "professional thief" Chic Conwell (see note 12 above) concluded that all that is necessary to be a successful con man is to be "a good actor, a good salesman, and have good manners and a good appearance." In editing Conwell's manuscript, Edwin H. Sutherland added the observations of another confidence man that they also needed "great egoism [and] if they cannot put on this veneer of culture, they cannot make it go. A confidence man must live by his wits" (see *The Professional Thief*, op. cit., 56). There is no evidence that it takes unusual

abilities to lie and defraud investors of money. Average people lie and steal as effectively as those below average or above average. Madoff seemed unaware that he was a failure as an investor; during his career he was not able to increase the wealth of his clients through investing.

There is a discrepancy between the magnitude of Madoff's crime—a career of defrauding investors of money, laundering money, and evading paying taxes—and the mediocrity of the man and his accomplices. It is difficult for some to grasp that many times an individual may not be as great as his or her deed. When the Madoff narrative was being created, one journalist in the Introduction in an early book referred to him as "a financial mastermind," although no evidence of this could be found. She later wrote in Chapter Two: "Bernie Madoff didn't need to be a crook. ... In the world of stock brokers, Bernard Madoff was a real, legitimate big-league player. He and his brother had built from scratch one of the most successful broker-dealer firms in New York. ... Bernie Madoff was a very astute businessman." Of course, this is all myth and nonsense (Erin Arvedlund, *Too Good to Be True: The Rise and Fall of Bernie Madoff* [New York: Portfolio, 2010], 8, 30). It cannot be forgotten that almost all of what Madoff and his backstage accomplices did was routine, what employees in any Wall Street office do. However, they were not processing the records of the actual trading of securities, but the records of the make-believe trading of securities. One can only speculate as to why such an unremarkable man as Madoff seemed to hold himself in such high regard. Having fooled so many, thus reducing the stature of others, for so long may have given him an unrealistic sense of his worth and self. Living the life of a highly successful financier for so many years surely added to his self-deception. A half dozen years after incarceration, he continued to boast to journalists that he has remained a celebrity with his fellow inmates, and continued to offer advice and instruction about a number of current events—social, economic, and political.

29. See Andrew Kirtzman, *Betrayal: The Life and Lies of Bernie Madoff* (New York: HarperCollins Publisher, 2009).

30. Tarde, *Penal Philosophy.*

31. Gresham M. Sykes and David Matza, "Techniques of Neutralization: A Theory of Delinquency," *American Sociological Review* 22, no. 6 (December 1957): 664–70.

32. Ibid., 666–67.

33. Ibid., 667–69.

34. Robert A. Kagan and John T. Scholz, "The Criminology of the Corporation and Regulatory Strategies," *Enforcing Regulation,* ed. Keith Hawkins and John M. Thomas (Boston: Kluwer-Nijhoff, 1984), 67–96.

35. James Truslow Adams, *The Epic of America* (Boston: Little, Brown, and Company, 1933 [1931]), 185.

36. Emile Durkheim, *Suicide: A Study in Sociology* trans. John A. Spaulding and George Simpson (Glencoe, IL: The Free Press, 1951), 256.

37. Karl Marx, *The Poverty of Philosophy* (New York: International Publishers, 1963), 34.

38. Robert K. Merton, *Social Theory and Social Structure* (Glencoe, IL: The Free Press, 1957), 136.

39. Durkheim, *Suicide*, 257.

40. Merton, *Social Theory and Social Structure*, 139.

41. Ibid., 140–57.

42. Steven F. Messner and Richard Rosenfeld, *Crime and the American Dream* (Belmont, CA: Wadsworth Group, 2001), 79.

43. Ibid., 133.

44. Ibid., 141.

Index

About the Author

LIONEL S. LEWIS, MA, PhD, is professor emeritus and former chair of sociology at State University of New York (SUNY) at Buffalo. Previously, he also taught at the University of Texas at Austin and the University of Nevada at Reno. In addition to writing 150 research papers, essays, and reviews, Lewis is the author of six previous books, including *Con Game: Bernard Madoff and His Victims*. He was admitted to Phi Beta Kappa and named a Woodrow Wilson Fellow at Washington University, where he majored in sociology; his graduate degrees from Cornell University and Yale University are also in sociology. Lewis was the recipient of a Social Sciences Research Council Faculty Grant and received a Myers Center Award for the Study of Human Rights in North America.

5/16